The CIA's Black Ops

The CIA's Black Ops

Covert Action, Foreign Policy, and Democracy

John Jacob Nutter, Ph.D.

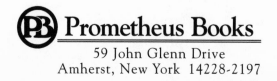

Prometheus Books

59 John Glenn Drive
Amherst, New York 14228-2197

Published 2000 by Prometheus Books

Inquiries should be addressed to
Prometheus Books, 59 John Glenn Drive, Amherst, New York 14228–2197.
VOICE: 716–691–0133, ext. 207.
FAX: 716–564–2711.
WWW.PROMETHEUSBOOKS.COM

04 03 02 01 00   5 4 3 2 1

Library of Congress Cataloging-in-Publication Data

Nutter, John Jacob.
    The CIA's black ops : covert action, foreign policy, and democracy / John Jacob Nutter.
        p.   cm.
    ISBN 1–57392–742–2 (cloth)
    1. United States. Central Intelligence Agency. 2. United States Foreign relations.
I. Title. II. Title: Central Intelligence Agency's black ops.
JK468.I6N88   1999
327.1273'009'045—dc21   99–40404
                                                                                CIP

Printed in the United States of America on acid-free paper

For Ian

Contents

PART I: THE THIRD OPTION

PART II: COVERT OPERATIONS: RED, WHITE, AND BLACK

Acknowledgments

Ilearned a great deal from my students at Michigan State University, and am especially indebted to those who contributed to my senior seminar, Democracy, Foreign Policy, and Covert Action. There is probably a piece of each of you somewhere in this book. I have also benefited from some wonderful and perspicacious academic colleagues, including Colleen Tremonte, Robert Aponte, Donald Lloyd, Linda Racciopi, Norman Graham, Peter Dorman, Kenneth Walzer, Jessica DeForest, and Dixie Platt. I am also grateful to a number of friends who have helped maintain sanity (I think) through some difficult times, including Steve DeVore, Brian Rowe, Mark Bellaire, Matt Thompson, Alec Lloyd, and Randy Cowell.

In the course of producing this work, I have learned a great deal from the current and former intelligence officers and operators who have spared the time to educate me in some of the nuance and nitty-gritty of black ops. You will not agree with all of my analyses or conclusions, but I hope you think your contributions improved them nevertheless. You know who you are, and you have my gratitude. This research has also been deliberately obstructed by a number of people and organizations, and is produced here in spite of their malignant efforts. You are who you are, and nothing I can say can be worse than that.

I am particularly grateful to my agent, Sheree Bykofsky, and to Janet Rosen. Your encouragement and belief in this work, as well as your efforts in teaching a novice author some of the trade, have helped make *The CIA's Black Ops* a reality I have also enjoyed the editorial skill of Meghann French, who has made this a much better work, and a much better experience.

Most importantly, my family has been my reason for writing as well as the rock upon which I have stood during some trying times. My wife, Susan, has put up with so many evenings and weekends while I pounded the keyboard, and is still here. My mother's faith in her son never wavered, and that is worth a lot. It has been most difficult for my son, who nonetheless has been understanding beyond his years for the times his dad has had to forego playing pirates while writing about spooks. Well, from now on, "Yo ho ho."

Introduction

A Tale of Two Operations:
SUCCESS and Failure

LOOKING GLASS WAR

The rebel DC-3 came in low and fast,[1] a gray-green shadow thundering out of the jungle and across the rooftops of the Guatemalan town, its twin Pratt and Whitney engines shaking loose the red roof tiles as the campesinos in the marketplace scattered for cover. Wind buffeted the face of the "bombardier" through the open cargo door as he took aim, then released his "payload"—an empty Coca-Cola bottle. It exploded on the worn cobblestones of the market square with a startling "boom" that quite resembled a bomb burst. "Mission accomplished," the pilot might have thought to himself in Chinese (for he was a Taiwanese soldier of fortune) as he turned the cumbersome aircraft toward home. He planned to enjoy the sunshine on the way back, for there were no enemy fighters in the sky; the Guatemalan air force was grounded by the most dangerous weapon of all: propaganda. It was just another day for the secret army of OPERATION PB/SUCCESS, a United States covert action that proved you *could* overthrow governments with smoke and mirrors—and a few Coke bottles.

This is the story of the secret operations of the cold war. It was a war fought with exploding seashells, fake sex films, Frank Sinatra letters, and yes, Coke bottles. It was a war fought with student front groups and with the world's largest airline. It was a heartless war, with guns supplied by Americans and Soviets and blood supplied by Kurds, Cubans, Hmong, Montangards, Afghans, and Miskitos, who would each in their turn be cast aside. It was a war for the highest ideals; it was a war for the lesser evil. It was war through the looking glass; it was the war of *black ops*.

11

OPERATION PB/SUCCESS[2]

In November 1950, the people of Guatemala freely and fairly elected as president Jacobo Arbenz Guzmán, a populist with genuine concern for the lives of the impoverished Guatemalans. By August 1954, Arbenz had fled the country, both his regime and the democratic institutions of Guatemala destroyed by a coup d'etat, largely psychological in nature, which was created and implemented by the Central Intelligence Agency. In fact, the operation was so effective that casualties were virtually nil, except for the accidental sinking of the British ship *Springfjord*, whose owners were compensated by Lloyds of London. OPERATION PB/SUCCESS, as it was code-named by the CIA, became a model for future covert actions against uncooperative foreign regimes.[3]

Jacobo Arbenz assumed office aiming to improve the lot of his people, a desire that crashed head-on into a brick wall of interests called the United Fruit Company (UFCO). UFCO was Guatemala's largest landowner, and also controlled the nation's railroads, ports, and telephone facilities. *La Frutera*, as UFCO was known locally, followed a traditional practice of U.S. corporations in Latin America; it bought land not only to grow crops, but also to keep it out of the hands of other fruit companies. More than half a million acres of the finest agricultural land in Guatemala lay uncultivated while native Guatemalans starved. To remedy this, Arbenz nationalized some 400,000 acres out of the 550,000 held by *La Frutera*.[4] Yet this was no gunpoint expropriation, for Arbenz paid for the land. United Fruit, however, was not amused by the compensation, which was the taxable value that UFCO had assigned to the land.

It was at this point in 1953 that Thomas Corcoran (aka "Tommy the Cork") chief counsel to UFCO (and to Civil Air Transport, a CIA proprietary airline), discovered the "Communist threat" in Guatemala, bringing it to the attention of Undersecretary of State Walter Bedell Smith (who was the former director of Central Intelligence *and future director of the United Fruit Company*). As Arbenz had recently legalized the small Guatemalan Communist Party in addition to his expropriation of land, Secretary of State John Foster Dulles and President Eisenhower were easily convinced that immediate action had to be taken to stamp out the "Soviet beachhead" in our hemisphere.

The action was OPERATION PB/SUCCESS. The CIA moved rapidly to assemble a group of legendary covert operators, including Allen Dulles, "Rip" Robertson, Al Haney, Richard Bissell, David Atlee Phillips, and E. Howard Hunt (yes, *that* E. Howard Hunt). The operation relied mainly on psychological operations (*psyops*) to strip Arbenz's regime of support, especially from the middle class and the army. Operational assets consisted of a radio station, a couple dozen aircraft, a replacement president (Carlos Castillo Armas), and an "army of liberation" that "overran" the border in six trucks and a station wagon. It was a "smoke-and-mirrors" affair, and it worked.

The crux of the operation was Dave Phillips's propaganda shop, which ran a multifaceted psychological campaign aimed at the military, the general population, and Arbenz's fear. Posters and leaflets were posted all over the country which simply said "Is this *Your* Wall?"; the message was that this was where dissidents would be stood up when Arbenz unleashed his Stalin-like reign of terror. The radio station broadcast popular music mixed with propaganda aimed at creating distrust of Arbenz's regime and fear of the invading forces, boasting of the size, quality, and success of the "forces of liberation." One particularly clever ruse was to announce that all those who supported the rebels should leave their lights on all night. When Arbenz responded by prohibiting this, the rebels announced that night bombing would *only* hit the dark areas of the towns. The lights burned all night. The station also employed black propaganda (fake announcements that seemed to be from Arbenz's government) by "snuggling" (broadcasting on a frequency very close to the official government frequency), and cleverly using denials to start rumors, e.g., "It is *not* true that the waters of Lake Atitlan have been poisoned."

The second key to the operation was an aerial blitz by a small, ragtag, yet by Latin American standards, powerful air force, including roughly six P-47 Thunderbolts, three P-51 Mustangs, a dozen C-47 transports, a Cessna 180, and a PBY-5 naval patrol bomber. These were supplied by the United States, flown by CIA contract pilots (mostly Americans but also several Taiwanese soldiers of fortune who spoke only Chinese) secretly based in Honduras and Nicaragua. Ordnance (i.e.,, bombs) was limited, but then the primary purpose of the air force wasn't to actually fight, but to create the illusion of a powerful rebel force. To this end, the bombers resorted to dropping hand grenades, sticks of dynamite, and empty Coca-Cola bottles. During "bombing runs" over Guatemala City, a tape of bombing sounds was blasted over loudspeakers hidden on the roof of the American embassy.

At a critical moment, the rebel air force lost three aircraft, almost crippling the air offensive. Without constant bombing to show the populace that a rebellion was underway, the operation would collapse. While CIA Deputy Director Charles Cabell pressed for deployment of U.S. aircraft, CIA Director Allen Dulles believed that this would expose the United States as the true "rebel," and he had promised President Eisenhower that the role of the United States would be invisible. "Tacho" Somoza, "president" of Nicaragua, came to the rescue by supplying two Nicaraguan P-51s on the condition the U.S. would replace them. When Allen Dulles reported to Eisenhower that the chances of the operation succeeding were zero without the additional aircraft, Ike approved and the air offensive continued.

Once Arbenz believed that an actual force was attacking his regime, he made a fatal error. He had purchased a shipload of generally useless weapons from Czechoslovakia, including railroad guns, antitank guns, and some small arms, and on 25 June 1954, he announced that he would arm the peasants to aid in the fight against the invaders. This infuriated the officers of the Guatemalan army, who saw this as an insult to their manhood as well as a threat to their social status. Amazingly, the Guatemalan army chose to remain neutral during an invasion of their own country; the army remained in its barracks, to all intents and purposes handing the CIA the keys to the presidential palace. Without army support, who would stand against the rebels?

As things turned out, the key to the whole operation was that the Guatemalan air force remained grounded. On 18 June 1954, rebel commander Castillo Armas led his intrepid band of 150 "liberators" across the border from Honduras into Guatemala, moved about six miles into Guatemala, and stopped to see what would happen. Meanwhile, Dave Phillip's "rebel" radio fabricated breathless reports of fierce combat ending in rebel victories; simulated radio transmissions between dozens of nonexistent rebel units filled the airwaves. If Arbenz had gotten a single aircraft in the air, he might have discovered the trivial size of the rebel "army" and the true outcome of the "battles." Yet his aircraft, like his army, remained at home. How had the CIA achieved this coup de main?

Realizing early on that the linchpin of the operation would be control of Arbenz's information, CIA propaganda broadcasts continuously reported defections of pilots from Communist Bloc nations, thereby planting the seeds of mistrust in Arbenz's mind and ideas in the minds of Guatemalan air force pilots. Eventually, one Guatemalan pilot *did* defect. When asked by the CIA to appeal to his fellow pilots via the rebel radio, he refused, fearing for his family, who had remained in Guatemala. Not to be put off, CIA operatives got the man drunk one evening and asked him "hypothetically" what he would say to encourage more defections. They secretly taped this conversation, then sent it out over the rebel radio.[5] Fearing that all his pilots would fly off to Honduras, Arbenz grounded his entire air force. Thus blind, when rebel radio reported columns of well-armed insurgents converging on the capital, the beleaguered president believed them. On 27 June 1954, as the army demanded his resignation, Arbenz turned the government over to Colonel Carlos Diaz and fled to refuge in the Mexican embassy. Shortly after that, Diaz relinquished authority to Castillo Armas. PB/SUCCESS had lived up to its name. Soon after, when Dave Phillips stopped in Guatemala City, he borrowed a pair of especially comfortable golf shoes during a round at the country club. The shoes that fit so well had belonged to a former member: Jacobo Arbenz.

Nothing Succeeds Like SUCCESS: OPERATION ZAPATA[6]

PB/SUCCESS, along with OPERATION AJAX (the 1953 overthrow of Prime Minister Mohammad Mosaddeq in Iran), convinced the CIA that a little force, a few million dollars, and plenty of American "can-do" could shape world events. Even a "covert" fiasco in Indonesia (1957, see chapter 3) failed to dampen the enthusiasm with which such actions were advocated, and when doubts about Fidel Castro's political leanings arose,[7] the first impulse was to dispose of him with "the Guatemala scenario." Thus was born OPERATION ZAPATA.

The regime of Fulguencio Batista imploded on New Year's Day 1959, and Fidel Castro, guerrilla prince, marched triumphantly into Havana to assume the mantle of power. A former lawyer and baseball pitcher (a lefty, naturally), Castro espoused *Fidelismo*, ostensibly a form of nationalism that was not Marxism, but he quickly aroused the wrath of American economic concerns (both legitimate and Mafia) by confiscating hotels, casinos, sugar mills, and plantations. By March 1960, President Eisenhower's National Security Council and the "54/12 Group" (a group of advisors that supervised covert actions) considered Castro a Soviet puppet in the Western Hemisphere, and began a program of guerrilla infiltration and support of indigenous insurgents against him. This program was run by many of the guiding lights of PB/SUCCESS, including Director of Central Intelligence (DCI) Allen Dulles, Deputy Director for Plans, (DDP) or head of covert operations, Richard Bissell, Assistant Deputy Director for Plans (ADDP) Tracy Barnes, David Phillips, J. C. King, and E. Howard Hunt (yes, *him* again). In an overzealous and perhaps fatal effort at secrecy, the CIA's own intelligence analysts were excluded from the operation.[8]

By November 1960, the CIA realized that its halfhearted guerrilla campaign was failing, due to the continuing popularity of Castro, his repression of those dissenters who remained in Cuba, and problems in keeping the guerrillas supplied (in particular, efforts to parachute-drop supplies consistently failed). Therefore, the guerrilla *program* metamorphosed into an invasion *plan*, in which the CIA would secretly train a "brigade" of several hundred troops who would enter Cuba by amphibious assault near Trinidad, a town of about eighteen thousand on the southeastern coast. The brigade would be supported with its own tanks and, most importantly, an air force of B-26 bombers. While these aircraft were World War II surplus, they were common throughout the world, and had been modified by the addition of a "pack" of six .50 caliber machine guns in the nose. This weaponry provided devastating firepower against troops and tanks on the ground. The cumbersome aircraft were not designed for aerial combat, however, so these planes were intended to knock out Castro's small air force by strafing Cuban airfields before the landing, and thereafter be free to annihilate Castro's ground troops.

The biggest problem seemed to lay in the size of the landing force. How could fourteen hundred men, even well supported by air power, stand up for any length of time to Castro's forces, which numbered over two hundred thousand? While denied by operators in the CIA, there is substantial evidence today that shows Dulles and Bissell counted on the landings to ignite popular rebellion against Castro, which would sweep him from power. Even though analysts from the CIA's analysis branch assessed the chances of this as very small, the prospects for an uprising were prominently featured in briefings to President Kennedy and his advisers. Indeed, provisions were made for landing arms for thirty thousand additional men. What if the uprisings did not occur? In that case, the brigade was expected to "melt into the hills" near Trinidad and "go guerrilla." Moreover, CIA documents consistently spoke of the necessity of United States armed forces support should the rebel Cubans get in trouble, and on Inauguration Day in 1961, Ike had told JFK, "This must not fail." Kennedy, however, explicitly ruled out any U.S. military engagement, because he didn't want to commit American lives to a bloody invasion; "It would be a fucking slaughter," he told his brother Bobby. Despite what their written plans said, no one from the CIA ever told the president that the plans virtually required U.S. military intervention.

Another difficulty with the plan as inherited by President Kennedy was the "noise" it was expected to create. JFK came to office hoping to erase the "bully of the North" image the United States had in Latin America (in no small part precisely because of operations like SUCCESS and ZAPATA). Therefore, he wanted any intervention in Cuba to appear to be a completely Cuban operation. TRINIDAD (the name of the landing plan at the town of Trinidad) smacked too much of *The Longest Day* (the movie about D day, World War II). The town was sizable, which would inevitably draw media attention, and it had no airfield that B-26s could fly from, thus exposing the fiction that the operation was solely Cuban and revealing the substantial U.S. role in the invasion.

The CIA agreed that, in the interests of a "quiet" operation, a new landing site would be found. The change in site took place on 16 March 1961 (about thirty days before the assault), and the selected alternative was the Bahia de Cochinos, or Bay of Pigs. This bay, near the tiny seaside hamlet of Giron, had a runway that could accommodate B-26s. It was also surrounded by the Zapata Swamp, through which passed only three narrow causeways, and the beachhead could therefore, theoretically, be defended by merely sealing off the three approaches through the swamp. Whereas Trinidad was only three miles from the escape hatch of the Escambray Mountains, however, the Bay of Pigs was eighty miles away on the other side of a swamp. Turning into guerrillas would be impossible, but no one told Kennedy. Finally, President Kennedy asked that the amphibious assault take place at night so as to produce a less spectacular event. No one told him that the United States had *never*, even in World War II, carried out a nighttime amphibious assault. In the end, the CIA presented Kennedy with a plan that was developed in two days.

The initial air strikes began on D-2 (two days before the Brigade landing, 15 April 1961), hitting Castro's three main airbases and destroying about five aircraft. However, the bulk of Castro's air force remained undamaged, including a couple of prop-driven Sea Furies. More critically, several T-33 jets, which, unbeknownst to the CIA, had been armed with rockets and machine guns, survived. A B-26 painted by the CIA to resemble a Cuban plane landed that morning in Miami with the cover story that defecting pilots had attacked the Cuban airfields and then fled to Miami. However, discrepancies in the aircraft (wrong nose cone, gun barrels taped over and not fired through) and cover story (how did two defecting pilots simultaneously attack three airfields?) were soon discovered by the press, and the web of deception began to unravel.

Since making an amphibious assault and holding a beachhead would be almost impossible without command of the air, a second air strike was necessary to complete the destruction of Castro's air force. Yet no second strike was ever carried out. Why not? The orthodox explanation is that President Kennedy "chickened out" and canceled the second air strike due to the ruckus raised by Cuba in the United Nations. However, accounts by both David Phillips and Howard Hunt, who were hardly Kennedy apologists, suggest that the second strike was spiked by Deputy Director of Central Intelligence (DDCI) Charles Cabell, who was unsure that a follow-up strike was authorized. When CIA executives finally acted to request a second strike, Cabell and Bissell approached Secretary of State Dean Rusk, not JFK. Unwilling to make the decision himself, Rusk asked if they wanted to press their case to the president, but they refused. Thus, Castro's aircraft survived to play a key role in the debacle to follow.

Concurrent with the first air strike on the night of D-2, a diversionary landing was scheduled for the Oriente Province on the southeast coast of Cuba, about thirty miles from the U.S. naval base at Guantanamo Bay. This group of about 160 recruits was to draw Castro's "reaction forces" farther away from the true landing site. A series of snafus resulted in the failure of this operation, and no diversion took place. Besides, the CIA and independent exile groups had been constantly raiding Cuba for months, and Castro's forces had become quite efficient at responding to reported landings.

On the morning of the landing, 17 April 1961, Brigade 2506 frogmen tried to go ashore to mark channels for the landing craft. Although DDP Bissell had promised President Kennedy that there "wouldn't be a white face on the beach," the two Underwater Demolition Team (UDT) groups were personally led, in the finest tradition of U.S. Special Forces, by CIA contract agents Rip Robertson and Grayston "Gray" Lynch. Before it touched land, Lynch's team was spotlighted by a Cuban patrol. Lynch opened fire with a Browning Automatic Rifle (BAR), and a fierce night firefight took place. Robertson's team was also discovered, and what little surprise that remained in the operation slipped away.

As dawn broke, the rebel Cubans launched from their "mother ships," heading toward three separate beaches in and around the Bay of Pigs in landing craft and aluminum and fiberglass pleasure boats hastily purchased days before. The CIA had discounted evidence of offshore reefs, but they were real, and the boats frequently hung up on coral one hundred or more yards from the beach, forcing the commandos to wade the rest of the way in. Critically, almost all Brigade radios were ruined by seawater, depriving the commanders of the ability to control their forces, to obtain timely resupply, and to keep the CIA and President Kennedy informed of events.

Even though they were discovered earlier than planned, the initial troop deployments went well, with paratroop detachments seizing key points along the narrow Zapata Swamp causeways and successfully ambushing small groups of Castro troops who were already heading for the landing site. Three problems quickly became apparent. First, Castro, who had been aware of the impending invasion for weeks, responded much more rapidly than the CIA had planned.[9] The Brigade had been told not to expect any serious resistance until two days after they had landed (D+2), yet Castro's alert forces assaulted the beachhead almost immediately. Second, due to poor training in transportation and cargo handling, the rebels could not land their complete force and supplies before daybreak so that their ships could escape out to sea; they would be caught in daylight. Third, with Castro's air force still flying, both the rebel ships and ground troops became easy targets, as the Brigade B-26s were no match for Castro's T-33 jets in air-to-air combat. Several rebel aircraft were shot down, and where the exile forces had expected aerial gunfire to devastate their enemy, they were instead on the receiving end.

The CIA had decided not to arm the rebel ships, since the plan assumed that all of Castro's aircraft would be preemptively destroyed. However, Gray Lynch had, on his own, provided some light machine guns and BARs to the crews. Although suddenly exposed and vulnerable, the rebels on the ships succeeded in shooting down one or two of the attacking Castro planes, but then disaster struck. An FAR Sea Fury braved the withering small-arms fire to bury a single, catastrophic bomb in the *Rio Escondido*. The *Rio's* deck was loaded with aviation fuel, and the ship ignited quickly, taking with it most of the Brigade's spare ammo. There would be no resupply. Photographs of the burning *Rio* would become symbolic of the disaster. A second ship, the *Houston*, was hit and forced to beach inside the bay, and the rest of the fleet fled over the horizon.

To make matters worse, the rapid response of Castro's forces required the invaders to fire off ammunition at a much higher rate than anticipated, and by the morning of D+2 (19 April), the rebel Cubans had been forced back almost to the sea into a few isolated pockets of resistance. With no food, water, ammunition, or air cover, Commander Pepe San Roman gave the order to disperse. There was no contingency plan for "going guerrilla" or for evacuating by sea. Indeed, there was no contingency plan at all. Ultimately, about twenty-six rebels were picked up by U.S. destroyers that cruised close to shore looking for survivors. In doing so, they risked a provocation that could have led to something far more serious. As it was, the American ships were shelled by Cuban tanks, but did not return fire, and there was no Cuban equivalent to the Gulf of Tonkin incident. About twenty other survivors set off on an epic sailing voyage, landing in Mexico weeks later. More than eleven hundred rebels were captured.

A stunned America watched as President Kennedy, barely three months in office, shouldered the responsibility for the fiasco, and the CIA swiftly spread the "explanation" that the president had "chickened out" on the air strikes; the agency never acknowledged the folly of sending fourteen hundred men against twenty thousand. Kennedy himself established a study group, headed by Maxwell Taylor, to perform the official "eyes only" postmortem. The resulting report merely reinforced the cold war mindset that had produced the Bay of Pigs operation, focusing on the question of "how to do it better next time." Despite this fiasco, covert operations had become such an integral part of U.S. government policy that their raison d'etre remained unquestioned.

COVERT ACTION: WHAT THIS BOOK IS ABOUT

In July 1947, Congress created the Central Intelligence Agency, granting it the authority "to perform other such functions and duties related to intelligence affecting the national security as the National Security Council may from time to time direct." Within six months, the CIA was airdropping guns to rebels *inside the USSR* (one can imagine our reaction if, say, Libya was supplying machine guns and missiles to, say, the Michigan Militia). The agency would eventually plot assassinations of foreign heads of state; recruit, train, supply, and deploy private armies; conduct foreign wars by proxy; instigate and sponsor coups d'etat; wreck the economies of foreign countries; manipulate the political processes of allied countries such as England, Italy, and Australia; and disinform the American people for political (and sometimes *partisan* political) purposes. Moreover, "retired" agency officers would in time establish shadowy, parallel intelligence operations and conduct their own private foreign policies. President Truman, who signed the CIA into being, would later protest that "it [the CIA] has become an operational and at times a policy-making arm of the government. . . . I never thought . . . that it would be injected into peacetime cloak-and-dagger operations."

It is not much of an exaggeration, if any, to suggest that for much of the cold war, in much of the world, covert action *was* American foreign policy. Major covert actions were conducted in Albania, East Germany, France, Great Britain, Greece, Italy, the USSR, West Germany, Angola, the Congo, Egypt, Ghana, Libya, Afghanistan, Australia, Cambodia, China, Indonesia, Iran, Iraq, Lebanon, Morocco, Laos, North Korea, Pakistan, the Philippines, South Korea, Vietnam (North, South, and united), British Guiana (now Guyana), Costa Rica, Cuba, the Dominican Republic, El Salvador, Grenada, Guatemala, Haiti, Nicaragua, Dutch Guiana (now Suriname), Bolivia, Brazil, Chile, Ecuador, Peru, and Uruguay.[10] In some of these countries, a few actions were carried out, while in others covert action was nearly constant throughout the cold war (and continues to this day).

Many of these covert actions were, speaking legally or practically, acts of war. Yet they were generally undertaken with the purpose of avoiding war. They were part of "the secret war" that was never to be acknowledged; that's what made them "covert" actions. More formally, a *covert action* is an operation intended to change the political policies, actors, or institutions of another country, performed so that the covert actor's role is not apparent, and if that role is discovered, the actor can claim he was not involved (this is called *plausible deniability*). This includes paramilitary actions, terrorism, assassinations, manipulating or "fixing" election, arms supplying, and propaganda campaigns. (For a more thorough discussion, see chapter 4.) "Insiders" refer to such actions as "black operations," or black ops, for they are conducted outside the light of day, away from and deniable by the more "civilized" bureaucracies.

The CIA's Black Ops is about the issues raised by the concept and conduct of covert action. In the chapters that follow, I explore the questions raised by covert action in principle, by the conduct of covert operatives, and by the assumptions of the institutions that operated in secret throughout this era. These questions and issues include:

- Why did covert action become so prevalent after World War II? Did covert action become a substitute for a coherent foreign policy? Are the same motivations still present *after* the cold war?
- What is covert action, and what forms does it take?
- What are the implications of covertly creating or supporting private foreign armies? By encouraging and supporting oppressed peoples like the Kurds, Montagnards, and Hmong in rebellion, does the United States create political and moral commitments that it sometimes fails to honor?
- Why did the United States resort to assassination attempts on foreign leaders such as Patrice Lumumba, Fidel Castro, and Rafael Trujillo? Why did these succeed or fail? Under what conditions *might* assassination be an effective foreign policy tool? What are the practical and moral implications of such acts?
- Why did the United States turn to the Mafia and drug lords, and what were the repercussions of this? How does organized crime manipulate and "set up" intelligence agencies to evade prosecution? Under what conditions can one use criminal organizations in a covert action without getting "tainted," manipulated, or blackmailed?
- How do covert operators turn into "cowboys" who run their own private foreign policies? What made it possible for Edwin Wilson to use U.S. Green Berets to train Gadhafi's terrorists? How did a Marine Corps lieutenant colonel ignore U.S. law and the Constitution to fund and fight his own private war? What can be done about these activities?
- Why do secret institutions so frequently resort to covert action against their own people and government? FBI operations like COINTELPRO and CIA's CHAOS have shown that even innocent Americans can be the subject of American covert operations. How can the American people and American institutions be protected from this?
- What is the connection between covert operations and U.S. multinational corporations? Are covert actions sometimes undertaken to preserve corporate power and wealth, rather than the U.S. national interest? What is the influence of corporate power on American intelligence activities? What was the role of the United Fruit Company in the "Guatemalan" insurrection of 1954, or of the International Telephone and Telegraph Co. (ITT) in the overthrow of Chilean President Salvador Allende in 1973?
- Are covert actions as successful as we have been led to believe, or can successful operations be attributed to U.S. economic power? How much of the overthrow of Allende can be attributed to successful covert action,

and how much to U.S. government economic warfare? Was it the contras or the cutoff of foreign credits that defeated Nicaragua's Sandinistas?

- What are the ramifications of creating private armies in the United States for foreign adventures? How does one draw the line between private and governmental power? *Should* private "volunteers" be permitted to undertake such ventures?

- Why and how do covert operators create "off-the-books" funding for covert operations and organizations? Did the creation of Richard Secord's "Enterprise" or the army's YELLOW FRUIT operation damage the American democracy? What is the connection of the infamous Nugan Hand Bank to American covert operations and intelligence? What do these activities mean for democracy in the United States, and can they be controlled?

- Why do covert actions so often escalate into overt operations that ignore limitations imposed by legitimate authority? Did CIA executives try to force President Kennedy to invade Cuba in 1961 by sending out a purposely weak covert army? How did U.S. covert operations in Laos and Vietnam snowball into a major American war? If the purpose of covert action is to avoid open war, what can we learn from these experiences?

- How does the control of intelligence information by covert action institutions influence the political decision-making process?

- Will the end of the cold war reduce the United States's reliance on covert action? Why or why not?

- Is it even *possible* to control covert action institutions? Does secret power *corrupt secretly*?

Much of the history in this book will be little known to most readers, because our educational system doesn't teach it. Thanks to a dedicated group of researchers as well as the efforts of many professional intelligence officers who remember their oath to the U.S. Constitution, the true stories of covert operations have been revealed. The following pages, I hope, shed some light on what it all means. The cold war is over, and those peoples who win wars tend not to be self-reflective. It is enough to win; why dwell on things better left unsaid? This book is my response, for it is about you and me.

NOTES

1. Technically, the aircraft was the military version of the DC-3, designated the C-47. I've called it the civilian name here to help readers visualize the craft.

2. This account is drawn from Stephen Schlesinger and Stephen Kinzer, *Bitter Fruit: The Untold Story of the American Coup in Guatemala* (New York: Anchor Books, 1982); John Prados, *President's Secret Wars: CIA and Pentagon Covert Operations Since World War II* (New York: William Morrow and Co., 1986), chap. 6; David Atlee

Phillips, *The Night Watch: Twenty-Five Years of Peculiar Service* (New York: Atheneum, 1977), chap. 2; Gregory Treverton, *Covert Action* (New York: Basic Books, 1987), chap. 2.

3. "Uncooperative" covered a wide range of cases during the cold war: Soviet client states (Iraq), Third World "neutralists" (Indonesia), anyone who nationalized U.S. holdings (Guatemala, Chile—it was often okay to nationalize one's own holdings, however), allies with strong Communist parties (Italy), and allies who didn't like what the CIA was doing (Australia).

4. Importantly, Arbenz also nationalized most of his own family's landholdings to redistribute to peasants.

5. We have no record of what happened to the defecting pilot's family. See Phillips, *Night Watch*, chap. 6.

6. This account is drawn from Peter Wyden, *Bay of Pigs: The Untold Story* (New York: Simon and Schuster, 1979); Prados, *President's Secret Wars*; Taylor Report, Paramilitary Study, John F. Kennedy Library, Boston, Mass.; John J. Nutter, "To Trap a President: JFK, CIA, and the Bay of Pigs" (The Conflict Analysis Group, photocopy), available from author; Philips, *The Night Watch*, chap. 5; E. Howard Hunt, *Give Us This Day* (New York: Arlington House, 1973.

7. Although it should be noted that plans to oust Castro were well underway long before he turned to the USSR for aid, and the CIA's own directorate of intelligence, as late as early 1960, described him as a nationalist.

8. Also strangely cut out of ZAPATA, perhaps by his own choice, was Richard Helms, who was the chief of operations in the directorate of plans, i.e., the executive normally in charge of these affairs. It is also possible that the DCI and DDP cut out their own intelligence analysts because the analysts were telling them things they wanted neither to hear nor to have passed on to President Kennedy, such as the unlikelihood of a revolt against Castro.

9. There's nothing sinister here. Reports of the impending invasion had been in the Latin American and U.S. media for weeks; rebel troops had been openly recruited in Florida; the town near the the brigade training site in Honduras had numerous well-known Communists; the sudden disappearance of the brigade and closing of Nicaraguan docks to load ships with secret cargo must have been a tip-off to Castro; and it's likely that Castro had agents among the brigade anyway.

10. For the history of these actions, see Prados, *President's Secret Wars*; William Blum, *Killing Hope: U.S. Military and CIA Interventions Since World War II* (Monroe, Maine: Common Courage Press, 1995); Jonathan Kwitny, *Endless Enemies: The Making of an Unfriendly World* (New York: Viking Penguin, 1984).

Part I
The Third Option

Chapter 1

Like Moths to Light:
The Attraction of Covert Action

The bumper stickers were everywhere during the cold war: "Better Dead Than Red." For true believers, and there were many, the choices were that simple—nuclear war or Communist slavery—and they'd made their pick. The more clever policy makers expanded the options to *threatening* nuclear war, for which they coined the mildly comforting euphemism *brinkmanship*.

Into a world of such bleak choices rode the Central Intelligence Agency, charter in hand and ready to perform "other such actions" authorized by the National Security Council. Presidents latched onto the promise of covert action like a drowning man to driftwood, and every president since Franklin D. Roosevelt has engaged in significant and numerous black operations.

Why did covert action become so important that in many times and places it became a substitute for a coherent foreign policy? Why, even when it failed, did it retain a privileged position in the foreign-policy menu? Debacles in the Ukraine, Albania, Indonesia, and Cuba never dampened the enthusiasm for covert ops. Sometimes covert operations led down the slippery slope of disastrous escalation. United States involvement in Indochina began in the 1950s with "advisers," White Star Teams, and Civil Air Transport supply drops to Dien Bien Phu: it ended in Arc Lights, free-fire zones, and the Killing Fields.[1] Even when covert actions became highly public "proxy wars," as in Afghanistan, the very openness of the warfare was viewed as a benefit—"At least we're doing something."

To understand the possible future of black ops in American foreign policy, we must understand how they became the method of choice in the foreign-policy menu of the United States. There is no single reason why covert action became the "American way," raising up the CIA to a (or perhaps *the*) major foreign policy maker for the cold war. As conditions changed throughout the cold war, the motivations for covert action changed as well, but whatever the situation, the government and agents of the United States always found adequate justification for operating in the black.[2] These reasons include:

- a "bipolar" (two-superpower) international system, which created the perceived need to resist the Soviets *everywhere*;
- decolonization of European empires in Asia and Africa, creating the potential for dozens of "brushfire" (local) wars all over the world;
- the potential for nuclear war that required the United States to avoid overtly confronting the Soviets;
- a desire to avoid direct U.S. military intervention in the Third World after World War II, in order to maintain U.S. self-image, to buff up the American image abroad, to ease American "war weariness," and to limit the potential financial costs of confrontation at a hundred points around the globe;
- the Office of Strategic Studies (OSS) experience of the American "intelligence elite," and the importance they placed on World War II "special operations";
- the success of early covert actions in overthrowing "unfriendly" regimes (AJAX, SUCCESS);
- the fact that little domestic political cost occurred when some early covert actions misfired or were exposed;
- the prevailing view among American political elites that "the world is malleable" and Americans could do anything;
- the "Imperial Presidency" and the breakdown of bipartisanship in foreign policy, which exposed conflict between the president and Congress, leading presidents to try to circumvent controls and unilaterally make foreign policy;
- the belief that covert actions could circumvent domestic political constraints and that the administration could "get away with" actions that the American people and Congress would not support;
- covert action permitted decision makers to do *something* in difficult or ambiguous circumstances, and it allowed them to create the illusion of having done something where they didn't want to act;
- belief that "subversion" worked for the Commies, and that it could work for us, too;
- the rejection of "idealism" and morality, and the perceived need for a new approach, exemplified in NSC-68, the Doolittle Commission Report, and the Hoover Report; and
- the structure of the U.S. intelligence community, in which the agencies themselves largely controlled the government's problem definition, and therefore often "found" threats to the national interest that "required" covert action.

A NEW WORLD AND A NEW ENEMY

"These proceedings are closed," said General Douglas MacArthur when the final page of the armistice with Japan was signed, ending the terrible agony of World

War II and ushering in, it was thought and hoped and prayed for, a new era of peace. Evil had been vanquished, and on 26 June 1945, the Allies had established the United Nations as guarantor against a third world war.

Yet wartime alliances were already crumbling. The deep and inherent antagonism between the capitalist and communist worlds was reemerging. Within the West, conflicts between the United States and the European colonial powers (Britain and especially France) over decolonization in areas like India, central Africa, Indochina, and Algeria, threatened to break apart the Atlantic fraternity. A new international system had emerged with two superpowers and unpredictable conflict dynamics. President Harry Truman was fearful of the costs of sustaining a cold war economy, yet faced global military necessities. In this context, a new American approach to foreign policy developed.

BIPOLARITY AND THE GLOBALIZATION OF AMERICAN INTERESTS

Even before the end of World War II, the United States government and American elites had realized that the Soviet Union would emerge as the only rival to the United States in the postwar world.[3] With the prewar major powers England, France, Japan, Germany, and Italy in ruins, only the USSR remained to challenge the hegemony of the United States. Even though the Soviets had experienced a human and economic catastrophe, two things suggested that the Soviet Union would rise to confront America. First, the immense but largely untapped economic potential of the USSR remained largely intact, and in fact the war had enabled Josef Stalin to mobilize the country's bountiful resources and labor on a historic scale. Moreover, by pillaging Eastern Europe, the Soviet Union extracted the resources, physical plant, skilled labor, and technological and scientific know-how that enabled it to recoup the losses of the war with startling speed. Second, Soviet ideology was by definition the antithesis of American ideology, and thus conflict was inherent in the belief systems of the two goliaths. Even before the war's end, both allies were regarding each other with a considerable degree of hostility.[4]

This suspicion and animosity was aggravated by events that took place as the war neared its final act. Various German leaders had tried to arrange a separate peace with the Anglo-American allies, dangling the bait of Germany as a bulwark against Communism. Even though the Western powers ultimately declined such offers from Reichsfuhrer Heinrich Himmler and Admiral Wilhelm Canaris, the mere offer, as well as the fact that some in the West were willing to listen, ratcheted up Stalin's paranoia. Matters were not helped by the fact that the "separate-peace" offers had been sought out by Allen Dulles, who would become America's spymaster as director of Central Intelligence during the 1950s. Moreover, the United States *did* eventually protect and employ a substantial number of Germans, many of whom were known Nazis. Under the aegis of operations like PAPERCLIP, the United States eagerly sought the services not only of rocket scientists, but also the likes of barbarous "medical" experimenters and mass murderers. Neither was the atmosphere improved by the recruitment of Germany's expert on the USSR, master spy Reinhard Gehlen, who worked first for the CIA, then became head of West German Intelligence.[5] Certainly the Soviets also grabbed as many German experts as possible, and they had signed the nonaggression pact before the war, but to Stalin this was beside the point—Western employment of former Nazis merely reinforced his paranoia, and also supported Soviet ideological perceptions about the unity of capitalist states, whether authoritarian or democratic.

Feeding this fear, too, was the fact that there were many in the West who openly viewed the rise of Soviet power with dread and hostility. Truman himself had suggested that the Western allies should side with whoever was losing in the East, to prolong the war and bleed the two totalitarian states dry, and Churchill's unconcealed enmity toward the Bolshevik regime dated back to the days of Lenin. American intelligence was already planning for U.S.-Soviet conflict in any event: *Even before the end of the war, the OSS was stashing radios in the Soviet Union for postwar operations in Russia.*

Against this background, the United States emerged from the war in an unfamiliar position. It had suffered far less from the war than any other major power. It had the world's only functioning industrial economy. And it had the bomb. In short, the United States towered over the world like a titan.

The emergence of the United States as a global power, and the survival of the Soviet Union as the only logical and capable challenger, produced a structural change in the world system. Where the prewar world had contained several major powers, the new international system was dominated by only two, and the change from a multipolar structure (many powers) to a bipolar structure (two powers) created new conflict dynamics. Among the most important of these forces was that the United States and Soviet Union came to view the world in zero-sum terms. This meant that any gain for oneself was perceived as an automatic loss for the other side, and any loss for oneself an automatic gain for the enemy. By definition, then, the way to help oneself was to hurt the other side. Even if one might not capture new countries for one's own side, simply having small groups of guerrillas or terrorists raise hell in an enemy country forced the opponent to divert valuable resources and attention from core areas of the struggle, thereby automatically weakening the foe. Thus, the entire globe was "in play."

Another important idea arose to reinforce the zero-sum tenet of bipolarity: the Domino Theory. This was the simple concept that even though many countries might be inconsequential in and of themselves, each might nevertheless be a critical stepping stone toward subverting the vital countries. As Truman pointed out:

> If Greece should fall under the control of an armed minority, the effect on its neighbor, Turkey, would be immediate and serious. Confusion and disorder might well spread throughout the entire Middle East.[6]

On Laos, President Dwight D. Eisenhower explained that

> you have the broader considerations that follow what you might call the
> "falling domino" principle . . . you knock over the first one, and what will
> happen to the last one is the certainty that it will go over very quickly . . . the
> geographical position achieved thereby does many things. It turns the so-called
> island defensive chain of Japan, Formosa, of the Philippines, and to the south-
> ward; it moves in to threaten Australia and New Zealand.[7]

The implication of this shift in worldview was that there were no longer any
inconsequential countries. *Any* gain for the Soviets was a potential crack in the
dike through which would flood unstoppable Red hordes, and no backwater was
too remote to leave uncontested.

The possibility of falling dominos and U.S.-Soviet confrontation was dramatically increased by global decolonization and the wars of liberation that often
accompanied it. For roughly three hundred years, Africa, south Asia, Indochina,
and the southwestern Pacific archipelagoes had been ruled by European powers.
By the end of World War II, Great Britain, France, Belgium, the Netherlands,
and Portugal were hanging on to these colonies by their fingernails, if they had
not already lost them. The colonial powers were too weak from the war to hold
on long, and besides, hadn't the war been fought for "freedom"? In such circumstances, decolonization was going to happen, peacefully or otherwise.

Where there had been a few dozen colonies, each strictly controlled by a major
power and generally left alone by the others, recognizing one another's "spheres of
influence," decolonization produced one hundred or more sovereign states, the
majority of them small, poor, and weak, each with its own foreign policy, and
many of them charter members of the "revolution-of-the-month club." All these
countries represented new opportunities for the ruthless contest between the
United States and the Soviet Union. The new countries were now outside their
former colonial rulers' spheres of influence, and as such, were up for grabs.

Virtually none of these new entities were, in any sense, "nation-states."
While they had the trappings of sovereignty, many of the newly formed "countries" were loose conglomerations of disparate and often hostile peoples, tribes,
and nations, who had been thrown together by European statesmen drawing
lines on maps without regard to local history, politics, or custom. Such "states"
were highly prone to civil wars, coups, assassinations, terrorism, and guerrilla
warfare—in other words, each was a perfect opening for one superpower to challenge the other. As soon as one faction in a country called on the United States
for aid, the Soviets would immediately discover that the opposing side were pro-
letarian heroes worthy of brotherly socialist support, and vice versa. Ideology was
a secondary consideration, since Third World rebels generally lived by the motto
"Any Port in a Storm."

Coupled with the explosion in opportunity was a new internationalism in Soviet
politics. With the destruction of Germany and the establishment of an Eastern Euro-

pean buffer zone, the Soviet Union (and Russia, historically) was secure at last from European invasion (or capitalist counterrevolution, depending on your point of view). The Soviet Union now had both the inclination and the ability to look outward, with an eye toward imposing Soviet control where it could or simply raising a little hell where it couldn't.[8] By the early 1950s, the Soviet government decided to support "wars of national liberation," and it went about this task with vigor.

Confronting the vast assortment of nationalist, irredentist, and subversive movements that ignited across the postwar globe would have been financially ruinous for America. One solution the United States hit upon was the nuclear doctrine[9] of massive retaliation, according to which John Foster Dulles proclaimed that the American government would not fight brushfire wars all over the world, but would instead "go to the source" of subversion, the Soviet Union.[10] Thus, subversion in, say, Laos, would presumably be answered by nuclear airbursts over Moscow. However, the threat of nuclear retaliation in these circumstances rang hollow. Once the Soviet Union developed the bomb in 1949, there was little chance that the United States would nuke Moscow over, say, Laos, knowing that the Soviets could destroy Washington in return. The "Washington for Vientiane, followed by global annihilation" strategy was a loser.

Having defined the choices as nuclear war or surrender, the United States arrived at a third option: covert action employing coups and indigenous forces to resist the onslaught of subversion and insurgency. Covert action offered numerous advantages over the more conventional or nuclear approaches. First, there was (presumably) little risk of dragging the United States into a shooting war with the Soviets. U.S. and Soviet troops would not be directly engaged, and therefore the prestige of the two superpowers would not be put on the line. If a covert action didn't work out, one could simply withdraw with no loss of credibility, as one had "never been there" in the first place. The superpowers could compete in the Third World with comparatively little cost to themselves. It is always far better to make war with someone else's blood.

NUCLEAR WEAPONS AND COVERT ACTION

While the bipolar worldview required confrontation practically everywhere, the development of the Soviet bomb precluded confrontation anywhere. Although many contemporary strategists suggested that a nuclear weapon was simply a "big bomb" and would not change the face of warfare, political leaders seemed to intuitively sense that a nuclear war might well destroy all human life. The tension thus created between bipolarity and the potential for nuclear escalation required a careful balancing act between the two great and opposing American foreign-policy analogies of the twentieth century: Munich and Sarajevo. First, failure to respond to an opponent's encroachments, however modest and far away, smacked of Munich (1938), Chamberlain, and appeasement, and could lead an aggressor to believe that one did not have the will to actually fight. It would be even worse to attempt to defend insignificant areas with threats, but then back down. The consequent loss of credibility would only stimulate the adversary to ever greater demands and aggressions, in the belief that you were weak and vacillating.[11] On the other hand, military responses that engaged the armed forces of the superpowers against one another, or even staked the credibility of one against another, evoked images of 1914 and the "Guns of August." "Some damn thing in the Balkans"—Sarajevo and the assassination of Archduke Franz Ferdinand—had precipitated the Great War, as Bismarck had prophesied, and cold war leaders were painfully aware that small sparks could ignite the final global conflagration. Thus, one had to stand up to the foe *without* standing up to them. Covert action was the only policy that seemed to satisfy both conditions.

OSS BUCCANEERS AND THE INTELLIGENCE ELITE

The Central Intelligence Agency was created, as an agency and an ethos, by the men who had planned and executed the secret war against Germany and Japan. These operators, virtually all veterans of the OSS, had seen the effects of resistance, sabotage, guerrilla war, propaganda, and the rest of the covert menu firsthand, and they had been impressed.

Even before the United States was impelled into World War II, Franklin Roosevelt had recognized that American involvement was merely a matter of when, not if, and had asked his friend William "Wild Bill" Donovan to assemble the nucleus of an intelligence service. Donovan, a freewheeling Medal of Honor recipient from World War I, lived up to his nickname, establishing the prototype for the covert operator: audacious in action, heedless of authority, ceaselessly active, careless of administrative detail, loyal, and fiercely protective of his field operatives.[12] For Wild Bill, no plan was too outrageous to consider. On one occasion, OSS psychologists diagnosed that Adolf Hitler might be driven mad by massive exposure to pornography. To that end, the OSS accumulated an immense store of German pornography, with the intent of airdropping it around Hitler's headquarters, in the belief that he might stumble across some and go insane. In the end, the only thing that was dropped was the plan itself, when an American air commander refused to risk pilot's lives on such a scheme.[13]

When the CIA was established by the National Security Act of 1947, Donovan was the logical choice for director. He had argued for a centralized intelligence function since the 1930s. Wild Bill, however, faced two political enemies that cared little for his experience and acumen. Harry Truman disliked Donovan's postwar enthusiasm for continuing covert and special operations. Perhaps more importantly, J. Edgar Hoover opposed him because: (1) Donovan had scrapped for every advantage he could during the war, including using known or alleged socialists and Communists in the OSS; (2) Donovan had made some accommodations during the war with leftist guerrillas (Tito, Ho Chi Minh, and some Italians); and (3) Hoover wanted the job for himself. Nonetheless, the CIA and its operating ethos was invented by the alumni of the OSS. Foremost among these was the "great white case officer," Allen Dulles, who served as director of Central Intelligence from 1953 through 1961. Dulles was legendary even before World War II. He had, as a fledgling foreign service officer during World War I, opted to keep a tennis date and skipped a meeting with a Russian expatriate seeking his help. The man turned out to be Vladimir Illyich Lenin. During World War II, Dulles not only ran espionage networks into the Third Reich, but also conducted clandestine political actions, including negotiations with German leaders (e.g., Canaris, Himmler) for the removal of Hitler, and attempted to aid German groups who were trying to assassinate *Der Fuhrer*. Other key CIA figures with OSS experience included:

- William Colby, director of Central Intelligence (DCI). Colby parachuted into occupied France as a member of Jedburgh team BRUCE and blew bridges and railways on the right flank of General Patton's epic sweep across France to prevent a German counteroffensive. Later, Colby parachuted into Norway, leading sabotage operations against the Germans (mainly blowing up bridges) to pin down German troops who could have participated in the last-ditch defense of the Fatherland.[14] During Vietnam, Colby for a time ran the PHOENIX program, and later, as DCI, became the "Man Who *Didn't* Keep Secrets," revealing to Congress and the world evidence of assassination plots, mind-control experiments, and domestic surveillance operations.
- William Casey, who was responsible for all OSS activity in Germany from 1944 on, organizing the Jedburgh operations that delayed German reaction to the Normandy landings, and guarding Patton's southern flank by destroying bridges and railways. He would write ". . . it is important today to understand how clandestine intelligence, covert action, and organized resistance saved blood and treasure in defeating Hitler. These capabilities may be more important than missiles and satellites in meeting crises yet to come, and point to the potential for dissident action against the control centers and lines of communication of totalitarian power."[15] Casey would later act on his belief and experience; as Ronald Reagan's DCI, he was a key figure in the Iran-Contra affair.
- Ray Cline, deputy director for intelligence (DDI), a staunch CIA defender who would go on to found "Agents for Bush."
- Frank Wisner, first chief of CIA special operations, who penetrated Rumania during World War II, served as a major allied intermediary with both King Michael and the head of the Soviet security service, and whose detailed reporting of the Soviet takeover convinced many in government that World War II would soon be followed by another.[16]
- Tracy Barnes, an Allen Dulles protégé and former Jedburgh who rose to assistant deputy director for plans (ADDP)—"plans" was the early euphemism for covert operations. Barnes oversaw such operations as the Bay of Pigs.

- Lyman Kirkpatrick, inspector general of the CIA, vilified within the CIA for his still-classified Bay of Pigs postmortem, who would be offered the job of DCI by President Jimmy Carter.
- Thomas Karamessines, DDP during the operations against Salvador Allende in Chile.
- Lucien Conein (aka "Black Luigi"), legendary operator and key CIA player in Vietnam and later in the CIA's drug war in Southeast Asia.
- Kermit "Kim" Roosevelt, OSS analyst to Supreme Allied Headquarters and official historian of the OSS.[17] He planned and organized the overthrow of the Mosaddeq regime in Iran in 1953, and refused the Guatemala operation.
- E. Howard Hunt, who served with OSS Detachment 101 in Indochina, and would play major roles in the Guatemala coup, the Bay of Pigs, and Watergate.
- Sherman Kent, deputy director of Central Intelligence (DDCI) and influential chairman of the Board of National Estimates, whose memoranda were ignored by the Bay of Pigs planners.
- James Jesus Angleton, famous (or infamous) CIA chief of counterintelligence. In the OSS, Angleton served as the chief of the Italian Desk, and his agents (named, among other things, ROSE, PANSY, and BLOOM, after Angleton's love of flowers) sought out Nazi "stay-behind" agents and burgled suspected enemy agents.[18] As the CIA's chief of counterintelligence, his "molehunt" (investigation for Soviet spies within the agency) nearly destroyed the CIA, and never revealed a single enemy agent.[19] Ironically, Angleton was a close friend of Kim Philby, who *did* turn out to be a Soviet spy.

The exception to this list is former DCI Richard Helms. He served in OSS, but came away with a different conclusion: The gains from special operations weren't worth the cost.[20] To Helms, penetration of enemy military and political secrets cost less and paid off far better. This natural caution played out during the Bay of Pigs, when Helms, nominally in charge of operations, was omitted from the planning and execution of ZAPATA. It was during Helms's tenure as DCI that the CIA began to turn more toward intelligence gathering and away from covert action, a trend that would not be reversed until the directorship of William Casey, some seventeen years later.

With the exception of Helms, special operations left a highly favorable impression on OSS veterans because the actions were so successful and apparently consequential to the outcome of the war. Some operations involved starting small armies, such as OSS Detachment 101, which organized the Kachin tribes in northern Burma against the Japanese. By the war's end, the group had inflicted over ten thousand casualties on the invaders at a cost of about two hundred of their own.[21]

Perhaps the most famous European operator exemplifies the spirit of buccaneering audacity that permeated the OSS. Raised in France, Marine Corps Major Peter Ortiz spoke the language like a native and was a five-year veteran of the Foreign Legion. Parachuting into France in 1943, Ortiz operated by day as a fashion designer, well liked by German officers. By night he led Maquis raids wearing his U.S. Marine Corps uniform. His audacity is best illustrated by the act of walking into a German-filled cabaret wearing his full uniform under a raincoat. Casually drawing a pair of .38s from his belt, Ortiz dropped the raincoat, and "encouraged" the Germans, many of whom had been his drinking companions, to raise a toast to Franklin Roosevelt and Allied victory. He then casually disappeared into the night.[22]

Former OSS men drew their conclusions about the efficacy of covert action not only from their own experience, but also from that of others in the war, especially the "cousins" (British). During the darkest hours of the war, Winston Churchill had chartered the Special Operations Executive (SOE) with the admonition to "set Europe ablaze." Two operations in particular illustrated the potentially decisive effects of small, strategic operations.

One of the these was the theft of a German Enigma cipher machine. Enigma was a typewriter-like machine that encrypted messages with nearly an infinite number of possible combinations, and was therefore considered unbreakable. However, in 1939, the Polish Secret Service had ambushed a German SS truck in the Danzig Corridor and stolen an Enigma machine. The Poles burned the truck and left a pile of mechanical parts that the Germans mistook for the remains of the cipher machine. With this machine in hand, brilliant Allied cryptanalysts sometimes presented Churchill with German intelligence before Hitler received it.[23]

The other key commando operation of the war was the destruction of the Norwegian heavy-water plant, the Norsk-Hydro, along with Germany's supply of heavy water—the crucial ingredient in Hitler's effort to build an atomic bomb—at Vemork, Norway, in 1943. Unwilling to risk the numerous Norwegian civilian casualties that might be inflicted by a bombing raid, Churchill and SOE sent in a group of thirty-four commandos to destroy the plant. Unfortunately, their gliders crashed, and the commandos were all either killed on landing or captured and summarily executed. Next, SOE sent in a small group of saboteurs, who penetrated the plant, destroyed all of the electrolysis tubes and half a ton of heavy water. However, this attack only delayed production, and within six months the plant was restored to full production. Worse, German security was increased to the point that no further commando or sabotage raids were possible. The Allied Combined Chiefs of Staff concluded that the only alternative was a bomber raid, but although seven hundred bombs were dropped, only two hit the plant. Norwegian casualties numbered twenty-two, and Norway's government-in-exile strongly protested.

Fortunately for the Allies, although the physical effect of the bombing was almost nil, the psychological effect was impressive. The Germans became convinced that Vemork was too exposed to both sabotage and bomber raids, and decided to move the whole plant and the entire stock of heavy water to Germany for greater security. The first part of the transport required crossing a deep Norwegian lake by ferry. A Norwegian SOE agent penetrated German security, planted a bomb aboard the boat and sunk it, along with Germany's atomic bomb project, in a thousand feet of water.[24]

Additionally, the potential for small Special Forces units was amply demonstrated during the war. While the United States regular military remained highly resistant to such "behind the lines nonsense," the forerunners of the CIA watched and learned. In North Africa, David Stirling's Special Air Service (SAS) was spectacular in penetrating through German lines across hundreds of miles of trackless desert, to cripple Erwin Rommel's supply lines and air force. On one raid, SAS drove a convoy of land rovers down the runway at a German airbase, shooting up dozens of aircraft. In Asia, Orde Wingate's Chindits and Frank Merrill's Marauders operated solely on airborne resupply and what they could capture to range far into the interior of Burma, capturing or destroying crucial Japanese installations and rail facilities.

Finally, the operators in the OSS emerged from the war with a grasp of the possibilities of revolutionary warfare.[25] OSS men had worked with highly successful resistance movements in France, Yugoslavia, Greece, Indochina, and China, among many others, fighting side by side with Mao Tse-tung, Ho Chi Minh, and Tito. In some areas, insurgent forces practically liberated themselves. By June 1945, six entire provinces in Tonkin had been liberated from the Japanese by Vo Nguyen Giap's Viet Minh.[26] Tito's Partisans freed islands, towns, and large tracts of land from the occupying German *Wehrmacht*, operated their own railroad and mail system, and tied down more than 300,000 German and Axis troops.[27] These lessons were not lost on the OSS veterans who invented the CIA. Even if indigenous forces behind the Iron Curtain could not liberate themselves from Soviet occupation, experience showed that they could tie down large numbers of troops, who would then be unavailable to threaten Western interests. The OSS also created an intellectual underpinning to their brand of revolutionary liberation. As part of their wartime study, the analysts for the OSS had come to know theorists of revolution such as Harvard historian Crane Brinton, whose *Anatomy of a Revolution* would be consulted by the CIA in the 1950s as a "how-to" book.[28]

In summary, the men of the early CIA were inspired by the courage and audacity of the OSS and SOE, and emerged from that experience convinced that decisive outcomes could sometimes be effected by small, cleverly directed groups of specialists.

THE BREAKDOWN OF BIPARTISANSHIP AND COVERT ACTION

For much of American history, foreign policy was conducted in a spirit of bipartisanship, perhaps best exemplified in the words of Senator Arthur Vandenberg, who said that "politics stops at the water's edge." This expressed the sentiment that the United States needed to present the world with a single, unified voice, and that this unity was so important that mere partisan political disagreements should be put aside. We are, after all, all Americans. Bipartisanship was also fostered by the substantial foreign-policy consensus that emerged in the aftermath of World War II. Gone were the vituperative debates between the interventionists and the isolationists. Having been "dragged" into two European conflicts in twenty years, the people and leaders of the United States concluded that the country *could not* stand outside these wars, and that it was better to become a global leader to deter World War III than to be inevitably sucked into yet another European inferno. Thus, a consensus of anti-Communism and globalism (active involvement in world affairs) arose, cutting across political boundaries and essentially defining attempts to use foreign policy issues for partisan point scoring as "un-American."

Two related issues began to break down this consensus in the 1960s: the Vietnam War and the "Imperial Presidency." Opinion about Vietnam was divided early on, not only between doves and hawks, but also between those whose hawks who felt Vietnam was a test of America's credibility and willingness to fight Communism, and those who felt it was a diversionary attack to "bleed" America before the real attack in Europe. Later, when Congress became aware of the complete history of U.S. involvement in Indochina, it deeply resented having been manipulated. This feeling ran deep against Lyndon B. Johnson for the Gulf of Tonkin incident and resolution, and against Richard Nixon, who in 1968 had promised a "secret plan" to end the war, which he then allowed to drag on for five more years.

These two administrations came to be called the "Imperial Presidency." The term connoted the belief that the presidents had vastly overstepped their constitutional and traditional powers; that they had less in common with "We the people" and more in common with *l'etat c'est moi* ("I am the state"). While most Americans continued to accept the idea of presidential preeminence in foreign policy, these presidents came to treat their domestic opposition contemptuously, often viewing political disagreement as akin to treason. The conduct of the Vietnam War, essentially divorced from Congress and its authority to declare war, contributed to this. Additionally, both Johnson and Nixon employed domestic agencies, such as the Federal Bureau of Investigation and the Internal Revenue Service, to persecute political foes. Each also identified himself and his political fate with the national interest of the United States. Finally, there was Watergate, which was much more than the "third-rate burglary" portrayed by Nixon apologists. Revelations about the Committee to Reelect the President (CREEP) revealed that Nixon's cronies had performed domestic covert actions to sabotage enemies, and that Nixon planned to use the full weight of presidential power (*not* "authority") to "screw his political enemies." For these reasons, by the mid-1970s, Congress overwhelmingly felt the need to rein in the power of the presidency.

Global events also contributed to the breaking-down of bipartisanship.

During the 1950s, it was easy to get on the anti-Communist bandwagon, and virtually everyone did. Communism was perceived as monolithic and omnipresent, and every bad thing for the United States could (and generally was) interpreted as the result of the global Communist conspiracy. Senator Joe McCarthy could wave a blank envelope as "evidence" of Communist conspiracies, and no one dared challenge it. Whittaker Chambers took us to his garden to reveal his "pumpkin papers," purported proof of massive Communist infiltration of America. Hollywood portrayed allegorical Communists as thinly veiled bodysnatchers (in the movie *Invasion of the Bodysnatchers*). In 1963, however, the traditional enmity between the Russians and Chinese broke through their ideological and expedient alliance, resulting in the highly public and hostile split in the Communist bloc. While some believed the split to be a ploy, it soon became clear that previous fears of a unified, implacable enemy were overblown, to say the least. In the face of a unified foe, everyone was expected to hop into line. With the two major enemy powers at each other's throats, there became room in America for differences of opinion.

One upshot of the breakdown of bipartisanship was an increasing congressional assertiveness over foreign policy issues. In 1973, Congress passed the War Powers Act in an effort to limit the power of a president to engage American armed forces while bypassing the "declaration of war" authority of the Congress (Article I, section 8). In 1975, the "Year of Intelligence," the Church Committee began stripping away the veils of secrecy surrounding the CIA (and other intelligence organizations, such as the FBI), revealing a history replete with assassination plots, disinformation campaigns aimed at influencing the American people, complicity with organized crime, domestic surveillance, blackmail, and subversion. By the 1980s, although Congress supported aid to the Afghan mujahedin, it generally opposed operations to undermine the Nicaraguan Sandinistas, passing the Boland amendments in 1982, which prohibited the United States from any action aimed at overthrowing the Nicaraguan government, and thus specifically limiting the president's covert authority.

The result of Congress's efforts to impose ever greater controls over the presidency, foreign policy, and intelligence institutions was an increasing presidential reliance on covert action. Particularly in the Reagan administration, "plausible deniability" came to mean not that an action was deniable to America's enemies, but rather that congressional oversight committees couldn't prove who was responsible, and even if they could, it was impossible to successfully prosecute the perpetrators. The primary, but not only, example of this is the effort to circumvent both congressional oversight and the Boland amendments that led to the Iran-Contra operation run by Richard Secord's Enterprise. Ironically, one reason the president and his cronies chose to work outside the formal intelligence organizations is that congressional oversight was working, and the "cowboys," such as William Casey and Elliot Abrams, feared that the professionals within the CIA would refuse to lie to Congress or break the law.

Finally, several administrations have performed covert actions to pursue policies that were either blatantly illegal, unconstitutional, lacking support by the American people, or the opposite of what the presidents themselves have publicly declared. The people of United States did not believe that the Sandinista government posed a serious threat, and did not support any kind of overt U.S. military action. Moreover, fearing another Vietnam-like quagmire, most opposed even covert action, and Congress passed the two Boland amendments, forbidding members of any U.S. intelligence agency from acting to overthrow the government of Nicaragua. For these reasons, Reagan and his advisers turned to a private covert action run out of Bill Casey's vest pocket and Ollie North's office, keeping the CIA itself out of the loop. (Similarly, Presidents Johnson and Nixon had feared the domestic backlash of open U.S. military intervention in Laos [a "widening of the war"], and therefore chose to operate with a clandestine army and air force.) Ronald Reagan came to office vowing to never bargain with terrorists; he ended up ransoming a few hostages for thousands of missiles.

In each of these cases, there is a clear and deceitful reason for keeping the operations covert: *to keep them from the American people.* In the case of the secret war in Laos, or Phoenix in Vietnam, or the mining of Nicaraguan harbors, or the secret arming of Iraq in the 1980s, or the arms-for-hostages swap with Iran, "the enemy" knew what was happening in each instance! It was only to keep these activities from the American people (i.e., voters) that these operations were conducted secretly.

COVERT ACTION: THE SEDUCTIVE OPTION

The attraction of covert action is probably inherent in our system of government. Power is diffuse, and presidential problems tend to be complex and full of uncertainty. Covert action promises a simple, or "clean," solution to a problem. It is one of the few exercises of power that is largely held within the sole purview of the executive, avoiding the need for messy, unsatisfying compromises and the need to answer hard questions from congressional committees. Even the "problem definition" part of the decision-making process becomes simpler, as problems can be narrowly framed, e.g., "that bastard Castro," and the solution then seems to suggest itself. Finally, covert action offers the benefit of limited accountability, for even if it fails, one cannot, presumably, be blamed.

Another institutional reason for the attractiveness of covert action is the nature of American politics. Presidents rarely come to office with foreign-affairs experience, and are confronted with managing a complex set of problems and competing bureaucracies. Facing the president are covert executives and operators with long years experience in not only covert activities, but also bureaucratic warfare. It is not coincidental that the Bay of Pigs plan was never presented to President Eisenhower, who would have hesitated scarcely a millisecond in overruling Allen Dulles and his plan to send fourteen hundred men against Castro's two-hundred-thousand-man army. Instead, the plan was created out of whole cloth in November 1960—after the election of Kennedy—and presented to the president-elect. The complex circumstances of world and domestic politics always contain the possibility of a neophyte president and inexperienced staff simply being overwhelmed by the mystique of covert operators. Novices often do not know the questions to ask (neither, sometimes, do experienced executives) and have not developed a feel for when something is being left unsaid. If Richard Bissell, CIA legend and "one of the smartest men in government," tells you that the worst case is that the Cuban Brigade will simply move to the mountains and "go guerrilla," who are *you* to dispute him?

SUBVERSION, ROLLBACK, AND COVERT ACTION

Covert action was also given a substantial boost by the political winds of the forties and fifties. The Communists had expanded their empire not only through outright armed occupation of Eastern Europe, but also through an active and effective program of subversion. They had promoted civil insurrection in Iran, Turkey, and Greece, and had successfully created puppet regimes by subversive methods (*their* acts are "subversion"; *ours* are "covert action"—semantics are important in politics). In 1948, a Soviet coup overthrew a nominally democratic government in Czechoslovakia, and similar events occurred throughout Bulgaria, Poland, Hungary, and Romania.[29] It must have seemed as though such tactics worked (see the comments by John Foster Dulles below).

Nineteen forty-nine was a momentous year. Mao Tse-tung's revolution in China finally succeeded, and America sought scapegoats for "losing China." It found them in President Truman, Secretary of State Dean Acheson (labeled the "Red Dean" by the American right wing), and in the "hundreds of Soviet agents" that riddled the State Department. The year also witnessed the explosion of a Soviet atomic bomb, several years before U.S. intelligence had predicted, in part because Soviet agents had stolen the atomic secrets from the United States. The capture of the atom bomb spies Rudolf Abel, Klaus Fuchs, David Greenglass, Harry Gold, and Julius and Ethel Rosenberg seemed to confirm the existence of a web of deceit across the United States, and the "revelations" of "Tail-Gunner Joe" McCarthy and Martin Dies only heightened this belief. Whittaker Chambers became a hero (to some) by telling stories of Alger Hiss. In 1958, J. Edgar Hoover, America's number one anti-Communist, told us "how to spot the communists" in *Masters of Deceit*.[30] Subversion seemed to work, and with the choices limited to nuclear war or surrender, covert action must have seemed a pretty good third option.[31]

Finally, although American policy through the cold war has largely been identified with *containment* (i.e., holding the line against the Communists), there was always an underlying longing for *rollback* (i.e., "kicking their red butts back to Moscow"). Ike promised to "never rest" until the enslaved peoples of the world could choose their own path. In 1953, Eisenhower's secretary of state, John Foster Dulles, told the Senate Foreign Relations Committee that we must always have in mind the liberation of these captive peoples. Now, liberation does not mean a war of liberation. Liberation can be accomplished by processes short of war. . . . Soviet communism itself, has spread . . . by methods of political warfare, psychological warfare, and propaganda, and it has not actually used the Red Army as an open aggressive force in accomplishing that. Surely what they can accomplish, we can accomplish.[32]

Dulles promised to use "all means necessary" to liberate Eastern Europe.[33] President John F. Kennedy's inaugural address was a masterpiece of rollback rhetoric, pledging the United States to "pay any price, bear any burden" to liberate the oppressed.[34] In an era of nuclear weapons, covert action is the ideal choice with which to pursue rollback. As one cannot risk pushing the opponent too far, a deniable operation in which neither side risks credibility or prestige is the *only* offensive option.

THE AGE OF CONFIDENCE

Covert action was also attractive because the postwar era was a time of unlimited optimism and confidence. The Axis had been vanquished, and while the United States had entered the war an ill-prepared sleeping giant, it now towered over the globe. It contained the world's only functioning industrial economy, the world's most lucrative markets, and the only currency widely accepted around the world. The United States had created the United Nations and the Bretton Woods international economic system, guaranteeing that the American idea of "free trade" would be the world's trading system. It had the world's most effective armed forces, and even if American armed might could not squash every bug, a judicious application of American skill and money might tip the balance in many places. It's no stretch to understand that American decision makers saw the world as a plastic, malleable entity, and covert action was a perfect tool for "fine-tuning."[35]

PUPPETMASTER'S DREAM: CIA IN THE FIFTIES

One might forgive the CIA for developing hubris in the 1950s. It had some notable successes: Italy in 1947, Iran in 1954, Guatemala in 1954, the rescue of the Dalai Lama in 1959. Perhaps from these experiences, one might justifiably draw the lesson that the world can be made the way we want it.

Moreover, covert failures seldom produced any political cost. Covert action misfired in the Ukraine and Baltic states (late '40s and early '50s), Albania (1949), and Indonesia (1957), among others. In each case, political costs were minimal to both the United States and, internally, to the CIA. If anything, failure was generally a prod to greater effort ("We'll get it right next time") rather than a spur to reexamine the underlying premises of covert action. After the spectacular fiasco at the Bay of Pigs, President Kennedy's first impulse was to tear up the CIA and scatter it to the winds, but he was quickly diverted by General Maxwell Taylor's postmortem report. Taylor, a retired general, was recalled to duty by Kennedy, and became a cold warrior of the first rank. JFK immediately plunged ahead into plans for another, better invasion and OPERATION MONGOOSE.

"LIE, CHEAT, AND STEAL": AMERICAN POLICY PAPERS

Abstract concepts are important to Americans: right and wrong, fair and unfair, just and unjust. Deep in the American psyche is a belief that our country operates with honesty, fairness, and integrity. "Gentlemen," said Secretary of State Henry Stimson, "don't read each other's mail."[36] On the other hand, the Soviet Union was an enemy who was implacable, cunning, merciless, and godless, a Borg-like entity whose sole purpose was to assimilate everything and everyone into a single, robotic, obedient mass. In a winner-take-all fight for survival, could the United States struggle with one hand tied behind its back?

The answer was that it couldn't—it was necessary to fight fire with fire. Explicitly, America had to reject the Idealism characterized by Stimson and epitomized by Woodrow Wilson. Justification for this was provided in a series of documents that represented the change in mind-set thought necessary to fight the cold war. These documents were "The Sources of Soviet Conduct," by "X," National Security Council document 68 (NSC-68), and the Doolittle Commission Report.

One of the first documents of the cold war was the famous "X" article, "The Sources of Soviet Conduct," by George Kennan, in which he laid out not only the motivations for Soviet expansionism, but also what must be done about it:

> . . . the Soviet pressure against the free institutions of the western world is something that can be contained by the *adroit and vigilant application of counterforce* [emphasis added] at a series of constantly shifting geographic and political points.[37]

If the United States was to respond, however, then the existence of nuclear weapons, the size of the Red Army, and the fiscal conservatism of Truman (and later Eisenhower) meant that something other than overt military confrontation was required.

The second seminal document was NSC-68. Produced for the National Security Council in 1950 by cold warrior par excellence Paul Nitze, it expounded the view of an unrelenting Soviet Union assault on the free world, aiming at "the complete subversion or forcible destruction of the machinery of government and structure of society in the countries of the non-Soviet world and their replacement by an apparatus and structure subservient to and controlled from the Kremlin."[38] While the preferred policy of NSC-68 was one of a massive arms buildup leading to strategic superiority, only the arms buildup, but not the superiority, was possible. However, the overall affect, or feeling, of a mortal threat, endured.

The most direct endorsement of the cold war perspective of the secret warriors was from the "Special Study Group on Covert Activities," from a group chaired by General Jimmy Doolittle of "Thirty Seconds Over Tokyo" fame. The Doolittle Report "rang the gong" for the covert operators:

> It is now clear that we are facing an implacable enemy whose avowed objective is world domination by whatever means and at whatever cost. There are no rules in such a game. Hitherto acceptable norms of human conduct do not apply. If the United States is to survive, long standing American concepts of "fair play" must be reconsidered. We must develop effective espionage and counter-espionage services and must learn to subvert, sabotage and destroy our enemies by more clever, more sophisticated, and more effective methods than those used against us. It may become necessary that the American people be made acquainted with, understand, and support this fundamentally repugnant philosophy.[39]

This approach was taken to heart within the CIA, at least within the directorate of plans (or operations). In 1977, former DDP Richard M. Bissell commented that as DDP, he had believed that any tactics were justified to defeat the Soviet Union.[40]

DOMESTIC POLITICS AND COVERT ACTION

Domestic considerations also made covert action attractive to the postwar presidents. Covert action was presumably cheap in both dollars and lives. As fiscal conservatives, Truman and Eisenhower were fearful of bankrupting the country with an endless arms race. President Truman listened to judicious economic advisors and imposed a ceiling of $13.5 billion on defense spending. He was finally spooked out of his caution by NSC-68, more than tripling the defense budget in one year, from $13.5 billion in 1950 to $48.2 billion in 1951.[41] President Eisenhower respected the military establishment, but he also understood the budgeting process (which we might encapsulate as "estimate what you need and double it") and refused to support extravagant budgets. "The foundation of military strength is economic strength," he said, and "a bankrupt America is more the Soviet goal than an America defeated on the battlefield."[42] Even with the growth of a permanent wartime economy, both presidents were aware that the United States could not sustain intervention everywhere. Thus, covert action could not only bridge the gap between war and surrender, but the financial solvency gap as well.

A second domestic problem that militated against a massive military solution to the problem of widespread subversive war was the general war weariness of the American people. They had sacrificed and fought hard for four years. In 1945, the men came home, intent on making up for lost time. The baby boom was one result of this, but there were others. The GI Bill helped these men go to school and obtain good jobs. The economy was booming, and who would want to reenter the service when not only had he already done his duty, but there was also a lot of money to be made? Thus, a major personnel buildup would have been both difficult to implement and unpopular.

As it was, the United States engaged in an unprecedented peacetime buildup, essentially maintaining a wartime economy. The percent of the gross domestic product absorbed by the newly named Department of Defense rose from a prewar 1.5 percent and would never again in peacetime drop below 5 percent. However, along with the larger military came increased commitments. The most important was Western Europe, and it would have been unthinkable to "strip" America's NATO forces to fight brushfire wars in Africa, Asia, and Latin America. Therefore, even with a larger military, the United States didn't have the ability (in its own perception) to fight everywhere.

Covert action promised a solution to both the multiplicative problems of limited finances and numerous, unbreakable military commitments. With a few million dollars here and a dozen advisers there, a small band of highly skilled operators might contain and even roll back Communist subversion. It was an impossible temptation to resist.

THE LEADER OF THE FREE WORLD

Emerging from the war as the only superpower, with the ability to create new "rules of the game," the U.S. government hoped to lead by example, rather than by stomping around the world as the "global policeman." It had a major image problem in Latin America, where the people were used to seeing American troops invading their countries at the drop of a hat. U.S. troops had intervened throughout Latin America and the Caribbean sixty-four times between 1850 and 1940, in many instances to establish or prop up oppressive regimes favorable to American governmental or commercial interests.[43] In the 1930s, FDR had instituted the "Good Neighbor" policy, and at Montevideo in 1933 and Buenos Aires in 1936, Secretary of State Cordell Hull had committed the United States to nonintervention in the affairs of Latin American countries. Furthermore, if the United States continued to invade its neighbors, how could it excoriate the USSR for doing the same?

Again, covert action provided the solution. Local troops weren't U.S. troops, and Guatemalan or El Salvadoran colonels weren't the U.S. Marines. The illusion of nonintervention could be maintained, with the concomitant good will of the region, while still ensuring the interests of the United States.

CONCLUSIONS

Across time, American presidents have found it difficult, if not impossible, to resist the call of covert action. A world of bipolarity and nuclear weapons has required a policy of numerous, simultaneous, unprovocative actions. The nature of American politics has encouraged presidents to pursue foreign policies outside traditional channels and to minimize defense budgets by implementing smaller operations. The intelligence elite, on whom a president must rely, has a predilection for covert activity. Perceptions of the antagonist as ruthless and inexorable have broken down ethical barriers. These reasons, in concert, have impelled every American president since FDR to engage in widespread, numerous covert actions.

NOTES

1. White Star Teams were teams of advisers that led Hmong guerrillas against the Pathet Lao in Laos; Civil Air Transport was a CIA-operated airline, the forerunner of Air America; an Arc Light is a massive bombing raid by B-52s; the Killing Fields, of course, refers to the genocide of the Pol Pot regime, in part created by a CIA-sponsored coup and by the instability created by the massive "secret" American bombing campaign in Cambodia.

2. This is not to suggest that these rationales were all made up out of whole cloth. To the contrary, they were often well-founded. There are many instances, however, when decisions to conduct a covert operation were justified ex post facto.

3. I suggest that, given the potential for the "rise of misplaced power," the USSR emerged as the *necessary* challenger as well.

4. For a discussion of the origins of the cold war, see Thomas Patterson, *Major Problems in American Foreign Policy: Documents and Essays*, 2d ed., vol. 2 (Lexington, Mass.: D. C. Heath and Co., 1984), chap. 8; Walter Lefeber, *The American Age: United States Foreign Policy at Home and Abroad Since 1750* (New York: W. W. Norton and Co., 1989), chap. 13–14.

5. See Lisa Hunt, *Secret Agenda: The United States Government, Nazi Scientists, and Project PAPERCLIP, 1945–1990* (New York: St. Martin's, 1991).

6. Harry S. Truman, "The Truman Doctrine," Address to Congress, March 12, 1947, reprinted in Paterson, *Major Problems*, p. 309.

7. Dwight D. Eisenhower, press conference, April 7, 1954, reprinted in Paterson, *Major Problems*, p. 478.

8. The USSR had to this point been very limited in its foreign adventures, focusing instead on the development of "socialism in one country," which was Stalin's policy, rather than the "continuing world revolution" policy of Trotsky. This policy difference was a primary cause of the two Soviet leaders' falling out and the eventual assassination of Trotsky by the NKVD, forerunner of the KGB.

9. A "declarative doctrine" is a strategic doctrine in which one publicly states what one will do in particular circumstances, and is not necessarily the same as one's "real" doctrine, which is what one would *really* do in those circumstances. For example,

during most of the cold war, the United States had a declarative doctrine of "assured destruction," implying that the United States would destroy Soviet cities in the event of a nuclear war, while virtually all U.S. nuclear assets were in actuality targeted at Soviet military facilities.

10. John Foster Dulles, "The Evolution of Foreign Policy," *Department of State Bulletin* (January 25, 1954): 107–10.

11. James Payne, *The American Threat: National Security and Foreign Policy* (College Station, Tex.: Lytton Publishing, 1981), chap. 1, 2.

12. Joseph Burkholder Smith, *Portrait of a Cold Warrior* (New York: Ballantine Books, 1976), chap. 1.

13. Ibid., p. 222. This operation might have foreshadowed the CIA's operation dubbed "Elimination by Illumination," which was aimed at Castro.

14. See William Colby and Peter Forbath, *Honorable Men: My Life in the CIA* (New York: Simon and Schuster, 1978), chap. 1.

15. William Casey, *The Secret War Against Hitler* (Washington, D.C.: Regnery Gateway, 1980), p. xiv.

16. Burton Hersh, *The Old Boys: The American Elite and the Origins of the CIA* (New York: Charles Scribner's Sons, 1992), pp. 196–97.

17. United States War Department, Strategic Services Unit, *The Overseas Targets: War Report of the OSS*, vol. 2, ed. Kermit Roosevelt (New York: Walker and Co., 1976).

18. See Tom Mangold, *Cold Warrior: James Jesus Angleton: The CIA's Master Spy Hunter* (New York: Simon and Schuster, 1991), chap. 3.

19. Smith, *Portrait of a Cold Warrior*; G. J. A. O'Toole, *Honorable Treachery: A History of U.S. Intelligence, Espionage, and Covert Action from the American Revolution to the Present* (New York: Atlantic Monthly, 1991), chap. 32.

20. Thomas Powers, *The Man Who Kept the Secrets: Richard Helms and the CIA* (New York: Pocket Books, 1979), p. 28.

21. O'Toole, *Honorable Treachery*, pp. 406–407.

22. See Barbara Nolen, *Spies, Spies, Spies* (New York: Watts, 1965).

23. See William Stevenson, *A Man Called Intrepid* (New York: Ballantine Books, 1976), chap. 6, 7.

24. Casey, *The Secret War Against Hitler*, chap 4.

25. O'Toole, *Honorable Treachery*, pp. 420–21.

26. Robert Asprey, *War in the Shadows: The Guerilla in History* (Garden City, N.Y.: Doubleday, 1975), chap. 45.

27. Ibid., pp. 478–79, chap. 36–37.

28. Smith, *Portrait of a Cold Warrior*, p. 193.

29. See Lefeber, *The American Age*, p. 457; Senate, *Final Report of the Select Committee to Study Governmental Operations with Respect to Intelligence Activities*, Book 1: Foreign and Military Intelligence, 94th Cong., 2d sess., 1976, S. Rept. 94-755, 105.

30. J. Edgar Hoover, *Masters of Deceit: The Story of Communism in America and How to Fight It* (New York: Henry Holt and Co., 1958).

31. For a discussion of this period, see William O'Neill, *American High: The Years of Confidence 1945–1960* (New York: Free Press, 1986), chap. 3–6.

32. John Foster Dulles, tesimony before the Senate Foreign Relations Committee, January 15, 1953, reprinted in Paterson, *Major Problems*, pp. 473–74.

33. See O'Neill, *American High*, p. 207.

34. Theodore Sorenson, *Kennedy* (New York: Harper and Row, 1965), pp. 245–46.

35. See O'Neill, *American High*, pp. 1–7. O'Neill calls this sense of confidence the "American High."

36. O'Toole, *Honorable Treachery*, p. 337.

37. "X" [George Kennan], "The Sources of Soviet Conduct," *Foreign Affairs* 25 (July 1947): 575.

38. NSC-68, reprinted in Ernest May, *American Cold War Strategy: Interpreting NSC-68* (Boston: Bedford Books, 1993), p. 26.

39. "Report of the Study Group on the Covert Activities of the Central Intelligence Agency" (Doolittle Report), 30 September 1954, declassified 1 April 1976, pp. 1–2.

40. Bill Moyers, *The Secret Government* (Washington, D.C.: Seven Locks Press, 1988), p. 42.

41. This was, in the view of Truman, a temporary explosion, ending around 1954 (the "year of maximum danger"). See Fred Kaplan, *The Wizards of Armageddon* (New York: Simon and Schuster, 1983), pp. 138–41.

42. Glenn H. Snyder, "The 'New Look' of 1953," in *Strategy, Politics, and Defense Budgets*, ed. Warner Schilling, Paul Hammond, and Glenn Snyder (New York: Columbia University, 1962), pp. 289–90.

43. See William Blum, *Killing Hope: U.S. Military and CIA Interventions Since World War II* (Monroe, Maine: Common Courage Press, 1995), app. 2. I didn't count instances of chasing pirates or occupying foreign-held colonies to protect them during World War II.

Chapter 2

The Wars That
Came in from the Cold

Covert action is as American as apple pie. From George Washington, Thomas Jefferson, and James Madison to the OSS buccaneers Bill Donovan, Allen Dulles, and William Casey, covert action has helped create American and world history. This chapter provides an overview of significant U.S. covert actions, emphasizing major operations and themes. It is not a complete recounting of U.S. covert action, as there are already several fine books that do that, but rather provides an outline of the key operations and programs that characterize American black ops, focusing on post–World War II actions.[1]

AS AMERICAN AS APPLE PIE:
BLACK OPS BEFORE THE CIA

"I Cannot Tell a Lie—
But Kidnapping is Something Else . . ."

One of the finest intelligence operators the United States ever had was George Washington. Although mythologized as the great truth-teller, and despite being completely untrained in intelligence,[2] Washington matured from early amateurish efforts (e.g., Nathan Hale with spy notes hidden in his shoes) to run complex, highly skilled, effective espionage networks. He was a master of disinformation, developing on his own the idea of fooling opponents by feeding them the same false information through several seemingly independent sources.[3]

The most nefarious plot hatched by the father of our country was a kidnapping (in modern parlance, a "snatch") of perhaps the only man George Washington ever truly hated, Benedict Arnold. Once the most talented and courageous of American battlefield leaders, Arnold's extraordinary act of betrayal seared Washington so deeply that the commander in chief sought out every opportunity to "get" the traitor and try him for treason. When British commander Sir Henry Clinton refused to exchange Arnold for the captured British officer John André (a favorite of Clinton's, and sentenced to hang), Washington secretly offered to release André if Clinton might send Arnold on some risky mission to allow his capture by the Americans.[4] Clinton refused this too.

Washington then turned to a black op, conspiring with Light Horse Harry Lee to send Sergeant Major John Champe of Lee's Legion to New York to abduct Arnold. The plan was for Champe to "defect" to the British (as a "false defector" in modern parlance), get close to Arnold, and snatch him.

Champe's defection, known only to Washington and Lee, was so authentic that the sergeant major was nearly shot down by enthusiastic American cavalry as he attempted to "desert," all in front of British horse soldiers. Presenting himself to the British with fresh bullet holes in his clothes, Champe had little trouble in convincing them of his bona fides. As a former sergeant major of an elite unit, Champe was quite a catch for the redcoats, and he was quickly encouraged to join Benedict Arnold's American Legion, a cavalry unit comprised of American loyalists. Spying on Arnold, Champe observed that the traitor visited his backyard privy every evening near midnight. The American agent planned, with another secret agent (whose identity remains unknown to this day), to clobber and bind the traitor and slip him aboard a waiting boat, which would ferry Arnold across the Hudson River and into American hands. Unfortunately, the very night the operation was scheduled, Arnold's American Legion received orders to embark; Champe spent the night on board a British transport. With the deployment of Arnold's unit to Virginia, the plot was scratched, and Champe "redefected" to the Americans in Virginia, retiring from service to avoid British retribution.[5] While ultimately this operation failed, it illustrates the audacity that future intelligence operators would try to emulate.

The Revolution also provided the first American experience with a *proprietary company*, a corporation used as cover for a covert action. Hortalez and Co.[6] was invented by the French playwright (and secret agent) Pierre-Augustin Caron Beaumarchais and American diplomat (and secret agent) Silas Deane as a deniable mechanism for the government of France to support the American insurgents without causing an immediate war with England. Through Hortalez, France sent money and arms to the thirteen colonies, including perhaps 90 percent of the weapons used in the critical battle of Saratoga, which brought France openly into the war as a U.S. ally.[7] The significance of the Hortalez operation is still recalled by the CIA: when William Colby was called to testify before the hostile Church Committee in 1975, he began his statement with a recounting of this story.

The Shores of Tripoli

One of the most famous lines in martial music, ". . . to the shores of Tripoli," originated from a covert action ordered by President Thomas Jefferson. Barbary pirates off the coast of North Africa preyed on American shipping as early as 1785, often seizing Americans to hold for ransom. In fact, George Washington actually paid some ransoms from the "contingency fund," an account authorized by Congress for secret activities. Congress eventually settled on a "treaty" that paid the corsairs a regular stipend (i.e., "protection fee") to not plunder American shipping, but in 1803 one of the Barbary states, Tripoli, repudiated the "treaty." The United States retaliated with a blockade, but the USS *Philadelphia* ran aground in Tripoli harbor, its crew taken hostage by Yusuf, pasha of Tripoli. While the captured *Philadelphia* was ultimately destroyed by American sailors in a raid led by Stephen Decatur, burning your own ships is hardly the way to build international prestige. President Jefferson had had enough.

It was a classic covert operation.[8] Jefferson delivered orders to his envoy, William Eaton, in such vague, un-Jefferson-like language as to allow plausible deniability. Eaton then arranged for a cadre of nine U.S. Marines to raise an army of local dissidents and mercenaries ("indigenous forces") and lead them against Tripoli to "restore" the "rightful ruler" of Tripoli, the pasha's brother Hamet, to the throne. After an epic desert march, the rebel, or proxy, force stormed and captured the city of Derna, Presley O'Bannon himself leading a bayonet charge of his few dozen men against hundreds of defenders—and routing them. The assault would forever enshrine O'Bannon's name in Marine Corps lore. This victory led Yusuf to sue for peace before the U.S. proxy army could march on Tripoli, and the United States accommodated him. As it would later with the Hmong, Montangards, and Kurds, among others, the United States abandoned the indigenous fighting men, who had fought and won for the Stars and Stripes.[9]

The Founding Father Goes Covert

When one associates U.S. presidents and covert action, the first name to come to mind is not James Madison. Yet the primary author of the Constitution demonstrated, on occasion, a willingness as president to use underhanded means to obtain his ends. The following operation is distinguished from Washington's and Jefferson's in that Madison employed a covert operation against a country with which the United States was at peace—Spain.

In 1811, the United States and England were on the slippery slope leading to war. On the southern flank of the United States remained the Spanish colonies of East and West Florida, and Spain was essentially defenseless after a devastating war with France. Since England still held Canada, the United States might be caught in a "red sandwich" between English territories should the British seize Florida.[10] Congress authorized President Madison to "temporarily occupy" Florida to forestall this—and, in the lights of some Americans, to begin fulfilling the manifest destiny of the United States as a continental nation-state.

At first, Madison claimed the executive right to occupy Florida in the name of national security, a rather astonishing assertion for the father of the Constitution. When this was denied by Congress, he sought its consent, requesting

". . . the expediency of authorizing the executive to take temporary possession of . . . the territory. . . . The wisdom of the Congress will at the same time determine how far it may be expedient to provide for the event of a subversion of the Spanish authorities."[11] On 11 January 1811, Congress authorized an operation to take possession of East Florida if requested by "local authority" (a nice touch, considering that U.S. citizens had been recently flooding into the area, and could manufacture a receptive "local authority" expeditiously). Moreover, the president could employ U.S. armed forces as he deemed necessary.[12]

Madison appointed George Matthews, former Revolutionary general and governor of Georgia, as a special emissary to the Spanish authorities. Matthews thereupon raised an army of volunteers, marched into Spanish territory, and declared the "Republic of Florida." When the Spanish ambassador protested, Madison insisted that Matthews had misunderstood his instructions. However, the Americans were not withdrawn from Florida for fourteen months.[13] Although this operation, similar to the way Texas became a state, ultimately failed, it illustrates the problem that all presidents face: No matter how principled one might be, the temptation to employ secret and inexpensive power is often overwhelming.

Conclusion

Whether or not covert action is explicitly recognized in the Constitution, the primary founders of America—Washington, Jefferson, and Madison—all employed secret means to achieve what they felt to be critical national goals. Congress even went so far as to recognize this necessity by authorizing the "contingent fund," which was accountable only to the president. From such early beginnings, American covert action was born.

COVERT ACTION IN THE COLD WAR

From its sporadic use in the early days, covert action moved to the top of the foreign policy menu during the cold war, ironically coming to exemplify the backstreet competition between the United States and the Soviet Union. Whereas in the past covert action had been mere flavoring, from the late 1940s onward it became the main course.

The Forties: From OSS to CIA

To many people, the end of World War II signaled hope for a new beginning, yet as discussed in chapter 2, it instead merely initiated a new round of deadly serious competition. Although the precise shape of new American intelligence organization(s) remained blurry for a time, few questioned the need for permanent intelligence institutions. Even though Harry Truman and J. Edgar Hoover cut Wild

Bill Donovan out of the new organization the most logical people to establish the new agency were the veterans of the OSS. They hit the ground running.

The primary target was Russia. Since the Soviet Union was a "denied area,"[14] the United States was at first forced to rely heavily on intelligence provided by the Gehlen Organization.[15] However, by 1947 it was clear that while covert paramilitary or political action by outsiders might be impossible, the Soviet Union was experiencing a series of large-scale regional insurrections in the Baltic States and the Ukraine. With the Lithuanian "forest brotherhood" reaching an active strength of about fifty thousand, the United States and England began supplying agents similar to World War II Jedburgh teams, air dropping the commandos or infiltrating them by boat under cover of the British "Baltic Fisheries Patrol." Baltic, Ukrainian, and Russian émigrés were also trained and returned to lead the resistance, and radios and small arms were provided. By the end of 1950, however, it was clear that the insurgents (partisans) could not stand against the NKVD[16] military units created especially to put down the uprisings, and that without outside military intervention, the subject peoples could not win their freedom. Although the uprisings must have been a costly diversion for the Soviet Union, resulting in Soviet/NKVD casualties of between twenty thousand (by Soviet admission) and eighty thousand (partisan claim) and something fewer than one hundred thousand partisan and civilian casualties, the U.S. program was a political, military, and intelligence failure.[17]

In the end, these missions failed not only because the circumstances were hopeless, but were also fatally wrecked because (1) the Gehlen Organization was heavily penetrated by the Soviet NKVD, and (2) the émigré organizations were saturated with Soviet agents. Thus, the NKVD was frequently waiting for the teams as they hit the ground, sometimes "turning around"[18] the captured agents to lure the next mission into Soviet hands. Moreover, as became clear to the partisans over time, the United States would not intervene militarily, even with a nuclear monopoly, and the CIA agents sent in were intelligence officers generally intent on gathering intelligence. There was no serious plan to liberate these areas.

This program had two major implications. First, the CIA concluded that in extremely repressive countries, paramilitary action was doomed to failure. Second, if there were to be more operations of this nature (as there would be in 1949 in Albania),[19] professional planning and training must be provided, and clear goals established.

Another defining operation began in 1947. Italy, key to the Mediterranean, was troubled yet again by political instability, with elections forthcoming in 1948. Most troubling for the United States was the fact that the Italian Communist Party, which had been the most effective antifascist resistance organization during World War II and was therefore quite popular, was expected to win the election.

To head off this calamity, the U.S. government engaged in a two-pronged program. One prong was *overt political action*.[20] U.S. loans were pledged, provided the country did not go Communist, and the United States promised to support

Italian "trusteeship" of former Italian colonies Ethiopia and Libya. The U.S. government sponsored a massive propaganda effort in which U.S. citizens with Italian relatives (a letter-writing campaign), Frank Sinatra, and labor leaders extolled the virtues of capitalism and friendship with the United States. Specially produced free movies extolled the benefits of friendship with the United States. The Italian military was given U.S. money, arms, and technical advice, creating close and binding ties to the United States military.

The second prong was *covert political action*. More than ten million dollars was secretly funneled to centrist politicians, especially the Christian democrats, and to Socialists who would split the Socialist/Communist vote. Election officials were bribed. A classic piece of *black disinformation* (information purported to come from one's enemies) was produced—the "Zorin Plan." This document, supposedly purloined from the Soviet Union, outlined Soviet Ambassador Valerian Zorin's program for Italy once the Communists had won, including strict dependence on the USSR and Yugoslavia; rigid Soviet-style repression of social, political, and economic affairs; and the execution of priests who failed to conform to Moscow's control. Further efforts included stories planted in the U.S. media, e.g., *Time* magazine, suggesting that the United States would not permit Italy to go Communist, even if military intervention were necessary. This grey propaganda effort was supported by conspicuous port calls by U.S. and British warships.[21] Finally, it has been suggested, although definitive evidence has not been found, that elements within the Italian military would have staged a U.S.-supported coup should the Communists have won.

There are three telling features of this operation. First, the CIA, through the "Office of Special Operations," conferred on itself the authority to perform this covert political action. DCI Roscoe Hillenkoetter proceeded with the operation despite the opinion of his counsel that it was beyond the authority of the CIA and the National Security Act. Thus, the CIA created its own license, and future "authority" would be established by this precedent. Second, the CIA established the model of using other branches of government for clandestine purposes. In this case, the money channeled to Italy was "obtained" from the Economic Stabilization Board and laundered through the Internal Revenue Service. Third, the operation worked, and thus established covert action as a viable menu choice for American presidents.

The Fifties: Heyday for the Operators

The 1950s must have been heady times for the operators. Covert actions routinely and easily overthrew intransigent regimes, and even when they failed, there was no penalty. The decade was an era of explosive growth for the covert side of the CIA, such that, although chartered as an intelligence coordinating organization and then as an intelligence-gathering one, the majority of the CIA's budget was directed to covert operations (then called the directorate of plans).

OPERATION AJAX was the first key covert action of the decade, resulting in the overthrow of the government of Iran, placing the shah on a throne he would hold for twenty-six years.[22]

In 1951, Iran rebelled against British dominance by electing a well-liked populist, Mohammad Mosaddeq, as prime minister. Mosaddeq moved quickly to end British exploitation of Iran, in which a British company, the Anglo-Iranian Oil Company (AIOC), earned ten times as much profit as it paid in royalties to Iran. Mosaddeq nationalized the country's oil facilities, reduced the young shah to a figurehead, and legalized the small Iranian Communist Party, the *Tudeh*. Although Mosaddeq offered compensation to the AIOC in the form of 25 percent of profits, the British wanted their oil company back. Britain organized a boycott of Iranian oil, but this failed to have immediate political effect, so it then turned to the United States, and the CIA, for help.

Kermit "Kim" Roosevelt, grandson of Theodore Roosevelt, was selected to head the operation. Roosevelt perceived the need to secure the support of both the people and the army of Iran. The former might prove a difficult task, given the relative popularity of Mosaddeq who, the *New York Times* observed, was "the most popular politician in the country," and had "a reputation as an honest patriot."[23]

First, economic pressure was stepped up, eroding the Iranian standard of living. When Mosaddeq appealed to the United States for economic assistance, he was refused. He then turned to the USSR, thereby increasing the urgency with which the CIA forged ahead toward his overthrow—even though Mosaddeq had occasionally brutally repressed *Tudeh*, one time killing more than one hundred *Tudeh* demonstrators in the process of breaking up a demonstration.

The aid of the shah was secured, promising him a return to effective "rulership" of Iran. Reza Shah Pahlavi got the ball rolling by dismissing Mosaddeq as prime minister. Mosaddeq defiantly ignored the writ, declared the shah had sold out to "foreign elements" and had attempted a coup d'etat, and that Mosaddeq himself was therefore compelled to assume emergency powers. The shah, believing that discretion was the better part of valor, immediately fled the country.

Roosevelt swiftly set in motion covert political operations to create popular support for the "restoration" of the Peacock Throne (the traditional name for the rulership of Persia). Leaflets proclaimed the Communist nature of the Mosaddeq regime. Bodybuilders, who had been recruited from Tehran health clubs, were paid to beat up any demonstrators supporting Mosaddeq. Drivers were asked to drive with their lights on if they supported the shah, and since those without their lights on had their cars demolished by paid gangs of roving thugs, *everyone* drove with them on. The United States literally purchased demonstrations supporting the shah against Mosaddeq by paying march organizers and demonstrators.

The army moved, impelled by the notion that "the people" wanted Mosaddeq removed, with the substantial material assistance of the United States. Boots, uniforms, blankets, electrical generators, medical supplies, weapons, trucks, armored cars, and radios were all supplied to the pro-shah army faction. The pro-shah military assaulted Mosaddeq's residence, using armored vehicles to win a nine-hour battle in which three hundred people were killed. Mosaddeq was captured, and the shah returned from Switzerland to ride a triumphal procession through Tehran. Reza Shah Pahlavi quickly moved to restore more "orderly" oil production, although he infuriated the British by reducing the AIOC share to 40 percent and turning over another 40 percent to an American consortium, including Gulf Oil. Kermit Roosevelt was made vice president of Gulf Oil in 1960.

Throughout the 1950s, CIA covert actions multiplied, and the agency continued to expand its portfolio. A year after AJAX, in 1954, the CIA launched SUCCESS to overthrow the Arbenz regime in Guatemala, as recounted in chapter 1. These two operations, coming so close together, having such great effect, and apparently succeeding so easily, produced an operational hubris that would lead to later disasters.

The 1950s also witnessed a burgeoning role for the CIA in Indochina. The CIA had participated with the French in the region since 1950, channeling U.S. weapons and equipment to the French, and by 1954, the United States was providing 78 percent of the French budget for the war against the Vietminh.[24] Covertly, when the French army established its ill-fated base at Dien Bien Phu in November 1953, the troops were flown in by the American pilots and aircraft of Civil Air Transport (CAT), a CIA proprietary airline that was the forerunner of the more well-known Air America. CAT pilots flew 684 perilous aerial resupply missions into the narrow, flaming valley of death called Dien Bien Phu.[25]

Shocked by the debacle at Dien Bien Phu, the French negotiated a settlement in 1954, agreeing to a temporary division of Vietnam into North and South, with full national elections to be held later. The United States immediately stepped in to prevent the country from "going Communist." A propaganda campaign describing the horrors of life under Communism was begun. CIA sabotage operations in the North began, including contamination of the North's oil supply and the delayed destruction of the railroad. South Vietnamese were selected to begin U.S. military and intelligence training.[26]

Another important covert battleground was Laos. The CIA instigated coups in Laos in 1958, 1959, and 1960, often by withholding monthly payments to Laotion troops.[27] By the mid-1950s, the CIA was arming the hill people known as Hmong, or Meo, against the Soviet-backed Pathet Lao, eventually creating a secret army of roughly forty thousand tough combatants. Starting in 1959, the CIA sent in White Star Teams comprised of U.S. Army Special Forces (Green Berets) to train and lead the Hmong.[28] All these actions presaged the secret war CIA would fight in Laos in the 1960s.

The "lost lesson" of the 1950s was Indonesia. This was an operation which failed miserably, created a backlash which strengthened the very person the CIA was attempting to bring down and left plausible deniability in tatters, yet failed to temper the CIA's hubris.

Achmed Sukarno, president of Indonesia, was a hero of the Indonesian struggle against both the Japanese and the Dutch. As president, he had attempted to maintain a precarious balance between East and West, struggling as one of the early leaders of the nonaligned movement. In the eyes of U.S. Secretary of State John Foster Dulles, there was no room in the middle—one chose either good or evil. Since Sukarno had not chosen the good side, his leaning was obvious.

Several attempts were made to dispose of Sukarno in creative ways. Some evidence suggests the CIA kicked around the idea of assassination, but the idea was apparently dropped.[29] Sukarno was known as an outrageous womanizer, so the CIA hit on the idea of filming him in a compromising act, thus blackening his name in the eyes of the conservative Muslims that comprised Indonesia's populace. First, the CIA scoured the Los Angeles underground for "blue movies," looking for films that starred swarthy, middle-aged, bald men with beautiful blonde women. Failing this, the agency then produced its own porno films with a Sukarno look-alike, but the look-alike did not look enough alike. The CIA then tried to film using an actor in a full face mask, but the final cut, entitled "Happy Days," was never released.[30]

In December 1956, a group of Indonesian colonels based on Sumatra declared themselves independent, and soon were joined by forces from the Celebes, named PEMESTA (after the Indonesian acronym for Charter of Common Struggle), who openly broke with Sukarno in April 1957. Early on, the colonels didn't make much progress, prompting John Foster Dulles to think about withdrawing U.S. recognition of the Sukarno government and giving it to the rebels, using the excuse of "protecting U.S. lives and property" to send in the marines to effect a change. Apparently, he chose to rely on his brother, DCI Allen Dulles, instead.

PEMESTA declared itself the government of Sumatra, Celebes, and Java on 15 February 1958. A major CIA support operation was set in motion immediately, including airdrops of weapons and supplies, the use of U.S. submarines to supply rebels and drop off liaison officers, and the provision of an air force of fifteen sterilized B-26 bombers, modified to carry a "pack" of eight .50 caliber machine guns in the nose, that could devastate opposing ground support.

Sukarno and his forces moved with greater speed and enthusiasm than expected, and by the end of May 1958, the rebellion had been put down. Most damaging for the United States was the fact that U.S. complicity was conspicuous. One obvious problem for deniability was the materialization of an air force, even though none of Sukarno's pilots had defected. Most embarrassing was the capture of a conspicuously American pilot, Allen Lawrence Pope. All CIA contract pilots were carefully searched before takeoff to prevent them from carrying incriminating papers, yet Pope was captured with a U.S. Air Force ID card, a Civil Air Transport ID card, his Civil Air Transport contract for the operation, and a post exchange card for Clark Air Force Base in the Philippines. On 27 May 1958, Sukarno presented this evidence to the world, exposing the U.S. president and secretary of state as liars.[31]

What is important about the Indonesian operation is what *didn't* happen. The operation failed. It wasn't remotely deniable. The president got caught lying about it. *And nobody cared!* There was little international outcry, and no backlash at all in the United States. Indeed, few in the United States were even aware of these events. Allen Pope was quietly repatriated in 1962; within six months, he was flying CIA missions for Southern Air Transport.[32]

What were the lessons of the 1950s? To the operators and the executives they served, it seemed that the world could be manipulated with some ease, by a small group of operators, if they were smart enough and tough enough. Even if plans sometimes failed, the costs were minimal, even when plausible deniability broke down. The confidence produced by these successes would lead to the disasters of the following decade.

The 1960s: Icarus Falling

With the collapse of the ZAPATA plan at the Bay of Pigs in April 1961 (see chapter 1), the CIA might have entered a period of crisis, retrenchment, and reflection. President Kennedy had angrily threatened to shatter the CIA into a thousand pieces and scatter it to the winds. Yet the savvy operators turned JFK's attitude around with impressive speed. The key was the president's brother Robert. The official postmortem to the Bay of Pigs was a small, "ultrasecret" affair directed by Jack Kennedy's favorite cold warrior, Maxwell Taylor, and included Robert F. Kennedy, Allen Dulles, and Admiral Arleigh Burke. RFK emerged committed to covert action, and to doing it right next time. Indeed, the report even chides President Kennedy for failing to take whatever steps were necessary (i.e., sending in the marines) to overthrow Castro. For the operators, the price of failure was the dismissal of Allen Dulles.

Immediately, a new program to eliminate Castro was begun. Initially, it included a bigger, better Bay of Pigs–style operation. By the fall of 1961, this operation was dead in the water, and for his conduct of ZAPATA and the faltering post–Bay of Pigs program, DDP Richard Bissell was fired. Kennedy hired legendary operator Edward Lansdale, conqueror of the Filipino Communist insurgent *Huks*, to depose Castro. The new operation was called MONGOOSE.

MONGOOSE was conceived as an orderly six-step program, beginning with intelligence gathering, building to small political actions, and culminating with a major insurrection and march on Havana. In practice it turned into a series of disjointed raids, acts of sabotage, and assassination plots, which only intensified Castro's hold on the island at the cost to America of over $50 million a year.

MONGOOSE was run from a front company called Zenith Technical Enterprises, based out of the University of Miami and supervised by up-and-coming CIA officer Ted Shackley. It became rather common to see carloads of camouflage-clad men riding around Miami with automatic weapons. Traveling in speedboats from bases in Miami and the Keys, Cuban-exile commandos attacked ships, boats, and coastal buildings in Cuba, sometimes sneaking ashore to plant explosives, and other times simply cruising the coast, machine-gunning anything that moved.

A second aspect of MONGOOSE was covert economic warfare, conducted in an effort to strangle the Cuban economy and strike down Castro's popularity. Cuban sugar shipments were contaminated, ruining Cuba's trade. Cuban mines were bombed, and buildings, such as Havana's largest department store, were burned. Sugarcane fields were torched, sometimes by tying burning rags to the tails of stray cats and letting them run. The CIA attempted to counterfeit Cuban currency. A German factory was paid to sell Cuba "off-center" ball bearings.[33]

The third element of MONGOOSE (not part of Lansdale's "official" plan, but perhaps the major component nonetheless) was a program to assassinate Fidel Castro. This had been proposed by Howard Hunt as part of ZAPATA, although, as far as is known currently, Hunt's recommendation was not specifically acted on. The next two years, however, were filled with assassination plots, including plans to kill Castro with exploding seashells, exploding cigars, poisoned wet suits, bazookas, and even ordinary bullets, prompting Lyndon Johnson to observe that "we were running a goddam 'Murder Inc.' down there."[34]

MONGOOSE was notable for its fallout. First, agents of the United States government actively carried out acts of war against another country from U.S. soil.[35] A precedent was set for violation of U.S. laws under the cloak of national security, including the Neutrality Act, weapons laws, customs laws, and U.S. treaty obligations. Second, MONGOOSE produced a sizable legion of well-trained, well-armed soldiers not strictly under the control of, or accountable to, the United States (or anyone, for that matter). These men would later be involved in other secret wars: Vietnam, Laos, the Congo, Angola, Nicaragua, El Salvador. Some would engage in acts of terrorism abroad and in the United States, bombing Cuban airliners and embassies. Others would turn their talents to a more lucrative enterprise—drug running. Several of them, including Bernard "Macho" Barker, Rolando Martínez, and Frank Sturgis, became Watergate burglars. Third, the concept underlying covert action, plausible deniability, was almost completely ignored. The Cuban-exile commandos operated more or less openly in Florida, essentially conducting their own war from the safe haven of Miami. Dave Phillips, propaganda master for PB/SUCCESS, would later write that one of the biggest headaches of the operation was the near-continuous need to post bail for carloads of heavily armed Cubans who had been arrested joyriding around Miami. Fourth, a precedent was established for encouraging private funding of such activities. As a longtime sponsor of right-wing causes, the Luce publishing empire used *Life* magazine to provide money for attacks on Cuba, with the stipulation that a *Life* photographer got to ride along. *Life* got the story, including the last hours of famous Cuban-exile guerrilla "Eddie Bayo," who disappeared while on a raid in Cuba.

A second feature of covert action in the 1960s was a series of assassination plots against foreign leaders. Aside from Castro, several other foreign leaders were expressly targeted in this decade. Rafael Trujillo (Dominican Republic), Ngo Dinh Diem (South Vietnam), and Ngo Dinh Nhu (South Vietnam) were killed by conspirators who had been given the go-ahead for a coup d'etat by the

United States, and General Rene Schneider (Chile) was killed by assassins who had been in close contact with the CIA. Patrice Lumumba, prime minister of the Congo, is probably the case in which we can most confidently say that a U.S. president, Dwight Eisenhower, approved outright assassination.[36]

Consequent to the interest in assassination was the development of an "off-the-shelf" assassination capability, initiated in early 1961.[37] The idea was that one should have a small, professional team of assassins ready all the time, so that when they were needed, one didn't have to spend time training them or waste effort with amateurs. This executive action group, codenamed ZR/RIFLE, was recruited and run by legendary CIA operator William Harvey. ZR/RIFLE recruited at least one agent, QJ/WIN, who is believed to have been Jean Soutre, a member of the Corsican Mafia (the *Unione Course*), and who reportedly served as a "talent-spotter," looking for assassins. As head of ZR/RIFLE, Harvey also seriously compromised the CIA by recruiting the Mafia for plots to assassinate Castro.[38]

In Latin America, a small but significant operation occurred in Bolivia in 1967. Famed Argentine guerrilla Ché Guevara came to Bolivia to begin the revolution there, employing his concept of the revolutionary *foco* (the idea that the mere demonstration that resistance to tyranny is possible will bring about mass revolution). He was especially targeted by a CIA group that employed high-altitude infrared photoreconnaissance to locate Ché's tiny and faltering guerrilla band. The reconnaissance photos showed even the tiniest specks of heat given off by, say, cooking fires in the jungle. Armed with this data, U.S.-trained Bolivian special forces, supervised by CIA contract agent Felix Rodriguez, captured Ché, and against the advice of Rodriguez (at least by his own account), executed him.

Another notable Latin American effort was aimed at stopping the election of Socialists and Communists in Chile. Most of this was covert political action, and managed to forestall the election of Salvador Allende for several years. Chile was subject to a major propaganda campaign, painting Allende as a Stalinist. Flyers depicted an Allende victory as a victory for "godless, atheistic Communism," an especially effective plea in Catholic Chile, and a radio spot played the sound of a machine gun followed by a woman's voice crying, "They have killed my children—the Communists."[39] More directly, the CIA subsidized anti-Socialist groups of unions, students, and intellectuals, and actually owned several media outlets. Money was also funneled to a splinter Socialist group to divide the Socialist vote. From 1958 until 1970, such tactics helped keep Allende from the presidency.[40]

The two enormous actions of the decade were Vietnam and Laos. Deeply involved in Vietnam since the French withdrawal in 1954, the United States stepped up its covert activities. Counterinsurgency expert Ed Lansdale was assigned, and he quickly organized "civic action teams" that built wells, schools, health clinics, and hospitals. Covertly, the United States began an air war against the Vietcong (VC), secretly employing the 4400 Combat Crew Training Squadron, known as the "Jungle Jim" unit, to attack Vietcong targets (OPERATION FARM GATE). American SEALS and Green Berets "advised" the Army of the Republic of Vietnam (ARVN) and also carried out missions in South and North Vietnam.[41] Aside from the full-blown war and special operations within it—such as the "over-the-fence" commando operations in Cambodia, North Vietnam, Laos, and China, and OPERATION IVORY COAST (the raid on the POW camp at Son Tay)—the notable CIA operation of the war was PHOENIX.[42]

PHOENIX was intended as a program to destroy the Vietcong Infrastructure (VCI), e.g., the tax collectors, local commanders, and so on. The original idea was to capture members of the VCI, interrogate them to reveal and unravel the VC organization, and perhaps even gain their trust and "turn" them via the Chieu Hoi ("Open Arms") program. This program was supposed to be run by Vietnamese Provincial Reconnaissance Units (PRUs), which would capture (i.e., kidnap) suspected VCI members and turn them in to Provincial Interrogation Centers (PICs). Unfortunately, even in the eyes of its creators and supporters, PHOENIX took on a dirty life of its own. PICs were notorious for the actions of interrogators (e.g., bamboo under fingernails), and produced little intelligence of value. Moreover, family vendettas ran strong in Vietnam, and "VCI suspects" were often betrayed to the PRUs based more on family animosity than Vietcong intelligence value. It is likely that many suspects didn't talk because they were, in fact, innocent.

Finally, while the CIA vigorously objects to its characterization as an "assassination program," PHOENIX, without dispute, resulted in the outright killing of many suspects, with no pretense made of attempting capture or interrogation. PRUs and American special forces were sometimes specifically assigned to shoot suspects. Even former head of PHOENIX and DCI William Colby reports the number of "suspects" killed during the operation as about twenty thousand, while other estimates range as high as forty thousand. Tellingly, two army officers assigned to PHOENIX obtained discharges from the army after persuading a federal court that they had been ordered to fulfill a "kill quota" of fifty bodies a month.[43]

Laos was truly the secret war—a wholly-owned subsidiary of the CIA. The agency adopted Colonel Phoumi Nosavan, who had his own personal CIA adviser, John Hazey. White Star Teams, commanded by future legend Arthur "Bull" Simons, began training and leading combat units in 1959. Other White Star legends included Grayston Lynch (first ashore at the Bay of Pigs) and Charlie Beckwith (founder of the top-secret Delta Force, an army unit that focused on counterterrorism). In autumn 1960, the CIA allied with the Hmong tribes, who flocked to receive the benefits of civilization, including CIA training, transistor radios, free rice, retail stores, and automatic weapons. Under General Vang Pao, the Armée Clandestine, as the Hmong forces were called, numbered more than forty thousand by 1968, fighting the indigenous Pathet Lao as well as harassing North Vietnamese on the Ho Chi Minh Trail, which twisted its way through Laos along the Vietnamese border. The Armée Clandestine was well supported by Air America, which flew in a thousand tons of supplies monthly in 1960, increasing this load to six thousand tons and sixteen thousand passengers a month by 1966. In the latter year, the United States Air

Force also flew 7,316 strike sorties in support. For a time, due to the demands of the war in Laos, Air America literally became the largest airline in the world, operating hundreds of aircraft. Some of the covert operators, and a lot of the covert aid, were provided under cover of the United States Agency for International Development (AID). The Hmong fighters were tough and victorious, nearly driving the Pathet Lao into North Vietnam in 1968. The next year, the Pathet Lao and North Vietnamese went for the jugular, the Hmong bases, striking hard and driving the Armée Clandestine across Laos, while the United States refused to support them with B-52 strikes. In February 1970, the secret war was exposed, triggering a public and congressional outcry in the United States. Under the glare of the spotlight, support for the Laotian war was slowly withdrawn, and Vang Pao and the Hmong were sold out in the cease-fire agreement of 1973. In the end, the secret war cost the United States more than 400 dead and 556 missing in action, with 17 Air America pilots killed. The Pathet Lao were victorious, and a few thousand Hmong (out of a quarter million in 1960) made it over the border to Thailand, to be scattered in small pockets across the United States.[44]

What may be most remembered from the Laotian operation is the fact that American actions were sullied by involvement with drugs: heroin, opium, and morphine. Northern Laos is part of the "Golden Triangle," the source of most of the world's opiate supply. Poppy growing was a centuries-old part of Hmong culture and their major cash crop. In the war-torn country, Air America provided the Hmong with the only reliable means of getting the drugs to market, as well as returning with payment (often as bags of gold dust).[45]

The 1970s: Rogue Elephants and Red Sandwiches

Many of the operations and programs of the sixties continued into the next decade, including the activities in Indochina. They became ever less covert and deniable, and this, combined with general exasperation and outrage over the Vietnam War, as well as public revelations that some covert operations had been undertaken precisely to keep them secret from the American people, created a major backlash against United States intelligence institutions.

All the machinations to keep Salvador Allende from rising to the presidency of Chile failed as he won a plurality victory in 1970. Allende was certainly a Socialist, and set out a program of aiding the lower classes, including food subsidies and free milk for children. He also nationalized some industries (c.g., copper, telephones), although *this occurred after plans to overthrow him were underway*. Even though Allende had been fairly elected and was certainly no Soviet puppet, Secretary of State Henry Kissinger had commented, "I don't see why we need to stand by and see a country go communist due to the irresponsibility of its own people."[46]

The CIA realized that a coup would probably be necessary, yet found it difficult, in the words of a CIA report, to overcome a troublesome hindrance: "the tradition of military respect for the constitution."[47] This obstacle was removed, however, when General René Schneider, leader of the proconstitutional military, was assassinated by men who had been supplied with sterilized weapons by the CIA (although it has not been proven that the CIA provided the actual weapons used in the assassination). With Schneider dead, the vital bulwark against military dictatorship was eliminated.

Ultimately, Allende was disposed of through a combination of overt and covert methods, both political and economic. Richard Nixon instructed the CIA to "make the economy scream," and the agency was highly successful. The Import-Export Bank, the Inter-American Development Bank, and the World Bank withheld loans and credits, and the United States pressured private banks to reject loans. Since Chile already owed foreign banks billions of dollars it could not pay back, these policies insured that practically all foreign trade with Chile halted—Chileans had no dollars or hard currency to pay for imported goods, and who would accept Chilean money? Busses and taxis shut down for lack of spare parts, and the cumulative effect of shortages in cigarettes, soap, and even toilet paper added up to an unhappy populace. Allende suffered tremendous political damage from a trucker's strike that lasted a year even though the union had no discernable strike fund. To this day, the CIA insists that it did not finance the strike, but no other source of funding has ever been discovered. Political propaganda was provided by media outlets that, in some cases, were actually *owned* by CIA, and by media assets that called for someone to save the country from the evils of Communism. The standard propaganda campaign was initiated, including foreboding accounts of Soviet-occupied countries, and of what the Communists would do to Catholics. The International Telephone and Telegraph Company (ITT), via former DCI John McCone (then a member of ITT's board of directors), contributed over a million dollars to the program. Perhaps most importantly, CIA operatives secretly assured leaders of the Chilean military that the United States would support a coup and that plentiful U.S. dollars would flow to a regime that undid Allende's reforms.

In September 1973, the Chilean military "stepped in" to rescue the nation, and Allende "committed suicide" in the presidential palace. While denying complicity, the CIA later admitted it had been in contact with the plotters throughout the summer. Moreover, U.S. military personnel actually accompanied Chilean army units during the coup. A new word, *destabilization*, entered the lexicon.[48]

Angola was the last major covert effort of the decade. Gaining its independence from Portugal in 1973, the country immediately plunged into a triangular civil war among three roughly Marxist factions, although the nature of all their ideologies was, in fact, fuzzy anti-imperialist nationalism. By 1975, although the United States was hesitant to enter a new guerrilla war after the Vietnam debacle (the "Vietnam Syndrome"), Henry Kissinger predicted serious damage to U.S. interests if Soviet proxies were allowed to prevail. The result was OPERATION IA/FEATURE.

The United States ironically selected to support the most radical faction,

Jonas Savimbi's UNITA. Through the next two years, the CIA supplied weapons, vehicles, and mercenaries. Some weapons were provided through Zaire, which skimmed off the best hardware, including M-113 armored personnel carriers and most of the modern assault rifles; and through South Africa, in violation of U.S. law, an act of cooperation which harmed U.S. relations with practically all of Africa. To the embarrassment of the United States, several CIA-paid American mercenaries were captured in Angola and sentenced to death.[49]

The Angolan affair provided the world with one of the cold war's most paradoxical and amusing outcomes. By the late 1970s, several thousand Cuban troops were guarding Angolan oil facilities, which were owned and operated by Gulf Oil and Texaco, from UNITA attacks paid for by the CIA (and thus, American taxpayers)!

Through the mid- and late 1970s, the United States scaled back covert action considerably. President Jimmy Carter was not a secret warrior at heart, and his director of Central Intelligence, Stansfield Turner, refocused the CIA on intelligence gathering and analysis. Americans were gun-shy over Vietnam, and Congress had conducted several investigations into U.S. intelligence institutions. In these, it was revealed that the CIA, the FBI, the IRS, and other government organizations had systematically flouted the law, engaging in thousands of illegal acts against political opponents: surveillance, thousands of black-bag jobs at home, blackmail, assassination plots, mind-control experiments, and so on. The CIA was in disrepute. Perhaps most dangerously, Stansfield Turner cut back on the operations branch of the CIA, putting more than eight hundred covert operators out on the street (but certainly *not* out of "business").

The 1980s: The Real Phoenix Rises

It took less than four years to change that. Nineteen seventy-nine was a momentous year, as United States experienced:

- the abdication of the shah of Iran and his replacement with a blatantly hostile Khomeini regime;
- the Soviet invasion of Afghanistan;
- the fall of Nicaraguan dictator Anastasio Somoza and his replacement with the Socialist Sandinista regime friendly to Cuba and the USSR; and
- the seizure of American hostages in Iran.

Each of these events ratcheted up the "anxiety quotient" of the American people, who concluded that the world no longer feared the United States; perhaps, as the famous Reagan advertisement said, there *was* a bear in the woods; perhaps Communism *was* on the march. Coupled with this was a decade-long concern over terrorism. Ronald Reagan rode this wave of fear to victory in the 1980 presidential election, promising to stand tall, make America great again, and to "unleash" the CIA. Turning Jimmy Carter's human rights policies on their head, Reagan proclaimed that terrorism was the world's greatest human rights problem.

Ronald Reagan's national security apparatus left the idea of covert action in shambles, as thinly veiled U.S. actions were called covert merely to protect the president and his staff from those annoying "checks and balances." To evade accountability, Reagan privatized covert action to a greater degree than ever before, contracting out both operations and funding to private citizens, corporations, and shadow organizations.

Afghanistan was the first major operation Reagan's team took over. Covert actions against the Soviets in Afghanistan had been initiated by President Jimmy Carter, and backing for Carter's policy was bipartisan. This policy was supported by "liberal interventionists" as a matter of principle (support for self-determination), and by "realists" as a way to "bleed" the Soviets and get some "payback" for Vietnam. Initially, Carter's program was indeed covert. The funding came from covert sources, and weapons and some training were obtained from the Egyptians and Chinese.

Assuming office in 1981, Reagan immediately raised the ante. By the end of the year, the mujahedin were attacking the Soviets with antitank missiles and caseless mines (which can't be found by mine detectors), and by 1985 the Afghan operation was receiving as much as $250 million a year. The Soviets, like the United States in Vietnam, relied heavily on overwhelming firepower, usually delivered from the air. Thus, the most important aspect of the war became the mujahedin struggle against Soviet aircraft, and it was U.S. Stinger missiles, lightweight and fired from the shoulder, that turned the tide against the invaders.

Three things stand out about this operation. One was the efficacy of modern technology in some settings: Once the Stingers were supplied, the mujahedin virtually imprisoned Soviet troops in the cities. Second, a huge proportion of U.S. aid was skimmed off in Pakistan. It has been estimated that anywhere from 20 to 90 percent of U.S. weapons and equipment were siphoned off by the Pakistani military and by local police; the mere range of estimates is indicative of the lack of control and accounting. Moreover, the Pakistani government insisted on supervising the distribution of weapons, and disbursed them with more of an eye toward favorite friends than the most effective fighters. Third, the program was successful in the sense of bleeding the Soviets and perhaps in some way contributing to the dissension that broke down the Soviet Union. However, it left behind a country devastated by war and torn by internal strife, with no end in sight.[50] It remains to be seen if the "lost" Stingers will be turned around by Islamic militants to shoot down planeloads of Americans.

Aside from the Evil Empire, the major bogeyman of the Reagan administration was Libya's Colonel Mu'ammar Gadhafi. In 1981, the CIA began cooperating with the French and Saudis to support Libyan opposition, eventually picking the National Front for the Salvation of Libya. In May 1984, the group attempted the assassination of the dictator, engaging Gadhafi's forces in a firefight in Tripoli. They were overcome in about five hours, and perhaps two hundred sympathizers were executed afterward.[51] After this, the United States shifted to more overt operations, eventually sending in the U.S. Navy and Air Force to bomb Gadhafi's home in what the Reagan administration claimed was *not* an assassination attempt.

The most notorious operation of the Reagan administration was the Iran-Contra affair. While the Iran and contra ends of the operation began separately, they gradually merged in the White House basement as Marine Corps Lt. Col. Oliver North essentially ran American foreign policy.[52]

Anastasio Somoza Debayle's father had been installed as "president" of Nicaragua in the 1930s by the United States Marines, who had trained the Nicaraguan "National Guard" to secure his regime. With the aid of American Marines and corporations, the Somoza family ruled Nicaragua until 1979, when a broad-based coalition of Nicaraguans, sickened by Somoza's joyous pillaging of his own people, arose to oust the dictator.

The future of the revolution was determined in no small part by special operations provided by American mercenaries and a few active-duty Special Forces troops, who succeeded in killing off most of the frontline Sandinista leadership near the end of the insurgency. This left the fledgling government in the hands of the second bananas, many of whom were committed Marxists (although generally not Soviet puppets, as they would be portrayed by ideologues of the American right).

The American-supported contras ("counterrevolutionaries") came into being about a year after the final Sandinista victory in 1979. In fact, some of the original contras had also been original Sandinistas, including the most famous surviving leader, Eden Pastora, known as "Commander Zero." The initial contra movement, however, was controlled by former Somocista National Guardsmen, who had a clear history of brutality and murder and were generally viewed by the Nicaraguan people as simply a way to restore a Somoza-like regime. Early contra efforts were haphazard and ineffective, as the number of troops, their quality, and their hardware were all minimal.

The election of Ronald Reagan changed the nature of the rebellion. In March 1981, President Reagan signed his first "finding"—a document that a president is required to sign to authorize covert activities; it also requires that the action be disclosed to a congressional oversight committee—on Nicaragua, ostensibly with the goal of cutting off Sandinista support to the El Salvadoran guerrillas, the *Frente Sandinista de Liberación Nacional* (FSLN, Sandinista National Liberation Front). From 1981 through 1984, the United States provided about $80 million and aircraft, ships, Green Berets, and CIA contract agents to the contras. Early on, the United States also got Argentina on board as a source of training, and the influence of the "experts" from Argentina's "dirty war" became clear.

By early 1982, machine guns, mortars, and automatic rifles began arriving in the contra camps, and they were quickly put to use. By mid-March, two important bridges had been blown up by the contras, and the Sandinista government declared a state of emergency. While the contras were active through

1984, however, they were unable to achieve their goal: to take and hold territory within Nicaragua and declare a provisional government. Instead, their counter-revolution descended to looting, rape, and terrorism against coffee pickers, teachers, local officials, and anyone riding in a vehicle. Dozens of Nicaraguans disappeared. The contras also waged an indifferent air campaign, raiding Managua and Nicaraguan ports, but with no overall purpose and producing little effect. The Sandinistas had learned from Arbenz, and would not be panicked by rather transparent psyops.

By 1984, the contras were badly lagging in the CIA timetable which scheduled contra "liberated zones" by the end of 1983. Frustrated by the lack of progress, DCI Bill Casey proposed the idea of mining Nicaraguan harbors, thereby isolating the Nicaraguan economy and destabilizing the government. The CIA purchased a "mother ship," from which speedboats and helicopters operated. Ultimately, mines were laid by either CIA contract agents or U.S. military personnel (SEALs). The mining was more effective than anything else, damaging the Nicaraguan fishing industry, and eventually a Japanese freighter. To evade congressional control, Casey had purchased the mother ship out of the DCI's contingency fund.

One of the major problems the contras faced was that they were so closely identified within Nicaragua with Somoza's brutal National Guard. The first military commander of the contras was Enrique Bermúdez, a former colonel in the National Guard and founder of the Fifteenth of September Legion, a contra unit composed entirely by former Guardsmen. The prevalence of Guardsmen, especially among the contra leadership, so tainted the cause that by 1982, Pastora moved to Costa Rica and began his own organization rather than associate with them.

The unsavory nature of the leadership and the brutality of the contras could not be disguised. While some in the United States compared them to America's founding fathers (e.g., Adolfo Callero was the George Washington of Nicaragua), they more often behaved like the terrorists the Reagan administration was so quick to condemn. The unpopularity of the cause in the United States was the initial reason why Reagan had to certify (in the March 1981 finding) that U.S. covert action was only aimed at interdicting supplies to El Salvador. By December 1982, the House of Representatives passed the first Boland amendment, prohibiting the CIA or the Pentagon from using any funds for the purpose of overthrowing the government of Nicaragua, by a vote of 411 to nothing.[53] That year, Congress had appropriated $24 million to the contras, but by 1983, congressional support had run bone-dry. The House cut off additional money and passed Boland II, prohibiting the CIA, the Department of Defense, or any other entity of the U.S. government engaged in intelligence activities from providing any military or paramilitary support for the contras.[54]

The cutoff of funds was a crucial blow, as the contras had no real means to sustain themselves (they couldn't "swim like a fish among the peasants," to use Mao's phrase), and they quickly ran out of steam. Encouraged by President Reagan, Lt. Col. Oliver North of the National Security Council (NSC) began conspiring with elements of the intelligence underworld, including Richard Secord, John Singlaub, Ted Shackley, Thomas Clines, Albert Hakim, and Manucher Ghorbanifar. North was a "can-do" Marine, and when the president asked him to keep the contras together "body and soul," he resolved to get the job done no matter what.[55]

The answer was "Project Democracy," a covert program to raise money, buy weapons and supplies, and provide military training for the contras. Project Democracy, more importantly, was a major effort to privatize foreign policy and circumvent the U.S. Constitution and law. First, the contras hired a public-relations firm to "sell" them to the American people and Congress, in hopes of eventually restoring formal U.S. support. Second, funds were solicited from private individuals, groups, and foreign governments. In the United States, the contras received substantial cash from the Cuban-exile community and from wealthy individuals like Joe Coors of the Coors Brewing Company.[56] Carl "Spitz" Channell, prominent in Republican politics, was a particularly effective fundraiser for the Endowment for the Preservation of Liberty, bringing small groups of prospective donors to the White House for "special intelligence" briefings by Ollie North, at which Ronald Reagan appeared twice and Undersecretary of State Elliot Abrams appeared frequently. North himself was a tremendous asset as a fundraiser, exploiting the prestige of the National Security Council to imply that donors were serving the national interest and had official government sanction. Unleashing his natural talent for hyperbole, Ollie painted a terrifying picture of Soviet beachheads and Sandinista atrocities, rousing the privileged listeners to give freely. Training (and perhaps some weapons) was provided by private paramilitary groups such as the Alabama-based Civilian Military Assistance Group (CMAG).

Funds were also raised from foreign countries. Typically, someone like National Security Advisor Bud McFarlane would "mention" the U.S. problem to foreign diplomats. Understanding the way that international quid pro quos work, Saudi Arabia and Brunei contributed millions of dollars. North also worked through retired General John Singlaub and the World Anti-Communist League, and it was this connection that obtained Taiwanese aid.

Finally, money and arms were provided by the Enterprise, a shadowy, private covert-action-support organization run by retired Air Force General Richard Secord. Secord was a covert operator from way back, having run the secret air war in Laos, and had been a key figure in the aborted Iranian hostage rescue mission in 1980. The Enterprise was useful simply for its international arms connections, but provided a more valuable service as well—facilitating arms transfers to Iran in exchange for cash and hostages.

Coming into office with strident "tough on terrorism" rhetoric, Ronald Reagan was embarrassed when seven American citizens in Beirut were snatched by Hezbollah, a radical Islamic group sponsored by Iran. Critically, the first victim was William Buckley, CIA station chief in Beirut. Buckley had been involved in numerous CIA operations around the world—he knew a lot of secrets, and the CIA and the Reagan administration were desperate to get him back.

Although the origins of the idea are disputed, the NSC via Oliver North soon developed the notion that one might curry favor with Iranian "moderates" by selling them some weapons for Iran's ongoing war with Iraq (despite the fact that other elements in U.S. intelligence were simultaneously shipping money, equipment, and intelligence to Iraq). Perhaps then the "moderates" might use their influence to help get the American hostages released. The first shipments of arms to Iran came from Israeli inventories, with the guarantee that the United States would replace the weapons for Israel. After a second shipment of 408 TOW antitank missile systems, one American, Reverend Benjamin Weir, was released on 15 September 1985—not Buckley, as the administration had so fervently hoped. In fact, Buckley was already dead.

Ironically, North had failed to ensure that the man he wanted was still alive and available. After shipping 2,008 TOW antitank missiles, some HAWK anti-aircraft missiles, and some spare aircraft parts to Iran, two more American hostages were released—whereupon Hezbollah went out on the streets of Beirut and simply snatched four more Americans, along with British mediator Terry Waite. The arms-for-hostages deal was a bottomless pit; there was a large pool of potential hostages for Hezbollah to draw from. North had been suckered, and the self-proclaimed "good Marine" had given thousands of missiles to the same people who had blown up the Marine Corps barracks in Beirut.

The weapons sales were managed by Secord's Enterprise, and it was North's idea to link the Iran and contra operations: why not sell the weapons to Iran and divert the payments to the contras? Secord himself sweetened the deal by charging the Iranians exorbitant markups on the weapons; purchasing the TOWs for $3.7 million and selling them for $10 million—more than a 200 percent profit after expenses, perhaps not the best way to make new friends—then keeping the "excess" for "operating expenses." Profit, he'd tell the Iran-Contra congressional committee, is the American way.

It all came apart when Secord attempted to arrange further shipments to Iran behind the back of Manocher Ghorbanifar, a prominent Iranian exile who had served the lucrative role of middleman. Ghorbanifar took his revenge by making the arms deals public, igniting a firestorm of scandal in the United States.

The American hostages were released later on when they no longer had any use, i.e., no more arms deals. Ultimately, Violetta Chamorro's *Unión Nacional Opositiona* (UNO) Party defeated the Sandinistas in the Nicaraguan election of 1990, largely on the back of both U.S. economic actions that destroyed the Nicaraguan economy and massive American campaign funding. It was scarcely observed in the United States that the election was *allowed* by the supposedly totalitarian Sandinistas, and that when they lost they surrendered power to an opposing political group, an act of extreme rarity in modern Latin America.

The winner of the "swept under the rug" award (covert action category) for the 1980s goes to the illegal and generally ignored efforts of the United States in arming and supporting Saddam Hussein's war with Iran. At the outset of the decade, the State Department had placed Iraq on the list of "terrorist" nations for its patronage of groups like the Abu Nidal cell, led by Abu Nidal, responsible for numerous acts of international terrorism. There is an old saying, however: "The enemy of my enemy is my friend," and when Iraq went to war with Iran in 1979, Baghdad began the political transition from Soviet client to American intimate.

First, Iraq was removed from the "terrorist nation" list in February 1982. During 1982 and 1983, U.S. equipment, including ammunition, computers, spare parts, and defense electronics, was secretly shipped to Iraq in an operation run from the White House. There was no presidential finding related to these transactions. The relationship with Iraq was handled strictly "off the books." In June 1982, the United States also began secretly sharing intelligence information with Iraq, including highly classified satellite photos and Airborne Warning and Command System (AWACS) data aircraft that contain the most sensitive radar, enabling the user to "see" virtually everything in the air in real time. These were first passed to Baghdad through the Saudi government, but eventually the U.S. government built and staffed a special electronics center right in Baghdad to directly download electronic intelligence to pass to the Iraqi government. Eventually, the United States would begin covertly funneling money and critical military equipment to Iraqi, first through "agricultural loans," and ultimately through the Atlanta branch of the Italian-based *Banca Nazionale del Lavoro* (BNL). In the euphoria over the outcome of the Persian Gulf War, BNL's connection with the American covert arming of Iraq became a forgotten scandal.[57]

The 1990s: Get Saddam!

Saddam Hussein, however, never became America's bulwark of stability in the Middle East. Always operating on his own agenda, the Iraqi grabbed world oil markets by the throat by seizing Kuwait in August 1990. To the apparent surprise of former Director of Central Intelligence George Bush, Saddam became the "next Hitler." During the war, the United States attempted several hits on the Iraqi dictator, despite the ongoing presidential ban on assassination, targeting his known headquarters with numerous air strikes. All failed. President Bush also appealed directly to the Iraqi military to remove Saddam from power, but in Saddam Hussein's Iraq, anyone who doesn't praise the dictator loud enough is quickly stood up against a wall.

Having failed to eliminate the "Butcher of Baghdad" during the war, the Bush administration began several programs of covert action to terminate him (no real intelligence officer ever says "terminate with extreme prejudice"—this is an invention of fiction writers). These programs operated along two conflicting themes: a popular uprising largely ignited by the Kurds in the northern "safe haven," and a military coup.

Using the northern no-fly zone as a base, the two main Kurdish factions, often at war with each other, created a state-within-a-state, built their own armed forces, and planned for an uprising that would exploit the willingness of many

Iraqi military units to turn against Saddam. In this they were encouraged by CIA officers stationed in northern Iraq. According to the Kurdish leadership, American officials told them explicitly that their "safe haven" was guaranteed by American air power—while the Kurds couldn't kill Saddam's tanks, American aircraft would. It is unclear what the Kurds were promised,[58] but on the very eve of their insurrection in September 1996, the rug was pulled out—Washington sent word that there would be no American air cover. With the skies clear, the Kurds pressed Saddam's forces for four weeks; then Massoud Barzani, leader of one Kurdish faction, the Kurdish Democratic Party (KDP), struck a deal with Saddam Hussein. Opening the door for the Iraqi army, the KDP allowed the dictator's armored forces to take command of the struggle. Eventually the dictator's forces rolled through the "safe haven," destroying the fledgling Kurdish state, and slaughtering thousands of people who had put their trust in the United States. The night before the Iraqis arrived, the officers of the CIA station fled, leaving behind electronic gear, computers, and a television station. In a belated, pathetic response, the Clinton administration launched a cruise missile attack against Iraqi radar installations in southern Iraq, a so-called measured response that achieved the goal of avoiding another shootout with Saddam.

During the six-year flirtation with a popular uprising, a second covert track followed attempting to create and support a coup d'etat by senior Iraqi military commanders. This endeavor was the more attractive to senior American officials, promising to minimize the chances of a bloody civil war that could allow Iran to expand and to maintain the organizational integrity of the Iraqi army. Thus, the decisive goal of "regional stability" would be maintained. While Saddam periodically shot a general or two to maintain discipline, the CIA focused on a group of expatriate Iraqi military men called "the Accord," who promised to use their influence within the Iraqi army to oust Saddam Hussein. Much like other operations of this kind, however, the Accord was critically infiltrated with Saddam's agents. All the efforts of this group have produced, as of this writing, is a series of executions in Iraq.[59]

CONCLUSIONS

The United States, either through the CIA, other government agencies, or private organizations, conducted hundreds of covert operations during the cold war. This chapter has summarized some, and many others will be detailed later as specific issues about covert action are discussed. While we might all agree that the most important thing about the cold war was winning, the record of covert action makes it clear that the way one wins is also critical, for it determines what the future brings. In the following chapters, we will explore the way the war of black ops was fought, and the consequences we shall live with for many years.

NOTES

1. Some good histories are: John Prados, *President's Secret Wars: CIA and Pentagon Covert Operations Since World War II* (New York: William Morrow and Co., 1986); William Blum, *Killing Hope: U.S. Military and CIA Interventions Since World War II* (Monroe, Maine: Common Courage Press, 1995); G. J. A. O'Toole, *Honorable Treachery: A History of U.S. Intelligence, Espionage, and Covert Action from the American Revolution to the Present* (New York: Atlantic Monthly, 1991).

2. Of course, Washington's colleagues and opponents were likewise unskilled, as such unprincipled activities were things gentlemen simply didn't *do*.

3. See John Bakeless, *Turncoats, Traitors, and Heroes* (New York: J. B. Lippincott, 1959), chap. 13.

4. Washington's complicity in this offer has never been proven, as the offer was made through Lafayette.

5. See Bakeless, *Turncoats, Traitors, and Heroes*, chap. 21.

6. In French, Hortalez et Compangie.

7. See O'Toole, *Honorable Treachery*, pp. 29–30 for a summary.

8. It is also reminiscent of later U.S. operations, as in Laos in the 1960s.

9. See Robert Barr Smith, *Men At War: True Stories of Heroism and Honor* (New York: Avon Books, 1997), chap. 15; O'Toole, *Honorable Treachery*, pp. 97–101.

10. The "red sandwich" quote is after Nixon, who in 1970 feared that Latin America could be caught in a "red sandwich" between Cuba and Chile.

11. Joseph Burkholder Smith, *The Plot to Steal Florida* (New York: Arbor House, 1983), p. 113.

12. Smith, *The Plot to Steal Florida*, pp. 115–16.

13. See Senate, *Final Report of the Select Committee to Study Governmental Operations with Respect to Intelligence Activities*, Book 6: "Supplementary Reports on Intelligence Activities," 94th Cong., 2d sess., 1976, S. Rept. 94-755. The United States finally obtained Florida in 1817 by a simple overt military invasion.

14. CIA parlance described the Soviet bloc as "denied areas" because they were extremely difficult for outside intelligence agencies to penetrate due to their rigid oppression.

15. The Gehlen Organization, later referred to simply as The Org, began as a German espionage network in the Soviet Union during World War II. When Germany collapsed, Reinhard Gehlen, the German intelligence chief for Russia, bartered the network to the United States, aided by the fact that Gehlen had been befriended immediately after the war by Allen Dulles. As the USSR had been virtually impenetrable for the United States, the Gehlen Organization was viewed as nearly providential. Gehlen and his hand-picked associates, some of them unrepentant Nazis, were given a fresh start. Eventually, Gehlen and his organization were absorbed into West German Intelligence, which Gehlen was picked to head. The actual intelligence contributions of the Gehlen Organization are a matter of some dispute.

16. Forerunner of the KGB. NKVD stands for *Narodny Komisariat Vnutrennikh Del*, or People's Commissariat for Internal Affairs.

17. This section is drawn from Prados, *President's Secret Wars*, chap. 2.

18. "Turning around" is forcing the captured agents to cooperate, often by sending back radio messages as if nothing were wrong. Thus, the Soviets could learn about other missions, as well as feed false information back to the United States and Britain.

19. The Albanian operation crashed and burned, in large part, because one of the planners was the British traitor Kim Philby, who was simultaneously planning the action and relaying the plans to the Soviets.

20. This entire operation was strikingly similar to that conducted against Chile in the 1960s and 1970s (without the coup, as none was needed).

21. See O'Toole, *Honorable Treachery*, pp. 435–37; Blum, *The Forgotten CIA*, chap. 2.

22. This account is drawn from Prados, *President's Secret Wars*, chap. 6; Blum, *The Forgotten CIA*, chap. 9.

23. *New York Times*, 18 January 1953, IV, p. 8.

24. *New York Times*, 21 March 1954, p. 3; 11 April 1954, IV, p. 5.

25. Prados, *President's Secret Wars*, p. 115; Blum, *The Forgotten CIA*, p. 135; Christopher Robbins, *Air America* (New York: G. P. Putnam and Sons, 1979), pp. 59–62.

26. Blum, *The Forgotten CIA*, pp. 137–38.

27. Ibid., pp. 156–57.

28. Prados, *President's Secret Wars*, p. 265.

29. Senate, *Final Report of the Select Committee to Study Governmental Operations with Respect to Intelligence Activities*, Book 4: "Supplementary Detailed Staff Reports on Foreign and Military Intelligence," 94th Cong., 2d sess., 1976, S. Rept. 94-755, 133.

30. *New York Times*, 26 January 1976; Blum, *Killing Hope*, p. 111.

31. See Prados, *President's Secret Wars*, pp. 140–44; Blum, *The Forgotten CIA*, chap. 14; Robbins, *Air America*, pp. 88–94. It is not surprising that pilots violated the prohibition against carrying ID cards. If they were captured without identification, they were liable to be legally executed as spies or war criminals, whereas as American pilots, they might hope to be treated either (at worst) as prisoners of war or (at best) as valuable bargaining chips with the United States.

32. See Joseph Burkholder Smith, *Portrait of a Cold Warrior* (New York: Ballantine Books, 1976), p. 197.

33. See Blum, *The Forgotten CIA*, chap. 30; Prados, *President's Secret Wars*, pp. 208–17; Warren Hinckle and William Turner, *Deadly Secrets: The CIA-Mafia War Against Castro and the Assassination of J.F.K.* (New York: Thunder's Mouth Press, 1992), chap. 4–5.

34. See Hinckle and Turner, *Deadly Secrets*, p. 320.

35. The 2506 Brigade (the Bay of Pigs group) was trained in Guatemala precisely to avoid this legal, as well as practical, problem.

36. See Senate, *Interim Report of the Select Committee to Study Governmental Operations with Respect to Intelligence Activities*, Book 6: "Alleged Assassination Plots Involving Foreign Leaders," 94th Cong., 1st sess., 1975, S. Rept. 94-465.

37. ZR/RIFLE was apparently initiated around 25 January 1961, in the interim period between presidential administrations. As it is unlikely that President Eisenhower would have started a project like this as he was leaving office, and also unlikely that President Kennedy would have started it so soon after taking office, questions about precisely who authorized *executive action* remain unanswered, intriguing, and worrisome.

38. See Senate, "Alleged Assassination Plots," 181–90. Using the Mafia for these plots made the men who authorized them subject to blackmail or graymail by the Mafia, who could threaten to expose the plots and the cooperation with gangsters.

39. Paul E. Sigmund, *The Overthrow of Allende and the Politics of Chile, 1964–1976* (Pittsburgh: University of Pittsburgh Press, 1977), p. 297. (And we think U.S. campaigns are sleazy!)

40. Senate, *Staff Report of the Select Committee to Study Governmental Operations with Respect to Intelligence Activities*. Book 7: "Covert Action," 94th Cong., 1st sess., 1975; Prados, *President's Secret Wars*, pp. 315–22; Blum, *Killing Hope*, chap. 34.

41. Prados, *President's Secret Wars*, pp. 239–48.

42. I include Phoenix as a covert operation because it was covert from the American people, and many of its operations were ideally hidden from the enemy as well, although certainly the Vietcong knew there was someone "out there" hunting them.

43. Prados, *President's Secret Wars*, pp. 308–11.

44. Ibid., pp. 288–95.

45. Robbins, *Air America*, pp. 229–32, chap. 9.

46. Prados, *President's Secret Wars*, p. 317.

47. Senate, "Alleged Assassination Plots," p. 240.

48. See Senate, "Covert Action"; Blum, *Killing Hope*, chap. 34; Prados, *President's Secret Wars*, pp. 315–22.

49. See Prados, *President's Secret Wars*, pp. 347; Jonathan Kwitny, *Endless Enemies: The Making of an Unfriendly World* (New York: Viking Penguin, 1984), chap. 9.

50. See Prados, *President's Secret Wars*, pp. 356–63.

51. See ibid., pp. 382–83.

52. This account is drawn from ibid., chap. 28–29; *Tower Commission Report* (New York: Random House, 1987); Jonathan Marshall, Peter Dale Scott, and Jane Hunter, *The Iran-Contra Connection: Secret Teams and Covert Operations in the Reagan Era* (Boston: South End Press, 1987).

53. Theodore Draper, *A Very Thin Line: The Iran-Contra Affairs* (New York: Simon and Schuster, 1991), p. 18.

54. Ibid., pp. 23–24.

55. I do not mean here to insult the many "can-do" Marines who take their oath to the Constitution seriously—something North did *not*.

56. See Joseph Coors, testimony at Joint Hearings before the House Select Committee to Investigate Covert Arms Transactions with Iran and the Senate Select Committee on Secret Military Assistance to Iran and the Nicaragua Opposition, vol. 100-3 (Washington: Government Printing Office, 1987), pp. 126–29).

57. See Alan Friedman, *Spider's Web: The Secret History of How the White House Secretly Armed Iraq* (New York: Bantam Books, 1993), chap. 1–3.

58. This is extremely reminiscent of the conflicting stories reported by the Cubans, CIA officers, and military personnel involved in the Bay of Pigs.

59. For more detail, see "Unfinished Business: The CIA and Saddam Hussein," *Peter Jennings Reports*, ABC News, broadcast 26 June 1997.

Chapter 3

Covert Action:
The Black Ops Menu

I t's nearly impossible to overestimate the lengths to which the governments of this world will go to have their own way, punish their enemies, and enrich their friends. No tactic is untried, and while practically all governments claim high moral purposes, practically all go by the book—Machiavelli's *Prince*, that is. Machiavelli's viewpoint, one shared by most national leaders, is that the highest morality is the preservation of the state and its power; therefore, in the service of state survival, any low blow is justified.

The variety of covert operations is wide open and limited only by human imagination (which, as we shall see, is almost no limit at all). What follows illustrates some of the choices available to a president: the black ops menu.

WHAT COVERT ACTION IS

To begin with, *covert action* is an act, operation, or program intended to change the political policies, leaders, institutions, or power structure of another country, performed in a way that the covert actor's role is hidden or disguised, and if that role is discovered, the actor can deny responsibility. In other words, as long as no one can *prove* you did it, it's okay. This basic concept is known in the trade as *plausible deniability*. This differs from a *clandestine action*, which is an act or operation in which the deed itself is hidden, so that only the people carrying out the action know that it is taking place. For example, a guerrilla war is apparent to all observers, and if the identity of the belligerents and their supporters is disguised, then it is covert action. Photographing a codebook is a clandestine action, in that if it is done properly, the enemy will never know that the action even took place (as is necessary in such deeds, since if they know you've got their codes, they just switch to new ones—which is why one copies, rather than steals, codebooks). When a spy secretly slips across a border, the enemy (ideally) doesn't know he did it, making this a clandestine act. Note that for an action to be covert, the identity of the perpetrator need not be absolutely anonymous. In many cases, it is merely necessary to establish and preserve the fiction that one is uninvolved, so as to not provoke one's enemy (which might require a response and perhaps escalation) and to avoid getting caught in an outright lie.

All political actions are not covert actions. *Political action*, intended to influence political processes (usually elections) in foreign countries, may be covert or overt. If the hand of the influencing government is visible and acknowledged, then it is simple political action, as for example, when the United States cut off Chilean access to the International Monetary Fund (IMF) in 1973, or when it publically promised financial aid to Nicaragua only if Violetta Chamoro was elected in 1990. Political action becomes *covert political action* when the influencing government hides its role. Examples of this include forming and subsidizing political groups like "Christian Women Agitators for Truth" in Jamaica (1976), and conspiring to overthrow the prime minister of Australia.[1]

One final distinction should probably be made between a covert war and a proxy war. A *proxy war* is one that is fought with the overt, acknowledged assistance of an outside power. The foreign power merely uses the people and land of another country to fight (or often, to "bleed") a third country. For example, United States support of the mujahedin in Afghanistan was more properly a proxy war than a covert action. Although American involvement began covertly by supplying sterile arms acquired from third countries, e.g., Egyptian AK-47s, eventually the U.S. government made little or no effort to hide its involvement. At the end, once it had supplied over a thousand Stinger antiaircraft missiles to the Afghans, the only effort made was to avoid direct U.S.–Soviet engagement

Conversely, a *covert war* is one in which the covert acting power takes pains to avoid the appearance of direct involvement. The Bay of Pigs is one example of this, as is the U.S. intervention in Laos with the Armée Clandestine in the 1960s. In the latter case, American special forces in civilian clothes fought alongside native Hmong tribesmen, and transportation was provided not by U.S. military aircraft, but by Air America, acting as a supposedly private airline.

In general, I also distinguish between covert action and *special operations*. Special operations are small-scale military actions carried out overtly, usually during wartime: commando raids to blow up bridges, capture electronic "black boxes," and so forth. The raid on the Son Tay prison camp in North Vietnam is one example, as is OPERATION EAGLE CLAW, the attempt to rescue the American hostages in Iran. They're not meant to be deniable, and they generally take place during wartime, so they're not really covert actions. Even during wartime, however, some special operations can be covert operations, especially in "limited wars." For example, during the Vietnam War, the United States often sent teams of SEALs into North Vietnam and China. These actions were never acknowledged by either side, since they would be considered serious provocations (somehow, thousand-pound bombs from B-52s wouldn't start World War III, but a half-dozen SEALs with M-16s would; go figure).

Finally, covert action is not espionage. *Espionage* or *intelligence gathering* is an action or program designed to obtain strategic information. Some intelligence gathering is essentially open (i.e., everyone knows you do it), such as reading and analyzing foreign magazines and newspapers, "debriefing" citizens who have traveled to strategic countries, or taking pictures from spy satellites. Open intelligence gathering also includes: signal intelligence (SIGINT, listening to others' radio and telephone transmission); traffic analysis (TRAFINT, analyzing where their trucks and trains go); electronic intelligence (ELINT, analyzing their electronic emissions); and cryptanalysis (codebreaking). These are called "open" mechanisms because, although the process and product of such activities are highly secret, the fact that we do them—and, generally, when and where—is not. Espionage is a clandestine kind of intelligence gathering aimed at obtaining information that the opponent is trying to conceal or protect. This includes the most important (usually) intelligence source: spies.[2]

Intelligence gathering is related, however, to covert action. First, intelligence is always a critical aspect of a successful covert action. For example, if a coup depends on the support of the military, one had better be certain of military support. Second, covert actions (or more properly, clandestine actions), are often performed to obtain intelligence, as when one does a black-bag job to photograph secret documents or install a phone tap. A real-life example is the American program of assistance to the Baltic rebels (Ukranian and Estonian, mainly) in the late 1940s: While the nominal goal was to liberate these nations, in reality the Americans did little more than use the partisans to gather information on conditions inside the Soviet Union.

COVERT ACTION: THE MYRIAD WAYS

We generally think of paramilitary operations as covert action, but black ops comprise many different kinds of activities, performed singly or in combination. Some operations are simple, focused, and short (e.g., disrupting the Communist Party rally in Bogota), while others are long-term programs (e.g., fighting a war in Laos and keeping it a secret). Generally, covert action can be grouped into five categories:

- Asset Development
- Political Action
- Propaganda and Disinformation
- Economic Warfare
- Paramilitary Action

Asset Development

While we might not think of developing assets as a covert action per se, this activity is critical to every covert action. For a government to deny an opera-

tion, it is always helpful to have some evidence that points the finger at somebody else. The best method of keeping the U.S. government from being identified as the source of an operation is throwing suspicion in another direction,
allowing the United States to say, "See, *they* did it." Thus, assets as we mean it
here are largely covert operators who have no immediate, provable link to the
U.S. government.

The most common kind of asset is the single individual who holds some
position that is or could be useful to a covert operation. This could be a journalist, editor, soldier of fortune, customs official, banker, business owner, the vice
president, and so on. The development of assets is a tricky business, as one can
rarely walk up to an important foreign official, hand her a roll of cash, and tell
her you're going to build a secret airbase in her country so you can secretly bomb
neighboring countries. In some cases, of course, individuals approach known
CIA officers, offer their services, and hold out their hand. Typically, however,
people of real importance are powerful and sophisticated enough that they must
be carefully cultivated.

In the ideal case, individuals are first carefully but surreptitiously investigated for attributes or circumstances that would disqualify them, including:

- can't keep his mouth shut;
- already under suspicion or surveillance by her own government;
- rabidly anti-American or pro-Soviet (unless this looks to be a "cover," or
  there's a good reason to believe he has had a change of heart);
- too good to be true (in which case she is probably being "dangled"—
  which means she is an agent for somebody trying to infiltrate *your* organization).

The features that make an individual especially suitable to become a U.S.
asset include:

- holding an influential position in government, the military, business, or
  the media, or having good "contacts";
- reliable and disciplined;
- having no or few vices (a mistress is okay; a cocaine addiction generally
  isn't), unless you can use the vice to blackmail the target;
- a taste for the "good life" (and the need for a little extra cash);
- pro-American sentiment (but not visibly *too* pro-American, or he can't be
  useful as an agent of influence).

If an individual is deemed suitable, the approach is made cautiously. In the
subtle approach, a recruiter, often the case officer running the recruitment, will
arrange with a third party (some mutual friend, ideally) to meet the potential
asset (the *target*) casually, perhaps at a party, business meeting, club, or theater.[3]
Later, the recruiter might have a "chance encounter" at a restaurant, club, or bar,

where they'll discuss mutual interests (the recruiter, from the background inves- tigation, knows the likes, dislikes, and interests of the target). A friendship is struck up, but no deals are made for a while. At some point, the recruiter will do a favor or two for the target, purposely asking nothing in return—perhaps providing a small gift for the target's child (something generally not available in that country), working out a visa problem, and so on. In some cases, the recruiter might secretly arrange a problem for the target (e.g., a truck accident that keeps the newsprint from getting to the newspaper owner's plant) that the officer can then conveniently remedy. Proceeding slowly, the favors increase in scale, until it's obvious to the target that he is receiving some truly valuable "gifts." At this point, the target will often ask to reciprocate. If he doesn't, then the recruiter will go to him with his *own* "problem," which the target is positioned to rectify. Once the target has performed one or two small favors for the case officer, the stakes are raised. Having established a friendly relationship involving recipro- cated favors, the recruiter will start asking for the *real* goods: "inside" informa- tion, a slant to a news story, holding up contract negotiations with the truckers, allowing a shipment of "oil drilling equipment" to pass through customs unin- spected, and the like. These are things that might be illegal, but generally are designed to cost the target nothing; the recruiter doesn't want to scare him off. Once the target has begun providing something to the recruiter, he is hooked, because now he has done things he won't want his own government, corporation, or constituency to know about. At this point, the recruiter begins providing pay- ments, often in the form of money transferred to a foreign bank account or small gifts of cash. This merely cements the relationship, for the unspoken threat of revealing his collusion with a foreign intelligence service is probably enough to maintain an asset's cooperation.

Of course, there are less subtle ways of developing an asset. If someone has a "useful" vice (e.g., perhaps a drug addiction), he can be entrapped and black- mailed. However, in the case of a covert asset, as opposed to a spy, it's usually best to obtain his cooperation, and the subtle, friendly method is more reliable than coercion (at least in the view of the CIA; Soviet intelligence generally pre- ferred to blackmail or coerce assets when possible).

Finally, one of the most important methods of developing individual foreign assets is education and training of foreign nationals. When we think of an asset for a foreign country, we generally assume that this individual would behave dif- ferently if he weren't "controlled" by foreign intelligence; that he would view his country's "national interest" in opposition to the interest of his recruiter's country. However, suppose one could get him to view the world in such a way as to see his own national interest as coinciding with the interest of the foreign power? In this case, he'd do what the foreign intelligence service wants because he thinks it's best for *his* country, too.

Adopting the viewpoint of a foreign country occurs through a process political scientists call "dependency." By attending American universities and training schools, foreign nationals learn to view the world the way Americans do, thereby creating a *comprador elite,* an upper class that identifies more closely with the United States than it does with its own country and people. Under these conditions, it is quite natural for foreign individuals to volunteer as American covert assets. Throughout the cold war, the CIA kept a stable of "cleared" university professors who served as talent spotters, watching foreign students—especially foreign graduate students—for signs of the capacity and desire to become CIA assets.

Whether as intelligence sources or covert action assets, foreigners who work for American intelligence must keep the relationship secret. Almost always, their effectiveness relies on the fact that others don't know they're working for American intelligence. This is easy to understand: How would you feel if, for example, it were reported that Dan Rather, Jesse Helms, or the chairman of the Joint Chiefs of Staff was on the payroll of a foreign country?

A second kind of asset is the front organization, a group, company, foundation, or agency that is actually created and paid for by an intelligence agency. These might be cultural, social, business, or student groups, such as the Asia Foundation, the World Assembly of Youth, the International Student Conference, and the Congress for Cultural Freedom.[4] These groups were generally used during the cold war to combat Soviet-sponsored groups. Organizations of this nature are generally used for propaganda operations and to build general political support for a particular ideology.

In the past, the CIA also operated foundations and "educational" organizations on university campuses. During the 1950s and early 1960s, Michigan State University was the host to the Vietnam Advisory Group (the MSUVAG), a group of operators who helped develop counterinsurgency doctrine, trained South Vietnamese "police," and consulted closely with Vietnamese leaders. In fact, Vietnamese President Ngo Dinh Diem was at one time appointed to Michigan State as a consultant to the Government Research Bureau.[5] Several CIA operators (may we call them Spartan spooks?) were hidden in departments like human medicine and public administration and technically paid by the university.

Other front organizations are created for more violent operations. "Zenith Technical Enterprises" was stationed on the campus of the University of Miami (although not formally affiliated with the university), and was the base of OPERATION MONGOOSE, the post–Bay of Pigs program to either assassinate Castro, foster a rebellion against him, or create a provocation to permit the United States to overtly invade. Supervised by Ted Shackley, exiles raided the Cuban mainland from this base (called by the code name JM/WAVE), shooting up boats and the waterfront, and sabotaging Cuban infrastructure and the economy.

Finally, the CIA operates *proprietary companies*—business firms that appear independent, but are actually arms of the intelligence agency. The most famous of these was Air America, which became so well known that it spawned several books and a movie starring Mel Gibson. Air America, for a time the largest airline in the world (in numbers of aircraft), was used principally as a covert air force in Southeast Asia, running supplies, ferrying personnel, and actually conducting air strikes against enemy targets. Another CIA proprietary, still in operation, is Southern Air Transport (SAT), the Latin American version of Air America. When Eugene Hausenfus was captured by the Sandinistas after his aircraft was shot down over Nicaragua, his contract was with "Corporate Air Services," a front for SAT.[6]

Political Action

Political action is an endeavor designed to directly influence political processes, decisions, and institutions. It is comprised of political advice, psychological operations (psyops), subsidies to important individuals and organizations, non-monetary subsidies, and political training.

Political advice is often provided to friends and clients to help them establish or increase political support from their own constituencies. This advice is often provided in an electoral process, sometimes to prop up the popularity of a teetering regime with the landholders, or perhaps to ensure the loyalty of the military. In the Chilean elections of 1964 and 1970, CIA provided Madison Avenue-style campaign techniques to the Christian Democrats (the opposition to Allende), including slick American-quality campaign materials, voter registration drives, "get out the vote" drives, and professional survey research to poll public opinion. The general CIA attitude toward elections is perhaps best illustrated by the fact that a prominent election specialist was borrowed from the Chicago "machine" of Mayor Richard J. Daley.[7] The reason political advice is often given covertly is simply to avoid the appearance of American influence (or outright control) on foreign political processes. In the Third World, it's generally a bad idea to gain a reputation as "the Americans' candidate." It's no accident that the team of American election specialists employed by Boris Yeltsin was a closely guarded secret.

Another form of political advice concerns "how to govern." Many foreign leaders, mainly from the Third World, come to power with little or no experience in running a government. Often, as with Ngo Dinh Diem in Vietnam or President Napoleon Duarte in El Salvador, the regime is under immediate and immense pressure from insurgency or economic disaster, and simply managing the political and economic system requires substantial expertise that can only be obtained from outside the country. In such cases, the U.S. State Department and the CIA have often provided political "advisors" who counsel national leaders in an effort to "stabilize" their regimes.

This can be highly successful. In the late 1940s, American advisor Wulf Ladejinsky suggested that land reform was the way to undercut Communist Party support (or "steal Communist thunder," the title of his article) in Taiwan, Korea, and Japan. Following the redistribution program, which dispersed large landholdings to thousands of small-scale farms, virtually all support for the

Communists disappeared. In the 1950s, U.S. military advisor (and legendary CIA operative) Edward Lansdale[8] planned both the military and political strategy that cut the legs out from under the Communist *Huk* rebellion in the Philippines and solidified the regime of Ramón Magsaysay. American academics also served as political advisors in the postwar period, as university professors who were experts in the emerging fields of "modernization" and "stability" traveled the world, often funded covertly by the CIA, spreading the fruits of American social science. This kind of advice has often proven beneficial, even to the people of the target country: It's hard to argue with building of schools and hospitals or digging wells for clean drinking water. It doesn't matter that the advisor was provided by a foreign intelligence service, and that the purpose was to influence the indigenous people in favor of Uncle Sam.

As the cold war began, the United States inherited the role of protector of the global status quo, largely because the challenger to the status quo was Communism. The key concept in American policy toward Asia, Africa, and Latin America became "stability," which simply meant keeping current regimes in power, no matter what. A stable regime wouldn't go "Commie." Unfortunately, this often resulted in agents of the United States providing political advice based on a kind of "carrot and stick" approach to stability: The carrot was "how to govern," which included advice and money for schools, hospitals, and businesses; the stick was "how to oppress," which covered police operations, riot containment, infiltration of political opponents, and sometimes techniques of "hostile interrogation," i.e., torture. This combined approach was called the counterinsurgency doctrine, and came to the Third World from Britain and America, helped along by American universities. Some prominent scholars of "conflict studies" were involved in creating models of rebellion and political violence that seemed to suggest that the way for a leader to achieve stability (i.e., crush insurgency) was to effectively repress his people (*in*effective repression would only lead to greater rebellion). Indeed, it would later emerge that some American academics were on the CIA payroll during the time they developed such theories, and some training for counterinsurgency actually took place at American universities. The author has a list of "class supplies" from Michigan State University (1960s) that includes machine-gun ammunition, hand grenades (fragmentation), and recoilless rifles (small artillery).[9] It is also unfortunate that almost everyone in "conflict studies" was (wrongly) accused of serving the CIA as instructors of "oppression studies."

"How to oppress" (effectively) advice includes the nitty-gritty of oppression, such as the creation of secret police forces, support and denial of death squads, interrogation methods, torture techniques, assassination of dissidents, and state terrorism carried out by the government. Whether or not such activities were taught at American institutions like the School of the Americas at Fort Bragg, North Carolina, they were certainly provided by Americans, as well as American proxies such as the Argentines. When a manual called *Psychological Operations in Guerrilla Warfare*, produced by the United States and employed by the

Nicaraguan contras, spoke of "neutralizing" selected targets, such as mayors and teachers, everyone understood what it meant.[10] When the "elite" men of El Salvador's *Atlacatl* battalion sealed off a hamlet called El Mozote and slaughtered over eight hundred inhabitants (including hundreds of women and children), their U.S. Special Forces "advisors" were present.

The reasons *this* kind of advice must remain covert are obvious—it's repugnant to American ideals, alienates the people being oppressed, practically always gets out of hand, and frequently—to the local people—"American" comes to mean "death squad" and "torture." It's always best to be able to deny these activities. Typically, deniability is easy to come by here—one either contracts out the advising to proxies (e.g., Argentines, Taiwanese, Israelis, South Africans, Cuban exiles), hires mercenaries, or sheep-dips some Americans to do the job: "Sorry," says the undersecretary of state, "we can't control private citizens." Because these deceptions are standard operating procedure for black operations, rarely do active duty U.S. personnel get exposed, as they did at El Mozote.

Subsidies are another form of political action. Money can be paid to agents of influence, political parties, government organizations (e.g., police, military), and private organizations (e.g., businesses, chamber of commerce, media, and unions). Often subsidies, "retainers," "goodwill gestures," or bribes are paid to these entities regularly to provide continual support for the payer's policy objectives, or just to create a general climate of goodwill (or hostility to one's foes). Subsidization also includes outright creation and ownership of groups such as businesses, unions, and media outlets.

Subsidies to individuals are simply cash gifts to important people who can determine a country's policies or influence public opinion (in countries where that matters). If "subsidies to individuals" sounds suspiciously like "bribes," that is because that's pretty much what they are. Despite this, several foreign heads of state have been on the CIA payroll, including the shah of Iran, King Hussein of Jordan, Ferdinand Marcos, and Manuel Noriega. It is through such subsidies that one develops human assets.

Subsidies to political parties have been stock-in-trade for the CIA since 1947. Sometimes, money is supplied to win specific elections, while in other circumstances, CIA dollars flow almost continually to keep local parties "on top of things." The bulk of funding for Italy's Christian Democrat Party in the 1948 election came from the United States. In 1964, the CIA spent about $10 million to defeat Salvador Allende in Chile, which amounted to more per voter than was spent in the United States' own election that year.[11] Violetta Chamorro's UNO party received an undisclosed sum of money (certainly in the tens of millions) from the CIA, as well as private American sources, to win the 1990 election in Nicaragua. More recently, a substantial portion of the budget for the Iraqi National Congress, the opposition to Saddam Hussein (and now largely in exile), was paid out of U.S. black funds.

As a practical matter, such activity must remain covert, since the people of a country almost always want political leadership that owes allegiance to them, not to some foreign power. In rare cases, however, political aid is made overtly, as in Nicaragua in 1990. When such "overt-covert" aid is given, it is usually accompanied by dire overt threats, e.g., "your economy will be destroyed." In such cases, "the people" are indeed given a clear choice: Vote our way or starve.

Subsidies carry with them some risk. First, exposure of the foreign subsidy can cost the recipient—individual, political party, or business—domestic support or credibility. Would *you* believe a paid agent of a foreign power has your best interest at heart? Second, to assure long-lasting pliability, American practice has been to lean toward supporting parties of the extreme right wing. While they are reliably anti-Communist, the long-term political ramifications have frequently been horrendous, as these organizations often support death squads, torture of dissidents, and genocide. If such regimes fall, as most ultimately will, the revolutionary governments that replace them are practically guaranteed to hate the United States. Third, sending money to countries in which democratic institutions are weak often results in less than fair elections; politicos everywhere understand it is easier and more certain to *buy* elections than it is to *win* them. While this may produce short-term stability (i.e., those in power stay there), this is not the way to strengthen fledgling democracies, which could evolve into the most long-standing form of government: stable democracy.

Financing "private" groups is a time-honored method of mobilizing public support in a foreign country. To the end, the CIA has directly paid part or all of the expenses for foreign businesses, unions, media (television, radio, and print), and student groups. For example, the CIA fought the ideological war in Europe by creating the Congress for Cultural Freedom (CCF) in June 1950. While the CCF received money from many sources, former DDCI Ray Cline notes that it could not have survived without a steady CIA subsidy.[12] Throughout Latin America, the CIA operated to forestall what it viewed as labor radicalism and Communism through the American Institute for Free Labor Development, some of whose members were involved in the 1964 coup against the João Goulart government.[13] During the cold war, the CIA contained an International Organizations Division whose job it was to create "independent" social, political, and economic organizations to combat the ones being supported by Moscow.[14]

Support or outright ownership of media outlets is one of the most useful forms of subsidy. Sometimes this is obvious, such as the Voice of America and Radio Free Europe, which are open advocacy or propaganda organs of government (although it was many years before the CIA admitted involvement in these two stations). Usually, intelligence agency subsidies are hidden so that the media appear independent and therefore more believable. Use of these outlets can be subtle, such as slightly emphasizing bad news about the enemy and good things about the subsidizer's side, or blatant propagandizing, such as Radio Martí, a Florida-based radio station broadcasting dissident material into Castro's Cuba. Media assets can range from individual reporters or stringers who drop an occasional story to entire staffs of television stations or newspapers.

Nonmonetary subsidies are also a valuable tool. Weapons can be provided at little or no cost, and access to advanced technology not provided to others is a powerful inducement to cooperation. Another common nonmonetary subsidy, and one that is seldom thought of as a subsidy, is *selective nonenforcement of laws or policies*. Foreign leaders are sometimes exempted from investigation and prosecution by U.S. (or, in some cases, international) law enforcement agencies. Leaders of numerous groups from the "Golden Triangle" of Southeast Asia, including the Meo, Chinese Nung, and nationalist Chinese Kuomintang (KMT) forces have been protected from the United States Drug Enforcement Administration (DEA), even though they have played major roles in opium, morphine, and heroin trade to the United States. In some cases, agents of the United States government have actually transported these drugs (see chapter 9). Similar deals have been struck with Mafia figures. When the CIA recruited Sam Giancana and Johnny Roselli into its assassination plots against Castro, one implied bonus was immunity from prosecution. Indeed, when Roselli was being tried for card cheating in California, a representative of the CIA appeared at trial, asserting under oath that prosecuting Roselli would jeopardize national security. The charges were dismissed.

Another nonmonetary subsidy that has been quite effective for the United States is *access to restricted technology*, i.e., allowing a foreign government or group to purchase critical technology that is restricted from others. For example, the United States permitted the Saudi Arabian government to purchase AWACS aircraft; soon thereafter, the Saudis began funneling money to the Nicaraguan contras. This kind of quid pro quo was quite prevalent in the 1980s.

Finally, one might include *moral subsidies* as a form of support. A moral subsidy is simply not holding one's friends to the same moral standards as one's enemies. Thus, torture by "our guys" is an "aberration" or "occasional necessity," while torture by our enemies is an "outrage"; "good" death squads are simply "overzealous defenders of freedom," and slaughtering entire villages by "our side" is "state-making."

Psychological operations, or *psyops*, try to induce a specific reaction in a target audience, usually building or destroying political support for a regime or movement. They are generally part of a larger plan of political action. Some of the most creative psyops ever were aimed at Fidel Castro. One CIA plan was to dust the inside of his shoes with thallium salts, making his beard fall out and thereby humiliating him in the machismo world of Latin American politics. Another plan was to expose him to LSD right before he made a speech, so that he would ramble incoherently.[15] Perhaps the most creative was a plan to spread the word that the Second Coming of Christ was imminent. On the scheduled day, a U.S. submarine would fire star shells over Cuba. The Cuban people, thinking that this was *it*, and naturally knowing that Christ hated Communists, would then rise up and overthrow Castro. The plan was derisively labeled "Operation Elimination by Illumination."[16] Legendary counterinsurgent Edward Lansdale played on Filipino superstitions by spreading word that an *asuang* (vampire) lived in the area where the Communist Huk guerrilla were based. One of his squads then snatched a guerrilla from a Huk patrol, pierced his neck with two "vampire bite marks," and hung him up to drain. When he was bled out, they placed the corpse back on the trail—in short order, the guerrillas fled the area.[17] More subtly, the CIA once assigned colors on the Vietnamese ballot so that its candidate, Ngo Dinh Diem, was represented by red, the traditional color for good luck, while his main opponent's name was depicted in green, the traditional color of a cuckold.[18] Finally, a masterpiece psyop was carried out during OPERATION PB/SUCCESS in Guatemala. When "rebel" aircraft would fly over the capital, U.S. agents played a recording of bombs exploding over loudspeakers mounted to the roof of the U.S. embassy. No one knew where the bombs were falling, but everyone could hear them somewhere. In the end, it wasn't bombs that were falling—it was the government.

Propaganda and Disinformation

Propaganda is always a critical component of complex covert actions, especially coups and paramilitary operations. It is always necessary to gain the support of some element of a country's population, be it voters, landowners, organized labor, professionals, intellectuals, or generally most important, the military. Moreover, because covert actions are supposed to be veiled, i.e., "Hey, don't look at *us*," it is necessary in every covert action to provide a "legend," or cover story, that explains why the United States isn't involved, why the action (e.g., guerrilla war, election fixing, assassination) was in fact done by somebody else, and that even if we *did* do it, the president didn't know.

"Propaganda" is not simply a pack of lies. Although the word has negative connotations, (e.g., Nazis, Goebbels, the Big Lie), propaganda is simply any information used to influence someone to do something; it's the political equivalent of commercial advertising.[19] Like advertising, propaganda can be true, misleading (partially or technically correct, perhaps), or completely false. The meaning has become distorted over time because governments generally use the word "propaganda" to label things they don't like.

White Propaganda[20]

Propaganda comes in three varieties: white, gray, and black. The "color" of propaganda is determined by the apparent source of the information. If someone disseminates information openly and publically so that the true source is apparent, that's *white propaganda*, e.g., when a government spokesperson or the vice president makes a statement, you know the origins of the information. Thus, press releases from the United States Information Agency (USIA) or *Pravda* (which in Russian means "truth") are recognized for what they are: overt efforts to persuade someone (the world, a foreign government or population, or perhaps even the American public) of something. Usually, governments try to make white propaganda as true as possible so as to build credibility. For example, the general truth of the Allied news media during World War II proved to be a potent weapon in undermining Axis morale—many German citizens learned to tune in the BBC to find out what was really going on. It is no accident that leaders all over the world turn on CNN when a crisis breaks; often, its reporters are more up-to-date than intelligence services.

The effect of credibility as a weapon can be observed in the Gulf War and the Iraqi reaction to the supposed shooting down of its SCUD missiles by American Patriot missiles. While we learned after the fact that the Patriot success rate in intercepting SCUDs was perhaps 40 percent or even less, during the war we all sat mesmerized by CNN footage showing Patriot launches that appeared to destroy practically every incoming SCUD. The "truth" as presented was that Saddam Hussein appeared ever more impotent as one SCUD after another was "shot down." The fact that after-action reports showed that many SCUDs got through the Patriot antimissile screen simply didn't matter. While the reports of Patriot accuracy were false, they nevertheless created a reality for Saddam Hussein, and rather than look like a fool, he stopped firing SCUDs. This "reality" was established in his mind by the credibility of the American media.[21]

Sometimes, however, governments produce white propaganda that is blatantly false. They can do this because often no one bothers to check the facts in government reports, or even if major discrepancies are uncovered, not many people pay attention to the critics. A prime example of this is the infamous El Salvador "White Paper," an eight-page document released by the Reagan administration 23 February 1981. Claiming to be based on captured documents, the White Paper described the massive Communist conspiracy behind the insurgency in El Salvador. When examined in closer detail, however, the supporting documentation (which was not part of the White Paper) didn't support the conclusions and factual claims of the White Paper. The kindest thing that can be said is that the White Paper contained considerable amounts of what even the paper's own author came to call "mistakes," "guessing," and "overembellishment," not to mention speculation and wishful thinking.[22] The admissions of profuse inaccuracies received scarcely a mention in most newspapers.

Gray Propaganda

Gray propaganda is information spread by a "neutral" party so that it appears to be more credible. Thus, if a U.S. asset who happens to be a newspaper reporter from Honduras bases a story on unverified information provided by his CIA case officer, that's gray propaganda. Everyone thinks it originates from the Honduran reporter's own investigation, when it was actually written in Langley, Virginia. Professionals also distinguish three shades of gray propaganda: light gray, gray gray (or medium gray), and dark gray. Light gray propaganda is information attributed to a source that's known to be friendly to the subject of the story. A press release from, say, Jesse Helms's office, lauding the wonderful democratic record of El Salvador's Roberto D'Aubisson[23] (Major Bob, "Father of the Death

Squads"), would fall in this category. Gray gray is propaganda that comes from a supposedly neutral source, perhaps a foreign newspaper that is sometimes critical of the United States. Dark gray propaganda is propaganda favorable to your side disseminated by a source that is usually or always hostile. Naturally, developing a dark gray asset is difficult; why would a newspaper, television station, or foreign government spread information that seems to harm its own position? There are several answers. First, they might be convinced to do so because the information is so overwhelmingly true that it cannot be challenged. This is rare, however—in today's ideological marketplace, virtually anything can be denied, explained away, or massaged by spin doctors. Second, while a foreign media outlet, business, or government may be anti-American on the whole, individuals within the organization might be U.S. assets who can occasionally slip through a bit of pro-American propaganda. Naturally, these individuals can't do this very often, lest they lose their jobs (and therefore their effectiveness as an asset). Such assets must be carefully conserved for critical operations and circumstances. Third, while it is rare, intelligence agencies sometimes create their own "hostile" assets. For example, the CIA might set up a radio station that continually berates America until a strategic moment, when it broadcasts critical information supporting a U.S. action or harming an opposition action or organization.[24]

A recent example of gray propaganda is the book *The Rape of Kuwait*, a lurid account of the atrocities committed by Iraqi troops when they invaded the tiny country. Few knew at the time that the book was subsidized by the Kuwaiti government; it was promoted as journalism.[25] Similarly, the vivid account of babies ripped from their incubators and dashed on the floor, splashed in painful detail before the American public, was also a fabrication, wonderfully acted out by "Nayirha," who happened to be the daughter of the Kuwaiti ambassador to the United States (and a member of the ruling al-Sabah family, therefore certainly not an objective observer of the conflict). This incident, later proven false, was repeated so often by American policymakers, including President Bush, that most Americans probably still believe it.[26] Also hidden from the public was that the "witnesses" at the spectacular congressional hearings had been "supplied" by the public relations firm of Hill and Knowlton, who had been retained by the Kuwaiti government for the express purpose of getting the United States to go to war.

Black Propaganda

When an intelligence agency creates false information that appears to come from some other source, this is *black propaganda*. This false information comes in many forms, e.g., fake documents, enemy "defectors" that admit evil activities, fake video- or audiotapes, and fake radio broadcasts that appear to come from the enemy. Black propaganda, usually called *disinformation*, is generally used to make one's opponents look evil, essentially to "frame" them for something they didn't do. Today, for example, there are "U.S. government" documents, fabricated by the KGB in the 1980s, that "prove" the United States government created the AIDS virus to depopulate the Third World and kill off African Americans. Such "documents" were stock-in-trade for the Soviets, but the CIA is far from innocent in such practices. Shortly before the Italian election of 1948, the CIA "discovered" the "Zorin Plan," ostensibly written by the Soviet foreign minister, which "proved" that Italian Communists and socialists would Stalinize Italy, including plans for the execution of priests, concentration camps for shop owners, and confiscation of all property by the state. The document, of course, was produced by the CIA (although it's also fair to say that there probably *is* a document something like this buried in the bowels of the Kremlin, if nothing more than a contingency plan—just because our side did some bad things doesn't make the Soviets any less oppressive than they were).

Former CIA officer Joseph B. Smith tells of an operation he carried out to hinder Soviet relations with Indonesia. When the Soviet and Indonesian governments agreed to open a Soviet consulate in Djakarta, Smith drafted a "Soviet" message about acquiring two hundred houses in the city, and arranged for it to "leak" into Indonesian hands. The Indonesians, predominantly conservative Muslims, were aghast, concluding that the Soviets were planning to flood their country with spies.[27]

While in Singapore, Smith also had occasion to plant a classic piece of black propaganda using a foreign journalist asset. The CIA wanted to implicate the Red Chinese in arms smuggling and actually sending troops to help the Vietminh. He and the journalist worked out a story in which the journalist during a press briefing, publicly asked British High Commissioner for Southeast Asia Malcolm MacDonald about the reports of Chinese involvement with the Vietminh. MacDonald of course had nothing to say about the story; he didn't know anything. The reporter wrote that he "refused to elaborate." The news story read as if the High Commissioner himself had mentioned the issue; it was picked up by other news services and broadcast around the world, implying British knowledge of Chinese transgression.[28]

Another notorious black propaganda operation was carried out by E. Howard Hunt in Mexico City. Learning that the local Communist Party was having an "invitation only" reception for visiting Soviet officials, Hunt printed up three thousand extra invitations and distributed them throughout the city. When thousands of extra "guests" showed up, the red-faced Communists swiftly ran out of food and drink and were forced to shut the doors on the crowd. Instead of building friendship, the local Communists reaped ill will from both the Mexican people and the visiting Soviets (who perceived them as incompetent).[29]

Ideally, black propaganda is something a democratic government doesn't use on its own people. We expect authoritarian regimes to lie to their own people in order to increase both the numbers of people who will actively support the government and to heighten the fervor of those who already do. On the other hand, we also expect "democratic" governments to be truthful to their own people.[30] How can one maintain government "accountability," the very linchpin of democracy, without the ability of the people to know what elected officials are really doing and what's really happening in the world? Unfortunately, we have become all too familiar with the efforts of "democratic" governments to sway their own populations with (1) information the government knows is false, (2) information it fails to adequately verify (on purpose), and (3) false documentation it creates itself.

One example of black propaganda used by a government on its own population was created by E. Howard Hunt. In September 1971, Hunt used White House and State Department typewriters to produce a fake State Department cable, ostensibly from President Kennedy, implicitly approving the assassination of Vietnamese President Diem. The idea behind Hunt's act was to "prove" that President Kennedy was an unprincipled leader who intended to escalate the war in Vietnam. Showing Kennedy as the assassin and warmonger, it was hoped, would make Richard Nixon look good by comparison. Hunt tried to pass these documents to William Lambert, reporter for *Life* magazine, but skeptical editors doubted their authenticity, and they were never published. The White House plumbers, the "dirty tricks" squad established by the Nixon administration, also forged the infamous racist letter printed on "Muskie for President" stationery, and as part of COINTELPRO, agents of the FBI forged Black Panther documents in an effort to sow discord in that party (it worked).[31]

One might also consider the El Salvador White Paper as a serious effort at black propaganda. At the very least, (1) it was based on information whose origins were suspect, and (2) it was full of speculation that was written as if the captured documents actually said what the White Paper claimed they did. The White Paper, while a piece of white propaganda (it was an acknowledged U.S. government publication) employed the government's own black propaganda ("captured" documents actually produced by agents of either El Salvador or U.S. intelligence). Thus, the White Paper was white propaganda written around black propaganda.

Economic Warfare

Covertly raiding the economy of an enemy during "peacetime" is a long-standing human tradition. When Queen Elizabeth sent her "Sea Hawks" to plunder the Spanish Main, looting the riches that the Spaniards had pillaged from the Aztecs and Incas, she acted under the veil of plausible deniability: She simply couldn't control every pirate afloat, she declared, and she *did* chastise them, after a fashion (by accepting a percentage of the loot to compensate for the diplomatic problems they had caused her). Modern nations still employ covert economic warfare, even though the methods are often more sophisticated (but sometimes less sophisticated as well).

When it goes after a foe, the United States has an unmatched and impressive array of overt economic weapons it brings to bear. Since World War II, the United States has been in the enviable position of world economic director—perhaps America can't control every event, but there is a saying among international economists: When the U.S. economy sneezes, the world catches a cold. Foremost among American economic influence is its *structural power*, the power to "make the rules" by which international trade occurs, such as the philosophy of "free trade," "most favored nation status," and so on. Further, by virtue of its other attributes, the United States and its economic actors could specifically punish ill-behaved or hostile states. For example, simply by rating an antagonistic Third World country as a "bad credit risk," the United States could virtually shut off private foreign loans and investment to it. As the largest contributor to the International Monetary Fund, America assured that it controlled the amount of "special drawing rights" that debtor nations could obtain, thus selecting who can trade in the world market and who cannot. Simply by its position as the only industrial country at the end of World War II, America insured that the U.S. dollar would become the currency of international exchange. By controlling the flow of dollars, the United States could pick economic winners and losers (for a more thorough discussion of overt economic power, see chapter 13).

Frequently during the cold war, such tactics virtually forced Third World states into the arms of the Soviet bloc, where they exchanged one form of dependence for another. By turning to the Soviets, however, states like Cuba, Nicaragua, Vietnam, Ethiopia, and, to some degree, Iraq freed themselves from overt American economic influence. It is when the overt fails that American intelligence begins covert economic warfare.

Covert economic warfare is a euphemism for vandalism, pillaging, and destruction of opposing economic targets; the idea is to bleed their economy. This strategy meets three basic goals, in ascending order of importance. First, it forces an opponent to divert resources toward protecting economic targets. Instead of "spreading the revolution," enemy troops are standing guard over electric generating plants and sugar refineries. Covert economic warfare places them on the defensive. Second, covert economic warfare keeps opposing nations poor; starvation, inefficiency, and huge foreign debts are hardly what the people of other countries want to emulate. During the cold war, it was deemed critical to be able to point to the economic failures of the Soviet Union. Finally, bad or worsening economic conditions are widely believed to stimulate rebellion, revolution, and coups d'etat, especially when economic failure can be blamed on the government (rightly or wrongly—the *perception* of who's responsible is what matters).[32]

To this end, there are many paths. The simplest form of covert economic warfare is sabotage. In Cuba, for example, this might be using cats to set fire to Cuban sugarcane fields, conspiring with foreign companies to sell off-center ball bearings to Cuban industries so that their machinery would break down, or poisoning a shipload of Cuban export sugar to frighten potential buyers. In Nicaragua, the contras attacked coffee pickers, hoping to spoil the harvest and take away the government's only source of hard currency.

Attacking the opposition's financial system is a more sophisticated form of economic warfare. One common tactic is to counterfeit enemy currency, thus making their money worth less, or worthless. If done in sufficient quantity, counterfeiting can create enormous inflation, thus undermining the people's faith in their government. This was done by practically all the belligerents in World War II, and since the early 1960s the U.S. government has printed an undisclosed (but large) number of Cuban pesos. One of the reasons for the recent introduction of new style large-denomination bills in the U.S. is a concerted effort by Iran to flood the world with counterfeit U.S. dollars. A more subtle approach is to use propaganda to create inflation or hoarding, perhaps starting rumors of shortages or counterfeit currency. If the financial system is under any pressure at all, a well-constructed and publicized rumor can stimulate inflation all by itself.

Finally, covert economic warfare can take on truly fantastic forms. During the Vietnam War, the United States secretly engaged in cloud seeding in order to increase rainfall over North Vietnam during the monsoon season. The hope was that by flooding the country, the rice crop could be destroyed, bringing the North Vietnamese to their knees.

Paramilitary Action

The last category of covert action is the violent one: paramilitary action and small-scale violence. Discussion of these endeavors occupies much of the rest of this book, and therefore this section will be brief.

Covert paramilitary action includes less violent operations, such as providing intelligence to a friend or client (which they might use to make their own violence more successful). For example, before he was anointed "the next Hitler," Saddam Hussein received so much classified American intelligence on the Iranians that eventually the United States built a secret annex in Baghdad to reduce transmission time.

While Americans think of "terrorism" as the product of outlaws, crazies, and revolutionary movements, it is also frequently a central facet of covert action programs. Naturally, government spokesmen deny this, but then they also generally use the word "terrorism" to describe any action by someone they don't like.[33] For our purposes, "terrorism" consists of acts of anonymous bombing (hand delivered, usually), hijacking and bombing of civilian aircraft, hostage seizures and kidnaping for political concessions, and political assassinations. These acts are generally carried out by groups so small they cannot attract enough of a following to create an insurgency.

Terrorism is a useful covert action tool precisely because it is deniable. Few terrorists ever get caught, and there are indigenous terrorist movements in most countries; a government can provide money, arms, and intelligence (for planning operations) to the group though cutouts who can never be traced. Even training can be provided covertly in "neutral" countries by mercenaries or sheep-dipped intelligence or military personnel. The very maverick nature of terrorist groups allows governments to use them to pressure enemies without providing just cause for retaliation. Several of the Cuban exiles trained and supported by the United States. during Operations ZAPATA and MONGOOSE went on to bomb Cuban airliners out of the sky, machine-gun Havana hotels, assault Soviet ships in Cuban waters, and blow up a foreign diplomat right in Washington, D.C.

The remaining three paramilitary options are the kinds of operations most of us associate with "covert action": supporting guerrilla movements, sponsoring coups d'etat, and simply assassinating political enemies. These will be discussed in chapter 5, 6, and 7.

CONCLUSIONS

The range of black operations is truly impressive. Those discussed in this chapter are the subtle tackhammers of diplomacy. We'll turn next to coups and assassinations, the piledrivers of undeclared war.

NOTES

1. See William Blum, *Killing Hope: U.S. Military and CIA Interventions Since World War II* (Monroe, Maine: Common Courage Press, 1995), p. 265 and chap. 40, respectively.

2. Spying is the most critical because it is the most reliable way of judging the intentions of an enemy (or friend, for that matter). For the importance of assessing threat, see John J. Nutter, "Unpacking Threat: A Formal and Conceptual Analysis," in *Seeking Security and Development*, ed. Norman Graham (Boulder: Lynne Reinner Publishers, 1994).

3. Depending on the circumstances, it is also CIA practice to have the "approach" made by a separate recruiter rather than the case officer per se. This is so that if the target is offended or turns hostile, the recruiter can flee the country without jeopardizing existing assets or the in-country case officer.

4. Joseph Burkholder Smith, *Portrait of a Cold Warrior* (New York: Ballantine Books, 1976), pp. 138–39.

5. See Michigan State University Vietnam Advisory Group, "All Reports of the Michigan State University Vietnam Team in Public Administration," *Reports and Documents* (Saigon: Michigan State University Vietnam Advisory Group, 1995–1960), box 1, file 90, part 1, p. 1.

6. See Theodore Draper, *A Very Thin Line: The Iran-Contra Affairs* (New York: Simon and Schuster, 1991), p. 353.

7. Blum, *Killing Hope*, p. 234; Senate, *Staff Report of the Select Committe to Study Governmental Operations with Respect to Intelligence Activities*, Book 7: "Covert Action," 94th Cong., 2d sess., 1976, 9.

8. In covert action stories, Lansdale is virtually always referred to as "the legendary Ed Lansdale."

9. My thanks to Michael Canella for locating this.

10. It meant *kill them*! You didn't really have to look here to find that out, did you?

11. See Blum, *Killing Hope*, chap. 2, 49.

12. Ray Cline, *Secrets, Spies, and Scholars* (Washington: Acropolis Books, 1976).

13. See Blum, *Killing Hope*, p. 168.

14. Smith, *Portrait of a Cold Warrior*, p. 153.

15. Although one is tempted to ask, "Who could tell?" See Senate, *Interim Report of the Select Committe to Study Governmental Operations with Respect to Intelligence Activities*, "Alleged Assassination Plots Involving Foreign Leaders," 94th Cong., 1st sess., 1975, S. Rept. 94-465, 72.

16. Ibid., 142 n. 2. Origins of this plan are uncertain, although one source suggests that it resulted from a facetious suggestion by Ian Fleming (creator of James Bond) to Jack Kennedy and Allen Dulles over dinner at the White House. See John Pearson, *The Life of Ian Fleming* (New York: McGraw Hill, 1966), pp. 321–23.

17. See Victor Marchetti and John Marks, *CIA and the Cult of Intelligence* (New York: Dell Books, 1989), p. 25.

18. See ibid., p. 26.

19. Also, just like commercial advertising, it sometimes works, despite the cynicism toward advertising we often see among sophisticated consumers.

20. For an excellent discussion of the kinds and uses of propaganda, see Smith, *Portrait of a Cold Warrier*, pp. 76–78.

21. In fact, even if the U.S. government knew that the Patriots were failing, it would have been an excellent idea to report their success anyway. The idea, after all, was to get Saddam to quit shooting SCUDs, and all interceptions, real or imaginary, served that purpose.

22. See Jonathan Kwitny, *Endless Enemies: The Making of an Unfriendly World* (New York: Viking Penguin, 1984), pp. 355–71.

23. D'Aubisson is widely acknowledged throughout Latin America as the "Godfather" of the El Salvadoran death squads.

24. Subsidizing an entire organization is a costly tactic, however, as the first time it dispenses out-of-character propaganda it is "burned" and loses effectiveness. For this reason, rarely does an intelligence agency create an entire "enemy" organization for the sole purpose of spreading dark gray propaganda. These ventures usually serve other purposes as well, such as attracting hostile groups and individuals (to find out who they are, infiltrate and spy on them, and serve as a provocateur).

25. See Jean P. Sasson, *The Rape of Kuwait: The True Story of Iraqi Atrocities Against a Civilian Population* (New York: Knightsbridge Publishing, 1991).

26. See John R. MacArthur, *Second Front: Censorship and Propaganda in the Gulf War* (New York: Hill and Wang, 1992), pp. 58–59, 238–40.

27. Smith, *Portrait of a Cold Warrior*, pp. 86–88.

28. Ibid., pp. 164–65.

29. Ibid., pp. 85–86.

30. At least we're *taught* to expect truthfulness. That's what it says in the American government textbooks I used when I taught that course. My experience, however, is that many American students are pretty cynical about this. It is, however, a *selective* cynicism—they're cynical about claims and people they disagree with, and often quite trusting toward people and ideas that support their biases. (I am also proud to report that many of my students did exhibit a healthy skepticism toward their own viewpoints as well.)

31. On the Hunt forgeries, see Fred Emery, *Watergate: The Corruption of American*

Politics and the Fall of Richard Nixon (New York: Random House, 1994), pp. 71–73. On the Black Panthers, see Morton Halperin, *The Lawless State: The Crimes of U.S. Intelligence Agencies* (New York: Penguin, 1996).

32. Bad economic conditions, however, are not sufficient to create revolutions; social scientists have discovered that the causes of revolutions are far more complex. For a summary of the causes of rebellion and revolution, see Ted Robert Gurr, ed., *Handbook of Conflict* (New York: Free Press, 1980).

33. For a discussion of the uses of the word "terrorism" and a resolution to the "definitional problem," see John J. Nutter, "Terrorism: A Problem of Definition or Epistemology" (paper presented at the annual meeting of the American Political Science Association, Washington, D.C., September 1993), available from the author.

Chapter 4

Making New Friends:
The Coup d'Etat

The firing was closer now: the guttural *thumpthumpthump* of the machine guns, the sharper *pop . . . pop* of the automatic rifles. Inside the presidential palace the few remaining loyal soldiers held out grimly, firing single shots to conserve their ammunition, desperately praying for deliverance. Over the city hung a funereal cloud of smoke from the artillery; the generals had called it down to destroy the dying pockets of resistance. In a matter of hours the big guns would be wheeled up to finish off the men in the palace, too.

Except the president was denied even that period of grace. A fighter bomber from the national air force roared over the city, its bomb exploding in the heart of the palace, a dagger in the heart of the middle-aged man with the glasses. This was the final blow. The president had armed himself with a submachine gun, vowing to fight to the death, but now he sat alone on the steps in utter dejection as his remaining followers fearfully trooped out to surrender.

There is some dispute over how it happened. Some say the president shot himself; others claim he was executed by the victorious forces of the national army. Then, as now, the exact circumstances don't really matter: Salvador Allende was dead. Chile would be ruled by a brutal military dictator for the next twenty-five years; Henry Kissinger and Richard Nixon had saved Chile from "the irresponsibility of its own people."[1]

A *coup d'etat*, or more simply a *coup*, is the forcible overthrow of a governing regime by a small group of plotters. Typically this is performed by leaders of the national military, backed up by military and paramilitary units loyal to them. A coup differs from a rebellion, revolution, or civil war in a number of respects. A coup is a relatively quick phenomenon: Government offices are occupied, political leaders are arrested (or worse), and a new leader is installed within a matter of hours or days. Some open warfare may occur, as in Chile in 1973, but military resistance does not last long. While it is difficult to put an exact number of days on it, a coup rarely takes more than a week to accomplish. Implicitly, we define a coup by whether or not it succeeds; if it does, it is a coup. If it fails, it might immediately be put down. Alternatively, it might degenerate into a civil war or rebellion; in which case it is not a coup, since a victory by the antigovernment forces come through open warfare. Second, a coup does not involve large-scale combat. It is an endeavor of stealth and surprise—a sudden descent of insurrectionist forces on the presidential mansion, the parliament, the capital city army barracks, and the TV and radio stations.[2]

Throughout history, powerful states have sought to secure their interests through a variety of means, sometimes occupying the territory of potential enemies, now and then by creating or supporting "buffer zones," and often by simply being powerful. A more subtle approach is sometimes employed by the sophisticated: imposing friendly regimes on foreign countries by coup d'etat. During the postwar period of 1945–1967, there were more than one hundred coups or attempted coups around the world, most unrelated (directly) to the cold war; by another count there were over three hundred coups or coup attempts around the world from 1945–1986.[3] There were also a number of coups that were attempted, in one respect or another, with the encouragement, support, instigation, or outright control of the KGB or the CIA. It is perhaps comforting to imagine that coups only happen in small unstable backwaters, yet in the last fifty years the governments of several large or "advanced" states have been hit with violent coups or attempted overthrows, e.g., France, Greece, and Brazil.

This chapter lays out not only the history behind some of these overthrows, but also the nature of coups and techniques employed, the issues raised by blatant and sometimes brutal intervention in other states, the problems of supporting coup plotters (especially in the long term), and the effects of this kind of covert action on American foreign relations.

OUR SONS OF BITCHES TAKE OVER

"He may be a son of a bitch," said the president, "but at least he's *our* son of a bitch." There is perhaps no better appreciation of American cold war policy than this.[4] From 1945 on, the United States sought to shore up wobbling dominoes by many means,[5] but foremost among these was ensuring that foreign countries were ruled by regimes friendly to the United States, welcoming to international (especially American) capital, and sufficiently hostile to the Soviet Union. As long as those complementary orientations were fulfilled, the internal politics of the country were of less than no concern to the U.S. government. So America, the "Beacon of Liberty" and "Shining City on a Hill," often ended up in cahoots with sons of bitches who murdered and tortured their own people, who ran their countries not as free markets but as personal cash cows to be plundered, and to whom democracy meant infrequent "elections" to legitimize the president-for-life.

To ensure that foreign governments were anti-Communist, anti-Soviet, and generally compliant, it sometimes became necessary for American intelligence to change rulers by "irregular" means, i.e., a coup d'etat. There is substantial credible evidence that the CIA encouraged, supported, or manufactured coups d'etat in Indonesia, Greece, Guatemala, Iran, Iraq, Brazil, Costa Rica, Syria, Cambodia, the Congo, Chile, Bolivia, and Libya, among others.[6] One of the most critical and ironic helped create the war that defined a generation of Americans: Vietnam.

The Only Horse We've Got

Ngo Dinh Diem was spotted by CIA talent scouts in the early 1950s and carefully cultivated by various spooks, including Ed Lansdale and Wesley Fishel. During that decade, he had been appointed to the Vietnam Advisory Group at Michigan State University, and when the time came for a pro-American leader to step forward in Vietnam, Diem was there, assuming the role of Vietnamese president and American bulwark against Communism in 1955. He was, in the words of Lyndon Johnson, "the Churchill of Vietnam."[7]

In many ways, however, Diem was an unfortunate choice. He had a number of things going against him, not the least of which was that he wasn't Ho Chi Minh. While Ho had led the fight to liberate Vietnam from the Japanese, Diem had spent the Japanese occupation in suburban New York. In a land of Buddhists, Diem was a Catholic, and he removed several Buddhist cabinet ministers, replacing them with those of his own faith. Diem's brother and principal enforcer, Ngo Dinh Nhu, made a habit of sending gangs of thugs to break heads at the first sign of dissent. Nhu's wife, Madame Nhu, did not help the regime's popularity by taking conspicuous-consumption shopping trips to America. Finally, as 1963 wore on, Diem and Nhu began to assert their independence, hinting that they would like to see the United States withdraw from Vietnam; perhaps a "neutral" Vietnam would be preferable to a land ripped apart by war.[8] Ultimately, Diem's attempt at a counterinsurgency campaign was ill-conceived and badly conducted. To the White House, it was painfully obvious that to save Vietnam, Diem had to go. On 29 August 1963, U.S. Ambassador Henry Cabot Lodge cabled to the president:

> We are launched on a course from which there is no respectable turning back: the overthrow of the Diem government. . . . there is no possibility, in my view, that the war can be won under a Diem administration. . . . We should proceed to make all-out effort to get Generals to move promptly . . .[9]

Throughout 1963, American agents, including Lucien Conein and Ambassador Lodge, consulted with dissident Vietnamese army officers, finally advising them to remove Diem and assuring them that the United States would back them; instructions on this point came directly from the White House. Eventually both American money and weapons were passed to the conspirators. Finally, on 2 November 1963, a cabal of army officers led by the army's chief of staff, Duong Van Minh ("Big" Minh), ordered troops into the presidential residence, where they found that Diem and Nhu had fled, seeking refuge in a Catholic Church. The Vietnamese Army, however, was Buddhist, and ignored the "sanctuary" tradition of the Church. Diem and his brother were dragged out, blindfolded, and shot in the back of the head.[10]

While President Kennedy was reportedly shocked over the assassination (or execution, depending on your point of view), there was an overall air of celebration that the obstacle to victory, Ngo Dinh Diem, had been removed, and that the war could proceed. Vietnam, however, would never become stable; although he ruled the junta briefly, "Big" Minh wasn't Churchill, either. There wasn't one in Vietnam. The country would experience a half-dozen more coups in the next four years, and victory remained a stranger.

Brazil!

João Goulart was very concerned about the possibility of an American-inspired military coup; he expressed this concern to President Kennedy.[11] Indeed, he had reason to fear. Goulart was elected president in 1961, and, much as Jacobo Arbenz had in Guatemala, instituted a number of policies that reinforced Brazil's independence, including association with the "nonaligned" movement. U.S. Defense Attaché Vernon Walters complained that Goulart favored "ultranationalist" military officers over "pro-U.S." officers.[12] Moreover, the Brazilian leader nationalized a subsidiary of the International Telephone and Telegraph Company (ITT) and passed a law restricting the profits multinational corporations could take out of Brazil. As a social activist, he hoped to establish a mild program of land reform, which could scarcely have been called radical; it was far more moderate than that imposed on Japan by Douglas MacArthur.[13] Finally, much as Arbenz had, Goulart attempted to balance the power of the military elite by developing close relations with the army's noncommissioned officers drawn predominantly from Brazil's lower classes. As with Arbenz, too, this essentially severed the loyalty of the military to the presidency and the Brazilian Constitution.

By 1962, the CIA and the U.S. State Department had become concerned about these indications of Goulart's "dictatorial tendencies." In elections of that year, the CIA funneled perhaps as much as $20 million to Goulart opposition candidates.[14] A standard political and propaganda campaign was initiated: Mass urban demonstrations were organized, cooperative Brazilian newspapers published provocative articles, and a "mothers" rumor mill (a network of mothers organized to disseminate propaganda) was engaged to spread stories of the coming atrocities under the Goulart dictatorship.[15]

It is unclear that these tactics did much to influence the mass of the Brazilian people. The fabricated political unrest did, however, manufacture a pretext for the Brazilian military to "save" the country. By 1964, a Brazilian military cabal seeking American approval and support approached U.S. Ambassador Lincoln Gordon; the ambassador implied that if they could hold out for forty-eight hours, the United States would help them.[16] The coup would be led by

General Humberto Castello Branco, who had been cultivated by American intelligence since World War II and had a close relationship with Vernon Walters. In fact, a week before the coup, Castello Branco presented Walters with a paper that accused Goulart of planning to impose a dictatorship, which explicitly justified a military coup d'etat.

The United States would indeed help the insurgent officers out, providing petroleum, a U.S. Navy task force, arms, ammunition, and massive economic aid to blunt the possible impact of a general strike.[17] On 31 March 1964, the insurrectionist soldiers rolled into Rio de Janeiro amidst general military confusion. Loyal troops waited for the call to arms to defend their constitution, but Goulart was unwilling to declare open civil war, and the orders never came. The deposed president left the country for Uruguay, and Brazil was plunged into the darkness of the death squads. In the end, the coup in Brazil accomplished one certain thing: It replaced a "potential" dictatorship with a real one.

Down Under-Handed[18]

There is a marvelous *Doonesbury* strip in which the U.S. Joint Chiefs of Staff are defending the concept of contingency plans to invade friendly countries like Belgium. "The Soviets invade *their* allies all the time," the general says, ". . . you can't tie our hands."[19] While funny enough in its own right, the satire is even more biting; the United States, through the CIA, has on more than one occasion brought down the government of friendly countries. Here is one such case.

In 1972, the Australian people elected their first Labor Party prime minister in twenty-three years, Gough Whitlam. While committed to most of the Labor Party agenda, the new PM was scarcely a raving Red, although he did implement several policy changes. Whitlam withdrew Australian support for the Vietnam War and ended the cooperation of the Australian intelligence agency, the Australian Security Intelligence Organization (ASIO), with CIA covert operations, including the coup against Allende in Chile. He was also dismayed about the close collaboration between the ASIO and the CIA in which the two agencies collected and selectively disseminated derogatory information about Labor Party members. The CIA and the ASIO were taking sides in domestic politics.

Essentially, Whitlam's government and the Australian Constitution were being subverted by Australia's own intelligence service with the complicity of the "closest ally." Whitlam struck back, demanding an accounting of all CIA personnel and operations within Australia. The CIA provided a list of agents, but it was less than honest, and Whitlam could prove it. Moreover, the CIA essentially defied Whitlam by refusing to detail the purposes of PINE GAP, a CIA electronic surveillance and communications base in northern Australia. While it was represented to the Australians as a monitoring center for U.S. spaceflight and communication, Whitlam feared that it was a clandestine part of U.S. command and control system for a nuclear war, and he wanted no part of it. The crisis came to a head as the prime minister threatened to publicly reveal CIA operations to subvert and control Australian domestic politics on behalf of the opposition parties.

Australia, as a member of the Commonwealth, maintains a governor-general, a bow to the past. In 1974, Whitlam himself appointed John Kerr to this largely ceremonial position. Politically, Kerr was substantially to the right of Whitlam and the Labor Party, and perhaps the PM made the appointment to reassure people that while he was a Labor Party stalwart, he was a moderate and certainly no Soviet dupe. Unknown to Whitlam, however, Kerr had long been connected to American intelligence. Having worked with the OSS in Washington during World War II, Kerr was a member of the by-invitation-only Australian Association for Cultural Freedom after the war; in the 1960s, Kerr was the founding president of the Law Association for Asia and the Western Pacific (LawAsia). Both would eventually be admitted as CIA front organizations, and both would funnel money to Kerr for years. It is unlikely that Whitlam knew of Kerr's foreign intelligence attachments when he recommended him as governor-general.[20] It is also extraordinarily unlikely that Whitlam could have conceived that his own appointee would invoke an archaic, never-used law against him; but that is what happened.

As a member of the Commonwealth, Australia maintained a strictly pro forma constitutional clause that nominally permitted the governor-general to dismiss the prime minister at will. This power had *never* been invoked, and was widely regarded as a polite but empty nod to the past. On 11 November 1975, however, Kerr dismissed Whitlam as prime minister, dissolved both houses of parliament, and appointed Whitlam's opponent, Malcolm Fraser, as interim prime minister. It wasn't bloody, but it was a coup nonetheless.

While no "smoking gun" proving that Kerr's action was prompted by the CIA has ever been produced, the evidence provided by Christopher Boyce is highly suggestive. Boyce worked in cryptographic communications for TRW, a corporation that handled communications between CIA stations in Australia and Langley, and was able to read most of the secret CIA traffic about operations in Australia. Boyce, subject of the book and movie *The Falcon and the Snowman*, would become so disillusioned over U.S. covert operations against Australia, ostensibly an allied government, that he struck back by passing intelligence data to the Soviet Union. When Boyce was on trial, he was sharply cut off by government lawyers as he began to discuss CIA operations against the Whitlam government. In effect, he was not allowed to explain *why* he had sold out to the Soviets. If his information was untrue, one suspects there would have been no need to cover it up.

TAKING OVER THE GOVERNMENT: A PRIMER FOR PLOTTERS[21]

Undertaking a successful coup cannot be that difficult, for it is such a common occurrence; historically, the success rate is around 70 percent.[22] There is more to it, however, than getting a bunch of soldiers together and heading downtown. Occasionally, as few as 150 troops (e.g., Togo, 1963) or perhaps 500 men, with scarcely a shot fired (Ghana, 1966), can take a government. More commonly, though, there is not only violence but also some substantial planning and organization required. In many cases, especially those discussed in this chapter, foreign support is sought or required. To fully grasp the implications of a coup as a political tool, one must understand a bit of the mechanics.

The most critical element in staging a successful coup (or fending one off) is control of the military. One generally cannot stroll into the presidential palace and tell the president-for-life to take a hike; rare indeed is the dictator, even among the benevolent ones, who will step down without at least some threat to life and limb. To pull off a successful coup, then, it is necessary to:

- control enough of the armed forces to take immediate control;
- keep this control secret;
- remove the military leadership that would organize armed forces to resist the coup; and
- have a large enough and effective enough force to deter outside intervention if necessary.

A second essential element is the support of pivotal social and economic groups. Generally this means enough of the managerial class and technical workers so that public services and the economy can continue to function; the new government probably won't last long if it can't deliver food, water, power, and *Baywatch* reruns. As long as these things are supplied, the ordinary people will go to work and will be less likely to think about a counterinsurgency. Further, the economic, social, and military elites that weren't party to the coup will be more likely to jump aboard if the coup plotters demonstrate they can get things working again. This element is especially important if the economy under the previous government was "destabilized" or shut down (even if by outside forces).[23]

Finally, one must always remember that the state not only deals with domestic forces, but also with external demands and institutions (i.e., it faces both inward *and* outward). When one assumes the mantle of power, it is necessary to declare a foreign policy, reassure foreign investors, and satisfy multinational institutions (e.g., the International Monetary Fund).[24] If the regime in power has been at odds with foreign powers or in trouble with the IMF, perhaps the best thing the coup leadership can do is to adopt a cooperative foreign policy toward the United States and other foreign powers, and to immediately embrace the recommendations of the IMF. The latter will get foreign credit flowing and ensure at least the appearance of prosperity; this may be a critical point, especially to the economic elite, in building acceptance of the new regime. It is also crucial in politically "disarming" the majority of the population; if things work well enough, they'll decide that restoring the old boss isn't worth risking life, limb, and money.

Once these things are lined up, one can engage in the actual coup itself. The basic idea is for a small force to take over a large group of people. Generally, this means a sudden assault on the institutions of government control. In a well-thought out coup, one seizes the following targets:

- the president or prime minister;
- other political leaders who have substantial followings and might oppose the coup;
- opposing or independent military leadership;
- major military bases and especially armories;
- major communications systems (television and radio stations, the telephone system [today, also cellular systems if possible]);
- transportation systems (mainly trains in countries that are prone to coups); also, close the gas stations;
- banks; a run on currency is almost inevitable, and can destabilize the new regime, so the banks are closed;
- customs checkpoints; this keeps people from panicking and fleeing, and enables capture of dissidents, who could organize a revolt, and foreign agents, who might infiltrate to organize opposition.

Once the government has been seized, one must consolidate control and prepare for the counterattack. Consolidating control often involves restoring order and getting those not involved in the coup to accept the new leadership. For example, the military is sifted for dissidents, who are politely discharged (or a firearm discharged into them, depending on how ruthless the junta is). If the country is large, a counterattack is almost inevitable, as one can rarely round up all the opposition in one fell swoop. Sometimes, too, elements of the initial plan misfire, and some opponents remain at large. If the coup has been managed adequately, opponents will have difficulty mobilizing armed forces, as communications will be impossible, and getting large forces around the country will be difficult due to coup army control of the transportation "choke points" or bottlenecks, such as key highways, intersections, railroad depots, and gas stations.

If the plan has been well conceived and implemented, preparing for the counterattack means fortifying the likely locations the opposition will try to retake: military bases, armories, TV and radio stations. These places are where the counterattack will come. If there are large opposition forces still loose, one has to be more active; rather than merely fortifying, one must prepare solid defenses, including ambush sites to forestall or break up the assault if possible.

Finally, the coup leaders need to mobilize international assets as fast as possible. This is where prior arrangement with a major power, such as the CIA, can be critical. As soon as the new government is proclaimed, foreign supporters can act: prearranged financial aid and military supply packages can be delivered, foreign markets can be reopened, and so on.

In real life, most coups do not work this way. Many simply involve taking over the radio station and declaring the new government. Many other coups disintegrate at the first sign of resistance, while some turn into bloody, seemingly endless civil wars (e.g., Somalia, Ethiopia). The preceding outline, however, is the basic "master plan" one might find buried deep inside Langley, if it were declassified. Such plans are important, after all, as the CIA hates to back losers.

COUPS: SOMETIMES GOOD, USUALLY BAD, ALWAYS UGLY

Creating or encouraging coups in foreign countries carries great baggage, including the responsibility for the new government and its activities, the effect on one's relations with the affected region and the world, the damage to one's reputation, and the difficulty in assessing whether the overall operation was a success or failure (or even of assessing whether the concept of manipulating foreign governments this way is a beneficial activity). In the following section, we explore the issues created when one embraces the role of kingmaker.

Every Coup Isn't One of Ours

It is easy to connect the CIA to any coup d'etat that occurs anywhere in the world because the CIA has been involved in some way in so many of them. All connections are not the same, however; some are essentially innocent and unavoidable, while others are not. There are four kinds of connection one can have to a coup, each with its own benefits, drawbacks, ethical considerations, and escalation potential. The first (and lowest) level of involvement is the mere awareness of an impending coup. This means more than just knowing that there are coup plots "out there"; in many countries, the political culture consists almost entirely of nebulous coup plots. Instead, what is denoted here is knowledge of a specific insurrection about to begin. While this kind of involvement is not "active" per se, it is included here because knowledge of this sort cannot be neutral; knowing but remaining silent is a way of "taking sides," as it indirectly aids the insurgents by not exposing them. It is vital to understand, however, that the CIA (or any good intelligence agency) cannot remain separate from this knowledge. Indeed, it is the CIA's job to find out about these things, even though the finding out imposes choices on American policymakers that they might rather not have to make—at a minimum, a question of tell or don't tell, but also, in some circumstances, whether to support or forestall the coup.[25]

The second level, where true "involvement" begins, is encouragement of specific plotters or plots. Encouragement in this context is mainly verbal; assurances that the coup is supported (or is not opposed) by the United States, and that aid will be forthcoming should the revolt succeed. This is a conservative commitment to coup plotters, and is generally the limit of engagement when (1) the target regime is of little strategic value or not "on the front burner," or (2) the United States *cannot* be exposed (for example, in a major country that could have nuclear ramifications).

At the third level of involvement, an intelligence agency actively supports the coup group with money, weapons, supplies, logistic support, and perhaps most importantly, intelligence. At this point, the intelligence agency can get in pretty deep; if care is not taken, equipment, money, and agents might be exposed, wrecking foreign relations not only with the target regime, but also perhaps in the entire region. The low end of this scale is probably the level of U.S. involvement with the Iraqi Accord in 1997, in which the CIA provided encouragement, supplies, and limited cash. The high end might be represented by Iran in 1953 or Chile in 1973, in which the coups were the direct result of massive amounts of American aid and coercion.

At the highest level, the intelligence agency itself creates a coup that probably would not have happened otherwise. In other words, CIA agents solicit a coup by cultivating and recruiting military personnel. Recruitment follows a pattern similar to that described in chapter 4, with some slight modifications. First, several likely targets are spotted. These individuals are then carefully fed derogatory information about the regime indicating that the government is planning to repress the social, political, or economic class to which the prospective coup members belong, e.g., "I don't want to be critical, but this is just the way it started in Cuba." Eventually, subtle hints are dropped that the "patriotic" cabal "is not alone . . . ," i.e., strong allies await their action. This is where the political "education" provided to thousands of foreign military personnel by the United States pays off; now, many of them are primed to act, to perceive their country in terms defined by certain interests in the United States. When a working cabal is established, more explicit arrangements can be made, and the American representative can provide a variety of influential guarantees, such as money or credits from the IMF, World Bank, or Exim Bank; weapons; intelligence about the regime and its military dispositions; access to or control of media outlets; diplomatic recognition; and so forth. It is a powerful set of incentives.

Shooting Ourselves in the Foot

One unfortunate result of CIA involvement in so many coups is that it has become very easy to blame *any* coup attempt on the United States (except the obvious Communist or pro-Soviet coups). The world has enough historical experience with documented CIA coups that any claim of CIA involvement is (1) automatically believed by large numbers of people, and (2) at least considered possible by most of the rest of the world.

This perception of American activity wounds American foreign policy in two ways. First, when the United States cannot plausibly deny it had a hand in a coup, foreign governments and peoples grow to distrust America more and more. One can see this even in cases where a U.S.-sponsored coup would be a boon to the region and world. For example, most of the Middle East would love to see the video of Saddam Hussein slumped against a bullet-pocked wall (not available in stores!), but at the same time, Middle Eastern governments fear that every American intervention in the region makes the next easier, and that they could be the next victim. Thus, the profligate manner in which the CIA has carried out coups in the past limits reasonably justifiable actions.

Second, by sponsoring some coups, including a large number that have installed brutal despots, the CIA has made it possible for the United States to get blamed for every murderous bastard that comes down the pike.[26] Having more or less installed the likes of Suharto, Joseph Mobutu, Roberto D'Aubisson, Augusto Pinochet, Reza Shah Pahlavi, Humberto Castello Branco, and the various rulers[27] of Guatemala, and having denied responsibility in every case, the United States now has no defense. Plausible deniability isn't remotely plausible.

Even after the cold war, the American national security apparatus preferred military coups to potentially democratic revolutions; the U.S. government backed the Iraqi Accord, a cabal of guys pretty much like Saddam Hussein, rather than champion a potentially democratic coalition that might overthrow the Butcher of Baghdad, but produce a less "stable" (read that as "controllable") Iraq.

Covert Action, Successful Coups, and Backlash

Whatever the connection, it is vital that foreign complicity in coups be as deniable as possible. First, the very success of a coup often demands that it appear indigenous; coups *do* require the support, or at least the nonopposition, of large numbers of people. If a new regime appears to be the puppet of a foreign power, an opposition force can be more quickly and readily mobilized. In the longer term, one doesn't want to be identified with the kinds of repressive regimes that the CIA has often supported in the past, e.g., Suharto, Pinochet, Anastasio Somoza, Joseph Mobutu, Efrain Rios-Montt. Eventually despots fall, and when they do, the people of the country and the successor governments will hold the United States responsible for the years of repression. Sometimes this does not matter, since the United States is so powerful; these countries must deal with America on its own terms.

Further, he who pays the piper calls the tune. When a regime takes power as a result of foreign intervention, the new government is expected to align its policies with the wishes of the foreign power, sometimes (if not often) in contraindication to policies in the best interests of their own people. The covert nature of the coup is critical here, as a government will incur greater opposition if its population believes it is an agent of a foreign government. How would Americans feel if they believed the president, the Joint Chiefs of Staff, the Supreme Court, and the chairman of the Federal Reserve were all greatly indebted to a foreign country? Every action would be scrutinized, and there would always be the suspicion that the government was acting for someone else's benefit.

Perhaps the central problem with supporting and manufacturing coups is that even when one succeeds, backlash is nearly inevitable. Sooner or later the CIA-installed ruler will fall, and both the new government and the people of the country may, with justification, hate the United States for establishing the former regime. The Iranian regime of Reza Shah Pahlavi was far from the worst dictatorship created by the United States, yet look at the backlash of hostility, which will take many years to get past.

The Cold War and Counterfactuals

One of the central issues of contention between supporters and critics of CIA interventions is the overall effect of coup and "secret war" activities on the strategic position of the United States and on the outcome of the cold war.[28]

It is quite difficult to assess the effect of CIA-sponsored coups d'etat on individual countries, on American foreign relations, and on the outcome of the cold war. True believers in the CIA coups can generally point to one thing: The CIA-installed governments did not "go over" to the Communists. For the most part, this is fact, so it is hard to argue against. Moreover, the cold war was "won," so who's to say that the interventions in these countries weren't critical to forestalling an otherwise inexorable Soviet advance?

Critics of the CIA interventions argue that (1) the regimes would not have gone Communist if left alone, (2) the so-called Communist governments weren't really Communist anyway, or (3) even if the target regimes were "Communist" or "socialist," they weren't necessarily Soviet puppets, and therefore were not automatically a cold war threat. Further, critics assert that many (or most, or some) interventions were motivated more by the need to support American and Western corporations, and the capitalist system in general, than by desires to promote democracy and free markets. It is more difficult to assess these claims, since the countries *weren't* left alone. One is left examining *counterfactuals*; i.e., what would have happened if the CIA had *not* intervened. Was Arbenz truly another Stalin? Would Allende have turned Chile into a base for Communist subversion throughout Latin America? Was Patrice Lumumba a clever Communist agent, a Soviet dupe, or merely a naive former postmaster in way over his head? Because they were overthrown, we can never know for sure.

In trying to assess the worth of these actions, however, one must keep a critical point in mind: virtually every CIA coup was directed at governments that were essentially neutral, perhaps marginally friendly, and at the very least, not Communist. Generally, the targets of these coups were politically akin to social democrats, relatively similar to the governments of major U.S. allies and friends, e.g., Great Britain, West Germany, Italy, Israel, or Sweden. Throughout the cold war, many countries, including U.S. allies, had better relations with the Soviet Union than most of the governments overthrown in CIA coups. The shah of Iran maintained substantial economic relations with the Soviets, as did Canada, Japan, Sweden, France, and many others. Indeed, despite the justifications provided at the times of the coups by various policymakers and advisers, it is extremely difficult to distinguish the American allies from the "about to go Soviet" governments. Moreover, during the cold war, there were several governments that moved back and forth between the Soviet and American blocs, thereby demonstrating that a close relationship with the Soviet Union was not irrevocable. Egypt relied on the Soviets for years, and then kicked them out in 1970; Ethiopia and Somalia switched back and forth. The very premise that once a government "went over" it was gone forever is distinctly flawed.[29]

Another critical aspect of these actions is that some of the coups were carried out against allies, e.g., Vietnam, Australia, Greece. It is difficult to imagine an act more likely to permanently damage relations with fraternal allies. American reliability as an ally was often argued to be a principal reason for not abandoning South Vietnam, but this image is undermined by CIA-sponsored "friendly" coups.

Finally, it is easy to see the results of the coups themselves. Not a single one produced a democracy. Not a single one produced a "free market"; even in those cases where a socialist or social-welfare system was dismantled, it was generally replaced by what is sometimes described as a "kleptocracy"—a government in which a dictator controls most economic activity for a cut of the profit (see chapters 12 and 13 for the political economic background and outcomes). In practically all cases, the coups produced rulers who (1) brutally oppressed, tortured, and murdered large numbers of their own countrymen, (2) plundered the national economy, and (3) repressed economic competition. A prime example is recently deposed Indonesian "President" Suharto, who was greatly assisted into power by the CIA. Without firmer evidence that these countries would have gone over to the Soviets, and that this movement would have altered the balance of power in the cold war, one must conclude that on the balance, these activities were costly mistakes.

The Philosophy of Overthrow

At the most fundamental level of political analysis, the basic theory behind sponsoring a coup is problematic. When one overthrows a regime and replaces it with a new one, one must believe that the new regime has the power to substantially change the structure, orientation, and policies of the previous regime. In some cases this is obviously true: Pinochet was the polar opposite of Allende, and the Brazilian generals were drastically different from Goulart. This is most often the case in terms of domestic orientation. When it comes to foreign policy, however, the differences are often not as pronounced. A national leader, whatever his ideological predilections, must base his actions at least in part on a set of fixed national characteristics: the power of his own country, the hold he has on government, the fixed economic and geographic features of the country, a political culture that may demand certain policies of any leader, and so on. He also has to act with the approval of some set of national elites. The coup may change *which* elites must be courted, but the ruling class must always be heeded.

Conclusions

With the cold war won, there is a great danger that we shall remember the victory without reflecting on how it was accomplished or wondering if there might not have been a better way. Given the nature of the coups encouraged, sponsored, or initiated by American intelligence, it is difficult to imagine a more costly method of combating the Soviet Union and Communism, short of nuclear war. By imposing foul regimes on many of the peoples of the world, the United States, even in winning, has poisoned the well of friendship.

Notes

1. See "The CIA's Bay of Bucks," *Newsweek*, 23 September 1974, p. 51. The whole quote about Chile is, "I don't see why we have to let a country go communist due to the irresponsibility of its own people." Kissinger was referring to the fact that Salvador Allende had been selected in an election that was stacked *against* him.

2. Neither is a coup an assassination, although the two often go together. Assassination is simply the killing of a political leader; it need not be accompanied by a governmental takeover. For example, the killing of Anwar Sadat was an assassination; the overthrows of Allende and Diem were coups in which the losers were assassinated (or executed, depending on your perspective).

3. Exactly what is and is not a coup makes counting coups an inexact business (with a nod to Native Americans). Two sources of data are Edward Luttwak, *The Coup d'Etat: A Practical Handbook* (New York: Fawcett, 1969), pp. 204–207; and Gregor Ferguson, *Coup d'Etat: A Practical Manual* (Dorsett, U.K.: Arms and Armour Press, 1987), pp. 197–202.

4. This was first said, apparently, by Franklin Roosevelt in the 1930s (i.e., before the cold war), but has been used in some form or other in virtually every presidential administration since. FDR was referring to Nicaragua's Anastasio Somoza (father of the Anastasio Somoza deposed in 1979).

5. The catchphrase of the time was to "stabilize" shaky regimes.

6. This list includes only coups d'etat, narrowly construed; I've left out a bunch of "possible but we'll never know for sure" cases. It does not include CIA support of investigation of assassination, terrorism, guerilla war, or conventional civil war; strikes, riots, or public disorders; "legal" coups (i.e., Australia) and election rigging; or overt military intervention. Moreover, it only includes coups for which there is good, publicly available evidence. If we could root around in CIA archives for a while, the list would probably be considerably longer. For accounts of these coups, see William Blum, *Killing Hope: U.S. Military and CIA Interventions Since World War II* (Monroe, Maine: Common Courage Press, 1995); and John Prados, *President's Secret Wars: CIA and Pentagon Covert Operations Since World War II* (New York: William Morrow and Co., 1986).

7. Had he not been overthrown and murdered, it appears Diem might have instead become the "Neville Chamberlain of Vietnam," or perhaps the "Warren G. Harding of Vietnam"; the mind boggles at the possibilities, of which "Churchill" was never one.

8. See *Foreign Relations of the United States, Vietnam*, V.III (Washington: U.S. Government Printing Office) 223, 246.

9. *The Pentagon Papers* (New York: Bantam, 1971), p. 197.

10. In his *The Dark Side of Camelot*, Seymour Hersh suggests that Jack Kennedy knew Diem would be killed, and that JFK offered the Vietnamese president an option to flee the country under protection of the United States. See Seymour Hersh, *The Dark Side of Camelot* (Boston: Little, Brown & Co., 1997), pp. 416–17.

11. See Phyllis Parker, *Brazil and Quiet Intervention, 1964* (Austin: University of Texas, 1979), pp. 21, 45.

12. Ibid. Walters's observation is, of course, most amusing, and symbolic of the arrogance that characterized American dealings with the Third World.

13. Ibid., p. 40.

14. This is the figure reported by CIA "renegade" Philip Agee; see *Inside the Company: CIA Diary* (New York: Bantam Books, 1975), p. 321. Lincoln Gordon, American ambassador to Brazil, said the figure was perhaps $5 million (see Parker, *Brazil and Quiet Intervention*, p. 27).

15. See Blum, *Killing Hope*, p. 166.

16. Philip Siekman, "When Executives Turned Revolutionaries," *Fortune*, September 1964, p. 214.

17. Blum, *Killing Hope*, p. 167.

18. This account is drawn from Jonathan Kwitny, *The Crimes of Patriots* (New York: W. W. Norton and Co., 1987), chap. 9; and Blum, *Killing Hope*, chap. 40.

19. I'm paraphrasing here; my copy of this strip is long gone, but my memory of it remains vivid.

20. Technically, the governor general was appointed by the queen, who virtually always followed the recommendation of the prime minister.

21. For a tactical description in some detail, see Luttwak, *The Coup d'Etat*; and John J. Nutter, "The Blue Helmets are Coming! Local Insurrection in America" (The Conflict Analysis Group, photocopy, 1997), available from the author.

22. See Luttwak, *The Coup d'Etat*, p. 208. Percentage calculated by the author.

23. In some countries, it may be important to have the support of the intellectuals, but military juntas are likely (*very* likely) to simply throw them in jail (or worse) if they don't acquiesce, rather than trying too hard to get them on the bandwagon.

24. Why is this so important? Because most countries do not produce all that they need for survival; many Third World states import a large proportion of their food supply, and almost all their energy. Unnerving foreign investors, banks, and multinational institutions means no hard currency flows into the country; without hard currency, no food and gas can be paid for.

25. By knowing and not telling, one runs the risk that the target regime will find out you knew, and turn against you.

26. It is not always the CIA, of course; often the agency is simply doing the bidding of the president or his advisors.

27. In the case of Guatemala, "rulers" is a synonym for "butchers."

28. In this case, it would be too simple to label the opposing sides "pro-CIA" and "anti-CIA." There are many within the agency itself who doubt the wisdom of supporting coups, and who agree that installing brutal dictators is generally a bad idea. To their credit, many of these courageous individuals said so while the struggle was still in doubt.

29. The issue of how these governments were *perceived* by decision makers is explored in depth later.

Part II

Covert Operations: Red, White, and Black

Chapter 5

Exploding Cigars,
Poisoned Wet Suits,
and the Body in the Buick:
Assassination as Foreign Policy[1]

JOE FROM PARIS

H is name wasn't Joe, and while he had changed planes in Paris, he wasn't *from* there. His real name was Sid and where he was from wasn't impor-tant—who sent him was. The president of the United States had dispatched "Joe from Paris" to kill the prime minister.

Foreign policy is a complex and difficult phenomenon, and often a govern-ment just can't get other governments to do what it wants. It would be a far sim-pler political environment if one could simply kill a few opposing leaders, thereby reshaping the world in a more favorable image. Recently, we have wit-nessed numerous calls from American leaders, especially in Congress, to "remove" Saddam Hussein; others wish to "get" Osama bin Laden. This chapter explores the history of the assassination, as well as issues raised by that most drastic and spectacular foreign policy event. In particular, we shall examine the problem of assassinating foreign leaders and heads of state. Is making the world a better place so simple?

The Station Chief, the Scientist, and the Postman

It was the end of September 1960, and the soul of the Dark Continent was rest-less. The Congo, resource-rich heart of mystery, had declared its independence from Belgium on the thirtieth of June, and had elected Patrice Lumumba as prime minister in an election that was, by African standards, reasonably fair. Lumumba took power with the naive notion that the wealth of diamonds and copper mined from his country ought to somehow, in some proportion, benefit the people of his country. Belgium, the actual recipient of the wealth of the Congo, disagreed. When the Belgians dragged their feet in evacuating their armed forces from the

Republic of Congo, Lumumba pleaded for international help. Twice in July, the United Nations ordered the Belgians to leave; when they still resisted, Lumumba played the only card he had: He asked for Soviet assistance.

The prime minister, who only four years earlier was a simple postmaster,[2] had betrayed his ignorance of the brutal realities of the cold war. This was 1960: *Sputnik* beeped ominously overhead, there was an imaginary but nevertheless terrifying "missile gap," and every American statesman rumbled with baleful pronouncements of falling dominoes and power vacuums. Within days, perhaps fearful of what he had started, Lumumba withdrew his Soviet appeal, signed a lucrative deal with American business interests, and declared a nonaligned foreign policy.

The damage, however, had been done. Calling for Soviet assistance was tantamount to driving the national car off the cliff—irrevocable and disastrous. Lumumba might have been bluffing, but he had played the Soviet trump, and it was the death card.[3]

On 18 August, CIA Station Chief Lawrence Devlin cabled Langley that

> ... EMBASSY AND [CIA] STATION BELIEVE CONGO EXPERIENCING CLASSIC COMMUNIST TAKEOVER [of the] GOVERNMENT ... WHETHER OR NOT LUMUMBA ACTUALLY COMMIE OR JUST PLAYING COMMIE GAME TO ASSIST HIS SOLIDIFYING POWER, ANTI-WEST FORCES RAPIDLY INCREASING POWER [in the] CONGO, AND THERE MY BE LITTLE TIME LEFT IN WHICH TAKE ACTION AVOID ANOTHER CUBA.[4]

Eight days later (26 August), DCI Allen Dulles replied:

> IN HIGH QUARTERS HERE [coming from a DCI, this means the president] IT IS THE CLEAR CUT CONCLUSION THAT IF [LUMUMBA] CONTINUES TO HOLD HIGH OFFICE, THE INEVITABLE RESULT WILL AT BEST BE CHAOS AND AT WORST PAVE THE WAY TO COMMUNIST TAKEOVER OF THE CONGO WITH DISASTROUS CONSEQUENCES FOR ... THE INTERESTS OF THE FREE WORLD GENERALLY. CONSEQUENTLY WE CONCLUDE THAT HIS REMOVAL MUST BE AN URGENT AND PRIME OBJECTIVE. ...[5]

While "removal" might mean operations less final than assassination, DDP Richard Bissell testified that he believed the cable was a roundabout but nonetheless unequivocal way of saying the president wanted Lumumba killed.[6] This impression was bolstered in the same cable when Dulles granted "wider authority" to "act on your own authority where time does not permit reference here," meaning that Station Chief Devlin did not have to clear his plans with Langley; like 007, he had been granted a license to kill.

For while, it appeared that fate might intervene to prevent the United States from dirtying its hands. Congolese President Joseph Kasavubu dismissed

Lumumba as prime minister under a disputed and probably misinterpreted article of the untested Congolese constitution. When Lumumba refused to relinquish the reins of government, elements of the Congolese army, led by Joseph Mobutu, carried out a coup, suspended parliament, and deposed Lumumba anyway. The prime minister sought refuge with United Nations forces, and he was granted protective custody in Leopoldville (Kinshasa) in late September.

Still, the CIA was fearful of his natural leadership ability. When the issue of reconvening the Congolese parliament was raised, the United States did everything possible to prevent it; the Congolese legislators would have almost certainly reelected Patrice Lumumba. Throughout September 1960, CIA officers considered Lumumba, in their own words, ". . . ALMOST AS DANGEROUS IN OPPOSITION AS IN OFFICE . . ."; meeting with Congolese coup leaders, these officers suggested ". . . MORE PERMANENT REMOVAL OF LUMUMBA. . . ."[7] Matters were complicated, however; Lumumba was well protected by the UN forces, who surrounded his residence precisely to keep the Congolese army out. The CIA itself would have to act.

In August, even before the coup, DDP Bissell had asked CIA Science Advisor Sidney Gottlieb to prepare to assassinate or incapacitate an "unspecified African leader," telling the scientist that the project came from "highest authority." Gottlieb went to the Army Chemical Corps at Fort Detrick, Maryland, and obtained toxic chemicals that, if ingested in even minute amounts, would make death appear as from a disease indigenous to the Congo. While the precise toxin has never been revealed, it was probably a choice among tularemia (rabbit fever), anthrax, smallpox, tuberculosis, brucellosis, and Venezuelan equine encephalitis (sleeping sickness).[8] Under direct orders from the deputy director for plans, Gottlieb set out for Leopoldville to personally deliver the toxin. When he arrived in the Congolese capital, he phoned CIA Station Chief Devlin. Gottlieb was "Joe from Paris."[9]

It was up to Devlin to figure a way to get the poison in Lumumba's mouth. One suggestion was to put it in his toothpaste, but Africans of that day and age didn't use it. Even slipping poison into food was a problem, as the CIA had no agents who could stroll into Lumumba's kitchen. One plan to infiltrate Lumumba's residence was to use a Congolese native working for CIA and have him "take refuge" with Lumumba, thereby becoming an "inside man" who might slip the toxin to the prime minister. Failing this, the station chief cabled Langley:

IF CASE OFFICER SENT, RECOMMEND HQS [Headquarters] POUCH SOONEST HIGH POWERED FOREIGN MAKE RIFLE WITH TELESCOPIC SCOPE AND SILENCER. . . .[10]

Further, the Leopoldville station requested the immediate assignment of QJ/WIN, a CIA contract agent of foreign nationality (probably Corsican) who was known as a operative who would undertake risky assignments and, according to his CIA case officer in Leopoldville, was "not a man of many scruples."[11]

Before QJ/WIN or Station Chief Devlin could carry through on these Machiavellian schemes, Lumumba completed his own self-destruction; the CIA never did directly kill him. Leaving U.N. custody on 27 November 1960, the prime minister dashed to Stanleyville, a stronghold of his supporters. From there, fearful of arrest by the Mobutu-led army, he attempted to escape the clutches of Mobutu's forces, but was captured by Congolese troops loyal to Mobutu. Ultimately, they turned him over to his most bitter tribal enemies, who happened to be on the CIA payroll, and who happened to beat him to death. Lawrence Devlin later revealed that he drove around the streets of Lubumbashi with Lumumba's battered body in his trunk, trying to decide what to do with it—presumably to ensure that the CIA wouldn't get blamed for the murder. The CIA's man on the spot, Joseph Mobutu, took power, renamed the country Zaire, served as president-for-life for the next thirty-six years, and fled the country having plundered his people for a reported $5 billion.

There are two important features of the Lumumba assassination plot. First, this is one of three clear-cut cases in which the CIA attempted an assassination, the others being Fidel Castro and Abdul Karim Kassem.[12] While there are many cases of CIA officers, supported or unsupported by Langley, making contact with, and even promises to, groups that eventually killed or tried to kill foreign leaders, we are truly certain only that the CIA itself attempted political killing of heads of state on these three occasions.

Second, the Lumumba case is the only case that offers compelling evidence that a president of the United States explicitly authorized an assassination. It was during a meeting of the National Security Council (NSC) in the late summer of 1960, staffer Robert Johnson later recalled, that President Eisenhower ordered the assassination of Patrice Lumumba. Johnson testified to the Church Committee that while Ike never came right out and said "kill him," his meaning was plain enough that years later the NSC staffer recalled his shock at the event.[13] While there is some dispute over this, others at the meeting recalled language to the effect that Lumumba must be "gotten rid of." While this does not appear in the minutes of the meeting, it was common practice in Ike's NSC meetings to delete from the minutes anything of a highly sensitive nature. The importance of this kind of ambiguity is discussed below.

THE MAN IN HAVANA

When the corrupt kleptocracy[14] of Fulgencio Batista imploded on New Year's Day 1959, a small band of bearded revolutionaries marched triumphantly into Havana to assume the leadership of Cuba. Fidel Castro, onetime lawyer and base-ball player, had led his guerrillas through an epic campaign, supported early on by the American government. However, after his famous trip to New York, Castro was branded a Communist by Vice President Nixon after lecturing the vice president on how badly U.S. corporations had "exploited" Cuba, and the CIA was actually planning to undermine the guerrilla prince even before he attained power. In fact, the first discussions of assassinating Castro occurred in the Eisenhower "Special Group," a small group within the Eisenhower administration that advised Ike on covert operations.

Whatever Castro was, and is, to Americans he became a symbol of the forces of darkness, all out of proportion to the size and power of his island. Part of this is the result of the Cuban exile lobby, a powerful, well-organized, well-funded operation with the capacity to influence American politics at the national level. Part of it is also likely his mere presence as a Communist (a long-surviving one at that) and Soviet ally, sitting like a manure pile on America's front porch. Mostly, however, Castro's longevity as major bogeyman can be traced to his successful repulse of the Cuban/U.S. invasion at the Bay of Pigs and the fierce hatred this humiliation created in the minds of John and Robert Kennedy, as well as in the CIA as an organization. It was this disgrace that led to OPERATION MONGOOSE and the plots to kill Castro. The U.S. government admits to eight CIA operations to assassinate Castro between 1960 and 1965; Castro's former counterintelligence chief claims the number is over two dozen. This doesn't count the various *character* assassination psyops involving, among other things, LSD and radiation poisoning, recounted below. Given the predilections of some of the more radical (and uncontrollable) anti-Castro Cubans living in America, as well as the interests of the Mafia, the figure is almost certainly higher. We'll never know for sure. What is certain is that Castro has been the target of deadly serious, albeit often wacky, assassination plots for nearly forty years.

Getting Smoked by a Cigar

Operations to "get" Castro began early in 1960, when the CIA's Technical Services Division (the gadget guys, referred to as TSD) was asked by the Eisenhower administration to find some clever, deniable way of discrediting him. These early efforts, intriguing as they were, did not focus on killing Castro. That would come later.

Perhaps the first method considered was an aerosol that produced disorienting, LSD-like effects. The idea was to spray Castro with this substance immediately before he was to give a radio speech; the belief in Langley was that some incoherent rambling by the bearded revolutionary would somehow induce the Cuban people to rise up and overthrow his regime. This plan was ultimately scrapped because the spray LSD was unreliable. Failing this, an alternative plan was developed to lace a cigar with an agent "intended to produce temporary personality disorientation."[15] Once again, the concept was to entice Castro to have a smoke right before going on the air. It was never explained by officers from the CIA, at least publicly, how such behavior might logically lead to a Cuban counterrevolution.

Perhaps the most humorous plot involved the bearded leader's prized symbol of revolution: his beard. The CIA developed a plan to humiliate Castro in the eyes of Cuba by dusting his shoes with thallium salts, a low-level radioactive powder. When Castro put his shoes on, the radiation would quickly make his beard fall out. This plan was to take place on a trip outside Cuba (almost certainly New York), where the CIA would get Castro's shoes when he placed them outside his hotel room door at night to be shined. The CIA planned for this to take place during Castro's appearance on *The David Susskind Show*, to maximize his embarrassment. This plan got to the animal testing stage, but was aborted when Castro canceled his trip.

No More Mister Nice Guy

By the late summer of 1960, this series of *Get Smart* plots gave way to the serious business of statecraft: killing.[16] On 16 August, Dr. Edward Gunn[17] (Operations Division, Office of Medical Services) was handed a box of Castro's favorite cigars, along with orders to poison them. He used botulinum toxin to produce a cigar so deadly it didn't have to be smoked; put one in Castro's mouth and he'd be dead. Dr. Gunn did a careful "flaps and seals" job, gingerly opening the box and unwrapping each cigar, then resealing them perfectly so there was no trace of tampering. According to the CIA, the cigars were ready on 7 October 1960, and passed on to an "unidentified person" during February 1961, where they seem to have disappeared into the mists of history.[18] During the writing of the CIA inspector general's report on the Castro plots in 1967 (seven years after the cigar caper), one of the cigars was found. The botulin still tested out at 94 percent effective.

No one is certain who first suggested recruiting the Mafia into the war on Castro; or, in any case, no one has owned up to it. What is certain, however, is that sometime during the middle of 1962, senior CIA officials set about to use *la Cosa Nostra* to "hit" Castro (the merits and demerits of cloaking the Mafia in the U.S. flag are discussed in chapter 8). But instead of a simple gangland-style shooting—which would have been a suicide mission—the mafiosi suggested a familiar plan: poison.

La Cosa Nostra did bring one thing to the table in this plan: Santos Trafficante had someone close enough to Castro to actually slip something into his drink. Once again botulinum toxin fit the bill, but when Dr. Gunn tested the pills, they "did not even disintegrate, let alone dissolve."[21] CIA Director of Security Sheffield Edwards sent Gunn back to the drawing board, then off to the pet store for some guinea pigs, to insure that the poison would actually do the job.

Of course, the guinea pigs didn't die. This little "oops" was corrected by another member of the TSD, who pointed out that the little rodents were more resistant to the botulin than humans. The oversight was quickly rectified by tests on monkeys, with satisfactorily lethal results.

The new and improved pills were delivered to Johnny Roselli, hidden inside a pencil, sometime during February 1961 (probably not coincidentally, shortly before the Bay of Pigs landing was scheduled). Eventually, via Trafficante, the pills were passed on to a Cuban named Juan Orta, who nominally directed the

Cuban prime minister's office but was, in effect, Castro's private secretary. Once again, good luck was with Castro, as Orta was fired from his job before he could slip him the big mickey. Orta sought refuge in the Venezuelan Embassy, and eventually was allowed to leave Cuba in 1964. There were supposedly one or more other Mafia-organized poisoning attempts after this, including one using a Cuban who was a waiter in a restaurant frequented by the bearded leader. This too failed, apparently because after he received the poison, the waiter waited for a final "go signal" that never came.[22]

Thus ended the pre–Bay of Pigs plots. Today, there is considerable suspicion that the assassination of Castro was one of the primary components of OPERA-TION ZAPATA. While no documentary record of this exists in any declassified piece of paper related to ZAPATA, there are other indications that perhaps a critical part of the plan was to whack Castro. Certainly some of the early planning incorporated a Castro assassination as part of the operation. When Howard Hunt returned from a reconnaissance to Cuba, he presented a four-part plan to the directorate of plans; the first part was killing the Castro brothers (Fidel and Raul) and Ché Guevara.[23]

After the Bay of Pigs invasion blew apart all over the evening news, the Kennedy administration invested a new urgency to the Castro problem. Richard Bissell was first ordered to "get off his ass" and get Castro; failing at a quick solution, he was shuttled off to a dead-end job. William Harvey, CIA buccaneer extraordinaire, was selected to recruit and establish ZR/RIFLE, and the plans to get Castro became ever more bizarre (or clever, depending on your perspective).

Early in 1963, New York attorney James Donovan, who had negotiated the release of the Bay of Pigs survivors and had developed a useful rapport with the Cubans, was engaged in still further negotiations with the Castro government.[24] Knowing that Castro loved scuba diving, the CIA purchased a fancy new wet suit and scuba gear, and dusted the breathing apparatus with tuberculosis bacillus. The plan was to have Donovan present the wet suit as a gift to Castro, apparently forgetting that there would be no way to deny *this* assassination plot: Castro would have been killed by an overt gift from the United States. Once again, the CIA was forestalled, this time by Donovan, who, unaware of the plot, had already presented a new wet suit to Castro. Richard Helms, who had replaced Bissell as DDP, thought the plan was "cockeyed"; the contaminated wet suit never left the TSD lab.

Shortly afterward, Desmond Fitzgerald, chief of Task Force W, the CIA department specifically organized to run black ops against Cuba, concocted an even better plan: the exploding seashell. According to the CIA's inspector general,

> The idea was to take an unusually spectacular seashell that would be certain to catch Castro's eye, load it with an explosive triggered to blow when the shell was lifted, and submerge it in an area where Castro often went skin diving.[25]

Upon further study, however, the plan was no go. Caribbean seashells just aren't spectacular enough, and unfortunately are generally too small to hold enough explosive material. The explosion might rupture Castro's eardrums, but he'd live. Further, the plan required a midget submarine to plant the shell, but none in the U.S. fleet had adequate range to sneak in and out. There were two other critical flaws pointed out by CIA officer Sam Halpern. First, one couldn't be sure that Castro would be the one to find the shell, and thus the plan represented a serious risk to innocent victims (or at least to their eardrums). Moreover, like the wet suit caper, "death by exploding seashell" could scarcely be an accident; it would be an obvious assassination.[26] This plan too was left on the drawing board.

AM/LASH

Rolando Cubela was a major in the Cuban army who had frequent contact with Castro. He was also a CIA agent, having established contact with the CIA sometime in 1961, receiving the codename AM/LASH. By mid-1963, Cubela believed that Castro had to die, and solicited the help of the CIA for a method that would be less than suicidal. The CIA first offered him a special "pen" that could be loaded with poison, and that had a needle so fine that the victim would, in theory, not feel the injection. For Cubela, the method wasn't quite enough less than suicidal. Ironically, at almost the very moment AM/LASH was taking the pen from a high-ranking CIA officer, President Kennedy was being shot in Dallas. After the assassination of President Kennedy, the CIA seemed to evince some (temporary) skittishness about assassinating foreign leaders, but soon overcame it. By early 1965, Cubela had been supplied with a pistol and an FAL assault rifle, as well as silencers for both weapons; the weapons were supplied by an organization headed by Bay of Pigs leader Manuel Artime, who was serving as a cutout for the CIA. Cubela, however, was not what you would call tight-lipped, and his own bragging led Cuban counterintelligence to him; he was arrested before he could act.[27]

In addition to these plots, there were several other known plans to get rid of Castro. As a corollary to the treacherous tobacco caper, the CIA may have planned to create an actual exploding cigar that would literally have blown the head off the Cuban leader. According to CIA contract agent Antonio Veciana, the agency also planned for three assassins to pose as reporters from Venezuelan television. In a crowd, they would shoot Castro using a revolver that had been built into a movie camera. There was yet another poisoning plot, this time involving Castro's mistress, who had been recruited by CIA contract agent Frank Sturgis (yes, *that* Frank Sturgis).[27] According to the mistress, Marita Lorenz, Sturgis convinced her that Castro was going to kill her, and that she should get him first. To this end, she was supplied with poison to slip into Castro's drink. When Lorenz traveled to meet Castro, she secreted the toxic capsules in a jar of Pond's cold cream, where they promptly dissolved. Anyway, she reports, upon reuniting with the bearded revolutionary face to face, her resolution dissolved as well; "I am a lover, not a killer," she says today.[29] Finally, three CIA operatives managed to slip into Havana, where they obtained an apartment overlooking the presidential palace. On a day in which Castro was to make a speech honoring three visiting Soviet cosmonauts, the assassins planned to obliterate the speaker's platform by firing a bazooka from their apartment window. Unfortunately for them, the bazooka had gotten wet during their infiltration (aboard a rubber raft) and would not fire. They were apprehended by Cuban counterintelligence, who found explosives and submachine guns hidden behind a false wall in the apartment. In all, according to Castro's chief of counterintelligence, Fabian Escalante, there were at least twenty-six serious attempts on Castro's life; it is testimony to the difficulty of such activities that Castro is still alive.

HANKIES AREN'T JUST FOR SISSIES

Another CIA assassination plot against a different target was virtually over-looked in the Church Committee report: an operation in 1960 to kill General Abdul Karim Kassem, ruler of Iraq.[30] Kassem had led a coup in 1958, in which he had murdered his rivals wholesale, restored diplomatic relations with the Soviets, and legalized the Iraqi Communist Party. In early 1960, the chief of the DDP's Near East Division suggested a plan to "incapacitate" Kassem: a poisoned handkerchief.[31] Approved by Chief of Operations Richard Helms, the op went forward, with Sidney Gottlieb employing the expertise he had used in the Lumumba affair. This time, a handkerchief was impregnated with botulinus bacteria and mailed to the Iraqi dictator as a gift. We have no record of whether he received it, but the general certainly did not die from it; he was executed by firing squad on live television on 8 February 1963. One hopes some poor clerk in the mail department didn't take the hanky home as a gift for his wife.

LYING DOWN WITH DOGS

Aside from Lumumba, Castro, and Kassem, there are really no cases where one can prove that the CIA itself attempted to kill a head of state.[32] This is not to say, however, that CIA was not involved with other assassinations. In fact, there is a fairly long list of foreign leaders who have either been assassinated or had serious attempts made on their lives by individuals or groups associated with the CIA.[33] These include:

- General Rafael Trujillo (Dominican Republic), who was ambushed and shot to death on a highway on 30 May 1961 by dissidents who had been supported by the United States, and who possibly used weapons supplied by the CIA.
- General René Schneider of Chile, the roadblock to a military coup, who was shot to death when he resisted kidnapping in October 1970. The CIA had offered $50,000 for kidnapping the general, and had previously supplied Chilean plotters with submachine guns and grenades.[34]

- Ngo Dinh Diem, ineffective president of South Vietnam, who was ousted in a military coup on 1 November 1963, and was, along with his brother Ngo Dinh Nhu, murdered. The plotters had been strongly encouraged by legendary CIA operative Lucien Conein; Ambassador Henry Cabot Lodge had received direct orders, verbally okayed by President Kennedy and Richard Helms, to proceed with a coup. Judging by JFK's reaction to the news of Diem's murder, it is probably true that he thought he had authorized only a coup, *not* an execution.
- Salvador Allende, who was overthrown in September 1973, and was either murdered or committed suicide rather than surrender. The CIA was very deep in the overthrow (labeled Track II in the White House), although there is no direct evidence that the CIA or the Nixon White House explicitly ordered the death—as opposed to the ouster—of Allende.
- Charles DeGaulle, premier of France, who was the target of numerous assassination attempts by the Organisation de l'Armée Secréte (OAS), a group of dissident army officers who were violently opposed to DeGaulle's policy for Algerian independence. Frederick Forsyth's novel *Day of the Jackal* is built around these events. The CIA was at least in close contact with the leadership of the OAS, although there is no evidence that the agency supported or encouraged assassination attempts. There is also no evidence, however, that the CIA tried to discourage OAS efforts to kill DeGaulle, despite the CIA's close contact with the OAS and knowledge of its goals. This is perhaps a curious case of the dog that didn't bark.[35]
- Chou En-Lai, who eventually became premier of China. CIA officers in the Far East cabled a request to assassinate Chou in early 1955; they were rebuked in writing by Allen Dulles.[36] Chou changed planes immediately before a flight (aboard an Air India aircraft) later that year. His originally scheduled plane blew up in midair; a detonator was found in the wreckage, although no culprit was ever proven.[37]
- Gamel Abdel Nasser, president of Egypt, who was reportedly targeted by another of Sid Gottlieb's smokes. According to CIA officer Miles Copeland, he was provided with botulinus-laced cigarettes to give to Nasser, but refused. Interestingly, Copeland's account was published several years before the rest of the CIA poisoning plots were made public.[38]

Letting the Sunshine In

As DCI Richard Helms has voiced on many occasions, murder will out. In the wake of Watergate came 1975, the "Year of Intelligence." On 5 June of that year, the *New York Times* printed a sketchy summary of the "family jewels," details of secret CIA operations that even within the agency were believed to be illegal, immoral, or even unconstitutional: assassinations, coups d'etat, and illegal activities *within* the United States, including mind-control experiments on unwitting

Americans. The report, known as "the Skeletons" (i.e., in the closet) had been prepared at the request of DCI James Schlesinger in 1973, and its publication, even in vague form, ignited a firestorm. Ultimately, the result was that a sitting director of Central Intelligence, William Colby, sat before a televised hearing demonstrating air pistols that would fire toxic pellets a hundred yards and an umbrella that would do likewise. The agency was in a fight for its life, seeming to have become an out of control "rogue elephant" (as Senator Frank Church put it), or even the "American Gestapo" feared by members of Congress in the debate over the national Security Act in 1947.

In the end, the CIA survived, and it was another assassination that ended the bloodletting. This time, however, it was one of the CIA's own, Richard Welch, station chief in Athens, who was shot down on his own doorstep in December 1975. Welch had been identified as a CIA operative by the *Athens News* a month earlier, and also by *CounterSpy*, a U.S.-based anti-CIA publication. Although Welch made little secret of his job and exercised little in the way of security (e.g., he chose to live in the same well-known residence as the former station chief), the CIA and its congressional patrons seized upon the murder like a drowning nonswimmer to a life preserver. The agency's counterattack was more or less couched as, "See what you've done." Welch received an unprecedented funeral for a CIA officer, including a public return of the coffin to Andrews Air Force Base and interment in Arlington. Rather than blame the coups and assassinations and secret wars for Welch's death, for many in the CIA it was the *unmasking* of the secrets and the atmosphere surrounding the Church Committee that killed Dick Welch. Almost in stunned silence, the investigation was over. The committees would publish reports, and a succession of presidents would issue executive orders commanding that any agent of the United States refrain from assassination. There was great gnashing of teeth over the immorality, yet it was here the analysis stopped.

What is certain is that there continue to be powerful incentives for the United States to assassinate foreign leaders, most recently Mu'ammar Gadhafi and Saddam Hussein. What remains unexamined, however, are the issues raised by such nefarious activities, both moral and practical. It is to these we turn next.

ISSUES AND ASSASSINATIONS

On the face of it, assassination is a simple, direct solution to an irritating problem: If a problem is caused by an evil leader, get rid of her. This solution, however, relies on a simple and naive view of the world, replete with "schoolyard bully" and "cut out the cancer" analogies. Assassination of foreign leaders is a trail fraught with pitfalls; one that should be entered into with trepidation, if at all.

Deniability is Critical

If deniability is important to regular covert operations, it is absolutely critical to assassinations. It can affect (1) the ultimate success of the operation, (2) U.S. relations with other countries, and (3) domestic American politics and political leaders.

The success of an "executive action" on a foreign leader is often affected or determined by how well one can deny responsibility. In some cases, the leader who replaces the assassinated ruler will cooperate with U.S. interests and often will repress the local population enough that any resentment of American control of the government won't matter (e.g., Guatemala). In other cases, however, assassination of a beloved or popular political figure can backfire, turning the bulk of the local people, and even an entire region, against the United States. If they cannot manifest it immediately, suppressed hostility may still explode decades later, as it did in Iran in 1979.

Open knowledge of assassination plans or acts can also affect the relations of the United States with other governments. For example, the vast majority of governments would be delighted to see Saddam Hussein eliminated, provided a more stable and less predatory regime took over Iraq. Within the Middle East, however, there would be substantial discomfort over the precedent of the United States intervening in the affairs of any Arab or Middle Eastern state in such a drastic way.[39] Even though some of the countries in the region might nominally be friends or allies of the United States, the inevitable thought would arise: "I could be next." Even to governments outside the region, the exercise of raw power would be unsettling; after all, there *is* a country that might be powerful enough to take over the world, and its name is the United States of America.

Finally, a display of open brute force can seriously infect American politics. Many Americans would be opposed to such ruthless violence and/or intervention in the affairs of other states under almost any circumstances. This objection would be shared by Congress, possibly resulting in a nasty set of hearings. Currently, the United States has renounced assassination—virtually every DCI in memory is on record against it—and it would be illegal, in violation of a presidential executive order, at the very least (unless the president had secretly rescinded the order, which would open yet another can of worms). Aside from the rending hostility this would add to an already polarized citizenry, the perpetrators of the assassination and their supporters would likely instantly resort to the kind of jingoistic hyperbole that stains the American political system: The target is the next Hitler, just this once is okay, and anyone who disagrees must want to surrender. It is difficult to imagine that a foreign leader could do as much damage to the United States as its own people have done. Deniability, then is a critical component of any assassination plan, lest the short-term solution poison the well for the long-term future.

Unfortunately, deniability is difficult, if not impossible, to maintain in an assassination operation. In virtually every case where a government would want to assassinate a foreign head of state, there will be a long established record of mutual hostility; if such a leader were killed, the United States and the CIA would be at the top of the list of suspects. Without a very good cover story, such as an obvious fall guy, without probable or even suspected connections to U.S. intelligence or interests, to take the blame, America would receive the mantle of guilt. Moreover, it seems apparent that murder *will* out. Today, the entire world knows about past CIA assassination plots and involvement with assassins. Even though we might currently resolve to keep such things completely secret, we cannot know what the political environment will be in the future. Thus, deniability can never be permanently assured; it cannot even be assured in the short run.

CIA, Assassination, and Intelligence

Although the CIA has apparently never actually carried out an assassination, it has frequently established and maintained close connections to individuals and groups that have assassinated, or have tried to assassinate, foreign leaders. Such contact is an inherent problem for the United States, as even if the CIA has not encouraged assassination (a big "if"), mere contact creates the appearance that the agency and the United States are killing foreign leaders left and right (well, only Left).

It would be simplest to say that CIA should not be in contact with plotters and assassins who plan to overthrow their own governments, especially governments that are at least nominally friendly to the United States. This way, there would not even be the appearance of having had a hand in successful or attempted assassinations.

This position, however, is not only extraordinarily naive, but also a bad idea from a purely practical viewpoint. There will almost always be individuals within an intelligence agency that will maintain close contact with dissident organizations, even those in allied countries. A strict policy of "no contact" would be largely ignored by field operators. More importantly, however, *it is a critical job of the CIA to know about these groups*: who they are, how large and capable they are, what they plan to do, and when they plan to do it. Such organizations, whether they're from friendly or hostile countries, can and do create both problems and opportunities for the United States, and often do things that require a response from the president. Indeed, when the CIA doesn't forecast serious events like rebellions and revolutions, it is called an *intelligence failure*; professors and journalists write books about these failures.

If the CIA knows about revolutionaries plotting to assassinate a friendly leader, one might ask, why don't the officers on the spot turn them in? There are several reasons. First, unless an officer can be assured that the bulk of the dissident group and its leadership will be captured, all that might happen is that a few footsoldiers of the revolution get picked up, and the CIA will have lost its source(s) of intelligence. Second, when a local regime is shaky and already has a high likelihood of falling, it's good to be on the winning team. By not exposing the plotters, one can play both sides: If the government survives, we didn't know about the plan; if the dissidents prevail, we didn't rat them out. Either way, the regime in power thinks it has a friend in the United States.

The problem with being in contact with dissident groups and potential assassins is that often "in contact" looks like "in cahoots." If the CIA has provided advice or material support to insurrectionists, even if that advice was "Don't kill the prime minister," there is still the appearance of CIA control of the organization and its activities.

If the CIA is going to be involved with potentially violent insurgents (and this is probably an objective intelligence requirement), then the agency will almost certainly continue to be blamed for the actions of those it merely observes. Largely, this comes with the territory, for there is no "neutral" information about an assassination plot. Either you keep quiet, thus aiding the assassins or the rebels in their plans, or you expose them, thus helping the government in power. The claim that one can simply let "nature takes its course" is sophistry; once knowledge is acquired, a decision is required—and refusing to make a decision is the same as keeping quiet.

If the CIA continues to infiltrate and monitor rebellious foreign factions, it will undoubtedly run across such plots from time to time; having obtained information, it will be accused of having planned the whole assassination. There are only three answers to this, none of them very satisfying. Fist, one can lie and say that the agency didn't know. This isn't a convincing answer, however, and it's also one that can often be proven false; there may be a paper trail, or several witnesses that might corroborate the story. A slightly better option is to claim that while there was lots of talk about assassination, the CIA was never aware of any specific plan. The best claim, because its virtually always true, is this: Dissidents are *always* talking about assassination, and it's virtually always just that: big talk. In any unstable country, there are a hundred assassination plans hatched every day; should the CIA investigate every rumor? It's a practical impossibility, so once in a while there will be an assassination by someone who has been in contact with the CIA.

Peel off the next layer of the onion, however, and one finds the kind of "contact" that is substantially more troubling: the murder of foreign leaders after the assassins have gotten the "OK" from the United States. In some cases, e.g., Saddam Hussein, Gadhafi, Trujillo, and probably Diem and Allende, the United States has actively encouraged assassination or, at least, execution after the coup.[40] From an ethical standpoint, at least, this is a better position than actually performing the assassination; the people of a nation have the moral right to free themselves from oppression. Practically speaking, deniability is also improved, for these would not be U.S. operations. Win or lose, the blame would not be attached to the United States or the CIA, and in the event of success, the rebels might give some credit to American support.

Is there a solution to the dilemma of the CIA's reliance on potential assassins for intellignece and the resulting appearance of supporting them? For now, it is essential to create an evidentiary trail to show that, while the CIA has been in contact with such organizations, it has encouraged them to undertake some form of due process rather than outright murder (whenever possible; it is hard to imagine arresting Saddam Hussein alive). Perhaps the best option is to try to reestablish the reputation of the United States as a government opposed to assassination in principle. By so doing, we might at least undercut the notion that the CIA is behind every assassin.

The Morality of Assassination

When historians and "analysts" discuss assassination, moral considerations sit in strange opposition: Morality is either viewed as the only consideration or as completely irrelevant. To the "idealists," killing is generally immoral and unjustified by almost any circumstances. Further, the principle of self-determination requires that governments refrain from interfering in the internal affairs of other states. Contrary to this position, "realists" claim that morality is at best a minor consideration in any affair of state; the singular purpose of foreign policy is to increase the power of the state, and especially to eliminate threats to it. Between these two perspectives, debates about assassination often degenerate into "Killing is wrong!" versus "It's a dangerous world!" Such disagreement over first principles usually produces nothing in the way of intellectual progress or innovative policy, and is generally futile. There is, however, a rich tradition of moral ideas that can be brought to bear on the idea of assassination: the philosophies of *just war* and *tyrannicide*.

A long-standing and great moral tradition justifies killing a tyrant: Virtually all the moral theorists have asserted or accepted the right of a people to rid themselves of their oppressor, by violence, if necessary, when peaceful means are unsuccessful. Moral arguments about tyrannicide, however, have never applied to the assassination of a foreign head of state, even if he or she is a tyrant. Philosophers have always demanded that the oppressed people liberate themselves. There is a good reason for this: The motive of an oppressed people to kill their oppressor is sincere, just, and obvious. An outside government, however, may have ulterior motives, such as installing an oppressive regime under its own control. To avoid the potential conflict of interest, moral theorists have chosen a "bright line" test; *no* outside intervention is justified.

Two lines of moral argument can lead to "just intervention," however. First, one can claim that intervention in another state's affairs (in this case, assassination) is justified as a preemptive or preventive action. Just war theory is largely based around the idea that defending one's country, land, and people is moral—providing the political system itself is moral and therefore worthy of defense. In theory, however, "defense" does not always mean that one has to wait for the aggressor to strike first, as political philosophy accepts the notion of preemptive war. If a government is reasonably certain that a hostile nation is about to attack, it is morally justified in attacking first; just war theory does not insist that an impending victim of aggression take the first blow and try to recover. In this case, actual operations leading to war are assumed to be underway, so that the war has become inevitable and immediate. There is no formal time limit on this, but in general one would expect the attack to be launched within a week, or perhaps a month at most, for the preemptive justification to apply. Based on this, leaders can stake a moral claim that assassinating the leader of a state that is irrevocably and immediately committed to attacking their country is also morally acceptable. It is critical to note, though, that none of the U.S./CIA assassination plots, proven or alleged, fit this scenario.

A step further into the gray area leads to the concept of *preventive war*. This is a war launched because a government believes that war with an opposing country is inevitable (although not immediately imminent), and that it is better to fight it sooner than later. Preventive war has often been used as a defense of the traditional "balance of power" system in Europe, the idea being that since the overall balance provided a kind of freedom to the various states, anything that might upset the balance should be avoided, even at the cost of war. The difference between preemptive and preventive war is the time element; in a preventive war, the enemy attack is simply "sometime in the future." Prevention is the only justification that can be invoked in the CIA assassination plots, for none of these nations could in any sense threaten the United States by themselves. It was only in the context of a Soviet base that Cuba had strategic value; only in some very long-term calculus could the Congo become critical in the global balance of power in the 1960s.

To use this as justification is to tread dangerously spongy ground, ground that has almost universally been rejected by moral theorists.[41] How far off in place or time does the threat have to be? Trying to split these hairs is arguing about angels on pinheads.

Another aspect of just war is the distinction between civilians and soldiers. To be justified, acts of war, even assassinations, must be directed at those who have assumed the risks of war, i.e., soldiers. Traditionally, the intentional killing of civilians has been not only considered immoral, but generally viewed as a war crime. In the Western philosophic tradition, at least, there has also been a moral proscription against targeting specific military leaders, although this has restriction has declined substantially, from the attempts on Isoroku Yamamoto and Erwin Rommel to more recent attacks on Gadhafi, Saddam Hussein, and Osama bin Laden.

There is also a flip side to the moral position against killing the leader of an opposing country: If it's acceptable to kill thousands, perhaps *millions,* of soldiers in a war (at least according to standard just war philosophy), and these soldiers are mostly guys who had no say in whether to go to war or even in what the war is about, then why isn't it all right to kill the one person who *does* make the decisions? In fact, why isn't it *preferable*? From a moral standpoint, while any unjust death is bad, certainly one death must be better than millions.[42] Rejecting assassination essentially protects society's elite and wealthy members while marching the common man and woman off to the mechanized meat grinder of modern war.

One answer to this question is simply that during wartime, national policies on assassination change; countries *do* attempt to kill foreign leaders, but seldom succeed, as leaders are better protected during times of war.[43] In World War II, for example, Allied forces assassinated two foreign military men: Reinhard Heydrich, a Nazi architect of the "final solution" and probable successor to Hitler, and Admiral Isoroku Yamamto, soul of the Japanese Navy. Moreover, the British mounted a commando raid in North Africa in an effort to kill Rommell; it failed only because the Desert Fox was not at headquarters. Our discussion of assassination, however, has focused on peacetime, and most countries don't kill foreign soldiers during peacetime any more than they kill foreign leaders.

Some more hard-core "realists" might wonder why we even bother with a discussion of morality. Without moral guidelines, though, the policies of the mightiest country in the world simply float along rudderless. If the United States is to be any more than simply another major power guided by the basic principle that it is better to be feared than loved, then moral principles firmly held and lived out are a necessity that separates "us" (the good guys) from "them" (the bad guys).

Assassination and the Law

American presidents have gone to extraordinary lengths to safeguard their prerogative to order covert actions. Assassination, however, has been treated like a visitor with the black plague. Even though numerous presidents have ordered either outright assassinations or operations that they at least hoped would kill foreign leaders,[44] they have also generally taken great pains to *appear* opposed to political killings, often making explicit public pronouncements that they, and the U.S. government, would never stoop to such nefarious deeds. Nevertheless, presidents have also been vigorous opponents of any laws that would forbid assassination, as was proposed by the Church Committee in 1976. Instead, President Ford issued an executive order prohibiting assassination, which has been renewed by every president since then. Perhaps this order has the force of law; it can, however, be secretly rescinded at any time by the sitting president. In other words, assassination is illegal unless/until the president says it's not.

Where Do We Get Assassins?

The word "assassin" has such a negative connotation to most people that one wonders why anyone would want to become one. Virtually all assassins, however, think of themselves as soldiers serving a higher purpose; to them, the term assassin is simply a pejorative word used by their enemies, or else a term to be embraced as synonymous with "hero," much as World Trade Center bomber Ramzi Yusef boasted of his pride in being a "terrorist."

The word assassin comes from *hashishim*, Arabic for "hashish user." Legend has it that the old man of the mountain built a formidable force of assassins who would seek out and kill his enemies. To convince the assassins to take up his cause, he would ply them with hashish and, while they were in this drugged state, would introduce them to a delightful garden full of willing women. This garden was portrayed to the potential assassin as the reward for one who gave his life in the service of Allah and the old man. Such belief created a cadre of literally fearless assassins who would joyously sacrifice their lives in the course of a political killing. In the modern world, having generally evolved beyond the drugged-assassin stage, there are six groups one might consider as souces for useful assassins: the military, professional killers or international assassins, the Mafia, convicted murderers, intelligence agencies, and indigenous personnel from the target country or government.

The first source of assassins that often comes to mind is the military. Surely these men are trained to kill, trained to kill on order, and skilled with weapons, explosives, and even their bare hands; what better choice could one make? But this source makes sense only if one is ignorant of the professional military, especially the United States armed forces. As a practical matter, one could certainly find the necessary combat skills of an assassin among a number of special forces personnel, particularly within the SEAL Teams and the Green Berets (within them, particularly Delta Force). Further, all of these men have a more or less proven willingness to risk their lives, and a few will even volunteer for a "one-way" assignment (i.e., a suicide mission). Combat skills and willingness to die, however, are not enough. As an American assassin, one would need not only combat and weapon skills, but also the skills of a clandestine operator: breaking and entering, operating under a false identity, and most desirable, the ability to pass as a native of another country, including fluency in the language. This certainly narrows the field.

The greatest obstacle to finding assassins among the professional American military, however, is the American professional military culture: It is a matter of great pride among professional military people that they are *warriors,* not assassins. While some Americans, particularly from the political far Left, maintain the image of the professional soldier as a mindless, order-obeying automaton, the U.S. military has gone to great lengths to instill a moral code in its personnel: Don't shoot prisoners, don't kill civilians, and so on.[45] One of the elements of this code is that *killing is done in wartime on a battlefield.* In the moral lights of the code, war is fought against people who can shoot back. Warriors train for war; in the minds of most soldiers, assassination isn't war. There is a certain cold-bloodedness required for assassins that we hope to train out of our soldiers, sailors, and airmen. Doubtless there are individuals within special forces that could be found to carry out political assassinations. Even so, it might be difficult to disguise or "cover" the assassin enough. Even a sheep-dipped operative would almost certainly convict the U.S. as an assassin in the eyes of the world, and it would be difficult, if not impossible, to obliterate the origin of a U.S. serviceman or woman.

The best assassins are those that meet several criteria: skilled, dedicated, disciplined, and deniable. For the United States, that almost certainly means *not* an American. An ideal assassin should be a foreign national with special forces training, e.g., a British SAS trooper, a South African mercenary, or perhaps some out-of-work Soviet *Spetznaz* (Special Forces) for hire. Ideally, he should be hired by a cutout with a convincing cover story and limited resources—which would indicate that the employer is not a government—and he should never know what organization hired him.

Perhaps the most appealing option would be to hire a professional assassin, something on the order of the "Jackal" from *Day of the Jackal*. It's a highly inviting idea (at least in some hardhearted, arrogant circles) to slip a briefcase full of cash to an anonymous operative, have her use her brilliant disguises and multiple identities to infiltrate the enemy camp, nail the troublemaker, and slip off into the mists of history with full pockets and the surreptitious thanks of a grateful country. This isn't as easy as it sounds; there are very few, if any, such individuals that one would want to trust to (1) do a good job, (2) not get caught, and (3) be absolutely unconnectable to the United States government.

There are two major difficulties with this option. First, simply trying to contact one of these operatives would raise ripples in the international intelligence pond; word would get out that *someone* is looking for a top-notch professional assassin. Second, professional killers at the highest level generally take great pains to safeguard themselves. They are acutely aware that the best way to create deniability for an international assassination is for the contracting government to either kill the assassin once the job is over, thereby severing all ties, or—perhaps better—to arrange for the assassin to be shot while "resisting arrest," thereby providing a convenient denial of the crime: "See, he wasn't one of *ours*." To avoid this, a professional in the trade may secretly document his mission and the identity of those who hired him. This proof is then deposited in several places (e.g., with several attorneys) with instructions to make it public if the assassin does not contact the holders on a regular schedule.

The disadvantage to a government is obvious. Even if there is no intent to double-cross the assassin, there is still a substantial risk that the assassin himself will create proof of the government's involvement, and the mere existence of such evidence is probably an unacceptable risk. What if he *does* get caught? Or simply killed in an auto accident? Finally, a really slick assassination in which security is circumvented, the target is eliminated, and the assassin gets clean away certainly smacks of professionalism. If the target is an outspoken opponent of the United States and the operation seems too good, the CIA is going to get blamed anyway. If deniability is critical to an operation, professional assassins are not a good option.[46]

One can readily imagine the reasoning that went through the minds of Sheffield Edwards, Richard Bissell, and Allen Dulles when they hit upon the idea of using the Mob to hit Castro: "Hey, they've got killers; they know how to do it, they've got a built-in motive, and they have people who can get Castro any time—*this* is deniability." While access to the target is important, it is far outweighed by the liabilities. First, virtually no one the CIA would want to assassinate can be hit by a Mafia shooter. Political assassinations are generally complex operations, and political persons generally have security that would prevent the typical Mob hit. Moreover, the access to the target that seemed so valuable to the CIA in Cuba not only proved ephemeral there, but is practically an unheard-of circumstance. Where else besides Cuba does the Mafia have this advantage? Probably nowhere. Additionally, there are such liabilities to using the Mafia for *any* purpose as to make this option a certain loser (see chapter 8 for a full discussion).

Regular murderers have the two advantages: They're proven killers and the government controls them. It's safe to say, however, that virtually no murderers in the United States possess any of the other requisites for performing a successful, deniable assassination. Moreover, it's impossible to imagine that a simple murderer would be reliable enough for a sensitive operation like a political assassination. The ultimate disaster would be for the prospective assassin to get to the other country and turn herself in in exchange for asylum and probably a nice payoff. Thus, the criteria narrows to selecting only *patriotic* murderers, which begins to stretch the logic a little far.

Intelligence agencies are probably not a fertile field for assassin recruitment. One only has to look at the kind of people the CIA itself tried to recruit during the heyday of assassination in the late '50s and early '60s. None of them were professional CIA officers, and with good reason. Even for the operational branches of the service, the CIA itself is comprised of upper- and middle-class American college graduates, hardly a bloodthirsty group (unless, of course, there is a grade on the line). Moreover, as with American military personnel, American intelligence officers would be hard to disguise or deny. Further, should one be captured, the prospect of a CIA officer/assassin spilling his guts on videotape is not an appealing prospect, and one would have to look pretty hard to find one of these chaps who would willingly crunch a cyanide ampule between his teeth rather than be captured.

The final option is to recruit an indigenous assassin. Perhaps "recruit" is too strong a word, for in many cases, individuals willing to assassinate their head of state often volunteer, with the proviso that the United States will assist. Such assassins largely must be taken where they are found, usually from the local military or dissidents. In most cases, the CIA ought to be keeping tabs on these individuals and their support networks anyway. Indigenous assassins can be very effective. A carefully selected assassin, such as Marita Lorenz or Rolando Cubela, may have easy access to the target. Further, deniability is greatly enhanced, as local insurgents have an obvious motive to kill a leader—a motive that may mostly go unchallenged. If, for example, Felix Rodriguez *had* shot Castro, there would be little or no question that he had wanted to do so on his own, that the CIA didn't need to put him up to it. Such individuals may also have a local support network far beyond anything the CIA could produce on the spot, up to and including a coup organization.

One drawback to hiring local assassins is their relative inexperience. Often, they are not professionals, and may have no training in clandestine operations, killing, escape (if necessary), and resistance to interrogation.

Moreover, many of these volunteers prove unreliable in one way or another: Some get cold feet and can't go through with the assassination, others talk too much, still others don't really have the access that they claim to have to the target. Worse, some catch a bad case of conscience and tell their story publicly, although this is possible with any assassin. Even worse, indigenous assassins may turn out to be provocateurs dangled by the target government itself in a sophisticated sting operation designed to catch other governments plotting against them. These false assassins are often used to ferret out local insurgents, and worse, to embarrass opposing governments, e.g., the United States, should they take the bait. In its early years, the Soviet government under Lenin and Feliks Dzerzhinsky ran a false insurgent organization called "The Trust," which enticed many Russian dissidents and some foreign intelligence agents to their deaths. In the 1950s, the Soviet Ministry of State Security (MGB), predecessor of the KGB, stung the CIA's OPERATION RED SOX/RED CAP, a plan to foment rebellion in Eastern Europe, by creating an "underground" in Poland, the *Wolnosć i Niepodlenosć* (WIN; "Freedom and Independence"), which was controlled by the Soviets from the beginning. In 1952, the MGB pulled the rug out, arresting the WIN leadership and using the event for disinformation.[47] It is also almost certain that some of the anti-Castro plots have been instigated by Castro's own counterintelligence operatives, both to uncover the identities of anti-Castro conspirators and also to simply keep the active plotters busy on schemes that could never bear fruit.

While one should be aware of the strengths and weaknesses of the different kinds of assassins, historical experience suggests that the choice of assassin really depends on the method of assassination, and vice versa. There are two categories of assassination plot: *access* and *technical*. Access assassinations are those in which the killer must be close to the target. These include the two kinds of suicide attacks, up-close shooting (the kind that got Anwar Sadat and Pope John Paul II) and suicide bombing (the kind that got Rajiv Gandhi). These are what CIA documents call a "loss" assassination, i.e., one in which the assassin is "lost." Poisoning is also an access assassination, as the assassin must be able to either contaminate the food or drink of the target, or directly expose him through injection, dusting a surface with a skin absorbent toxin, or spraying with a toxic aerosol like prussic acid. The spraying assassination was for a time the favorite of the KGB, who used it to kill highly visible dissidents. A time-delayed bomb, such as the one planted by Colonel Claus Von Stauffenberg to kill Hitler in 1944, also generally requires access to the target (or at least to a location he visits or passes by). With poisoning and time-delayed explosives, there is an opportunity for the assassin to escape, although due to the limited number of people that are likely to be allowed near the target, there is also a reasonably great chance that the killer will ultimately be identified. These killings are virtually always "inside jobs," almost certainly employing a local turncoat who the target believes to be loyal.

Technical assassinations are generally more long distance and require a degree of technical skill, either a long-range shot (rifle or perhaps rocket launcher, as happened to Anastasio Somoza when his armored limousine was taken out by a bazooka) or a remotely detonated explosion. They also generally give the assassin a greater shot at escape, as the assassin need not be in the immediate vicinity of the target to kill her. The difficulty of technical assassinations is reflected in the very name; as a bit of technical work, they require individuals who are highly skilled. This narrows the field considerably, as discussed above.

For the most part, access assassinations are more reliable, as the assassin has greater margin for error (e.g., a pistol from five feet versus a rifle from two hundred yards). Access operations, however, depend heavily on circumstance. If one happens to have an asset (i.e., an undercover volunteer) near the target individual, all well and good. On the other hand, potential targets often arise suddenly, and it may be necessary to "get rid of" one immediately. One is left with the choice of either trying to recruit potential assassins from the other side or sending in a highly skilled termination team. The latter was the idea behind ZR/RIFLE, the off-the-shelf assassination team planned by the CIA in the 1960s.

Off-the-Shelf: Executive Action

His name was Bill Harvey, and while his girth would have made about three James Bonds, he otherwise lived the part. He drank often, and hard. Unlike almost any other CIA officer, he carried a gun: In the middle of a tense discussion, he might casually take it out and lay it on his desk, pointed at his antagonist, or twirl it around his finger gunfighter-style. Bill Harvey was a buccaneer; Bill Harvey was an operator. In 1961, if you needed an assassination team set up, Bill Harvey was the man.

Under enormous pressure to "get" Castro in early 1961, DDP Richard Bissell tapped Bill Harvey to set up ZR/RIFLE. According to Harvey, the initial plan for this executive action team was simply to enlist a "spotter," a contract agent who would serve the CIA as a talent scout for international assassins. Harvey picked the ubiquitous QJ/WIN, a man of whom Richard Helms said, "If you needed somebody to carry out a murder, I guess you had a man who might be prepared to carry it out."[48] ZR/RIFLE also was intended as a team that would "research" assassination techniques, but apparently never got that far; as Harvey took over Task Force W (the anti-Cuban operation), ZR/RIFLE's activities were folded into the overall plans to get Castro.

The history of CIA assassination plots is replete with amateurism and haste, i.e., it is a record of failure. To our knowledge, in its hitman heyday, the CIA (or CIA contract operators) *never* successfully pulled off an assassination. Each operation either required that the agency depend on unreliable local recruits or hurriedly scrape together some plan with contract agents. Such operations are doomed to failure, and worse, exposure.

To overcome this problem, from time to time, someone suggests that the

CIA develop an off-the-shelf assassination unit: a team of professionals trained and ready to hit America's enemies whenever the call goes out from the White House or Langley. An off-the-shelf hit team, however, would be a very dangerous entity to exist in a society that hopes to stay free. A professional hit team would be an extremely tempting tool to employ in almost any circumstance. If a president thought he[49] had a weapon that could easily eliminate an uncooperative foreign leader without being traced back to the White House, we might see a whole spate of political killings. It would be far too easy for killing to become foreign policy: If we don't like a foreign leader, kill her and get a new one. Don't like the new one? Next! Foreign policy, however, is complex; bullets are no substitute for brains.

Whether or not wholesale assassination of whomever the president deems to be "bad guys" would be a good thing—certainly there are some reading this book who think it would—such activity would be almost impossible to conceal in the long term. Individuals on the team might spill the truth after a few too many beers, might experience an attack of conscience and remorse that could only be expelled by confession, might try to use their knowledge to blackmail the president or DCI, or might want to secure their places in history by writing a book (to be published posthumously, of course, but there's always the chance of a leak).

The most dangerous aspect of an executive action team is the power such a team would have. To be useful, it would have to be very good; if it was that good, it would be a sword of Damocles hanging forever over the neck of *any* head of state. It could, in fact, become a "killer elite," choosing who runs what. What if the team decided that a president of the United States wasn't acting in the best interest of the country? A good executive action team would likely become so powerful as to be corrupted absolutely. Moreover, such a team would truly be above the law; the members would know such dark secrets that they could never be tried for anything.[50] Such men and women could never be "retired," save on their own terms, which could prove expensive indeed.

Could the CIA not find individuals who are above reproach, whose loyalty to the United States (and the Constitution) is so rock-solid as to mitigate these drawbacks? Perhaps, at first. Individuals with the dedication and the skills certainly exist; many could be found in the SEAL Teams and the Special Forces. The CIA would, though, have to trust them not only in the beginning, but also have faith that their experiences would not change them; that cold-blooded assassination would not make them jaded and cynical, eroding their idealistic belief systems.

One must conclude that the standing executive action team is a bad idea. It creates a source of power and terror that is ultimately unaccountable to anyone, even the government that gave it birth.

We Have Met the Enemy and He Is Us . . .

One usually overlooked aspect of the practice of assassination is the effect it can have on an organization's own intelligence officers. Killing an individual for political purposes, arranging or encouraging such a killing, or merely knowing that "our side" does these things can seriously damage the individuals involved.

First, should the assassination succeed, it can encourage a belief that political killing is a preferred means of operation: clean, simple, straightforward; killing *is* policy. We might think of this as a self-reinforcing outcome of assassination. It is far too easy to develop a myopic vision of the world that reduces all policy problems to a few individuals, from which it follows that to eliminate the individual is to correct the problem.

There are also negative consequences for a country's own citizens. Many will have moral qualms about assassination. This is generally a good thing, as this ruthless tactic ought to be reserved for exceptional circumstances and opponents; U.S. policy and interests can scarcely be served by a chaotic world of leaderless states. This inherent morality, however, is a problem when individuals participate in or are aware of political slayings by their own side. If "our side" uses the same practices as "their side," how do we tell the good guys from the bad? To be sure, we can avow that *our* assassinations are rare, necessary, and committed with the best of intentions; but every despot makes the same claim: Don't judge me by my methods, but by my lofty ideals. This criterion, applied in the real world, provides no distinction at all.

When individuals with a moral foundation against murder (in general) observe their own government acting in what Americans traditionally believe is an underhanded way, they often experience what psychologists call "cognitive dissonance": a feeling of internal conflict created by trying to hold two contradictory beliefs simultaneously, in this case, "my country[51] is good, assassination is bad." When people experience such internal conflict, it usually affects their psyche and their behavior. Some retreat into a mind-set of separate logics: They "wall off" the contradictions, so that only one belief at a time surfaces, thereby separating themselves, to an extent, from reality. Intelligence agents may become disillusioned and cynical, and quit the intelligence service convinced that there are no moral precepts worth keeping, no real "right and wrong." A few, such as Philip Agee and Christopher Boyce, feel so betrayed by the apparent immorality of their own government that they sell out their own side and actually help the opposition.

Perhaps the ultimate risk is that the government might inadvertently create a small, ruthless cadre of assassins who, reveling in the power of life, death, and high politics, begin to assert their own policy preferences and act beyond the scope of their authorized operations. Such an organization might begin choosing its own targets, or even become a private government in and of itself—a modern version of the *hashishim* making its own foreign policy and serving its own interests even while hiding behind the cloak of partiotism.

The Logic of Elimination:
Or, How Assassination "Works"

Assassination has a powerful appeal. It is simple, dramatic, and decisive. If a foreign leader is a problem, eliminating him will eliminate the obstacle. While our sparse records of actual CIA and National Security Council discussions of assassination indicate that their thinking isn't quite so simplistic, it remains that one who believes that assassination is an effective policy tool *must* accept the logic of assassination.

At its core, this logic concludes that one individual changes everything. "Waste" Castro and freedom comes to Cuba; "pop" Saddam Hussein and put an end to Iraqi anthrax factories. This is essentially the rationale behind the "great man" theory of history: The direction of the world is shaped by a few individuals, and without Stalin and Hitler and Roosevelt and Lenin and Churchill and Castro and Saddam Hussein, the world would be a very different place.

This is a popular belief, and one that is easy to support. Graced by historical hindsight, practically *everything* appears to be determined by individual leaders. This kind of personal determinism, however, ignores a whole variety of political, economic, social, and cultural dynamics that influence the directions that nations and governments pursue.

First, every ruling executive, whether a president, prime minister, chief, dictator, or president-for-life, has some constituency that has to be pleased (or at least kept below the "violent rebellion threshold"). In democracies, these constituencies can be quite large: big business, banking, organized labor, religious or social groups, and so on. Even in dictatorships, however, the ruler does not literally rule alone; at the very least, a small elite class and key elements of the army must be satisfied. In dependent states, a leader might have to maintain a favorable business climate for multinational corporations. Thus, even dictators do not usually have a completely free hand; there are limits even for them.

Beyond quid pro quo constituent politics, rulers are constrained by other domestic considerations. Most large governments are bureaucracies with standard operating procedures dictating how things should be done. It takes quite a radical shift in government to change these all at once, and even then there is likely to be substantial "bureaucratic inertia" that resists change.

Several aspects of a country's position in the world also inhibit rapid changes in political direction. One of these is a country's history. Over time, a country and the people that make it up develop orientations toward the world that divide other countries into friends and enemies (with a lot of "indifferent" in the middle). Changing friends into foes and vice versa *does* happen, but is not an easy matter, and often requires a drastic change in the other country rather than a change in leadership in one's own government. This is particularly true when the antagonism has been very intense and deep-rooted. For example, even though the new government of Iran might desire more amicable relations with the

United States, the two countries' history of antagonism and years of indoctrination will be very hard to reverse.[52]

Another largely fixed national attribute that restricts and defines a regime's policy direction is the simple physical geography of the country. While it is hard to argue that geography itself determines if a government is friend or foe to the United States, the behavior that geography can lead to frequently causes friction between countries. The Russian drive to the south, toward Afghanistan and Iran, has long been understood as in part due to the need for a warm-water port that doesn't freeze in the winter. The accident of geography that put Kuwait on one side of a line and Iraq on the other produced the Gulf War in 1991. Can we imagine that *any* Iraqi leader, faced with a burgeoning population and a desire for prosperity, would not covet the sea of oil under Kuwait?

A country's position in the global power structure is another trait that will affect any leader's policies and orientation toward other powerful countries and the world as a whole. Some countries have traditionally viewed themselves as global or regional powers, and practically any leader who arises will endeavor to follow what is perceived to be national destiny. For hundreds of years, Britain had to be the continental sea power; Germany viewed itself as the natural power of Europe; Japan and China seek to fulfill destinies as leaders of Asia; after World War II, the United States became the "leader of the Free World." Leaders of many states simply must adopt these roles, or else they will never be accepted as leaders in the first place.

Finally, if a country is somehow dependent in the global system, any leader may find her newfound power rather less powerful than she imagined. Some client countries become so interlinked with their more powerful patrons that they cannot easily break away, if at all. Economically, a country may receive virtually all its foreign imports from a single country, and rely desperately on those imports for food or petroleum, for example. Conversely, it may send practically all its exports to a single country or two; cutting off that foreign exchange might devastate the dependent economy. Military dependence also occurs. When a country's armed forces buy most of their hardware, including tanks, aircraft, ships, radar, and communications systems, from one country, it is extremely difficult to sever ties with the supplier. Where will spare parts and maintenance come from? How can different military systems from other suppliers be integrated with the old equipment? Moreover, the current military is probably trained to use the tactics of the supplier country, which match the hardware. In other words, such a change as this requires that almost everything be revamped. It is almost always simpler and safer to continue in the already established path, no matter who the leader is. Finally, in countries in which changing leaders might create rapid changes of political orientation, e.g., personalist or autocratic governments, the leader almost always rules at the sufferance of the military leadership. This military has generally been trained and indoctrinated by the military of the patron country, and will probably view a change of orientation as a betrayal.

A cursory study of history might lead one to believe that changing the direction of world governments is simply a matter of getting some new leaders at the top. It should be clear, however, that complex social, political, and economic systems not only give power to national leaders, but also exert power over them. Merely changing the head doesn't necessarily change the *brain* of the system.

The second principle of the logic of assassination is that dramatic political events, such as a sudden change in leadership or a sudden vacuum, have predictable consequences. To the extent that we believe the actions of political groups can be accurately predicted, assassination is a valid tactic (this isn't a moral judgment, but a pragmatic one).[53] To this end, one must satisfactorily answer three basic questions before approving an assassination:

- Who is likely to replace the assassinated leader?
- Will this person adopt a more favorable policy?
- *Can* this person adopt a more favorable policy?

These questions get at the heart of the matter. A political killing is a risky endeavor undertaken to result in a better circumstance. If one cannot be reasonably certain that the alternatives will be better, then why take the risk? This logically requires, then, a follow-up plan in place to assure that the anointed replacement actually gets the job. One wouldn't want to kill the established leader merely to leave a vacuum that might be filled by anyone. Even worse, it is always possible that the replacement leader might be even more hostile toward the United States than the dead ruler. This means, of course, that to assure a successful outcome, a real assassination operation requires far more than a simple (or not-so-simple) killing; there must be a follow-up plan in place to exploit the opportunity. This is where assassinations turn into complex projects that cannot be kept secret.

The kind of regime the potential target heads also makes a vital difference in whether an assassination can change the course of a government. We can think of types of governments as falling along a continuum. At one end are the *institutionalized* governments with set procedures, laws, enforceable constitutions, bureaucracies, rules of succession, and in many cases predesignated successors— for example, the United States and Great Britain, or the bureaucratized dictatorships such as the Soviet Union. At the opposite end are the *personalist* regimes, governments essentially controlled by one person or a small group, often family, whose word is law and who is answerable to no one, e.g., Iraq, Libya, Cambodia under Pol Pot, and Saudi Arabia. The logic is this: The more institutionalized the government, the less likely an assassination will substantially change that government's policies. Merely removing a single leader might bring a less competent person, or one with differing political views, to power, but the new leader will still be bound by the various constituencies and bureaucracies that make up the *system* of political power. Moreover, in such cases, the successor may be unable to change the policies of the predecessor precisely because the assassinated leader was "martyred." Kill a "maximum leader" (*el jefé maximo*), of a personalist regime, however, and power is up for grabs. Power-seeking individuals established by a "winner-kill-all" political system are prone be at each others' throats immediately; here, a well-prepared leader can step in (1) with some assurance, and (2) with the real power to change national policies and direction.

It is also very risky to assassinate the only leader who is stabilizing a country (e.g., Tito). If a country is likely to explode into violent anarchy (e.g., Yugoslavia, some of the former Soviet republics, and many Third World states), there is much to be lost by a U.S.-orchestrated assassination. Mass political violence, insurgency, and terrorism are weapons that just about anyone can use. By breaking down established order, an assassination can level the playing field, depriving the United States of its most powerful weapon: economic leverage, including access to technology and weapons. Moreover, if one is to require a certain policy from the government that succeeds that of the assassinated leader, there must first *be* a government that controls the institutions of state. Perhaps, in hindsight, we can imagine circumstances in which anarchy as a result of assassination would have been preferable to allowing a foreign leader to continue his rule—e.g., Hitler, about 1935—but such conditions are rare indeed.

The third requirement of the logic of assassination is that the assassination must "work." Whenever the CIA or American decision makers discuss assassination, there is always great concern that if the United States undertakes an assassination, that the plan work. Seldom, however, does anyone think about the critical underlying question: What do we mean by an assassination "working"? This is important because the purpose of the assassination *isn't* to kill someone; the end goal is to change a regime or its policies. Without asking the question "what is success?" one cannot ever be certain that assassination is part of a logical chain of events that leads to a desirable outcome.

We can consider success in assassination as having two levels: *tactical* and *strategic*. Tactical success means that the target has indeed been killed; strategic success means that the desired end result, e.g., a change in government policy, has been realized.

There are three levels of tactical success in an assassination operation. First, is the target eliminated? Is there a high likelihood that either the target will be disposed of or else the plan will remain unrevealed? Second, did the assassin get away, and leave no evidence of U.S. complicity? If one is evaluating an operation, careful attention must be paid to covering the assassin's tracks. Third, does the plan provide for a patsy to take the fall, or is there at least some evidence planted to mislead investigators and the press? This most difficult part of a scheme is also the most important, for without someone else to take the blame, the United States could be looking at another set of ugly congressional hearings. There is perhaps a fourth criterion for tactical success: Does the plan provide for relatively little collateral damage, i.e., does it avoid killing a lot of innocent bystanders? In a crisis or wartime situation, this might be less of a consideration, but for peacetime assassinations, wholesale slaughter is considered a bit of a bad show.

Assuming a plan can reasonably promise to achieve a tactical success—the target will be rendered biologically inoperative, the CIA will not be blamed—one can turn to the larger questions of strategic success. The first, and least successful, strategic outcome is that the United States prevented an outcome, government, or policy it didn't want. This doesn't mean that one gets a favorable outcome, merely that some foreseeable negative consequence has been averted. A slightly better outcome is that the killing allows someone more favorable to the United States, or to specific policies, to take over. Usually this is a national politician who is prominent and popular yet opposed to the assassinated leader, or a military officer who steps in to "restore order" for twenty or thirty years (e.g., Joseph Mobutu, Augusto Pinochet, Suharto, the shah of Iran). The third and highest level of strategic success is that the "friendly" regime created out of the assassination remains stable, i.e., it's on our side and will remain there without further intervention.[54] A fourth (mythical) level of strategic mastery would be to create a democracy out of the chaos left by assassination. This never seems to be a major concern of those plotting assassinations, however (at least in the U.S. government); besides, at least in the Congo and Chile, assassinations were conducted precisely to *nullify* democracy.

Historically, the U.S. government has gone to great lengths to combine various economic and political operations with assassinations and coups specifically to try to create stability out of an assassination or coup d'etat. Often, the target regime is economically and politically destabilized beforehand (see chapter 13); once the target nation's economy and sociopolitical system is beaten down, the ruler who replaces the corpse is provided with lavish aid and assistance from the United States, thereby producing, in the short term at least, a "miracle." The promise of plentiful American money is often made to potential political successors to encourage them to venture their own overthrow of unfavorable regimes.

There are, of course, other notions of success that have nothing to do with changing governments or policies. They are still, however, important to understand, because these motivations are often what drives a locally recruited assassin that our government might try to manipulate. One possibility is revenge: A local asset might simply be getting even for some wrong done to his family, village, or religious group. Beyond this, an indigenous assassin might act merely to make a point or draw attention to a cause. Finally, it is possible, from a moral perspective, that a native killer can act in the name of justice; according to Western political ethics, if it is executed by a citizen of the state, tyrannicide is not murder.

Why is it important to understand these motives? If the CIA can get a national to liquidate a mutual enemy, isn't that all to the good? Perhaps. Different motivations, though, might easily affect the way in which our assassin performs his task. Rather than escaping through a carefully prepared "rat line" (escape route), the killer might instead prefer a spectacular public death in car-

rying out the assassination. Perhaps he desires to be captured to promote a political position from the splendid soapbox provided by a public trial or execution.
He might ache for martyrdom. Such postassassination events, in particular, can
knock plausible deniability into a cocked hat. Spectacular assassins can be identified from videotape, perhaps as American sympathizers; captured assassins can
be tortured and forced to reveal their contacts. To select and vet an indigenous
assassin, therefore, it is critical to understand his motivation.

In short, assassination is never a simple affair, rather, it follows a logic that is
both inexorable and demanding, requiring predictable political outcomes, government systems with significant decision-making latitude that a single individual can control, and a follow-up program to ensure strategic success. Given the
practical risks involved in killing a foreign head of state, there are probably few
circumstances in which assassination can provide any benefit to the United States,
especially if considered in light of broad political goals and long-term objectives.
Finally, assassination is largely viewed, accurately, as a failure of policy; like terrorism, it is a tactic of weakness. It is to that consideration we turn next.

Assassination: Playing the Poor Man's Game

One of the major reasons not to practice assassination of political foes is precisely
because the United States is so powerful in other ways: economically, financially,
technologically, militarily. When an international issue is contested in these
arenas, the United States is almost certain to prevail. On the other hand, assassination is a game that virtually every country can play, and some perhaps better
than America. In some parts of the world, suicide bombers are almost a dime a
dozen; few Americans would so joyously embrace death. Moreover, the United
States is almost uniquely vulnerable to assassins. The president, of course, is
guarded as well as possible, but is still one of the most exposed heads of state in
the world. American presidents seem to feel an overwhelming urge to "work"
crowds—how can one be protected against the kind of suicide bomber that killed
Rajiv Gandhi? What if a foreign assassin were to fire into the president's car with
a shoulder-fired antitank missile (e.g., a light antitank weapon [LAW], or
Bazooka-type weapon)? Against government-supported assassins with money and
weapons and intelligence services behind them, the president is unguardable.[55]

Moreover, it's not only the president who is vulnerable to the assassin. Thousands of government officials and corporate executives might be targets of retaliation should the government of the United States be exposed as complicit in an
assassination. Foreign "rogue" regimes are perfectly capable of deciding that
assassinating the president is too difficult a task, and perhaps the New York Yan-
kees would make a simpler target. In a free society like the United States, with
unrestricted travel, relatively porous borders, and easy access to firearms and
explosives, virtually anyone could pay the price for a CIA-sponsored assassination.

Furthermore, assassination of a political leader is an act of war. Few countries capable of fighting would overlook such a provocation: Should an assassi-

nation fail, or fail to install a U.S.-friendly replacement, the prospects for terrorism and assassination against American targets is greatly increased, if for no other reason than to "satisfy national honor." By killing or even attempting to assassinate a foreign leader, the United States provides automatic justification for the target regime to assassinate U.S. leaders. Further, it allows third countries (those not part of the initial assassination plan) to point to U.S. actions as precedent; how can the United States condemn Libyan hit squads if America itself is sending out assassins?

Because of the volatile nature of assassinating a foreign head of state, it is generally undertaken in only two circumstances. First, if the government can be absolutely certain it will never be exposed, then the assassination won't create a *casus belli*—cause for war. In the world of international relations, however, there are few secrets. If two countries have been hostile, the leader of one is mysteriously assassinated, and the other has an established history of assassination, where else can the finger point? In this case, even if a government is completely innocent, the gasoline is spilled on the floor anyway. In practical terms, this means that if a government is going to assassinate a foreign head of state, it *must* set up a logical fall guy, or "patsy," to quote Lee Harvey Oswald. It's not enough that the leader dies; he or she must be positively seen to have been the victim of some third party. Otherwise, the government must prepare for war, terrorism, or assassination-in-kind.

Second, a government can assassinate the leaders of weak countries who have no powerful, reliable allies. If the weak country declares war, so what? There might be a bit of terrorism, but what is the Congo, or Iraq, or Chile going to do the United States? One has to ask, however, if the countries are weak to begin with, isn't there some better way that a powerful nation like the United States can deal with them? What's the purpose of being powerful if it all comes down to a single, sweaty shooter?

As the most powerful country in the world, the United States should strive to create international norms or rules of behavior that eventually come, by tradition, to constrain other governments. It is easy to scoff at the idea of international rules of behavior that all governments will obey. International politics is, to many, a cutthroat game with no rules except "win." The power of established ethics cannot be dismissed out of hand, however. By establishing *and following* a set of rules, the United States and other countries can achieve several objectives. First, the shield all dictators and assassins hide behind is this: "Everyone does it." Even more frustrating is the truth: "The United States does it." By demonstrating that *not* everyone does something, it becomes far easier to identify and isolate those who do. By distancing the U.S. government from the actions of the past, America regains the privilege of moral outrage that it sacrificed in the 1960s. Furthermore, it is a mistake to underestimate the power of moral outrage. While morality in itself may not move many (or any) of the governments of the world, it is a critical ingredient in mobilizing the people of those countries to undertake great efforts and bear sacrifice; martyrs are powerful symbols indeed. Thus, moral outrage is power, and should be nurtured.

Of course there will be nefarious regimes that continue to plot assassinations, just as there are those who will not give up land mines or anthrax or suicide bombers. Is it necessary, though, to base our own policies and morality on the actions of the most contemptible countries? Instead, we might recall that it is American *principle* that defines America. This is not a short-run strategy to attempt to raise the overall civilization level of international politics, but rather one that might, in the longer run, help raise it to a higher moral plane. In a crisis, it is usually easier in the short run to sacrifice all manner of things, like freedom of speech and press and a legislature and elections, to the demands of emergency. Yet the United States has survived both civil and world wars while maintaining a semblance of freedom.

One can cynically argue that the best practice is to publically condemn assassination, in hopes of limiting other governments, while at the same time privately reserving for ourselves the right to kill a foreign leader on rare occasion. After all, isn't that the point of plausible deniability? This would have some merit, except for two realities. First, when assassinations occur, they have to be performed by *somebody*: A specific fall guy must be set up to take the blame; otherwise, any assassination of a U.S. opponent will be blamed on the CIA. Moreover, aside from the convincing evidence that the fall guy did the killing, there must be absolutely persuasive proof that he had no connection to the United States government.

Second, it should be obvious by now that secrecy around an assassination plot is almost bound to fail. Ultimately, these things blow up in your face. Plausible deniability for such public acts of violence is a chimera.[56]

Assassination is where two of the fundamental laws of international politics converge: (1) the pursuit of power, and (2) reciprocity. These combine neatly in the phrase, "Do unto others before they do it to you." If the United States practices assassination, even only on rare occasions, then it has no right to complain if other countries try to kill American leaders. The high ground of moral outrage will have been sacrificed, and no amount of "they do it too" will regain it. Only by foregoing assassination does the U.S. government retain the right to condemn others for it.

Authorizing Assassination: No Paper, No Control

You'll never see a signed order from the president of United States to assassinate someone; it doesn't exist. Even decisions to cooperate, or merely keep in touch, with foreign groups who plan to kill their own government leaders are never put to paper or recorded on tape. There are good reasons for this.

Assassination is a grubby, dirty business, one that doesn't square with the American self-image of honor, decency, fair play, and other John Wayne-like virtues. Americans don't want to envision their president sitting in the White House saying, like a Mafia don, "Kill him"; American presidents know this. Thus, orders to kill must be held *very* close to the vest, and when given, must be carefully euphemized to permit plausible deniability.

For the patriotic assassin, this creates a dilemma. How does a CIA officer, Delta Force shooter, or obedient contact agent ever know for sure that his orders to kill are actually authorized by the president? Without a written confirmation, the person connected to the finger on the trigger has to rely on the chain of command; contrary to what happens in spy novels, assassins are not personally briefed by the president. Orders must be passed from the president to the DCI to the DDO (Deputy Director for Operations, the current title for the head of covert operations) and certainly through one or more other intermediaries before the person who actually squeezes the trigger gets the word. Each step of the way, it is possible for orders to be misconstrued, ignored, or most critically, invented. Because of the number of cutouts, there arises the unsettling possibility that someone in the chain can essentially order an assassination on his own, simply by asserting that the orders came from above, e.g., ". . . HIGHEST AUTHORITY. . . ." In such a case, it might be possible to check; when asked to serve as case officer for the Lumumba assassination, CIA officer Justin O'Donnell flat out refused, and reported the order to both his immediate superior in operations, Richard Helms, and to CIA Inspector General Lyman Kirkpatrick.[57] Kirkpatrick shared O'Donnell's aversion to assassination and took the protest to DCI Allen Dulles, who had, of course, ordered the assassination. Such challenges to authorization seem rare, however. Throughout the Lumumba operation, each individual operated on the assumption that his superior had specific authorization for the killing. Most often, however, assassinations have been and will continue to be carried out by contract agents, ideally unsure themselves who they're actually working for. This is the point, after all, of employing contract agents. By insisting on cutouts, however, there remains the inherent problem that a rogue officer or cowboy could order an assassination.[58]

This problem stems from two other issues. First, the need to maintain the image of the president and the United States means that such matters cannot be handled through the normal chain of command processes, which by its very nature generates reams of paper. Cabinet secretaries, the DCI, and even White House staffers would all take great pains to insulate a president from even the appearance of having issued an order to kill a head of state. John Eisenhower, the president's son and staff member who attended many of the NSC meetings, said, "I would not conjecture that the words 'disposed of' meant an assassination, if for no other reason than if I had something as nasty as this to plot, I wouldn't do it in front of 21 people."[59] Among executives at the CIA and the National Security Council, it is axiomatic as well as a source of pride that one would never reveal such a secret even under penalty of perjury.

Coupled with this is the president's own cognizance of appearances—with, perhaps, some perception of the dignity of the office thrown in. For this reason, presidents have relied on euphemism and beating around the bush when it comes to ordering a political killing; they have apparently depended heavily on their subordinates to grasp the real intent behind the circumlocution. The historical record seems pretty clear that when a president talks about "getting rid of" someone, it *can* mean killing them.

There is a clear path around this, should the president desire: He can speak of "getting rid of" political foes, as long as it's made explicitly clear that *this doesn't mean killing them.* A president might directly say, "This does *not* mean assassinate this individual." Presumably, the purpose of the presidential executive order prohibiting assassination by agents of the U.S. government is to make everyone understand what "get rid of" *doesn't* mean. Naturally, this doesn't eliminate the possibility of assassination, for the chief executive can always take aside the DCI to tell him, "Forget what I just said; that was for public consumption. Do whatever you have to. . . ."[60] However, short of this kind of wheels-within-wheels plotting, this method allows us to be relatively certain in the negative—there is no assassination authorized.

What happens in the event that a president *does* want to issue an assassination order? How does the president give a positive command while (1) preserving deniability, and (2) assuring the necessary individuals in the chain of command that the directive is indeed authorized "at the highest level"? It is probably impossible. Unless the president personally briefs the person who will do the killing, then each individual in the chain of command simply has to trust his superior. The only real protection against unauthorized assassination is an attempt to ensure that there are no cowboys in the organization.

Assassination of Terrorists and Others

Up to now, we have been discussing the thorny problem of assassinating foreign government leaders, but there is another issue much discussed lately: Why not simply exterminate terrorists like Osama bin Laden? While it's unlikely an American agent could get close enough to shoot him, perhaps a car bomb could do the trick. Would this not be a simple solution to one of the major terrorist problems faced by the United States today?

There are, for the most part, good reasons not to assassinate foreign heads of state. It is not necessarily true, however, that all these apply to assassinations where the target is not a head of state. Osama bin Laden and others like him do not necessarily warrant the same protected status as antagonistic foreign rulers. Governments and foreign political officials are accorded a special protected status by both international law and traditional practice. Some of this comes from common decency, but is mainly enforced by the threat of reciprocity: "If you do something to one of my diplomats, I might do the same to one of yours, and my retribution may be perceived as justifiable by the international community." Reciprocity, however, cannot easily be applied to private individuals, terrorists, and so forth; they have no country, no economy to embargo, no diplomats to expel, no assets to seize. Often they live in a country hostile to the United States under the protection of a foreign government. If the United States does not want to commit acts that may create a war against that country, or contribute to a climate of international violence, must it simply wait to be attacked again? *Why not* go after these killers?

There are numerous reasons why such people are excellent candidates for assassination:

- First: No matter how ironclad the evidence against a terrorist, and no matter how egregious the crime, the individual might find sanctuary or even be protected by a foreign government. In these cases, should the international community simply permit him or her to remain at large, free to plan, organize, and commit future atrocities? If a rogue country fails to live up to the obligations of civilized nations, should that state simply be regarded as a safe haven?
- Second: Swift, carefully directed, and public retribution in the form of a bullet or quarter pound of C-4 plastic explosive may not only disrupt a terrorist organization, but also serve to deter others who would attack U.S. interests. If well done, it might even destroy the insurgent or terrorist organization altogether.
- Third: Assassinating transnational terrorists, those who are based in several countries and flow easily across international boundaries, may actually be doing some of the terrorists' base-country governments a favor. Some of them have little actual control over their own territory, and do not necessarily want terrorist groups operating out of their countries, but are powerless to stop them. Others face political constraints, such as the popularity of the terrorist organization or leader, that may prevent the government from acting. Further, terrorist organizations often "reserve" base countries as targets; they do not perform violence within these states, with the implication that they *could* if their protected status in these "safe havens" is violated. Thus, in at least some cases, the United States could obtain the tacit approval and support of the "host" government.
- Fourth: Even if the United States desperately desires a public trial, an assassination might be a simpler option than a moonlight extradition. Moreover, once the target is dead, there is no chance that he will ever commit another atrocity; there is no chance that he might escape from prison; there is no chance that his minions will take hostages to exchange for him.
- Fifth: While assassination is currently illegal under U.S. law, (1) the law is only an executive order, and can be reversed at any time—secretly if necessary—by presidential directive, and (2) it only applies to foreign heads of state; there is no mention of other individuals.

As with head-of-state assassinations, however, there are substantial reasons to refrain from extrajudicial killings. Four of these are practical. First, by directly attacking terrorist leaders or their bases, the United States risks stimulating even more acts of terrorism against American targets as the terrorists seek retribution. Second, there is the chance that the assassins may be captured and expose the hand of the United States in such a nefarious business. This would not only cause some embarrassment in Washington and Langley, but might also cost the United States considerable foreign goodwill. Most importantly, such actions would allow other countries to use the United States's activities to justify their own assassination operations; the United States would again sacrifice the right to moral outrage when a U.S. citizen is murdered on a foreign street. Third, open U.S. violence in a foreign land always has the potential to destabilize the foreign government. Elites, the military, and the people at large may start asking why the government cannot protect the nation's sovereignty, why it accepts a slap in the face from the Americans. Fourth, it is always possible that a hit team might kill the wrong person, as happened to the Israeli "Wrath of God" unit, which killed someone in Sweden thought to be a ringleader of the Munich Massacre terrorists; the corpse turned out to be a waiter. As with any assassination attempt, there is also the potential for accidental death of innocents, which could turn into a very nasty international situation.

The most important reasons to refrain from assassinations relate to who and what the people of the United States *are*. If the United States goes around waging dirty little assassin wars, killing people without trial and slinking away like a thief in the night, then what is the difference between *us* and *them*? If the American system of government is a valuable example to humanity, it is because of the rule of law; in contrast, assassination operations smack of anger, secrecy, and revenge, not the majestic deliberation of justice. Besides, look at the list of governments that send out assassination teams: Iran, Iraq, Libya, the Soviet Union, Chile under Pinochet, Argentina, Guatemala, and Israel.[61] Is this the kind of company America wants to keep? Finally, such operations are, of course, illegal under international law. While there is little or no enforcement of this law, international order in general benefits the United States; anything that erodes order in the international system usually harms American interests.

Despite the drawbacks, if a government decides to run the risk of assassinating foreign enemies who aren't heads of state, the preceding discussion illuminates some ways to make the most of the slaying while minimizing potential costs. First, such actions should only be undertaken if they carry the promise of destroying the terrorist organization or disrupting pending violent operations. Second, there should be clear and persuasive evidence that the target is guilty of crimes against humanity and is planning more; this allows one the claim that the termination is either meting out justice or preemptive self-defense. Third, if the evidence is clear but cannot be made public (i.e., it is well corroborated but comes from a source who would be in danger if exposed), then the assassination should be carried out in the most deniable manner possible: (1) no connection with the United States, and (2) with a prepared fall guy to take the blame. Fortunately, patsies are often easy to come by in these circumstances, for often the individuals most deadly to underground militants are other factions of similar groups.

Given the potential risks of such activities, however, a government should be very certain that the game is worth the candle. While many of the benefits from refraining from assassination seem to be intangible, they nonetheless may have real effects. Foreign friends find it much easier to be cooperative and helpful, and to ally themselves for serious matters such as the Gulf War, when there is a clearly drawn line between the good guys and the bad. Whether it is assistance in a war or helping track and apprehend terrorists, such friendship should not be lightly sacrificed. Finally, it must be said that such assassinations must be *very* rare occasions indeed, and therein lies the rub. There is a clear line between "no assassinations" and "some assassinations." It is there for everyone to see, and intelligence operators down the chain of command can easily determine whether an order is lawful of not: If one is commanded to assassinate someone, it's an illegal order. The lines between "rare assassination," "some assassinations," and "a lot of assassinations," however, are blurry and difficult to maintain. For the patriotic, disciplined shooter, it becomes a tricky proposition to ensure that assassination orders are properly authorized. For the government, it becomes impossible to deny involvement in assassinations that it is *not* engaged in, since it *does* perform such undertakings. Finally, by engaging in any assassinations at all, a government jumps through a plate glass window and lands on a slippery slope: If Hitler, why not Saddam Hussein? If Saddam Hussein, why not Gadhafi? If Gadhafi, why not thirty other individuals down the list that have done evil things? It could become far too easy to drift into the habit of extrajudicial killing, degrading the very rule of law the policy is ostensibly intended to guard. Should that be the result, the terrorists will have won.

"We Don't Target Individuals": Nonassassination Assassinations

In recent years, the United States has tried to kill three foreign leaders: Mu'ammar Gadhafi, Saddam Hussein, and Osama bin Laden (there's no use denying this; we're not stupid). In each case, U.S. armed forces heavily bombed locations where the leaders were thought and hoped to be. In each case, too, the United States government denied that these assaults were assassination attempts, *because there was no effort to target the specific individual.* In other words, if we don't put the target reticle directly on Saddam's head, we didn't mean for him *specifically* to die, ergo, it's war, not assassination.

These attempted killings have been pursued under the cover of larger operations: in the case of Gadhafi and bin Laden, retaliation for prior acts by striking terrorist and military bases, and in the case of Saddam Hussein, as part of wartime operations aimed at enemy command and control centers. While these are useful cover stories, the U.S. government did, in fact, intend to kill these individuals.

There are two good reasons to deny this. First, military retaliation may be justified under both U.S. and international law, while assassination is not. If specific individuals are killed as part of justifiable retribution or a justified preemptive attack, the death can be considered merely the fortunes of war. For American officials, it is vital to claim that these were not exactly attempted assassinations, since assassination is illegal, although not as clearly so in the case of bin Laden, who is not a head of state. In fact, in 1998, the U.S. Department of Justice investigated a CIA operative who had been based in northern Iraq to determine whether or not he had conspired, planned, or assisted in an assassination plot against Saddam Hussein. It is unclear what would have happened had the agent been indicted, as this law has never been tested in court.

Because terrorism itself is such a difficult problem, with no obvious and identifiable enemy or targets, and therefore no way enforce "rules" by the threat of reciprocity, it is tempting to claim that one is not bound by the traditional rules of war and fair play. This is especially true when terrorists are accorded sanctuary and protection in foreign countries. Further, much as the argument goes with covert action, so too the argument can be made about these military strikes: they are low-cost operations in terms of risk to American personnel.

There is a real danger, however, in slinging around Tomahawk cruise missiles too freely. First, most of the arguments against assassination also apply to these "nonassassinations." Moreover, unlike a covert assassination, the identity of the perpetrator is apparent to the world. While this may desirable—e.g., we have nothing to be ashamed of, and we want our foes to know we will hold them accountable—acts of war may undermine the position of the United States throughout an entire region, much as U.S. interventions have, for example, in Latin America. Further, when one of these attacks fails to hit the *real* target, he may emerge politically strengthened by his survival, perhaps (usually) claiming divine protection. Such failures also reinforce the perception of the United States as (1) unwilling to take truly effective action, (2) unwilling to pay the price for effective action, or (3) not competent to perform effective action. In any case, it is difficult to see how this strengthens the position of the United States.

Nevertheless, nonassassinations are already a common U.S. tactic, not to be confused with an actual policy. They permit a president to show that *something* is being done. They cost relatively little and they risk no American lives. In a world in which terrorism is difficult or impossible to stop, they allow the American people to feel good about being so powerful, and reassure them that everything is under control. In a post–cold war world where the old assumptions no longer hold and where uncertainty abounds, this is the real reason that military strike nonassassinations are here to stay.

ASSASSINATION: A NOT-SO-SIMPLE OPTION

If you travel around Africa, you will find numerous statues of Patrice Lumumba. Had he merely been another failed prime minister of a resource-rich Third World country, he probably wouldn't even be a footnote in history. Patrice Lumumba, however, is remembered all over the Third World, even by the people of nominally unfriendly nations, as a man who stood up to the colonialists. The Soviet Union chose to name their school for subversion and Third World revolution Patrice Lumumba University. The CIA made Lumumba a hero and a martyr.[62]

Assassination will always be a seductive option when a government is faced with difficult foreign policy challenges, especially antagonists who are personally malevolent, such as Saddam Hussein. It promises to reduce complex situations to something manageable and simpler, e.g., personal relationships. It promises to eliminate the necessity of wise and patient exercise of power. Like those who pursued the Sirens of mythology, however, those who respond to the siren song of assassination are liable to wreck themselves, their nation's interest, and their nation's good name. There are, on the whole, *many* powerful reasons to refrain from assassination:

- One cannot be certain the replacement will be better, and she could be worse.
- The foreign government may continue on its present path despite a new leader, especially if the government bureaucracy is comprised of stable institutions.
- American government offices, businesses, and citizens are uniquely vulnerable to assassination and terrorist warfare, and it is best not to provide a provocation of such acts.
- Creating martyrs is often a bad idea; creating permanent enemies among other nations is even worse.
- Assassination is a game every government can play, and it is to the advantage of the United States to persuade governments to play in more formal "games"—e.g., economic competition, diplomacy, social and cultural saturation—in which the United States has distinct advantages.
- Assassinations are hard to keep secret, and hard to deny; it is too easy for a government to be forced to prove its innocence, which is impossible.
- It is difficult to find assassins who are deniable, can keep their mouth shut, can do the job professionally, and can get near enough to the target to finish the job.
- It is very easy to open the door of assassination; it is much harder to close it again, and to regain a good reputation in the aftermath.
- The process of authorizing assassination blurs the chain of command to the point where subordinates might easily order such acts on their own.
- The desire to undertake effective assassinations can easily lead to the creation of a professional assassination unit (ZR/RIFLE), an undertaking particularly hazardous to a democracy.
- Engaging in *any* assassinations blurs the line between the good guys and the bad; and allows the bad guys to use America as a precedent.

While there may be rare occasions in which assassination can achieve significant and long-term objectives, it should generally be viewed for what it is: a proclamation of weakness and an admission of failure.

NOTES

1. This chapter deals primarily with assassination of foreign leaders, rather than the killing or political murder of lower positioned individuals, e.g., military officers, editors, priests, and so forth. Killing of these individuals is so commonplace as to hardly be worth notice, especially when carried out by agents of repressive regimes, Left or Right.

2. A simple postmaster could rise to prominence so swiftly in large part because when the Congo achieved its independence from Belgium, fewer than a dozen citizens were college graduates.

3. An excellent account of the background to and story of the Lumumba assassination is Jonathan Kwitny's *Endless Enemies: The Making of an Unfriendly World* (New York: Penguin, 1984), chap. 4, 5. The account in this chapter is drawn from this as well as from Senate, *Interim Report of the Select Committee to Study Governmental Operations with Respect to Intelligence Activities*, "Alleged Assassination Plots Involving Foreign Leaders," 94th Cong., 1st sess, 1975, S. Rept. 94-465, pp. 13–67.

4. Senate, "Alleged Assassination Plots," p. 14.

5. Ibid., p. 15.

6. Ibid.

7. Ibid., p. 17.

8. Ibid., p. 21.

9. This is the same Sid Gottlieb who ran some of the CIA's mind control experiments under MKULTRA and ARTICHOKE.

10. Senate, "Alleged Assassination Plots," p. 17.

11. Ibid., p. 43.

12. It is my belief that the bombing of Gadhafi's residence is a blatantly apparent fourth case of attempted assassination. We're not sure what has been going on in Iraq, although it seems virtually certain that agents of the United States have encouraged potential coup leaders to assassinate Saddam Hussein.

13. Senate, "Alleged Assassination Plots," p. 55. It is somewhat ironic that the best defense of Eisenhower in this case is that he wouldn't be stupid enough to say such a thing to the National Security Council; in Ike's case, this is an important argument.

14. "Government by theft."

15. Inspector General's Survey of the Cuban Operation, October 1961, p. 11. Declassified 19 February 1998. Reprinted in Peter Kornbluh, ed., *Bay of Pigs Declassified* (New York: New Press, 1998).

16. For the information of the humor-challenged, I'm being facetious here; assassination is the result of failed statecraft.

17. It's his real name; you can look it up.

18. Inspector General's Survey, pp. 21–22.

19. Senate, "Alleged Assassination Plots," pp. 74–75. One presumes that Maheu would have been a poor detective indeed if he didn't know Roselli was "connected."

20. Ironically (or perhaps not), the CIA thought it was buying a "Jack Ruby" kind of shooting.

21. Inspector General's Survey, p. 25.

22. Senate, "Alleged Assassination Plots," pp. 80–82.

23. E. Howard Hunt, *Give Us This Day* (New York: Arlington House, 1973), p. 38.

24. It is unclear what these negotiations were really about. Commonly, they are

reported to have been aimed at normalizing U.S. relations with Cuba; however, this would seem to have been an unlikely goal for the brothers Kennedy.

25. Inspector General's Survey, p. 77.

26. See Thomas Powers, *The Man Who Kept the Secrets: Richard Helms and the CIA* (New York: Pocket Books, 1979), p. 190.

27. Senate, "Alleged Assassination Plots," pp. 89–90.

28. This is the same Frank Sturgis who was arrested as one of the Watergate burglars, and who many have claimed was involved in the assassination of John F. Kennedy.

29. Marita Lorenz, interview on *CIA: Executive Action*, Arts and Entertainment Network, 1992.

30. The best account I know of is in Powers, *The Man Who Kept the Secrets*, pp. 161, 163, and even this is very sketchy.

31. Certainly in *this* case, "incapacitate" was interpreted as "kill."

32. This does not include, however, the two attempted *military* asssassinations: the bombing raid attempts on Mu'ammar Gadhafi and the cruise missile attachs on Saddam Hussein during the Gulf War. Maybe these weren't cases of a lone sniper, but the U.S. government sure as hell meant to kill 'em.

33. One list, complied by author William Blum, contains 36 plots against individuals (or groups in a couple of cases). Unfortunately, not all the cases are well documented in his book. See William Blum, *Killing Hope: U.S. Military and CIA Interventions Since World War II* (Monroe, Maine: Common Courage Press, 1995), p. 453.

34. It's unclear why conspirators from the Chilean military would need to get weapons and grenades from agents of the United States, other than that the weapons served a bit like "earnest money" to ensure the involvement of the Americans, in the hopes that once entangled, the United States would be forced to support the coup rather than risk failure and the certainty of heightened animosity should the Allende government survive.

35. See the *Chicago Tribune*, 15 June 1975, p. 1.

36. It is unclear whether this was a sincere rebuke, or whether Dulles was merely establishing a deniable paper trail (as seems most likely). See Senate, *Final Report of the Select Committee to Study Governmental Operations with Respect to Intelligence Activities*. Book 4: "Supplementary Detailed Staff Reports on Foreign and Military Intelligence," 94th Cong., 2d sess., 1976, S. Rept. 94-755, p. 133.

37. Miles Copeland, *The Game of Nations* (New York: Simon and Schuster, 1969), p. 202.

38. Of course, the United States would *say* that this is not precedent, that it's a one-shot deal. It is hard to imagine, however, that some of the savvy and less-secure potentates of the region would believe it.

39. While the CIA was involved in both these assassinations, we must also allocate "credit" where it is due. Diem's "removal" was explicitly authorized by two men from President Kennedy's National Security Council, and Trujillo's assassins were cheered on by members of the U.S. State Department, including the ambassador to the Dominican Republic.

40. See Michael Walzer, *Just and Unjust Wars* (New York: Basic Books, 1977), p. 80.

41. Don't argue that the one death might not stop the war anyway; that's a *practical* objection, not a *moral* argument.

42. See Franklin Ford, *Political Murder: From Tyrannicide to Terrorism* (Cambridge: Harvard University, 1985), pp. 277–79.

43. "Probables" include Eisenhower (Lumumba), Kennedy (Castro), Reagan (Gadhafi), Bush (Saddam Hussein). Nixon (Allende, Castro) is a "good probable."

44. In the many times I have taught my class on covert action, I was always surprised at one belief often shared by many of the students: that finding cold-blooded killers in the U.S. military would be a simple task. While there almost certainly are some, *useful* cold-blooded killers are thankfully rare.

45. At least not unless they are a part of an operation that includes planting verifiable evidence that someone *not* the United States government did it.

46. See Burton Hersh, *The Old Boys: The American Elite and the Origins of the CIA* (New York: Charles Scribner's Sons, 1992), pp. 279–80.

47. Senate, "Alleged Assassination Plots," p. 182.

48. Or she, perhaps someday, but from historical experience I'm simply going to say "he" in this context. Besides, we all know that a woman would *never* resort to such dirty dealings—don't we?

49. One could, of course, try them in secret and then keep them incommunicado for the rest of their lives; or perhaps assassinate *them*. This sequence of events, however, doesn't seem like a promising way to defend democracy, which presumably was the point of forming the team in the first place.

50. Agee has spent roughly the last twenty years doing all the damage he can to the CIA and its operations. There is a fairly widespread feeling among CIA officers that he actually worked for the Soviets, perhaps even while he was still with the Company. To my knowledge, there is no hard evidence to support this. Chris Boyce was the subject of the book and movie *The Falcon and the Snowman*. He was so outraged by CIA interference in Australian politics that he began spying for the KGB.

51. In my academic foreign policy work, I describe this process as (1) forgiving (a function of developing shared values and of "friendship" developing because of mutual enemies), and (2) forgetting (a function of time and the intensity of hostility).

52. Not only assassination but *any* policy is predicated on the notion of prediction: "If I do *x*, then *y* will follow." To believe in the mere concept of undertaking a policy, one must, *by definition*, believe that the behavior of human individuals, groups, and nations is predictable.

53. No matter how many of its own citizens it has to kill to stay in power.

54. Ironically, it was President Kennedy who observed that practically anybody could get the president of the United States as long as they were willing to trade their lives for his.

55. It is also useful to have some consistency between what one says and what one does. While this may evoke notions of "foolish consistency," there is some power too in being someone who means what he says.

56. O'Donnell is identified in "Alleged Assassination Plots" by the pseudonym "Michael Mulroney." It is interesting to note that while O'Donnell said he opposed outright assassination, he had no qualms about arranging to have Lumumba captured by Congolese enemies who would certainly kill him. From reading his written testimony, it is difficult to tell if he's being disingenuous or merely naive when he suggests there would be some Congolese "court" that would condemn and execute Lumumba. (See Senate, "Alleged Assassination Plots," pp. 38–39.)

57. Why is this bad? Even assuming one believes assassinations are OK, remember that we are discussing killing the leader of a government the United States is at peace with.

58. Senate, "Alleged Assassination Plots," p. 64 n. 1.

59. This is the way it should be done anyway, if you're going to authorize an assassination. This way, the authorization is "legitimate" (more or less), but the president is covered.

60. I have included Israel because it has, in the past, sent out hit squads to kill Palestinian and Arab insurgents. Unlike the other countries on the list, however, there is no evidence that Israel has tried to assassinate its own political dissidents.

61. This is one of the most ironic cases in history, for given the state of the Republic of the Congo in 1960, it is quite likely Lumumba's regime would have fallen on its own. This is not to suggest incompetence, but merely that almost no amount of good management could have coped with the problems that beset the Congo in the wake of a brutal colonization and an economy highly dependent on extractive industries and Western capital.

Chapter 6

They Were Expendable:
Covert Armies

They looked like Sinbad's buccaneers as they squinted out over the arid plain, watching the ominous line of dust clouds converging on them. It wasn't the clouds; it was the Soviet-made tanks kicking them up that were the problem. A man couldn't help but look around at his scattered compatriots, a "force" in name only, garbed in the traditional turbans, baggy trousers, and cummerbunds of Kurdish men. Up and down the thin line of insurgents, the *pesh mergas* ("men who face death") snicked back the cocking arms of their AK-47s, and felt for the comforting handle of their *kinjhals*, the wickedly sharp daggers of Kurdistan. A few of them checked the sights on their RPG antitank rockets; RPGs wouldn't stop the T-62s of Saddam Hussein's Republican Guard, but might scare a few tank drivers; might buy a few more precious minutes of freedom.

Mostly, they watched the skies. American airpower had shattered the Iraqi Army in 1991, and the people of fledgling Kurdistan waited expectantly, aching for a glimpse of a black batwing aircraft, just like they'd seen on CNN, praying that America would once more turn an Iraqi desert into a blazing sea of death for the army of the Butcher of Baghdad. But the sky held only the sun. The Kurds had no oil. The Americans would not come.

They see the world through despairing eyes, with the look of men and women who have left loved ones—somewhere. It is the eyes that plead their case, and sometimes the American money flows; the weapons appear by the crate; and tanned, hard-looking men arrive, smart and dangerous and full of "can-do." Sometimes too, promises are made, or implied, or wished for so desperately that they seem real enough. Sometimes, too, the money dries up; the hard-looking men cry as they leave, but still they go.

These are the proxy armies; "nations" without a homeland. On both sides of the cold war, nations, tribes, and clans were armed and sent off to fight: Hmong, Kurds, Montagnards, Afghans, Cubans, Nicaraguans, Ukrainians. Although such peoples are most often abandoned, still their eyes glow at the appearance of

154

an American spook. Although American goals are vastly different from theirs, the U.S. government still seeks them out. Who are these secret warriors and why do they fight? Why does the CIA use them, or create them? How has this strategy worked? These are the issues created by raising secret armies.[1]

BLEEDING THE KURDS[2]

Look on a map of the world and you will not find Kurdistan, for Kurds—sixteen to twenty million people—comprise the largest nation on earth without its own country. Kurds share the same language, culture, and religion; most importantly, they identify themselves as Kurds—not as Turks, Iraqis, or Persians. Kurdistan is the unfortunate region where the borders of Turkey, Iran, Iraq, and Syria come togther, and though the Kurds are fearsome warriors, they have been unable to establish their own homeland. They were promised an independent Kurdistan by Woodrow Wilson after World War I, but the idea was overruled by the British and French governments, who were courting favor with the Turks as well as coveting the recently discovered oil fields in northern Iraq.

During World War II, the Soviets helped set up the Kurdish state of Mahabad in northern Iran in a thinly veiled attempt to seize Iranian oil and natural gas fields. Faced with the threat of nuclear weapons from Harry Truman, the Soviets pulled out shortly after the war, leaving the Kurds at the mercy of the shah of Iran (the father of Reza Shah Pahlavi, who abdicated in 1979).

In the latter half of the twentieth century, the Kurds have continued their struggle for a safe haven, waging intermittent war against Iran, Iraq, and Turkey in a struggle for self-determination; perpetual pawns whipsawed between the powerful and brutal. In 1972, the Kurds sought to take advantage of the border dispute between Iran and Iraq by obtaining arms from Iran. Unwilling to trust the shah, however, they requested the help of the United States. While America, through the CIA, would provide some of the weapons, the main purpose of U.S. involvement was, in the words of the Pike Commission, to serve as a "guarantor that the Kurds would not be summarily dropped by the Shah."[3] The CIA pumped about $16 million into the Kurdish rebellion, much of it in sterilized Soviet- and Chinese-made weaponry. As the price of oil began to skyrocket from 1973 onward, the shah sought to bolster Iran's position within the Organization of Petroleum Exporting Countries (OPEC), and one way to do this was to reach an accommodation with Iraq on border issues. In March 1975, Iran suddenly and unilaterally cut off all aid to the Kurds; worse, no American aid was allowed through. The following day, Iraqi forces blasted through the Kurdish enclaves. Dazed at the sudden onslaught combined with the stab in the back, the Kurds implored desperately for the CIA and America to keep its word:

> Our people's fate in unprecedented danger. Complete destruction hanging over our head. We appeal you [CIA] and USG [United States Government] intervene according to your promises. . . .[4]

They also appealed directly to Secretary of State Henry Kissinger, who had played a large role in the American promise; the only response was silence. Tens of thousands of Kurds were killed, and hundreds of Kurdish leaders executed by the Iraqis. When challenged about the United States's apparent betrayal of the Kurds, Secretary Kissinger reportedly delivered the quintessential comment on foreign policy, black operations, and honor: "Covert action should not be confused with missionary work."[5]

This was not the last time the Kurds would be betrayed by the United States. With the destruction of the Iraqi army in 1991, several ethnic groups in Iraq seized the opportunity to throw off Saddam's yoke. One of these was the Kurds, who set aside their internecine quarrels to seize a chunk of traditional Kurdistan in northern Iraq, around the Agros Mountains, with Irbil as their capital. They counted on two things to secure their newfound freedom: the unreliability of the Iraqi army, many of whom are ethnic Kurds, and the promise of support from the United States. Irbil was soon home to a not-so-secret CIA station. We still do not know what, if anything, was promised to the Kurds, but in August 1996, they began an offensive they hoped would split apart Saddam's forces—many of whom did not want to fight anymore—and win the rest of Iraqi Kurdistan. Most likely aware of the operation, the CIA may also have encouraged the Kurds, trying to finally bring the revolution to Iraq and eliminate Saddam completely. The Iraqi army, however, proved more reliable than U.S. support or Kurdish unity, and after four weeks Saddam's forces, led by the Republican Guard—which the Americans had not been allowed to destroy in 1991— as well as helicopter gun ships flying in defiance of the American "guaranteed" no-fly zone, rolled up the defiant but thin Kurdish resistance and into Irbil. Aside from the casualties in combat, many Kurds also died during terrified flight to the Turkish border, where they were largely turned away. Hundreds of Kurds, especially those who had trusted the United States, were executed by the Iraqis.

The Kurds, however, will keep on trying, for there is a phrase that is ingrained in the earliest memories of the young men and women, *Kurdistan ya naman*: Kurdistan or death. It is their version of "next year in Jerusalem."

HMONG MEANS "FREE"[6]

We do not know if it is the mountains that make the people long for freedom, or if people who long for freedom naturally gravitate to the mountains.[7] In many cases, to be sure, the mountains are a refuge from the tyranny of the lowlands. Whatever the motivation, the Hmong of Laos, like the Kurds, are a mountain folk, steeped in family tradition and independence who, before the coming of the *farang* (foreigners), lived a "prewheel" existence. Like the Kurds, their language was different from that of the lowlanders, even though they shared the same "country" (it would be going too far to claim that the power of the Laotian government, like that of the government of Iraq, actually extended into the land of the mountain people). Like the Kurds, and virtually all other mountain peoples, the Hmong have a saying that roughly translates, "Every mountain is a fortress."

In the late 1950s, the Hmong (often called the Meo)[8] lived much as their ancestors had lived for a thousand years, hacking a meager but adequate subsistence out of the mountains in northern Laos, growing rice on mountainsides instead of in paddies, raising pigs, and planting poppies between rows of corn (the corn shades the fragile young poppy plants). For most Hmong, the poppy growing was a small yet vital commercial enterprise. The raw opium, appearing much like liquid latex, could be bartered for the few items the Hmong did not produce for themselves; a small ball of the stuff would supply a person with life's necessities for an entire year. For generations, the Hmong had successfully fought off the Chinese, Vietnamese, Japanese, and lowland Lao using traditional Hmong warfare: hit and run, ambush, live to fight another day. When threatened, they operated as small-scale guerrilla units, using what weapons they could make (including handmade firearms, mainly flintlocks), capture, or trade for. When a village was threatened, the Hmong would simply melt into the forest and wait for the occupiers to go away, or simply move the village altogether. In World War II, the Hmong had fought the Japanese; after that, some had been with the French at Dien Bien Phu. In the late 1950s, the Americans came.

His name was Bill Lair, a shy and soft-spoken CIA operator from Texas who respected the ways of the native peoples. Working in Thailand, Lair had created the Police Aerial Resupply Unit (PARU), a highly skilled guerrilla force that fought bandits, drug lords, and insurgents of all stripes. Most importantly, the PARU taught the local villagers how to protect themselves, developing a three-day training course that turned simple farmers into the Armeé Clandestine—an effective, village-based militia system. Lair introduced the PARU to the Lao in 1960, where they trained and fought beside the Hmong as the North Vietnamese became ever more aggressive in northern Laos. The PARU were skillful trainers, and the Hmong courageous fighters who could run the ridges all day without tiring. The PARU not only understood the ways of the mountain people, but also looked like them; there was no need for "white faces." The method of warfare taught by the PARU was perfectly adapted to the Hmong; hit and run, avoid stand-up fights, and simply make the cost of incursion so great that the North Vietnamese would give up. It was an ideal match, and a classic covert operation: no Americans (well, almost none), deniable World War II surplus weapons, and little cost.

Running a lean operation this way had enormous advantages. This secret war was virtually self-sustaining, and could therefore be carried out indefinitely. The Hmong had to rely mainly on themselves and their traditional way of life, thereby remaining essentially independent of American supplies and combat support. Since the Armeé Clandestine was village-based, there were no large bases to provoke a major North Vietnamese assault; there were no targets *worth* a major offensive. It was classic guerrilla warfare: a swarm of gnats.

Ultimately, it was the success of the Hmong that set up the disaster. Led by the energetic and creative Vang Pao,[9] Hmong units disrupted North Vietnamese operations inside Laos, one time literally blowing up over a kilometer of painfully constructed roadway. To make these units even more effective, the CIA began providing air support to bomb and strafe Pathet Lao (Laotian Communist) and North Vietnamese troops and convoys. These sorties was largely flown by U.S. Air Force pilots who had enlisted in the covert "Steve Canyon" program; disappearing from the air force, they turned up in Udorn, Thailand, in a new uniform, the Hawaiian shirt.[10] Airpower multiplied the effectiveness of the Hmong forces, but also changed their thinking about warfare. They could call down lightning from the sky, and began acting more like regular army units, trying to "fix" enemy units in place and then call in air support to destroy them. Further, as the war in Vietnam moved into the mid-1960s, the Americans began to ask more from the Hmong.

In 1962, to go on the offensive, the CIA encouraged the formation of Special Guerrilla Units (SGUs), that would forsake the traditional regional-defense strategy of the Hmong in favor of wide-ranging attacks on North Vietnamese and Pathet Lao targets. The SGUs gathered in military-style bases, rather than living in their home villages, and the CIA provided for their families.

A second feature of the upscaled war was a dramatic increase in air activity. The Steve Canyon pilots and Thai "volunteers" flew dozens of sorties daily. To supply a Hmong army that eventually would grow to forty thousand combat troops, the CIA employed its proprietary airline, Air America; at the height of the secret war, these aircraft were flying into the secret airbase at Long Tieng at the rate of one *per minute*.

It was the bases that eventually became the problem. When the war was a low-key affair, their was no real ground to hold, and no real reason for the Hmong to stand and fight. They could ambush an enemy column, kill a few dozen Communists, shoot up some trucks, and melt away into the mountains, having suffered little themselves. If they were surprised or outnumbered, they could simply abandon the combat, living to fight another day. The advent of the airbases, which supported the large-scale war effort and provided the supplies the Hmong families came to depend on, gave the Hmong places that *had* to be defended. The North Vietnamese could now pin down the Hmong in stand-up combat.[11] North Vietnam had a nearly limitless supply of expendable soldiers, and the will to expend them. This was their kind of war.

This was exacerbated by the American impulse for nation-building: bringing the benefits of civilization to the backward. This included schools, hospitals, permanent homes, and even retail stores. All these helped to cement the Hmong in place.

Two installations were symbolic of the trend: Long Tieng and Phou Pha Thi. Long Tieng was the key airbase in the war, complete with long runway, taxi strips, shopping center, several windowless buildings with funny antennas,[12] and an air-conditioned officers club. Phou Pha Thi was a mountain near the Vietnamese border, craggy and steep, sacred to the Hmong. It was also less than one hundred fifty miles from Hanoi (as the bomber flies), and was a perfect spot for a piece of hardware called the TSQ-81, a "blind bombing device" that could direct U.S. aircraft to targets in North Vietnam with surgical precision, day or night, regardless of weather. To some, such as Bill Lair, it was obvious that the North Vietnamese would do anything to eliminate this threat, but their warnings were ignored. When the North Vietnamese assault was completed, over a dozen U.S. servicemen were dead, along with hundreds of Hmong, and the top-secret equipment was captured by the Communists.

Stand-up combat proved a disaster for the Hmong. While the North Vietnamese and Pathet Lao could endure thousands of casualties and keep on coming, the Hmong simply could not; entire clans were wiped out. The war of attrition ground them down until they were fielding forces comprised of thirteen-year-olds and indifferent Thai mercenaries. With the American pullout from Vietnam, the Hmong position simply collapsed, leaving the loyal and devastated "free people" to fend for themselves.

The Hmong have survived, but their culture has been largely destroyed. In Laos, they have been hunted down; kept in slave-labor gulags; massacred with poison gas; had their wives and daughters publicly gang-raped as a form of political message; had the children of the rapes removed to be raised as "government children," taught to hate the Hmong.[13] Thousands who managed to flee to Thailand have been forcibly repatriated to the "Lao People's Democratic Republic," where their fate can only be guessed at. A few lucky "free people" with enough bribe money managed to purchase a reprieve in Thailand, for as long as the money holds out. In 1991, Vietnamese military aircraft used a Hmong village for target practice.[14] The most fortunate managed to receive asylum in the United States; the 1990 census showed about one hundred thousand Hmong in America. Today, there is still ongoing Laotian government effort to completely wipe out the Hmong.

THE MONTAGNARDS: SONS OF THE MOUNTAINS

The Montagnards of Vietnam's highlands are, like the Kurds and the Hmong, mountain people; *montagnard* is French for "mountaineer." They come from about eighteen ethnic groups, without a common name for themselves, although more and more are adopting the name *Ana Chu*, which means "Sons of the Mountains."[15]

The Americans called them "yards" when they came to the village of Buon Enao in October 1961. The concept was simple; to train the villagers to defend themselves from the Vietcong (known as the VC). For this purpose, Montagnard men were formed into Civilian Irregular Defense Groups (CIDGs); these were so effective that within two months they had cleared an area containing about forty villages. A year later, over two hundred villages were effectively protected by the CIDGs; to handle larger-scale VC attacks, some of the villagers were organized into mobile strike units called Mike Forces. By October 1964, the Montagnards were supported by about a thousand American Green Berets. The first Medal of Honor awarded in Vietnam was to Special Forces Captain Roger Donlon for the defense of the Montagnard village of Nam Dong. The Montagnards proved to be courageous, resourceful fighters, and often supremely loyal to the Green Berets who came to live among and train them, and to the country those men represented.[16]

Conflict between the Montagnards and the lowland Vietnamese was (and remains) a thousand-year tradition; the lowland call the mountain people *moi*, meaning "savages." By the end of 1964, the government of South Vietnam was concerned that the success of the CIDGs would allow the Montagnards complete independence from the central government. Indeed, the Montagnard understanding was that the United States was guaranteeing them autonomy after the war was won, and their military prowess, substantially superior to that of the regular Vietnamese army, seemed to assure independence. To forestall this, the South Vietnamese government attempted to take control of the CIDG forces in September 1964. The Montangnards rebelled, taking control of six CIDG camps, killing some sixty South Vietnamese soldiers.

As the United States began "Vietnamization"—turning the war over to the South Vietnamese and withdrawing U.S. combat forces—in 1969, the withdrawal of the Special Forces gradually undercut American support for the Montagnards, and within a year, the CIDGs were integrated into Vietnamese Ranger battalions. The collapse of South Vietnam was particularly hard on the Montagnards; as the fiercest opponents of the Communists, the Montagnards received the fiercest retribution. Villages were regrouped to organize for "sedentary farming": one-third of the crop to the state, one-third to the village, and one-third to the grower. Village leaders, teachers, and lower-ranking military officers were sent to "reeducation" camps. Some Montagnards still resist, hiding among the spectacular mountains; there are legends that a few of the Green Berets, at least, did not abandon them.

CONFLICTING GOALS: THE POLITICS OF TRAGEDY

It is really not possible to mitigate these tragedies. They cannot be undone; they will recur in some distant land. It is possible, however, to move beyond the well-deserved moral condemnation of a powerful nation exploiting desperate people and then leaving them holding the bag. If we can learn anything from these events, it is critical to understand why such things happen in the first place: because the aims of the proxy nations and the United States tear against each other.

The crux of the tragedy is that the goals of the United States and its allied nations are sometimes so clashing that one wonders how they can be on the same side. There is an old saying in international politics—and life—that "the enemy of my enemy is my friend." In many times and places, however, simply being *against* the same thing is not enough.

Perhaps the key problem that is virtually unavoidable when one recruits or supports secret armies is this: The Americans sent to consult, train, and even lead the forces almost always promise more than the CIA can or the United States will deliver. This occurs so regularly one suspects it is a natural phenomenon. Advisors are generally committed, can-do operators who deeply believe in the rightness of their cause and the United States. Sadly, this belief often leads them to inadvertent exaggeration about American commitment to the conflict. Sometimes, too, hyperbole is necessary to get reluctant native armies moving at all.[17]

The indigenous people, on the other hand, see the mere presence of American advisors as something of a promise. Certainly when the expensive weapons start to arrive, and radios that can call down the lightning from the sky, they must feel like they just hit the lottery. Throughout the Third World, indigenous peoples view the United States as almost supremely powerful, and cannot comprehend that millions of dollars in aid and dozens of Special Forces advisors could be so lightly written off.

The stateless proxy nations generally seek independence from the government that controls their communities and land, e.g., the Kurds aspire to break away from Iran, Iraq, Turkey, and Syria. This dream often conflicts with broader U.S. goals. While the United States might encourage Kurdish rebellion in Iraq, the American government will never seriously support an independent Kurdistan. A sovereign Kurdish homeland, even carved out of Iraq and Syria, would serve as a base for Kurdish insurgency in Turkey; and Turkey is too important an ally for the United States to disturb.

Even the lesser goal of an "autonomous region" within an existing country is often problematic for the United States. Carving out such regions within sovereign states might merely set up civil wars (or "wars of reunification," depending on one's perspective) in the future; and would almost certainly create a base for insurgency against the larger states in the future. It is difficult to imagine, for example, a Montagnard state set up within the borders of South Vietnam; such a division would create two nonviable states. Depending on the political and economic geography, the new state might cut off the former sovereign from important economic resources or transportation networks, and might even militarily weaken a border with an enemy country. Kurdistan, for example, not only contains some of Iraq's oil wealth, but also lies astride the most efficient route for the proposed Middle Eastern oil pipeline. Finally, such newly created zones would likely rely on support by outside (i.e., American) forces, and thus result in a potential commitment the United States would not or could not keep, such as in the Kurdish Autonomous Zone established in the wake of the Gulf War.

Luring nations within other sovereign states to the U.S. banner with promises (express or implied) of independence or autonomy is also a good way to create friction and even outright hostility in the government of the "host" country. In Laos, the Hmong were traditional antagonists of the lowland Lao people; the Montagnards of the Vietnamese highlands had been the target of Vietnamese oppression for centuries. Even today, the Kurds living in Turkey are forbidden to speak Kurdish or even to refer to themselves as Kurdish; they are "Mountain Turks." The United States could scarcely get these nations to fight without promises of homeland and independence; but these enticements always get back to ears in the capital city, where they are viewed, accurately, as pledges to divide up the country. Typically, this kind of political game produces a civil war in the midst of the conflict with outside forces, which is hardly the best way to strengthen a government's hand with its "official" allies.

Finally, one of the goals of *all* proxy forces is to openly involve the armed forces of the United States. This is, of course, the polar opposite of the aims of the United States, which will always seek to avoid these entanglements; the CIA engages proxy forces expressly to avoid the boot-sucking morass of risking American prestige and bloodshed by involving the armed forces. For the proxy army, though, securing U.S. involvement may be the only way to insure that its national goals are achieved. Liberation is the primary goal; but dragging in U.S. forces is better than losing. Thus, there is *always* tension in relations between the United States and the nations it uses to fight proxy wars. CIA operators and American Special Forces must be essentially "invisible,"[18] while the indigenous people seek to expose their role and thereby secure greater American intervention, which they often naively believe will insure victory.

The United States's goals, on the other hand, are substantially different, and often directly opposite. If the decision is made in Washington to operate a covert war, then the fundamental goal is to avoid overt confrontation with the enemy. While American troops operated in Laos, Afghanistan, and the Kurdish enclave, among others, their primary objective was to avoid entangling the United States at all costs, including their own lives: "If you or any of your IM Force are killed or captured, the secretary will disavow any knowledge of your actions."

A second goal is often *not* to win the war, but merely to bleed the enemy or wage a "spoiling action": to make the cost to the enemy so high in lives and money that it gives up, as did the Soviets in Afghanistan. Sometimes, too, a spoiling action is aimed at merely hurting the opposition: One knows the enemy cannot be defeated, but in a *global* political game in which the politico-military balance is calculated across the world, if the opponent pays too much *here*, they may not be as aggressive *there*. Thus, what is a war of survival for a proxy nation force is viewed as a mere diversionary tactic in Washington.

Corollary to this is that for the superpowers, sometimes the goal must explicitly be to *not win*. Against the background of the cold war, with fingers ready to push the button at the fall of the first domino, both superpowers operated on a fairly simple rule: "You can't have one of my countries." We cannot be certain that the Soviet Union or the United States would have actually gone to nuclear war over Laos, or Korea, or Taiwan; we cannot be certain that they would not have, either. Therefore, the Americans did not march upcountry in Vietnam; the Soviets marched out of northern Iran. In a world perpetually on the brink, a small "win" threatened to produce a big loss, and both powers frequently played for a tie. The status quo was always better than *The Day After*.

Third, if any particular conflict is important enough, the United States will engage its own forces anyway. In the places Uncle Sam chooses to send the CIA rather than the marines, it is generally true that the United States wants to fight the conflict on the cheap. This means that there will be limits on American money and equipment, and even stricter limits on the number and visibility of American fighting men (perhaps even as trainers). If the fighting gets too expensive, the Americans can always cut their losses and go home.

Finally, as a patron, the United States can be expected to view every local situation in terms of regional and global strategy. In the 1960s, the Hmong were enticed to abandon their traditional and successful hit-and-run approach to warfare to support the U.S. politico-military strategy in Vietnam. By fighting major infantry and artillery engagements, the heart of the Hmong Armeé Clandestine was shattered. In northern Iraq, the United States will never support the establishment of an independent Kurdistan; it would create too much instability for America's critical ally in the region, Turkey.

One final consideration is critical, however. If the United States is going to pursue global goals, then it must look at these conflicts through the lenses of global strategy. It is often not enough to win, even if we properly define winning in a global context. Instead, we must always consider the *way we have won*. If a covert war sows the seed of future disaster, what has been "won"?

VICTORY AND ITS AFTERMATH

Of the covert actions of the last twenty years, the real success is probably Afghanistan. United States support of the mujahedin, especially in providing Stinger antiaircraft missiles, indisputably turned a simple throat-cutting insurgency into a bloodsucking quagmire that played a substantial role in shattering the Soviet Union.

Afghanistan, however, also played a key role in the spread of increasingly lethal armaments, especially high-tech weapons. While the wars of the 1960s and 1970s produced a global glut of automatic small arms, the secret wars of the 1980s and 1990s created a windfall for terrorists and drug lords. Explosives and antitank missiles proliferated in the hands of civilians; mortars, excellent terrorist weapons, became widespread; particularly troubling is the prospect of Stinger antiaircraft missiles falling into the hands of terrorists. It has been estimated that as many as one thousand Stingers intended for the Afghan mujahedin are "missing." Of course, given the ideological predilections of the Afghan Taliban "government," even if they had received the Stingers, there might be some reason for Americans to worry. It is a great mistake to lump all zealous Islamic movements together, but even if the Taliban (or whoever emerges as the government of Afghanistan) don't share the same beliefs or militancy of, say, the Islamic Jihad, it is deadly certain that some Afghans do. Without strict weapons controls, such as those found in Western nations (and not found in less-developed countries such as, say, Afghanistan), some highly potent weapons are *certain* to reach the hands of men who want to kill Americans by the planeload.

In addition to the armaments, the creation of a secret army requires training; to be effective, they must receive up-to-date instruction on explosives, weapons, and tactics from the best U.S. Special Forces. To the extent that the trained individuals stay loyal to their cause and to their Special Forces instructors, everything is A-OK. Should the indigenous forces be simply an army of convenience (i.e., they oppose our enemy, but don't have any great loyalty to the United States or democratic ideals), then training them may simply be training the next generation of terrorists who will come after *us*. This is almost certainly the case with some of the Afghans. The costs of the victory in Afghanistan will be adding up for some time to come.

DEFEAT

When the battered remnants of the Hmong people reached the Thai border, they called in vain for the Americans to help them. Some still used their American radio call signs: Snowball, Hammer, Lucky. As with the Kurds, there was no response: The thunder from the sky was still.

One of the critical issues for a defeated proxy army is simply where to go after the war. In most cases, staying in their traditional homeland is a quick way to find out if there is really life after death. Unfortunately, adjacent countries are usually loathe to allow thousands of armed insurgents to flee over their borders, since it might provoke the opposing army to follow the insurgents in hot pursuit. Moreover, often the country across the border has its own share of insurgents, and is fearful that the refugees will simply reinforce its own domestic independence movement. Even the best case is dreadful: The people wind up in squalid long-term refugee camps, with nowhere to turn to. A few thousand lucky ones may be granted special status to emigrate to the United States.

Such outcomes cannot have a good effect on the reputation of the United States and of the CIA. The abandonment of loyal allies is hardly the way to build trust among other peoples and states, or to assure aggressors that the United States is a serious, dogged opponent. If U.S. instigation or involvement in secret wars will be exposed (and it is reasonable to believe it almost always will be), and if such involvement will be perceived by the world at large as a moral and political commitment (as it commonly is), then the United States must either be certain of victory or not play in the first place. "When you commit the flag," President Eisenhower said, "you must win." Given the relatively dismal outcomes common to secret wars, there are probably very few situations where this strategy is justified.

Moreover, the perceived abandonment of loyal peoples has a devastating effect on the Americans involved with them. Some excellent CIA officers left government service in disgust over what they were forced to do to indigenous forces; some Special Forces men refused to abandon their comrades-in-arms and stayed behind in Laos. In the future, every CIA field operator must understand, in the back of his mind, the possibility of running out on his brothers-in-arms. This is scarcely the best way to establish the esprit de corps necessary to produce winning armies.

Training insurgents has perhaps a greater consequence if the insurgents lose. Loyalties may change if the commitment of the United States to the indigenous force changes. In other words, should they feel betrayed, it would not be surprising if some of the "allies" turned on the United States for vengeance.

Finally, win or lose, massive infusion of American money, arms, supplies, and personnel virtually always breaks down traditional cultural, social, economic, and military patterns among indigenous people. This is not to argue that every native superstition is a treasure akin to Shakespeare's sonnets. The diversity of human culture has value of its own, but one cannot go very far making this argument in Washington or Langley. Instead, one must realize that rending the fabric of indigenous cultures creates practical political and military problems that may very well outweigh the potential benefits of a major covert action.

American supplies tend to break down traditional economic patterns, which often have the virtue of being self-sustaining. Thus, when indigenous people come to depend on American food and clothing, and the Americans go away, the remaining "indigs" are faced with either starvation or dependence on the surviving central government. Moreover, American weapons and tactics distort traditional modes of warfare. These traditional modes, such as intermittent insurgency and banditry, have proven sustainable over hundreds of years, and have often created a "balance" in the country, allowing the insurgents to more or less hold their own land. Modern weaponry, by increasing the military capacity of the insurgents, encourages them to go on the offensive, where they often take more land than they can hold once the Americans leave. Ironically, once CIA aircraft stop dropping ammunition, the insurgents are often worse off than they were before, since they have likely lost many of the skills (e.g., guerrilla tactics, gun and ammo making) that initially created the balance with the government forces.

Finally, by hitting a central government too hard without winning, by over-expanding, and by becoming too powerful, the indigenous nation invites a counterattack by the opposing forces. Had they stayed small they might have remained on the central government back burner as they hade been for centuries. Attacking and failing, however, makes them a problem of the first order; one to be dealt with immediately and brutally.

DEFEAT ISN'T ALWAYS LOSING

The one group that has substantially benefited from serving as a CIA proxy has been the Cuban exiles. Perhaps they would have done better back in Cuba, but they have certainly prospered in the United States, both economically and politically. The United States has provided a safe haven for more or less open warfare on Cuba by the exiles. Attacks that would be labeled "terrorism" if carried out by the Popular Front for the Liberation of Palestine (PFLP), such as blowing up civilian airliners, are virtually ignored by the U.S. press and the perpetrators hailed openly as heroes in Miami. Cuban exile groups have been permitted to openly flout U.S. law, e.g., the Neutrality Act, which says individuals and groups cannot commit, plan, or train for acts of war while based on U.S. soil; weapons laws; violations of paramilitary training statutes; customs laws; and many others. This "legal forgiveness" has been a boon to the active belligerents among the exiles, and has also allowed the exile community to develop enormous political clout within the American political system; the Cuban voting community is so powerful that U.S. representatives, senators, governors, and presidents cater to their desires rather than risk losing the mass of Cuban-American votes.

Cubans, however, can (and did) get to Florida in boats. They also had a substantial American political constituency to support their claims for asylum, and the arrival of tens of thousands of Cubans made them an irresistible voting bloc. This is a special circumstance of politics and geography, and one that cannot be emulated by any other national group.

THE FUTURE OF "SECRET ARMIES"

Even with the end of the cold war, the United States continues to spend over a quarter of a trillion dollars a year on American armed forces. Having witnessed the breathtaking efficiency of that military in the Gulf War, one might wonder why there will be any need for proxy armies in the future. When a hostile government acts against the interests of the United States, why not simply send in a few Tomahawk cruise missiles and blast 'em?

If enforcing the will of the U.S. government were merely a matter of pushing a few buttons, we might indeed witness the "end of history." As we have seen in the Persian Gulf, however, problems do not always yield to brute firepower. One can hurt an enemy army from the air, but the ageless maxim still applies: To take and hold territory, you need ground-pounders (infantry). Historically, an enemy army has *never* been slaughtered from the air like the Iraqis in 1991; but even in that case, it was the Allied foot soldiers who had to take back Kuwait.

The reasons the United States has and will continue to employ proxy armies are the very reasons it engages in covert action in the first place. It is always better to use someone else's blood for warfare. This has become important since the Vietnam War, and is even more important since the end of the cold war; now, the stakes don't seem as high, and the American voting public will not tolerate large-scale bloodletting of its sons and daughters. In addition, a proxy army does not carry the American flag—and American prestige—with it. If the Kurds fail, it is their failure, not America's, and the United States is not obligated to try to rectify the mess with American lives and treasure. This is the presumed virtue of plausible deniability (when it holds up). Furthermore, since the United States was "never there," it does not run the risk of a direct confrontation that could escalate into a shooting war against a well-armed foe. This seems less critical in 1999 than it did when the word "escalation" was always preceded by "nuclear," but there are still some governments with weapons—either nuclear, chemical, or biological—that could inflict mass casualties on the United States, and the list is continually growing. Finally, there are simply some parts of the world that are not worth a drop of American blood. When these regions are threatened by an unfriendly power, the CIA will continue to be called on to fight spoiling actions, the small wars that bloody the nose of an aggressor and make the cost of fighting so high that it quits and goes home.

THE INEVITABLE ATTRACTION

In the long run, the effect of American abandonment of indigenous allies may have little impact on the ability of the United States to attract similar forces in the future. These allies rarely *choose* the United States or the Central Intelligence Agency—almost always, it has been a case of "any port in a storm." Abandonment *may* affect future proxy forces that have a choice, such as mercenaries, or insurgents not under any great pressure. In these cases, given the experience of the Kurds, Hmong, and others, the track record of the CIA and the inconstant viewpoints of American political leadership, a wise insurgent leader would do well to steer clear of Uncle Sam. There are really two choices. First, the insurgents might obtain a clear-cut commitment, which by now we should realize is neither verbal nor even material; it has to be Americans on the ground, in substantial numbers, getting killed. Otherwise, it is far too easy for the U.S. government to simply wash its hands. The other choice is to make do without substantial U.S. aid, and only commit to a conflict that can be sustained more or less independently of outside powers. For most stateless nations, this probably means maintaining the same low-level insurgency and banditry they have engaged in for centuries. Upping the stakes by obtaining outside support, however, has often proven disastrous.

If there is an ironclad lesson from the secret wars of the last fifty years, it is that these operations always come into the light of day. Sometimes it is through a reporter; sometimes through one of the indigenous leaders, seeking to force the United States into a greater commitment; sometimes through a politician in Washington, hoping to embarrass the president or the CIA, or else to slyly reassure constituents that "yes, we *are* doing something." In the past, reports of a secret army in Laos could have been denied and laughed off for years; today, ignoble abandonment of Iraqi Kurds has its own Peter Jennings report within months. Ultimately, if the CIA is going to continue to aid insurgents, it will have to find a way to fight them in the open.

NOTES

1. The exploitation of proxy forces is not unique to the United States. The Soviets employed them all over the world, the best-known being the Cubans. In fact, some of the same nations discussed in this chapter as American clients have also been Soviet clients, such as the Kurds in northern Iran. China, too, uses these people: It supported the Hmong in their struggle against the North Vietnamese after 1979, and in the era of Sino-Vietnamese conflict, China also armed the Montagnards. Iran has used the Iraqi Kurds, and Iraq has used the Iranian Kurds. This is only a small sampling.

2. This account is drawn from John Prados, *President's Secret Wars: CIA and Pentagon Covert Operations Since World War II* (New York: William Morrow and Co., 1986), pp. 313–15; William Blum, *Killing Hope: U.S. Military and CIA Interventions Since World War II* (Monroe, Maine: Common Courage Press, 1995), chap. 39; David McDowall, *The Kurds: A Nation Denied* (London: Minority Rights Press, 1992); and *CIA—The Pike Report* (Nottingham, U.K.: Spokesman Books, 1977).

3. *Pike Report*, p. 196.

4. Ibid., p. 215.

5. See William Safire, "Son of 'Secret Sellout,'" *New York Times*, 12 February 1976, p. 31.

6. The sources for this section are two excellent books: Roger Warner, *Backfire: The CIA's Secret War in Laos and Its Link to the War in Vietnam* (New York: Simon and Schuster, 1995); and Jane Hamilton-Merritt, *Tragic Mountains: The Hmong, the Americans, and the Secret Wars for Laos, 1942–1992* (Bloomington: Indiana University, 1993).

7. It is certainly true. My grandmother taught me early on the motto of my native state: *Montani Semper Liberi*.

8. *Hmong* is their own word for themselves; it means "free." Outsiders called them *Meo*, a corruption of the Chinese *Miao* ("barbarians").

9. If the war had not been "secret," Vang Pao would have been called the "George Washington of Laos," which would have been far more accurate than some of the other leaders the name has been applied to, e.g., Ngo Dinh Diem of Vietnam, Adolfo Calero of Nicaragua, Jonas Savimbi of Angola.

10. The Steve Canyon Program, a covert program to supply USAF pilots to fly combat support missions in Laos, was named after the fictional hero of the comic strip. Pilots in the program were called *ravens*, and "raven" was used as their call sign. The best source on the program is Christopher Robbins, *The Ravens: The Men Who Flew in America's Secret War in Laos* (New York: Pocket Books, 1989).

11. "Stand-up combat" is when the two sides stay in place and shoot it out, each side hoping its firepower can kill more of the enemy than the enemy can kill of them. It is the opposite of "hit and run," where one side tries to catch an enemy force by surprise, kill some of them, and then run away before it suffers any casualties.

12. This is what CIA paramilitary installations look like the world over. Thirty-five years later, it is still how one could find the spooks in Irbil, Kurdistan.

13. Hamilton-Merritt, *Tragic Mountains*, chap. 25.

14. Ibid., p. 505.

15. Gerald Cannon Hickey, *Free in the Forest: Ethnohistory of the Vietnamese Central Highlands, 1954–1976* (New Haven: Yale University, 1982), p. xv.

16. See Prados, *President's Secret Wars*, pp. 252–55.

17. After all, they have been fighting in small-scale insurgencies for centuries, and at least surviving using their own methods and equipment. Why change the status quo and risk bringing down greater wrath on their own heads?

18. American operators and cadre forces are seldom unknown to the enemy, whether it's Saddam Hussein or the Soviet Union. Rather, these individuals and groups must take great care not to publicly commit an act that would force the other side to *acknowledge* their presence. In the world of international politics on the brink, unacknowledged insults do not require a response.

Chapter 7

An Offer You Can't Refuse:
Organized Crime and the CIA

They could have been any two shuffleboard seniors sitting there in the bar of Miami's Fountainbleu Hotel; maybe retired from the Ford plant in Detroit, moved to the land of sun. One introduced himself to the stranger as "Sam Gold"; the other called himself "Joe." They didn't talk much, mainly waited for the stranger to make his pitch. Just looking at them, it would have been hard to believe that together they had either killed or ordered the cold-blooded murder of dozens of people, perhaps hundreds. That, of course, was why they were here. Someone had made a discreet inquiry about a certain hit, and these two "gentlemen" were interested. "Joe" was Santos Trafficante, godfather of the Miami Mob; and "Sam Gold" was Sam Giancana, head of the Chicago syndicate and most powerful mafioso in the United States.

The stranger looked them over, but not too carefully, for it is not healthy to stare at men like these. His name was Robert Maheu. He was a former FBI agent, and was now working as a contract agent and go-between for the CIA; on behalf of the United States government, he was offering the Mob a $150,000 contract to kill Fidel Castro.[1]

Organized crime and American intelligence have, as they say, some history. Since before World War II, U.S. intelligence agencies have yielded to the allure of easy solutions: using organized crime organizations for "national security" purposes. The temptation must be enormous, for men who should know better keep yielding. Why is exploiting the Mafia bad for the United States? Why not use them, and in effect get some payback for what they do to our country? In this chapter, we'll explore those issues, as well as the dangerous government flirtation with the mob. It all began . . .

ON THE WATERFRONT[2]

It was hard to believe. The steel shell of the great ship crackled from the heat as flames consumed the doomed vessel. A mighty gasp rose from the crowd as the dying behemoth groaned, then rolled on its side, flooding the New York pier with the water it displaced; many a rat breathed its last that day. The *Normandie*, pride of France, was dead.

It was 1942 and the United States had just entered the war. In every part of America walls were plastered with posters warning of the menace of Nazi saboteurs, and it did not take long for the authorities to conclude that the *Normandie* blaze had indeed been set on purpose. Moreover, hard evidence fingered the culprits; an alert investigator discovered some German coins that had apparently been dropped at the scene by a careless or panicked Nazi saboteur. J. Edgar Hoover took this as a personal affront, but it was the Office of Naval Intelligence (ONI) that was responsible for securing the waterfront. From these docks steamed the ships that kept England alive; from these docks flowed the men and arms who would deliver freedom to Europe. The waterfront had to be *untouchable*.

Securing the docks and safeguarding the ships was not an easy task, however, for while New York Harbor was American territory, it was Mafia *turf*. Ships could arrive and depart whenever they pleased, but no cargo moved on or off without the approval of the New York Mob; the longshoremen's union amounted to a wholly owned subsidiary of the Genovese crime family. For years, government agents had tried to penetrate the closed dockside organization without success. Now it was a matter of national survival, and the ONI was ready to deal.

He wouldn't have to feel this damned denim on his body any more. Lucky had to smile, for he had once again lived up to his name; his pal, Meyer Lansky, had just left the visitors' room at the state prison, and Charlie Luciano, "Lucky," would soon follow. The ONI was ready to deal, and Lucky held all the cards.

The bargain was simple. Luciano, the head of the Genovese crime family and *la Cosa Nostra* "Boss of Bosses," was serving a thirty- to fifty-year prison sentence at Clinton State Prison in far upstate New York. For the duration of the war, the government boys promised, he would be moved to Great Meadow Prison outside Albany. By the standards of the time Great Meadow was a "country club," and it was far closer to Luciano's base of operations, New York City. Presumably, this would allow him to supervise the Mob's patriotic "dockwatch"; it would also, of course, let him maintain command of his criminal enterprise. While the evidence today is inconclusive, it is likely that Luciano was promised a pardon after the war; this is the kind of deal he would have demanded. In exchange, Luciano would allow the government to infiltrate agents among the longshoremen, the eyes of the Mafia would watch the docks, and there would be no longshoremen strikes during the war. As a bonus, when the war got to Italy, any contacts the crime families had inside that country, especially during the invasion of Sicily, would cooperate with the Allies. The Mafia would in effect become the Allied resistance behind German lines.

To all appearances, Luciano kept his word. The docks were undisturbed for the duration, with virtually no instances of successful sabotage. When Allied forces hit the beach in Sicily, local Mafia guides were there to meet them; throughout the campaign, Mafia contacts escorted Allied forces, perhaps directing them toward the best avenues of attack.

The government, however, double-crossed the Mafia boss. Thomas E. Dewey, governor of New York, could not bring himself to issue the pardon for Luciano; it would have been political suicide for Dewey, who had been the prosecutor that nailed Luciano in the first place, and who would soon run for president. In the end, Luciano was granted his freedom, but was forced to exercise it in Sicily after he was deported in 1946.

The double-cross may have worked both ways, however, for it is still today unclear precisely how much help Luciano and his organization actually provided. It is difficult to find any evidence that the strong men on the docks made any difference in the number of ships that were sabotaged. The sheer incompetence of German efforts to infiltrate saboteurs was astonishing; many were picked up practically right on the beach. Moreover, the ultimate impact of the Sicilian connection is arguable at best. The people of the United States were perfectly capable of winning World War II themselves, and basically did. While the Italian campaign was a bloody, vicious affair and the men who fought it were among the most valiant of the war, in the end it was not decisive; it distracted some German forces, but never proved to be the stab into the "soft underbelly of Europe," as Churchill hoped it might.

In fact, it is entirely possible that the government was suckered into the bargain by Luciano. The men who set the *Normandie* fire have never surfaced, even today, when German intelligence records from the war are an open book and everyone is trying to sell a spy story. Genovese longshoremen could have easily set the fire; the German coins found at the scene were a laughably convenient clue. Such a plan was not beyond Luciano, and with his control of the docks, it would have been far simpler for some Genovese guys than for German saboteurs. We shall probably never know for sure, but the possibility is all too probable and all too chilling.

CONTRACT ON FIDEL

No one is certain who first suggested recruiting the Mafia into the war on Castro; or, in any case, no one has owned up to it. If the Kennedy administration was as close to the Mob as Seymour Hersh suggests in *The Dark Side of Camelot*, one would expect the idea to somehow have originated with either JFK or, more likely, Robert Kennedy. According to those who testified to the Church Committee, however, the idea came from either Richard Bissell or Desmond Fitzgerald. What *is* certain is that sometime during the middle of 1962, senior CIA officials set about to use *la Cosa Nostra* to "hit" Fidel.

Robert Maheu, a former FBI and CIA operator, was selected as the cutout.

In 1962, Maheu was working as a security expert in Las Vegas for Howard Hughes, and was therefore believed (quite rightly) to have some access to the Mob. Maheu worked through a friend, Johnny Roselli, who he had known since the mid-1950s. While Maheu claimed he didn't know that Roselli was connected to the Mob, he *did* think that the debonair mobster was able to accomplish a lot in Las Vegas that other people couldn't.[3] Eventually, Roselli led the CIA contact to Sam Giancana, godfather of the Chicago Mob, and Santos Trafficante, head of the Mafia in Miami (formerly of Havana). A Mob hit, the CIA believed, was probably the best way to kill Castro; after all, the Mafia was flush with experienced killers. It also had powerful motivation to do the job, having been expelled by the Cuban dictator. This was *perfect* plausible deniability.

Bissell and Fitzgerald thought CIA was buying a simple gangland-style shooting. Giancana and Trafficante, however, demurred. While the standard "small-caliber bullets in the head" method might work in a club in Jersey or a Skokie parking lot, such an attack on Fidel Castro would be a suicide mission, and the mafiosi didn't think they could get anyone to undertake it. Instead, they suggested poison; to the conspirators at CIA (and in the White House), it must have seemed like deja vu all over again.

As detailed in chapter 6, however, all the Mafia plots came to naught. This result may be due to insufficient planning, or the fact that Castro was a difficult target, or just simple bad luck. These attempts, even though failures, ratcheted up cold war tensions and gave a considerable black eye to the CIA and the United States government. There was one winner in this whole sorry story, though: the Mafia itself. It is to that we turn next.

WHY TURN TO THE MOB?

There are numerous "good" reasons to exploit organized crime organizations for intelligence or covert action purposes. Underground crime organizations often have access to or control the "hidden" layers of society that would be difficult or impossible for intelligence organizations to penetrate, e.g., gun runners, corrupt politicians and law enforcement personnel (foreign ones, we hope), burglars, prostitutes, pimps, smugglers, and so forth. Moreover, crime organizations can bring these people into action *immediately*; there is no need to mount a major penetration operation to get a government operator "on the inside." Criminal organizations may also have high-level contacts in foreign governments, as the Mafia did in Cuba. These contacts may provide information, access to persons the CIA might want to "send to a better world," or political favors that can ease a covert action, e.g., a customs officer who looks the other way when the "machine tools" are imported. The Mafia membership also contains plenty of individuals who are accustomed to violence and nefarious activities. Covert action, after all, is crime; *why not* get criminals to do it? Professional criminals also travel the darkened byways that civil servants normally do not; they know, for example, smuggling routes, sources for false identities, ways to obtain sterile weapons in foreign countries without having to "pouch" them in, and where to procure a dozen prostitutes in a hurry.[4] Equally important, these Mafia thugs are deniable; whatever they do can be blamed on organized crime, thereby drawing attention away from an underlying government operation or objective. Should one of the Mafia plots have succeeded in killing Fidel, for example, it would have been perfectly believable that the Mafia did it on its own account. In that case in particular, even if the CIA had done it, the Mafia had such a strong motive that it probably still would have received substantial blame.

Finally, it would be difficult for the members of the Veterans of Foreign Wars to outdo the Mob in anti-Communism. Highly authoritarian regimes of any stripe are anathema to organized crime; they don't like the competition. During World War II, Mussolini's government nearly destroyed the Sicilian Mafia; important mafioso were forced to hide out in the hills like common bandits. Communist regimes have generally been even harder on the Mob. Castro kicked them out of Cuba and cracked down on the vice operations that were so lucrative. Secret police, extensive networks of informers, and an arbitrary "justice" system make it impossible for underground organizations to operate outside the law. As we can observe currently in Russia, organized crime is a facet of freedom. This reliable anti-Communism made the various criminal societies attractive CIA allies throughout the cold war (see chapter 9 for a full discussion).

YOU KNEW I WAS A SNAKE . . .

However, there are perilous drawbacks to engaging the Mafia as a co-conspirator. While covert action by definition breaks some laws, in general the rule of "moral necessity," as well as common sense, dictates that one break as few laws as possible, especially the laws of one's own country. Criminals, on the other hand, are not only accustomed to breaking the law, but often *prefer* illegal means (in the criminal world, it is always best to leave as few traces as possible). What they regard as standard operating procedures are what courts regard as felonies, and they are liable to commit all kinds of crimes without even noticing.

The government's previous use of the Mob for covert operations, however, should not be read as a precedent: "We did it before, and it worked out okay." Every instance of government partnership with organized crime has been fraught with peril. More importantly, even though there are no immediately apparent costs, cooperating with these societies always bears the weight of favors yet to be repaid.

Aside from the simple desire that individuals and agencies implementing government policy violate as few laws as possible, there is a practical consideration as well. Illegal acts attract attention. Whether it is a bunch of camouflage-clad men running around the woods with automatic weapons or unusual flights landing at a rural airfield at odd hours, law enforcement will take notice; then they'll have to be let in on the secret. It is hard to deny a covert action when the group carrying it out is noticeably flouting the law.

Intelligence agency employment of criminal societies also produces a critical overlap between the two organizations. Intelligence officers and contract agents make good contacts within the criminal community, and perhaps even make friends. It is not unknown for contract agents to work for both the CIA and *la Cosa Nostra*, sometimes at the same time. Many of the individuals involved in MONGOOSE, for example, also acquired ties to the Miami and New Orleans Mob. David Ferrie, a pilot who flew covert missions over Cuba during MONGOOSE, also served as a personal pilot for Carlos Marcello, don of the New Orleans Mafia. This blurring of lines is a critical problem. If a government operator moonlights for the Mob, what secrets and contacts does he take with him? If he tries to enlist other individuals into an operation, how can they tell if it's a government operation or a criminal scam? If a mysterious aircraft is seized by Drug Enforcement Administration (DEA) agents at a remote airstrip and the pilot can prove CIA affiliation, does this mean the particular flight or mission is a national security mission, or is it merely an operator making a few bucks on the dark side? This overlap cannot help but poison the relationship between law enforcement agencies and intelligence agencies as high-powered government attorneys order the release of individuals who essentially carry on criminal enterprises in the open.

A greater possible cost is the potential loss of moral compass among the government agents who cooperate with the wiseguys. While the money and lifestyle of the Mob might be tempting, few dedicated CIA officers, or even contract agents, turn over to the Mafia. There are cases, however, of government operatives, exposed to the criminal ethic, turning to crime on their own, for their own purposes (see the story of Edwin Wilson and Frank Terpil in chapter 10), or developing their own criminal methods to ostensibly serve some higher goal, e.g., the Secord/North/Hakim Enterprise (see also the story of the Nugan Hand Bank in chapter 15). Since covert officers essentially have license to operate beyond the law, it is vital that they start with and maintain a solid moral foundation. To do their jobs effectively, they must necessarily commit immoral acts. Only an officer with a sound ethical base, however, has the judgement to decide *which* immoral acts are necessary.

Finally, and most important, *la Cosa Nostra* is not a charitable foundation. If the Mafia agrees to serve as an agent of the government, they must think there's something in it for them, even if we don't see it. Any covert operation employing the Mafia will likely acquire a "parallel operation." *La Cosa Nostra* has its own agenda, and will piggyback some kind of bonus onto the affair: smuggling in a few weapons, perhaps a few kilos of heroin, storing up "favors" to cash in, settling a score by killing an old enemy under cover of government authority. In fact, there is evidence that major drug-running operations, including the "French Connection," discussed further in chapter 9, were established under cover of "patriotic mafioso."

The basic problem is inescapable; in dealing with organized crime, there will *always* be a quid pro quo. It will never be asked for up front; the mafia will always "be glad to do something for our country." Covert action, however, is not missionary work, even for *la Cosa Nostra*. The wiseguys will have paid the piper, and at some point they will want to call the tune. By and large, the melody will be a popular favorite among the boys: "immunity from prosecution." A government attorney will show up at the district attorney's office or in court and quietly explain that prosecuting this particular wiseguy represents a threat to national security, and no, the details cannot be explained. Case closed. Using the Mafia in CIA covert actions has one inevitable effect: It gives the mafioso a permanent "get out of jail free" card. With a history of cooperating with the government, Mob fellows can ask for "consideration" for their past services; with inside knowledge, they can *demand* amnesty else they trumpet the whole government/Mafia arrangement to the newspapers, the voters, and Congress.

Such is the power of a government "contract" (in many senses of the word) that the Mafia have probably sought to do favors for the CIA precisely to establish these relationships. As discussed above, it is unclear how much help the Genovese family really was during World War II, and the Giancana/Trafficante plots against Castro never produced an attempt on his life.

One can always try to outsmart the wiseguys, perhaps by engaging them through cutouts so that they can't be sure they are being officially solicited by the United States government. Any good intelligence agency would try this as a first option. One might have a cutout with a good story engage another cutout, who would talk to the Mob. Unfortunately, once the second the cutout began describing what he wants the crime organization to do, it would be almost impossible to conceal or deny the identity of the real patron. If the operation requires inside intelligence, special equipment, really good official documents, or a "temporary" exemption from state and federal laws, you might as well show up in a dark blue sedan with government plates.

That all these things happen when one engages the Mafia in intelligence operations is only to be expected. It is inevitable, for the Mafia is what it is: a criminal enterprise that will look out for itself first and foremost. To expect conventional, upright behavior is to expect the leopard to change its spots. One is reminded of the story of the viper who promises not to bite the man if the man will carry the viper across the flooded river. Halfway across, the viper bites the man, who, dying, asks the viper, "Why?" The viper replies, "Well, you knew I was a snake when you picked me up."

NOTES

1. Maheu's account can be found in Robert Maheu and Richard Hack, *Next to Hughes* (New York: HarperCollins, 1992), chap. 4.

2. This section is drawn from Rodney Campbell, The Luciano Project: The Secret

Wartime Collaboration of the Mafia and the U.S. Navy (New York: McGraw-Hill, 1977); Marvin Gosch and Richard Hammer, The Last Testament of Lucky Luciano (New York: Dell, 1981); and "Lucky Luciano," Biography, Arts and Entertainment Network, 1998.

3. Senate, *Interim Report of the Select Committee to Study Governmental Operations with Respect to Intelligence Activities*, "Alleged Assassination Plots Involving Foreign Leaders," 94th Cong., 1st sess., 1975, S. Rept. 94-465, pp. 74–74.

4. This can be a real necessity. During the Nicaraguan contra war, the contras often demanded that women be made available at their remote camps. During the training of Brigade 2506 for the Bay of Pigs operation, the CIA actually established a bordello at the training camp to prevent the commandos from making unauthorized nocturnal trips into town for women; it was thought these trips were a security problem.

Chapter 8

Just Say Yes:
Covert Action and Drug Empires

The story broke on 18 August 1996. Gary Webb, a reporter for the *San Jose Mercury News* published "Dark Alliance: The Story Behind the Crack Explosion," the first in a series of articles that seemed to charge that agents of the Central Intelligence Agency had facilitated, if not created, the crack epidemic that had swept America. Webb's story had three critical threads: first, that the drugs were sold to finance the contra war in Nicaragua; second, that this CIA operation was substantially responsible for the horrific crack epidemic in America; and third, that at the very least, the CIA knew of the operation, and at the very worst, the agency approved of it.[1]

The charges hit all of America like a hammer; they hit the African American community like a bomb. Proponents of white conspiracy theories had a field day, accusing the U.S. government of creating and selling crack, a cheap and dreadfully addictive derivative of cocaine, as part of a plan to degrade and destroy Black America.[2] At the peak of the ensuing political storm, CIA Director John Deutsch chose a remarkable course: he appeared before a boisterous and hostile public forum in South Los Angeles to try to refute the charges.

What made Deutsch's task all the harder was the established fact that CIA and American intelligence operatives have historically cooperated with and supported drug empires around the world. Under the guise of "national security," agencies of the U.S. government have provided security, weapons, protection from local law enforcement, covert or officially protected supply lines into the United States, immunity from prosecution (federal, state, and local), amnesty for convicted drug smugglers and dealers, and even the return of lawfully seized property used in or derived from drug activities.

What makes CIA involvement even more damaging is that the agency has not merely used drug syndicates on occasion, or only exploited small organizations. Instead, many of the largest, most far-reaching, and most destructive drug trafficking operations have benefitted from the protection and support of U.S. intelligence agencies, including:

- the French Connection
- Laotian heroin and opium networks
- Drug lords of the Golden Triangle (Burma)
- the Afghan mujahedin
- the Nicaraguan contras

U.S. intelligence connections have been critical to the development of these drug empires and pipelines into the mainline of the United States. While it is unlikely that anyone in the CIA, especially among the responsible officers, promoted the production and selling of drugs, the agency would be very bad at its job if it was not aware of the drug connections of both its contract agents and its allies. There is a saying when a government official or operator has to do bad things to prevent worse things from happening: "You can't make an omelette without breaking a few eggs." When it comes to drug-dealing allies, however, another homily is more apt: "You can't lie down with dogs without picking up fleas." The result of lying with *these* dogs, however, has been far worse than flea bites.

THE COLD WAR, U.S. INTELLIGENCE, AND THE FRENCH CONNECTION

Across south Asia, from the craggy peaks of Afghanistan to the forested mountains of the Burmese Golden Triangle, the routine is remarkably similar. A farmer examines the green seed pod sitting atop a three-foot stem. Using a special curved knife shaped like a large claw, he scores the egg-sized pod with several parallel cuts, allowing the white milky sap to seep out. It quickly congeals into a dark-brown rubbery gum. When the pod is drained, the farmer uses the knife to scrape off the almost black goo, rolling it into a ball; another pellet of opium has been harvested.

Not too many years ago, much of the crop would have been consumed locally, pinched off in tiny brown balls and fingered into a pipe. Most of it would have been smoked in the opium dens of cities with exotic names: Bangkok, Phnom Penh, Vientiane, Hong Kong, Peking,[3] Karachi, Jalalabad, or Istanbul. Today, however, though the rubbery ball looks brown, it is in fact gold. It will be transported to a local lab, where it will be processed into morphine weighing about 10 percent of the original opium. Loaded into a larger pack, it is hauled, often by mule train, over rugged mountain passes, to a sophisticated chemical lab. There the crystalline morphine is processed through several more stages, eventually emerging as "No. 4" heroin, a white flaky powder anywhere from 80 to 99 percent pure.[4] It is now ready to be shipped to America.

For the first two and a half decades after World War II, the shipment would probably have been handled by a legendary syndicate, the "French Connection." This was the name of a massive corporate organization based in Sicily and Marseilles that emerged after World War II to control the bulk of the world market for heroin. What most Americans know about the French Connection they learned from the movie of the same name, starring Gene Hackman. What few Americans know, however, is that the French Connection was established with pivotal help from U.S. intelligence agencies.

As Allied forces struggled across Sicily in 1943, they were aided by members of the Sicilian Mafia, who served as guides, scouts, and interpreters. Under Mussolini's fascists, the Mafia had nearly been wiped out, but their service to the Americans was to be rewarded handsomely; Mafia figures were awarded offices in the occupation forces and government, and in many cases given more political power than they'd had before the war. Vito Genovese himself served as an interpreter at Allied headquarters, while the head of the Sicilian Mafia, Don Calagero Vizzini, literally rolled across Sicily riding on George Patton's tanks, drumming up Sicilian support for the Americans. As the local force most likely to enforce public order, it must have seemed natural to the Allied occupation forces to turn to the Mafia.[5] Soon mafiosi were mayors, chiefs of police, and essentially the government of Sicily. The Mafia was back in business. All it lacked was a man of vision.

The man looked up at the hills of Sicily. It was 1946, and the war was over. He had left the island decades before, heading for the golden streets of America. Now America had cast him out. He had made a fortune in America from bootlegging, prostitution, and drug peddling, and for this he was expelled by his adopted land. He may have been cast out, but he wasn't through; his name was Lucky Luciano.

Although he was back in Sicily, Luciano was hardly back to square one. Working through contacts in Beirut, Lucky organized a heroin production and trafficking enterprise that was remarkable in many respects, not the least of which was that it was able to control major heroin production and shipping for over a decade without suffering a major seizure or arrest.

What really made the operation, though, was the connection Luciano established between the Sicilians and the Corsican Mafia, the *Unione Corse*, a syndicate of uncommon restraint and skill, operating in small, tightly knit clans, specializing in heroin smuggling, art theft, and counterfeiting.[6] Moreover, the Corsicans ran (and still run) a truly international organization, controlling most ventures from their base in Marseille (not, oddly, Corsica).

Like the Sicilian Mafia, the *Unione Corse* was substantially aided by U.S. intelligence. The Corsicans had nearly caused their own annihilation by siding with the Vichy regime during the war, but were soon rehabilitated with a substantial helping of American money and tolerance. In 1947, the French Communist Party imposed a boycott of U.S. Marshall Plan aid, and Party control of the dockworkers in the critical port of Marseille kept American goods sitting in the holds of cargo ships. To break the back of the Communist strike, Office of Policy Coordination (OPC, the precursor to the covert action arm of the CIA) operatives established a relationship with the Corsicans, who largely controlled the socialists. Backed by the CIA, Corsican strongmen engaged in a bloody street war with the Communists, eventually breaking the strike. In 1950, the Corsicans were organized and paid by the CIA to break yet another strike, receiving millions of covert dollars from the CIA. The support of the CIA not only paid financial dividends, but also practically gave the waterfront to the Corsicans. All cargo in and out of Marseilles either went through Corsican hands or it didn't go at all. For the Corsicans, as with the Sicilians, anti-Communism had resulted in (1) a substantial payoff from the Americans, and (2) survival, prosperity, and power for a criminal syndicate that had nearly been eradicated some months before.[7]

Once linked with the Sicilians, a relationship established by Luciano, the Corsicans quickly dominated the American heroin market; at its crest in 1965, the French Connection sent about 4.8 tons of high-grade heroin to the United States.[8] Luciano, working through Meyer Lansky in the States, quickly became a multimillionaire. Even the crackdown on Turkish opium growers in the mid-1960s failed to stifle this organization. The Mob simply turned to another source. In 1968, Santos Trafficante made a "diplomatic drug tour" of Asia, where he connected with the Golden Triangle. Smuggling routes were rearranged and the Sicilian/Corsican alliance continued to prosper. For twenty-five years, this connection provided the bulk of the heroin pumped into American veins.

Ultimately, the rise of a second generation of Corsicans brought down the French Connection. Until the late 1960s, the *Unione Corse* had secured their base in France by scrupulously refusing to sell heroin there; thus, they weren't a target for French law enforcement. A new cohort of Corsicans took power, however, in the mid- and late 1960s. By this time, the United States was engaged in a serious effort to stem the flow of heroin; the "import" business into America became more dangerous, difficult, and costly. To the new Corsican leaders, it was far easier to sell the heroin right in France, where it was made; the French Connection became a problem for France itself. The government responded, waging a war on the Marseilles drug labs that almost eradicated them by the mid-1970s.[9]

The French Connection was dead, but it had inflicted horrendous costs on America. Heroin use in the United States exploded in the aftermath of World War II, increasing from about 20,000 addicts in 1945 to 60,000 in 1952, and to about 150,000 in 1965.[10] According to the Federal Bureau of Narcotics, about 80 percent of this heroin came from the Corsicans.[11] The stake in the heart is that the organized-crime syndicates who promoted and provided this narcotic had survived through the cooperation and protection of American intelligence. Both the *Union Corse* and the Sicilian Mafia were on the ropes by the end of World War II. By playing on the fear of Communism and the almost blank check this gave them, these two associations not only survived and prospered, they helped poison a good number of Americans.

COLD WAR, GOLD TRIANGLE

The retreating soldiers were dirty, hungry, exhausted. They had been waging a fighting withdrawal through jungle—over mountains, across rivers—struggling to keep their army, their families, and their cause intact. For over twenty years they had fought, first the Japanese, then the People's Liberation Army (PLA) of

Mao Tse-tung. In the beginning, there were tens of thousands of soldiers. Now a few hundred backed against the border, having lost their final bastion in China's Yunnan Province.

This was not just any border, however; it was the place where China, Burma, Laos, and Thailand came together. The army, tattered remnants of Chiang Kai-Shek's nationalist Kuomintang (KMT) 97th and 193rd divisions staggered across the border into Burma. Unmolested by the Red Chinese, the KMT quickly established itself as the de facto government of this corner of Burma, in the face of a distant Burmese army too feeble to resist. It was 1950, and by the end of the year, Li Mi, the KMT general in charge, would hatch plans to invade southern China. Fearful that the red tide of Communism would sweep across all of Southeast Asia, President Truman authorized the OPC to beef up the KMT army in Burma and begin OPERATION PAPER, a supply and training project. Logistics were provided by Civil Air Transport (CAT), the soldier-of-fortune airline that would eventually gain fame as Air America.[12] Brandishing new American arms, the KMT army invaded Yunnan in April 1951, but were thrown back within a week. In the summer of 1952, Li Mi led some two thousand KMT troops about sixty miles into China, but they were again repulsed by the PLA without much difficulty.[13]

Two ineffective "liberations" did not endear the Burmese KMT forces to America or the CIA; it merely irritated the Red Chinese as well as the Burmese government, who feared the KMT forays would give Mao an excuse to hurl his endless hordes into northeast Burma. As Li Mi's outfit proved incapable, American funding dried up. For the KMT troops and their families, there was no bolthole, no final redoubt, no asylum in America. To safeguard themselves and their newfound lives, the army fanned out, seizing as much territory as possible; against Mao's army they were ineffective, but compared to Burmese troops they were tigers. Within months, the KMT was the de facto government of the Shan States, the heart of the Golden Triangle, which produced the bulk of the world's opiates. If the American government would not support the KMT, heroin profits would keep the dollars flowing.[14] To make ends meet, the KMT imposed an "opium tax" on the thousands of small farmers who produced the stuff. In turn, the farmers planted more poppies to make up for the new tax; the result was an explosion in opium production. This created a huge surplus of opium and morphine base for export, a surplus that would eventually hit the streets of America. It was these drug lords that connected with Santos Trafficante in 1968, and they would supply the American (and world) habit for roughly the next two decades.

By the early 1980s, the Golden Triangle was completely controlled by descendants of the KMT army; the former allies produced about 60 percent of the heroin sold in the United States. The drug lords of the Triangle controlled large, well-equipped armies and most of the important Burmese politicians. Even with the capture of the headquarters of the Shan United Army in 1994 and the "surrender" of chief drug lord Khun Sa, the Golden Triangle still supplied over half of the world's opium production in 1995.[15]

LAND OF A MILLION ELEPHANTS

Experienced CIA hands knew one thing about Laos: You could have a war against the Communists or a war against the drugs, but not both. If one wanted the Hmong to mobilize and fight, the cooperation of the Hmong warlords was necessary, and to the existing warlords, opium was the source of not only money, but of their power. It was, in other words, impossible to find (or create) Hmong leaders who were not involved, to some extent, in opium production. While there is considerable dispute about the involvement of the Hmong in the drug export trade, it is commonly accepted that the Hmong leader Vang Pao maintained a stash of opium against the day the Hmong might be abandoned by the Americans or forced to flee Laos.

The war itself also steered the mountain folk to poppy growing, as it took a substantial toll on Hmong agriculture. The Hmong understood that poppies were hardier than corn, rice, and other subsistence crops and could survive with less tending—a necessary trait, as the warriors often left to fight and the villages were forced to flee from time to time. Most importantly, the Americans would supply food, but they would not provide opium. Finally, as the war dragged on and the Hmong agricultural force became depleted by the heavy battle casualties of the late 1960s, Hmong families required crops that produced the greatest income for the smallest amount of labor: opium was it, hands down.

Perhaps the most recognized legacy of the Secret War in Laos is Air America, the descendent of Civil Air Transport and subject of the movie of the same name. Today, the very name "Air America" evokes the connection between drugs and covert action. In one way, this is too bad, for the Air America pilots who flew aging aircraft through sheets of gunfire in the 1960s were among the most courageous flyers to ever strap aircraft to their posteriors. While most former Air America personnel will deny it, it is also a sad fact that *some* Air America pilots did make drug runs; flying in rice and ammo, setting down on a mountainside on a strip the size of a Band-Aid, taking off again with foul-smelling containers of dark brown resin in the cargo bay. We cannot know for sure how much opium was flown out of villages in Laos, and how much of that ended up on Main Street, U.S.A. Considering the number of sorties flown by Air America planes each year, however, if even a small percentage transported opium, the tonnage may have been enormous.

Far more damaging than either Hmong opium production or Air America transport, however, is a covert activity still relatively unknown and unacknowledged. Simply keeping foreign agents of influence on the CIA payroll is one of the less sexy aspects of covert action, but for the running of heroin into Vietnam and the United States, it was critical. During the late 1950s and the 1960s, many of the men who controlled opium trafficking in Laos were on the CIA's payroll. In 1959, Phoumi Nosovan, a rightist politician, was selected by the CIA to serve as the bulwark against Communism in Laos. By the end of the year, Phoumi was both

a cabinet minister and a general, receiving substantial sums of U.S. money to organize the anti-Communist movement. Phoumi refused, however, to become part of
a coalition government with Laotian "neutralists" when the Kennedy administration sought to place Laos out of competition by allowing a nonaligned government. Cut off from U.S. funding, he turned to opium trafficking. By 1963,
Phoumi's empire was netting around $100,000 a month in opium shipped to
Vietnam alone, some grown in Laos and some merely transshipped from Burma.[16]
When Phoumi was overthrown in 1964, his aide, Rattikone Ouane, took over,
eventually forging an alliance with the KMT remnants in the Golden Triangle.
Under Ouane's direction, the Laotian/Burmese connection flooded South Vietnam
with cheap heroin, establishing and encouraging the addiction of thousands of
American soldiers who then brought the habit home with them.

THE GREAT GAME

The olive drab paint on the tank barely showed through the dust as it grunted
across the border; it had been the last Soviet armored vehicle in Afghanistan, and
now there were none. There had been others behind it, but they were flaming
wrecks somewhere back up the road. Like the tanks, the Soviet incursion to preserve a socialist regime was also a flaming wreck, shot down by Egyptian and
Chinese AK-47s and American Stingers.

Although the Afghans had "won," and although they had been generously
supported by the United States, the various mujahedin factions certainly did not
adopt American values and goals. Instead, the "liberated" Afghans turned to
flooding America's streets with heroin. In the mid- and late 1990s, the United
Nations Drug Control Programme estimates that there were about one million
Afghans producing opium, and that Afghanistan was responsible for about 40
percent of the world's opium supply. The "Golden Crescent" virtually replaced
the Myanmar (formerly Burma) as the world's largest opium supplier. One
might have thought that when the strictly Islamic Taliban emerged as the government of the country, along with beating unveiled women and inadequately
bearded men, they might have stamped down on opium production, a decidedly
un-Islamic occupation. Instead, roughly 96 percent of Afghanistan's opium came
from regions under Taliban control.[17]

During the war with the Soviets, the Afghans discovered that a guerrilla war
could be fought much more effectively if the guerrilla economy focused on
opium production instead of food production. Even with generous support from
the United States, several wealthy Islamic governments (e.g., Saudi Arabia), and
some generally anti-Soviet regimes (e.g., China and Egypt), it was still necessary
to supply food and minimal survival requirements to millions of Afghan families whose men were engaging the Red Army in prolonged guerrilla operations.
The poppy is a hardier plant than most foodstuffs, and the profits are liquid. A
small plot of poppies can provide food *and* guns.

During the war of liberation, Afghan opium production in general increased exponentially; the Afghan share of the world market rose to about 40 percent, and at the end of the 1990s the land of the Pathans rivaled the Golden Triangle. While the legacy of the liberation, civil war, rages on, there is little "economic development" occurring. Afghan families can expect a meager income of perhaps $100 per capita engaging in regular commerce and agriculture; they can make fifty times this amount (at a modest estimate) with a small poppy field. Such prosperity cannot be unlearned; you cannot unbite the apple.

In the long run, Afghanistan is (and will continue to be) a prime example of the problems with covert marriages of convenience. Not at all influenced by American values, the Afghans exploited American money and technology to achieve an important U.S. goal: to bleed and defeat the Soviet Union. Once that was accomplished, the alliance degenerated as quickly as that between the United States and the Soviet Union in 1945. Now Afghanistan is ruled by Islamic militants who have been well armed and trained by the United States and friends; its economy is largely run on opium, which provides virtually all of its foreign exchange and an estimated 30 percent of the monetary GDP.

Cocaine, Cowboys, and Contras

The men stood by the dirt and grass airstrip, waiting for the sound of approaching aircraft. The ground was littered with the last of their American cigarettes; here in Costa Rica, there was no need to fieldstrip the butts. Within a minute, the Cessna 402-B zoomed over the clearing, took a half-turn at the far end, and came in to land. As it bumped to a halt, the men in the green fatigues jumped into action, for time was important. The aircraft had to get in and out.

The door of the plane opened, and the pilot, Gary Betzner, stepped out for a moment to stretch his legs. As he did, the awaiting *Norté Americano* strode forward to greet him; his name was John Hull, and he owned this enormous spread of Costa Rican forest. Both men watched as crate after crate of weapons, ammo, and military supplies were manhandled from the cargo compartment of the Cessna. When the cargo bay was empty, neither man was surprised when the loaders turned to a nearby pile of duffle bags and began stacking them into the plane: Betzner counted seventeen duffles and five or six boxes. Within minutes, he was rolling, the aircraft clearing the end of the runway, and the airstrip melting into the lush tropical forest. Within hours, the Cessna reentered American airspace; there was no challenge, and the veteran smuggler had completed another run, cooly bringing in his shipment to Lakeland, Florida. Another load of contra cocaine was about to enter the bloodstream of America.[18]

"The ends justify the means," said Enrique Bermudez, and he meant it. He was first commander of the Nicaraguan contras, and the means involved shipping cocaine to finance the war against the Sandinistas. To win his war and regain his power, Bermudez, a former officer in Anastasio Somoza's brutal

National Guard, was willing to dump as much cocaine as necessary into American neighborhoods. He was a man who *lived* his credo.

Around 1980, cocaine became the drug of choice in America, acquiring a drug "market share" of about 37 percent. Between 1982 and 1985, the number of cocaine users in the United States increased nearly 40 percent.[19] These are also the years when the contras became involved in cocaine trafficking. This is perhaps coincidental, although one might think that the increasing street supply, in no small part provided by "secure" contra airlift, had something to do with the fact that by about 1985, crack was actually selling at less than cost.

In Central America, it is inevitable that a large-scale guerrilla war will become entangled in drug trafficking. Central America is the primary staging area for drug shipments to the big market, the United States. Well before the contras or Sandinistas, there were mule trails and narrow, perilous jungle landing strips, and dangerous men who knew the ways of the underground. The smugglers comprised an existing supply line, and the contras and their American supporters were quick to take advantage; once more, they proved out the adage that a supply line flows both ways.

There are two important ironies that come from the contra-cocaine connection. First, President Reagan understood that the American people viewed drug abuse and trafficking as a bad thing; to that end, his public statements often tried to link the Nicaraguan Sandinista regime to drug dealing. In his zeal, he went so far as to expose a government informant so that he could present photographs of a Sandinista official working with cocaine smugglers.[20] The irony is that there was practically no evidence of Sandinista cocaine trafficking, while Reagan's cherished "freedom fighters" were pumping tons of white corruption onto America's streets.

The second rich yet sad irony is that many Americans, and others, believe that the CIA was behind the contra drug operations. In fact, the contras probably turned to drug trafficking, as they turned to the Secord/North Enterprise, *because* the agency itself and individual CIA officers were generally law-abiding. Bill Casey came to the CIA with a buccaneering vigor, but found that the operating environment of the Company had changed; CIA officers *complied* with disclosure laws. Casey was faced with a dilemma: If he established a CIA operation to support the contras in violation of the law, agency officers would be obligated to inform the Congressional Oversight Committee (Casey, too, was obligated, but could probably could have mumbled his way through, as he did on occasion). On the other hand, he felt that the cold war and his own morality required him to sustain the contras. To resolve this, the director of Central Intelligence established a hip-pocket private program that evaded both the control of Congress and of the CIA's own internal control mechanisms.[21] It was the secret National Security Council operations, not those of the CIA, that provided the contras with secure drug pipelines into the United States.

The extent of contra drug trafficking is impossible to pin down precisely; given the weight of the evidence, however, it seems reasonable to say that as cocaine traffickers, the contras played a substantial role in the amount of "snow" on America's streets. We can also say with a degree of certainty that U.S. government officials knew the contras and their supporters were doing this; anyone can view the pages in Ollie North's notebook and see where he noted that at least some contra money was coming from drugs. National Security Council Officer North not only chose to overlook it, but continued to allow clandestine shipment of drugs into the United States by virtue of taking no steps to stop it. It is unlikely that CIA intelligence officers did not know of contra drug dealing, as one could scarcely move around the clandestine world in those years without tripping over the evidence. Whatever efforts were made to act on this information or pass it on remain agency secrets. Moreover, the Drug Enforcement Administration (DEA) certainly knew of some of the contra drug running and tried to stop it; they were simply told to sit down and shut up. Finally, the media publicized the issue enough so that, at the very least, inquiries could have been made, should the secretary of state or DCI been so inclined. In the end, the operating ethos of the contra supporters was characterized exactly right by Enrique Bermudez: "The ends justify the means."

DRUG EMPIRES: AN OFFER YOU CAN'T REFUSE?

There are enormous benefits to exploiting drug syndicates and cartels in covert-action programs. Many of the features that make "ordinary" organized crime useful—if not attractive—to intelligence agencies also apply to drug organizations. Operating underground drug empires have established intelligence nets, "own" numerous powerful individuals (politicians, military men, judges, police, intelligence officers, gunrunners, document dealers, and so on), and usually maintain well-armed private armies.

Further, drug producers, smugglers, and buyers are by their very nature anti-Communist. The control over every aspect of individual life represented by a Communist regime is anathema to the drug producers, who are, above all, entrepreneurs. Right-wing dictatorships can be accommodated with some cash in the right pocket, but the kind of totalitarian regimes generally established by Communists leave no room for either vice or private enterprise. Drug syndicates, in this light, tend to be reliable allies, for they have nowhere else to turn. Thus, for much of the cold war, partnership between U.S. intelligence and drug organizations was viewed as a natural collaboration.

Finally, one might also claim, based on historical evidence, that the alliance with drug syndicates, however unfortunate, has been justified by the outcome of the cold war in general and of specific regional conflicts in particular. U.S. support for the Afghans during the 1980s was undeniably critical in kicking the Soviets out of the country; it probably had some effect on the dissolution of the Soviet Union as well. Without the contras, others argue, Nicaragua might still be a Communist state. Moreover, while the United States did not emerge victorious, in the traditional sense, in Southeast Asia, the fierce war in Laos bled the

Communists so badly they were forced to stop there rather than sweeping on through Thailand, Malaysia, and Indonesia. France, critical to the coherence of Western Europe, did not fall to the Communists, in part because of CIA support of the Corsicans on the Marseilles docks. It is thus critical to understand, some might say, that in the big picture, the costs of the drug syndicate alliances were both necessary and, indeed, paid off.

You Knew I Was a Snake When You Picked Me Up . . . Again

It is hard to argue against all this, yet it would also be hard to imagine a more costly way to wage the cold war. The price of drug abuse to the United States, its people, and its families, is almost inestimable. The monetary expense alone of drug abuse includes the costs of:

- medical and emergency room treatment;
- police time and additional officers;
- incarceration of drug dealers, smugglers, and those who have committed drug-motivated property and violent crimes;
- interdiction (Coast Guard, DEA, Customs Service, U.S. military);
- U.S. support of antidrug efforts overseas;
- lost productivity from affected individuals;
- indirect costs of drug crime, such as higher insurance and security costs; and
- the development of organized crime and its attendant costs.

All these together run into the hundreds of billions of dollars annually. This does not even include the human wreckage:

- tens of thousands of dead Americans;
- millions of individual lives ruined;
- millions of families shattered;
- the death, danger, and trauma inflicted on law enforcement and medical personnel;
- fear of walking neighborhood streets;
- the millions of people injured and traumatized every year by drug-motivated crimes, in which the criminal is either on drugs or seeking money to buy more; and
- the corruption in government, law enforcement, and legal system engendered by the enormous influx of drug money.

It would be unfair and almost certainly factually wrong to lay all this at the feet of American intelligence. Left-wing writers often end up charging that the CIA is *responsible* for the various drug epidemics that have ravaged America. This would be hard to establish, and is almost certainly untrue. Drugs were being abused and smuggled into the United States long before the CIA was created; drug abusers would seek out their pleasure in any event, and drug producers and smugglers would try to meet this demand, and, to a degree, would succeed.

It would also be wrong, however, to assert, as many right-wing writers do, that American intelligence bears *no* responsibility. The Sicilian and Corsican Mafia were battered until the CIA/OPC picked them up; the Golden Triangle was a collection of small-time farmers until the KMT "Shan army" organized the production and collection of opium; opium from Laos would have arrived in the U.S. at a much slower rate and lower volume were it not for the air transportation provided by CIA aircraft; Afghanistan was not a major opium exporter until CIA support began to arrive; anti-Communist regimes and movements in Latin America receive CIA support while at the same time exploiting the drug-export economy themselves, often for personal gain rather than to sincerely aid their cause.

American support for drug trafficking organizations also deprived the United States of its moral standing on international drug issues; perhaps not so much globally as within certain regions. While the State Department and the DEA were pressuring countries such as Turkey, Laos, Thailand, Pakistan, Burma, and Colombia to stamp out their drug producers, the CIA was often funneling money, arms, ships, aircraft, and training to the very same drug organizations. To the foreign governments, it must have seemed as if the antidrug message was accompanied by a very obvious wink. Who could chastise France for tolerating the heroin labs in Marseille when America's own CIA supported the syndicate that owned the facilities? Who could blame Colombia for not pursuing the Medellín Cartel—a primary source for contra cocaine transshipped to the United States—when so much of Pablo Escobar's product was slipping into the United States on contra national-security-exempt aircraft? As long as the CIA continues to deal with drug syndicates, the moral standing of the United States to condemn other governments for tolerating drug production is exactly zero—or perhaps less, as such behavior only reinforces foreign perception of the U.S. government as hypocritical and self-serving.

America paid a substantial cost, too, in the development of organized crime. Drug profits have been an enormous windfall to the various criminal organizations; most could not exist without it. Sadly, some of these very syndicates, verging on extinction, were revived by the support of American intelligence agencies.

Without the CIA, the drugs would still have been produced; without the CIA, they still would have been shipped to America. Without the CIA, however, the process would have been much less efficient. The drug producers would not have become so centralized in the Golden Triangle and the Golden Crescent. The transportation routes would have been substantially more perilous if the national security blanket had not been thrown over them. High-level drug traffickers would have gone to jail (or gone much earlier) if the DEA had not received so many "hands off" orders from American intelligence agencies.

IS THE LEARNING CURVE FLAT?
DRUGS AND COVERT ACTION

No one has made a serious effort to assess the cost of covert action to the United States. In particular, it would be difficult—but not impossible, in my opinion—to estimate the proportion of America's drug problems that were caused or exacerbated by the covert activities of intelligence agencies. This does not mean, however, that nothing can be learned.[22]

One of the ironies of the CIA's involvement with the drug traffickers is that the narcotics syndicates are often the only groups that don't need American money to fight insurgencies. In many cases, insurgents began as regular proxy armies supported by the CIA—e.g., the KMT or the contras—and to some extent turned to drug trafficking because CIA largesse was cut off. In retrospect, it is practically an virtual iron law that indigenous forces from regions with high drug agriculture potential will either turn to drug production themselves or else co-opt existing drug growers. In the latter case, the takeover of drug agriculture by an armed force has always meant the centralization of drug production, increased agricultural efficiency, expansion of drug growing acreage,[23] and a more effective export system. In the long term, it would be wise to consider such possibilities before committing the United States to support of a proxy force in one of these areas.

It is quite tempting for intelligence operators to adopt a casual attitude toward drug trafficking by friends. In many of the historical cases, opium or coca was indeed part of the local culture. Moreover, a laissez-faire attitude about this often allows covert wars to be carried out on the cheap: Insurgents don't need as much money from Washington if they have a few million in heroin profits flowing in. Intelligence officers who fight winning, frugal wars figure to go far at Langley.

This is an extremely dangerous and deceptive argument, however. One cannot expect one's erstwhile allies to suddenly change long-established cultural norms, at least if one wants to keep them as allies. Narcotics *export*, on the other hand, is scarcely an established tradition. It may be necessary for survival or prosperity in lands ravaged by poverty and war, but it is nonetheless a fairly recent phenomenon. Even if it wins, a U.S.-supported regime or insurgent group may find it preferable to establish its own autonomy by taxing drug traffickers rather than stamping them out; this way, they can eliminate their reliance on the United States government. The expectation that a victorious ally adopt American values and policies fails to recognize a fundamental tenet of covert action: "Allies" have their own agendas.

Further, if the covert action is worth fighting, it should be worth funding. Whether or not the president, the DCI, or a lieutenant colonel in the White House basement likes it, money for covert action *must* be appropriated by Congress. Any other mechanism is extraconstitutional; any resulting action is simply the foreign policy of the people who pay for it, not the foreign policy of the United States of America.

What makes drug organizations different from other organized crime organizations, from the covert action perspective, is the fabulous amount of money they command. "Ordinary" crime syndicates carry on a lucrative business and can bribe or threaten individuals when necessary. It has been estimated, though, that drug cartels spend more than $100 million annually on bribes. This is not only a temptation to cops, judges, customs officers, and so forth; it *must* be a temptation to intelligence officers and contract agents who work with groups involved in drug trafficking. CIA officers, and generally contract agents, are reasonably well paid, and the government pension provides a good retirement. This is nothing, however, compared to what an agent can make off a single shipment of heroin or cocaine, not to mention the potential payoff for arranging security for a steady drug pipeline. No CIA officer has ever been convicted of drug trafficking, but contract agents have a decidedly less sterling record. From the government officials on the CIA payroll (e.g., Manuel Noriega, Phoumi Nosovan of Thailand) to the rogue pilots of Air America to the contras and the mujahedin, drug money has corrupted operations; CIA and intelligence expertise and support has made the allies' drug syndicates much more secure and efficient.

Much as the fatally flawed, brittle steel in the hull of the *Titanic*, cooperation with drug syndicates is an inevitable time bomb. *Losing* a covert war with drug traffickers as allies is bad—they'll need to stock up on cash before the war ends, and afterward will need a new base of operation, thereby spreading corruption to a new locale. If we support them and *win*, we have merely put drug traffickers in new positions of power, perhaps even legitimized them. Win or lose, cooperation with U.S. intelligence gives drug organizations resources, money, connections, security, clandestine or "protected" routes into the United States, and cover from prosecution. In the end, win or lose in local wars, working with the drug syndicates is an offer you can't *accept*.

NOTES

1. In fact, Webb never says that the CIA sold the drugs, nor claims explicitly that the promotion of crack and the protection of drug lords was official agency policy. See Gary Webb, "Dark Alliance: The Story Behind the Crack Epidemic," *San Jose Mercury News*, 18 August 1996. It can be found at http: www.sjmercury.com/drugs.

2. See, for example, Louis Farrakhan's *Final Call*, which includes articles about the Webb series and interpretations such as "Betrayal of the Highest Order." (See Finalcall.com, October 1996.)

3. I use Peking here because in the days when opium use was pandemic in China, the city was called Peking. With the coming of the Communists, the opium habit was mostly eliminated in China (mostly by eliminating opium users), and later the Western pronunciation of the city was changed to Beijing.

4. See Alfred McCoy, *The Politics of Heroin: CIA Complicity in the Global Drug Trade* (Brooklyn, N.Y.: Lawrence Hill Books, 1991), pp. 20–23.

5. See ibid., pp. 36–38.

6. Ibid., pp. 46–48.

7. Ibid., pp. 46–63; Tom Braden, "I'm Glad the CIA is 'Immoral,'" *Saturday Evening Post*, 20 May 1967, pp. 10–14.

8. U.S. Drug Enforcement Administration, "The Heroin Labs of Marseille," *Drug Enforcement* (fall 1973): 11–13.

9. McCoy, *The Politics of Heroin*, pp. 67–70.

10. Ibid., p. 38.

11. John T. Cusack, "Turkey Lifts the Poppy Ban," *Drug Enforcement* (fall 1974): 3.

12. The Flying Tigers were American soldiers of fortune who flew for the Chinese against the Japanese invaders from 1937 through 1940. Many of them were American Army Air Corps or Navy pilots who resigned from the U.S. Army to fight in China. This was a U.S. government-sanctioned covert operation.

13. See John Prados, *President's Secret Wars: CIA and Pentagon Covert Operations Since World War II* (New York: William Morrow and Co., 1986), pp. 73–77.

14. McCoy, *The Politics of Heroin*, pp. 171–73.

15. Thomas Constantine, "The Threat of Heroin to the United States," testimony before the House Committee on Government Reform and Oversight, Subcommittee on National Security, International Affairs, and Criminal Justice, September 19, 1996. This refers to world production, not American consumption.

16. See McCoy, *The Politics of Heroin*, p. 302.

17. See "Afghanistan's Gold," *The Middle East* (September 1997): ppTK.

18. See Senate Committee on Foreign Relations, Subcommittee on Terrorism, Narcotics, and International Operations, Drugs, Law Enforcement, and Foreign Policy, 100th Cong., 2d sess., 1988, S. Rept. S100-165, pp. 53–55.

19. All these figures are of course estimates. The market share is measured in dollars spent on illicit drugs in the United States; see William French Smith, "Drug Traffic Today: Challenge and Response," *Drug Enforcement* (summer 1982): 2–5. For the number of cocaine users, see U.S. Comptroller General, *Controlling Drug Abuse* (March 1, 1998): 7–9.

20. The informant was Barry Seal, an extraordinary pilot who became a DEA informant, by some accounts the best undercover agent the DEA ever had. Seal's exposure probably led to his murder by cartel hit men. His story was dramatized in the HBO movie *Double-Crossed*.

21. That is to say, evaded the controls in practical terms; in legal terms, he evaded the law by dying, for the operation was patently illegal.

22. Many people assume that since one cannot *precisely* measure the variables involved in intelligence-related drug trafficking, any attempt to estimate these costs is useless. Nothing could be further from the truth. One can work with estimates to produce a model, and then sensitivity test the model; use the most conservative estimates for a "low" figure, "high" estimates for the upper limit, and "likely" estimates for the most probable effect. It's hard, but not impossible. The alternative, of course, is to simply make whatever assumption one wishes for the most political advantage.

23. Internationally, this is usually measured in hectares.

Chapter 9

My Heroes Have
Always Been Cowboys

The waves lapped at the small boat as it quietly motored toward the beach. Midnight was black, moonless, and that was why the boat was coming in *this* night. By the time the sun came up, the big ships would be in the bay: the *Houston*, the *Barbara J.*, the *Blagar*, and the *Rio Escondido*. From their decks would come the landing boats, each crammed with highly trained, highly motivated troops intent on one mission: *Get* that bastard Castro. It was the early morning of 17 April 1961, and OPERATION ZAPATA, the landing at the Bay of Pigs, was underway.

This first small boat was critical. More than one amphibious assault had failed because landing craft got lost, scattering men and equipment along miles of coastline, turning a cohesive strike force into a confused, blood-soaked disaster. The United States had learned the hard way in World War II that a hard-hitting, coordinated amphibious landing required highly skilled pathfinders leading the way. This was the role of the Underwater Demolition Teams (UDTs), who would go ahead of the landing craft, slipping ashore under the very noses of enemy soldiers, marking channels and beachheads so that the troops would arrive at the right locations. Selected Cuban exiles, members of the 2506 Brigade, had been carefully trained for this critical job, and now, in the blackness, the Cuban UDTs in this boat strained for a glimpse of the beach.

ZAPATA was to be an all-Cuban operation. President Kennedy had been very clear on this, as had President Eisenhower before him. "There won't be a white face on the beach," promised Deputy Director for Plans Richard M. Bissell. This was a pivotal design element of ZAPATA. The United States did not want to provoke a confrontation with the Soviets, nor did it want to reinforce the image of the imperialist bully shoving around a small Latin American country yet again. What neither Kennedy nor Eisenhower counted on, however, was the intense fighting spirit of the American leader of the operation, Grayston Lynch. Lynch was a legendary Special Forces operator, and a natural choice to coordinate OPER-ATION ZAPATA in the field. He had lied about his age (fifteen years old) to join the army, and had hit the beach at Normandy on D day. After the war, Lynch joined the newly emerging Special Forces, eventually serving in the covert war in Laos. Retiring as a captain in 1960, he immediately plunged into CIA covert operations, starting with the 2506 Brigade of Cuban exiles. Despite Bissell's promise, anyone who knew Gray Lynch could have predicted where he'd be when the shooting started: right in the front of the first boat. Lynch had trained the UDTs, and, like the commander of any outstanding Special Forces troop, he was going to lead them.

On this night, however, Lynch was not running lucky. One of the red marker lights the UDT team carried suddenly began flashing. The startled frogmen managed to get it shut off, but a moment later, it began blinking again, until Lynch ripped out every wire he could find. As Lynch's small, vulnerable boat cut toward shore, a jeep pulled into sight, driving slowly along the beach. The Cuban militiamen had seen the blinking light and thought a local fishing boat was in trouble. They were trying to be helpful.

As the jeep approached, it aimed its headlights out into the inlet to assist the "fishing boat," and instead lit up Lynch's UDT boat, pinning them in the middle of the bay like sitting ducks. Another ten seconds and the frogmen were dead men. Lynch did the only thing possible: He opened fire, blasting the jeep with his Browning Automatic Rifle (BAR). In seconds, the UDTs were engaged in a fierce firefight as the call went out to alert Castro's forces; the jeep was shattered, and so was any chance of surprise. Gray Lynch was fortunate. None of the return fire hit him, and even when his command ship, the *Blagar*, was strafed by Castro's aircraft, he was unharmed. Moreover, Lynch's unauthorized exploit had not blown the cover off ZAPATA, although it could well have.

In the intelligence trade, men like this are sometimes called *cowboys*. The word conjures images of heroism, individualism, and wild, perhaps out-of-control, behavior. In the underground world of black ops, all of the above apply. "Cowboy," however, is not meant as a compliment. Even heroism, a relatively common trait among cowboys and covert operators, can be a liability when the point of a mission is first and foremost to conceal the involvement of the United States. When individuals step over the operational limits of covert action, the situation may go from bad to worse.

THE COWBOY WAY

There are many cowboys far more out of control than Gray Lynch: men who have sunk the ships of friendly nations; agents who have led indigenous forces into combat, risking capture; operators who have purposely attacked friendly countries hoping to provoke overt U.S. military intervention; and some who have gone over to the highest bidder, even as far as supplying terrorists with weapons and training.

In many respects, the men that intelligence officers call cowboys do indeed possess the traits of the stereotypical cowboy of the Old West. They are typically men of direct action, courage, powerful moral codes, and fierce loyalty to their country, their cause, and especially to their *people*. While these qualities are generally admirable, in a covert operator each is a double-edged sword.

Initiative, enthusiasm for direct action, and courage are all essential traits in an effective covert intelligence or paramilitary officer. These individuals must inspire indigenous people to undertake dangerous endeavors, perhaps breaking out of traditions dating back centuries. The difficult part for the covert operator, however, is that the same characteristics also impel the agent to *lead*. Perhaps the most difficult thing these individuals are asked to do is to mobilize, train, and earn the trust of their troops—and then send them off to combat while staying behind. Some simply cannot do it, and it is hard to fault them. No matter how difficult, however, it is a requirement of the job. Live Americans captured in combat who appear on CNN tend to blow the cover off covert operations.

RIP ROBERTSON: YOU COULDN'T MAKE HIM UP

The crew looked up as the aircraft zoomed over their heads, and the captain smiled and waved. Although it was 1954 and he was docked at San José, Guatemala, his ship, the freighter *Springfjord*, was loaded with coffee and cotton. There was no reason to fear. Then the hatch on the aircraft opened, releasing a load of—leaflets. It was a warning; the ship was about to be bombed. As the crew hastily fled ashore, the aircraft circled, allowing them time. Swinging his craft around, the American pilot, Ferdinand Schoup, lined up the ship for the bomb run, and stuck the bomb into the heart of the *Springfjord*. Five hundred pounds of high explosive blasted through the hull of the ship, opening huge a hole to the sea. Despite this, it didn't sink completely, although it quickly developed a sharp list to starboard. Schoup watched for the secondary explosions, for his intelligence had reported the ship was loaded with gasoline for Jacobo Arbenz's Communist hordes. As with so many other intel reports from PB/SUCCESS, this one was wrong too. The coffee and cotton, however, were a loss.

"Rip" Robertson, given name William, was the man behind the bombing. Several days before, Nicaraguan dictator Anastasio Somoza (father of the Anastasio Somoza overthrown in 1979) had told Robertson of the "gasoline" shipment and ordered Robertson to bomb the ship. Back at Opa Locka, Florida, the CIA base controlling the Guatemalan operation, cooler heads prevailed, suggesting that such a spectacular assault would draw unwanted attention to Guatemala and might result in exposing the role of the CIA. Better, they directed Robertson, to use a quiet commando raid or perhaps frogmen to quietly sink the ship without all the pyrotechnics.

Rip Robertson, however, was a classic cowboy: courageous, dedicated, impulsive. A couple years earlier in Korea, Robertson had trained South Korean guerrillas and, against strict orders, led them into North Korea. During PB/SUCCESS, Robertson led commando raids into Guatemala to sabotage and shoot up government trains. Seven years after the sinking of the *Springfjord*, Robertson would, like Gray Lynch, lead his frogmen ashore at the Bay of Pigs. Now, when the word from Opa Locka arrived, Robertson made a command decision: he'd ignore orders and bomb the ship anyway.

Unfortunately, the foundered vessel was *not* carrying gasoline; more unfortunately, it was a *British* ship. The government of Britain was perhaps more shocked than outraged, as was the shipping firm's insurer, Lloyd's of London. DDP Frank Wisner immediately went to the British Embassy to personally apologize, and the CIA quietly settled with Lloyd's for a million and a half. Robertson was discreetly cut loose (to be recalled for ZAPATA in 1961).[1]

"HAPPY (HO CHI MINH) TRAILS"

The North Vietnamese troops were about two hundred yards away. Some would take cover and fire, while others moved up, getting ever closer. The big ex-marine picked one of the crouching enemy and waited patiently, the front post (sight) of his M-1 carbine lined up where the Communist's head would appear when he jumped up to advance. The target showed, and the American squeezed the trigger; the target disappeared. Already, the American's combat-trained eyes were picking up the next mark.

He'd never bothered to officially change his name. He was born Anthony Poshepny, but to everyone, he was simply Tony Poe. Like all American advisors in the Laos during the 1950s and 1960s, Tony Poe was under unequivocal orders to stay out of combat. Laos was supposed to be neutral, and the U.S. government didn't want to give the Soviets, Chinese, or North Vietnamese an excuse to openly escalate the war; Laos was much closer to any of them than to the United States, and an open conflict would be very difficult and costly. Better to follow the adage of the U.S. Army, "Never fight a land war in Asia," and keep the war in Laos small, secret, and manageable. Moreover, word of American involvement could raise domestic hell in the United States. For Tony Poe, however, there was only one way to lead: from the front. The Hmong would fight like tigers if well and smartly led.

Poe was just the man for the job. Having experienced war from the sharp end of the stick as a marine in World War II, and wounded at Iwo Jima, he had joined the CIA soon afterward. The big American excelled at covert tradecraft and paramilitary operations, and was a standout graduate of his class at the Farm, the CIA clandestine training facility at Camp Peary, Virginia. He quickly put his natural talents and acquired skills to work, training the Khamba tribesmen of Tibet to fight against the Chinese occupation of that country; organizing a Chinese Muslim force for an eventually aborted covert action in China; crossing into China himself on missions that remain classified to this day; and participating in the 1958 CIA-sponsored rebellion against Sukarno in Indonesia. By 1965, Tony Poe was leading Hmong forces in Laos. That's how he ended up in a firefight at "Site 86," the village of Hong Nong.

Fired with methodical precision into the advancing North Vietnamese, Poe's slugs slammed into one Communist after another, turning back the North Vietnamese Army (NVA) advance virtually single-handedly; one of his Hmong compatriots counted seventeen bodies in front of the stalwart CIA man's position. Poe was moving forward to search them for intelligence information when the steel-jacketed bullet hammered into his hip; he went down hard and fast. Through teeth-clenching pain, he observed several North Vietnamese troops he hadn't seen before running toward him, probably eager for a trophy—a captured American would be a worldwide propaganda coup. Calmly, the big ex-marine eased three grenades off his harness, pulling the pin on the first but holding the spoon;[2] he would lay low, draw them in. When the Communists got close enough, Poe heaved the grenade, then the second, then the third. Three quick explosions followed, and the field was clear; Tony Poe had gotten them all. He wouldn't be taken this day.[3]

Though desperately wounded, Poe was still true to his moral code. An American "black" helicopter swooped in low to pick him up, but it was against American policy to use covert aircraft to evacuate injured "indigs." Tony Poe, however, would *not* abandon his men. He forced the American pilot to take on board thirteen wounded Hmong and fly the whole lot of them to safety, even though it burned out the engine on the chopper. "You can be the biggest prick in the world," he would later say, "as long as you take care of your people."[4] It's the code of the West.

BLACK OPS AND OPERATIONAL LIMITS

While the heroics of these cowboys are admirable, they also put the secrecy of the covert operation in jeopardy. There are many good reasons for covert action to be *covert*:

- to avoid provoking another country, either the target of the operation or its powerful ally;
- to avoid sinking a nation's reputation into an operation or secret war;
- if a government gets caught in a secret war, it will either have to abandon it and look ineffective and foolish or protect its reputation and credibility by escalating, and look bullying and foolish;
- to avoid getting caught in a lie (e.g., "We support the neutrality of Laos" or "We're not trying to overthrow the government of Nicaragua");
- to avoid embarrassing the president;
- perhaps even to evade the law or the U.S. Constitution.

At its core, the issue is this: Without deniability, a covert action is simply an act of war. Therefore, to stay with the accepted bounds of international affairs, intelligence agencies establish *operational limits* for each covert action. These are simply a set of rules laying out exactly how involved the United States is willing to get, what acts the field operators can undertake and what they cannot, what American assets will be available and which are out of play, and so forth. These limits are akin to the military "rules of engagement," serving to limit the responsibility of the United States for black ops should the action be exposed.

Operational limits are not usually written in a formal document. Some intelligence executives prefer hard-and-fast rules so that field operators know exactly where they stand. Other executives prefer operational limits that are implied but not specific, which gives the agency some flexibility; sometimes limits are negotiated *during* the operation when unforeseen needs arise. The latter approach may produce more overall "success," since greater resources can be dragged into the operation than might have been obtained when the plan was first put forth (e.g., "We're already involved, and we've got so much invested; just a half-dozen American planes will win the day"). Unfortunately, this approach also contains the spark of escalation, wherein the role of the government is exposed, the reputation of the country is put on the line, and the United States ends up fighting a full-scale, costly war in a highly strategic area such as, say, Vietnam.

The idea is to not get caught committing acts of war against a country with which the United States is supposedly at peace, so that the United States is not "accidentally" dragged into a war (or subwar violence) that it is not ready for or that is not worth the objective. For one example, a strict operational limit in ZAPATA was that no Americans would do anything that might get them captured and displayed to the world as "imperialist aggressors."[5] For another, pilots on black missions are required to fly without identification of any kind, so that they cannot be traced back to the United States if they're shot down. Sometimes these limits are obeyed, as by the Americans who flew during the Bay of Pigs, and sometimes they are not, as by Lawrence Allen Pope, who was shot down by Sukarno's Indonesian forces in 1957, carrying his Civil Air Transport contract, his U.S. Air Force ID, and his Clark Air Force Base (Philippines) PX card.

Typical operational limits run along these lines:

- No Americans can be caught or identified as American if killed. If they are, the United States will say they were cowboys or mercenaries acting on their own (i.e., they will be "disavowed").
- No identifiable American assets can be used, including vehicles, weapons, traceable money, clothes and uniforms, etc. Any matériel provided must be available on the world market, preferably purchased on the market by front companies that cannot be traced.
- All operations should be based outside U.S. territory; not even offices should be maintained on American soil (see chapter 14 for a full discussion).
- No American armed forces can be engaged in combat, or even called on in the direst emergency. Ideally, American forces should not even be in the vicinity, as it poses too great a temptation to the "indigs," the covert operators, the DCI, and the president.[6]
- Field agents should not promise any of the above to indigenous forces, especially American engagement.

Operational limits are the *essence* of covert action, for they create plausible deniability. If the people, equipment, and money in an operation are not American, or cannot be proved to be American, then it is at least possible that it is an independent venture. Once the limits are broken, exposure almost certainly follows. To make covert action work (at least as a *covert* action), it is necessary to treat operational limits as a plate glass window: Once it's broken, there is no going back. Once the role of the CIA or the United States has been exposed, secrecy *cannot* be reestablished. The government must either continue the operation as an essentially aboveground proxy war—and face the international political fallout, the political discord this is likely to create at home, and the problems created by proof of intervention[7]—or else withdraw and thereby abandon its indigenous allies, creating another set of political problems.

Some operators have argued that operational limits need to be flexible, as one cannot anticipate every contingency or emergency that might occur during a black op in the real world.

> I have seen a good many operations which started out like the Bay of Pigs—insistence on complete secrecy—non-involvement of the U.S.—initial reluctance to authorize supporting actions. This limitation tends to disappear as the needs of the operation become clarified.
>
> Allen Dulles[8]

> You can't take an operation of this scope [Guatemala, 1954], draw narrow boundaries of policy around them, and be absolutely sure that those boundaries will never be overstepped.
>
> Richard Bissell[9]

At first blush, this attitude seems like the only reasonable way to approach tricky political and paramilitary endeavors. History has mainly proved true the military aphorism that "no plan survives contact with the enemy," and perhaps the best label of what happens in combat is Clausewitz's "Fog of War." Further, the history of CIA covert actions shows the effect a little judicious rule-bending can have at a critical moment. In the Guatemalan coup of 1954, a few additional aircraft supplied by the United States may have tipped the scales,[10] as may a show of force by the U.S. Navy, which convinced Arbenz that he was doomed even if he defeated Castillo Armas's "army."

This path, however, can far too easily lead off the cliff. Operators or directors of black operations can become too readily convinced that any operational limits are not "real limits," i.e., they can probably persuade the president or DCI to scrap these limits—and, therefore, the "covert" aspect of an operation—whenever the need arises, as illustrated by Allen Dulles, above. This can lead to the trap of planning and executing poorly thought-out missions or missions with a low probability of "covert" success, in the expectation that if need be, the marines or navy can always pull the chestnuts out of the fire. There is some significant evidence that this occurred in the planning of ZAPATA,[11] where President Kennedy believed that operational limits *were* real but the intelligence executives did not. One of the keys to covert action is *failure*: If it fails, it will not damage the United States, *because the United States did not do it*. When operators pitch a black op as a "no-lose" situation while keeping open the possibility of open intervention as a (or *the*) contingency plan, they have the recipe for more Bay of Pigs fiascoes.

To make effective use of covert action, the decision-makers in government must understand the *kind* of covert operation they are being asked to approve, as well as the contingency plans in case of failure or exposure:

- *Strict Covert*: The role of United States cannot be acknowledged without jeopardizing the success of the mission. Overt intervention is likely to make matters worse.
- *Covert if Possible*: The operation should start and remain covert if possible, but the objective is so critical that overt intervention should be authorized if the covert action appears likely to fail, or if overt action will not create a serious foreign or domestic backlash.[12] Specific overt assistance and operations should be clearly described (and perhaps delimited) in the planning process.
- *Overt Action Required*: Covert action is likely to fail, reveal the hand of the United States, or simply drag out the process. In this case, it is best to go immediately to overt intervention, assuming the objective is suitably important and clearly defined, and either (1) American public support can be mobilized, or (2) the operation can be completed so swiftly as to obviate domestic public opinion.

Such a procedure would assist decision makers in avoiding the trap, often encouraged by proponents of black operations, of thinking that covert action is a "no-lose" proposition.

TO RIDE, SHOOT STRAIGHT, AND SPEAK THE TRUTH

Perhaps the critical problem with cowboys is that their actions often blow apart the "covert" part of covert action. In their zeal to get the job done come hell, high water, lack of ammo, no air cover, and indifferently motivated "indigs," they knowingly take risks that could get them killed, captured, or exposed as American operators. This cowboy nature is probably critical to mobilizing and leading indigenous troops in combat. Earning the trust of mountain people who have never received anything except lead from their own government (i.e., bullets) is a formidable task. Aside from convincing the local people that he is tough and fearless, can cause food and weapons to fall from the sky, and can eat truly disgusting things, there is one other problem the operator must surmount: loyalty. If he cannot persuade the tribe, village, or nation that he is *personally* deeply committed to them, he cannot lead them (and if *he* doesn't lead, they're not going to follow anyone else). In most cases, these peoples have been frequently betrayed by government representatives, perhaps for centuries; they will want proof that the American operator will stick. Often, a good way for the agent to demonstrate this is to openly defy orders from his own superiors. Unfortunately, the orders that are (1) easiest to "overlook," and (2) most useful to the indigenous people are precisely those related to maintaining a deniable low profile. As described in chapter 7, it is often in the best interests of the indigenous group that covert support from another country be exposed, in the hope that the allied power will have to escalate the conflict, and perhaps even overtly intervene, to avoid losing prestige. Moreover, simply by living, working, and fighting among people, a CIA adviser may come to identify with them more than his own country and government, and may even come to think of himself as one of them. It is not even unusual for an American operator to marry a native woman (or women, in some cases), and largely adopt their customs, way of life, and manner of warfare. A few even choose to permanently embrace their adopted people, to the point of refusing to return to the United States, even when American support is withdrawn.

Moreover, often the orders that come down from on high have no relation to reality. Ordering an operator to train troops, but not lead them, places the field agent in an almost impossible situation. Who is going to follow a leader who doesn't lead? In the macho world of many indigenous warrior tribes, such behavior is inconceivable. Further, the "indigs" will often not grasp the intricacies of "high politics," especially the desire of the United States to avoid confrontation. If America is so powerful, why does it care? Why does it not simply squash its foes like dung beetles? Try explaining the concept of plausible deniability to a village that only just discovered the wheel.

Back in the Saddle Again: Cowboy Foreign Policy

Cowboys need not be field operatives like Rip Robertson or Tony Poe. Some higher-level individuals also go off on their own, essentially making their own foreign policy. One example is General John Singlaub, former commander of U.S. forces in Korea, who retired after a public disagreement with President Carter. Singlaub went on to lead the World Anti-Communist League, a transnational organization of hard-core anti-Communists that provides training and material support for anti-Communist causes and governments around the world. When the United States government stopped supporting the contras in Nicaragua, Singlaub, supported by several private organizations, made sure the bullets kept flowing.

Cowboys operate even at high levels of the U.S. government. When National Security Advisor Admiral John Poindexter claimed that he had fostered an organization that provided money, supplies, and arms to the contras, he was admitting to being cowboy. This is so because he was aware of the potential illegality of his acts, and he thought he was doing what the president wanted, *but he didn't have real authorization from President Reagan.* According to Poindexter himself, he had exceeded his authority by making foreign policy decisions for the president.[13] Poindexter's claims are not new: When the CIA was plotting the assassination of Patrice Lumumba, DCI Allen Dulles apparently never received explicit orders from the president. To "protect" both the president and the presidency, Dulles simply inferred his authorization on the basis of veiled or ambiguous statements from President Eisenhower.

THE CODE OF THE WEST

It is also an unfortunate fact in the Machiavellian world of international politics that courageous men who follow orders and stay within operational limits are still sometimes labeled cowboys, sometimes by the very government whose orders they are carrying out. The nature of covert action sometimes means denying American agents and soldiers much as Peter denied Jesus: "I know him not."

This occurs in two circumstances. First, in many black operations, the intelligence agents understand that if they are exposed or captured, they are on their own. It is inherent in a deniable operation that the personnel cannot be acknowledged by the United States, else the role of the United States will be exposed, with all the attendant consequences. For intelligence operators, this comes with the territory; those who can't accept this should find another line of work.

The second circumstance is less respectable: American officers or agents are led to believe that the United States will support them as American operatives, but when exposed they are called cowboys and abandoned by the agency and government that sent them.

Deniability and the role of cowboys is even more confusing because of the government practice of sheep-dipping. To make an operation deniable, it is necessary that any of the personnel at risk (of exposure, capture, or death) sever all ties with the government and/or U.S. intelligence agencies before they undertake the mission or program. Frequently, highly skilled people at the peak of their careers "retire" for no apparent reason. Sometimes an operator will immediately hire on with a company with an ambiguous or meaningless name (e.g., The Dodge Corporation, Universal Export), based out of an office containing a single telephone—and no other furniture; the phone sits on the floor. Because of practices like this, there are hundreds or even thousands of individuals who may or may not belong to American intelligence, and there is really no way to tell (at least for the public, the press, members of Congress, and foreign governments).

BONANZA! WHEN SPOOKS GO PRIVATE

Tremendous difficulties arise when intelligence agents begin to operate on their own, either out of conviction or simply for the cash. These individuals are often dangerous fellows, with specialized and finely honed skills that could be put to good use in private wars (see chapter 14) or criminal endeavors, e.g., paramilitary tactics, terrorism, explosives, weapons training and use, breaking and entering (black-bag jobs), clandestine border crossing and infiltration, surveillance and surveillance electronics, forgery, bribery, blackmail, manufacturing false identity, and so forth. Further, agents operating in government covert operations also develop an extraordinary array of contacts, some savory and other less so (e.g., agents and officials of other governments; U.S. government officials, military personnel, and law enforcement personnel; government agents and intelligence personnel who don't know or don't care that the operators are off the government roll; drug traffickers; revolutionaries; arms smugglers; terrorists and assassins; mercenaries; Mafia wiseguys; illicit "money men"; and so on). While these contacts have been cultivated in the course of government business, agents cannot "un-know" someone. In some cases, these contacts extend well beyond professional acquaintance into the realm of friendship, and relationships continue even when the agent is withdrawn or "retired."

Fortunately, most CIA, U.S. intelligence, and covert-experienced military personnel also have enough ethics and patriotism to resist the urge to use these skills and contacts for personal gain or for personal foreign policy. In any group of highly motivated, highly trained individuals, however, one or two can certainly be found who are not bound by their oath of office nor by any recognizable moral code. These are the fellows who typically go private.

Going private is intelligence world terminology for working for yourself. This is more than selling Amway, though; going private means that a former government operator runs his own intelligence or covert-type operations. Historically, this has included bodyguard services, foreign "rescue" operations, private intelligence networks, small private or corporate armed forces, fraudulent financial institutions that fund off-the-shelf intelligence activities, and organizations that arrange to have U.S. Special Forces unknowingly train terrorists in Libya. Going private isn't necessarily a nefarious thing; some former or retired operators won't do *anything* for money. On the other hand, a few of them will.

TERRORISM 101

C-4 is perhaps the best all-purpose explosive in the world. It is highly stable: It can be dropped, stomped on, even shot, and it will not explode. It is also highly explosive: Given the proper detonator, a small amount of C-4 can destroy entire buildings.[14] It is plastic: It can be molded like putty to any shape and packed in small devices (e.g., a camera or tape recorder) or crevices (e.g., around a door lock). This is why C-4 is so eagerly sought by terrorists.

As the DC-8 descended, khaki-clad men waited in eager anticipation. Inside the plane in barrels labeled "Drilling Mud," they expected to find the C-4 they'd been praying for. They were not disappointed. The American-chartered cargo craft touched down on schedule at the airport in Tripoli, offloading twenty tons of C-4 into the hands of Mu'ammar Gadhafi. Ed Wilson, former CIA and ONI contract agent, had delivered.

Wilson had been able to pull off this operation, as he had others, because in his years of experience with the CIA, he had learned the tricks of the trade and had made extensive contacts in business, in the intelligence community, at the Pentagon, and around Washington, D.C. Eventually, he would produce a large shipment of arms to Libya, assist Libya's nuclear weapons program (although his efforts ultimately failed), organize a Libyan special forces raid against the French Foreign Legion during the Libyan war in Chad, provide former U.S. Special Forces troopers to train Libyan commandos, and organize assassination and kidnaping operations for Gadhafi.[15]

It is difficult to assess how much damage Wilson did to the interests of the United States during his time as a private operator. He is now serving a fifty-two-year sentence in the Federal Maximum Security Facility at Marion, Illinois, and the length of the sentence is perhaps only a small reflection of the ignoble schemes he attempted to pull off.

THE BLACK REVOLVING DOOR

One of the things that makes the role of cowboys and private operators so hard to get hold of is the revolving door between government service and private enterprise in the gray/black world. Many intelligence agents retire from the armed forces or intelligence agencies only to be immediately hired as contract agents by the very same agencies. Intelligence organizations seem to think this makes the agents deniable, as they are no longer formally connected to the government or the agency. Historically, however, a great number of intelligence agents and paramilitary operators have gone back and forth between government positions and private operations. Moreover, the widespread and widely known practice of employing contract agents means that anyone who has ever been a part of U.S. intelligence or armed forces is highly suspect. In most cases, even careful sheep-dipping is not enough to erase suspicion that the CIA is behind whatever schemes these individuals undertake.

Moreover, it is very difficult for people and organizations to know for sure when an operator is "retired" or "private" and when he is still carrying Uncle Sam's baton. This is critical, for intelligence agents often approach government acquaintances and offices for assistance: intelligence information, personnel, supplies, passwords (slipping past customs and the Coast Guard, for example), and even arms and troops (as illustrated by the Wilson scam above). By employing sheep-dipped "former" officers and "retired" contract agents, the CIA and other intelligence services have blurred the line between official government policy and private enterprise. This makes it more likely that government money, equipment, and even personnel will occasionally become "loaned out" or entangled in a private intelligence or paramilitary venture. This in turn increases the risk of unintentionally stepping into a morass created by a private operator (e.g., any U.S. involvement, even if tricked into it, raises suspicions and escalation potential). Finally, the use of sheep-dipped and contract agents has led to an inability to distinguish between official government agents and private ones. The important outcome of this is that virtually every nefarious act of any individual with even a distant connection to U.S. intelligence is blamed on the CIA or the U.S. government. The CIA has trained some very effective agents, and a few of the bad apples are capable of some *very* nefarious propositions.

CONCLUSIONS

As long as covert actions are undertaken, the risks of having cowboys blow the whole cover off is inherent. Good operators, by their nature, grab the bull by the horns; they are good operators precisely *because* they can overcome obstacles that force lesser men to give up. This characteristic is a primary, and perhaps the most important, selection criterion for Special Forces troops (SEALs, Green Berets, Marine Force Recon). In the field, the overwhelming temptation is to say, "The hell with those suits back in Langley." When *your people* are fighting and dying, the code of the operator is crystal clear: Get the job done and protect your troops. For the field operator, the "covert" part of the job is way down the list of priorities. This risk is built in, and rarely considered. With covert action, there will always be cowboys.

NOTES

1. For the story of Robertson and the *Springfjord*, see Stephen Schlesinger and Stephen Kinzer, *Bitter Fruit: The Untold Story of the American Coup in Guatemala* (New York: Doubleday, 1990), pp. 109, 193–94.

2. The "spoon" is the arming lever that springs off to start the timer on a hand grenade; once it is let go, the grenade will explode when the timer goes off.

3. Or ever. Today Tony Poe lives with his Laotian wife in northern Laos.

4. See Roger Warner, *Backfire: The CIA's Secret War in Laos and Its Link to the War in Vietnam* (New York: Simon and Schuster, 1995), pp. 91–93, 144–49.

5. As did Lynch, Rip Robertson, and numerous American pilots during ZAPATA.

6. If there were good reasons for engaging in a *covert* operation to begin with, there are good reasons for *keeping* the operation covert.

7. With a few exceptions, e.g., nearly all Americans, especially those in Congress, supported the Afghan mujahedin against the Soviet occupation.

8. "Response to the Bay of Pigs," Allen Dulles Papers, Seely G. Mudd Library, Princeton, N.J., Box 244.

9. Schlesinger and Kinzer, *Bitter Fruit*, p. 194; see also Richard M. Bissell, "Reflections on the Bay of Pigs: Book Review of Operation Zapata," *Strategic Review* 12, vol. 1 (winter 1984): 69.

10. The aircraft were supplied indirectly. Nicaraguan President Somoza provided airplanes from his air force to the Guatemalan rebels in exchange for new ones from the United States.

11. John Nutter, "To Trap a President: JFK, CIA, and the Bay of Pigs" (The Conflict Analysis Group, 1997, photocopy), available from author.

12. One example of this is the "overt" covert action in Afghanistan, wherein even with pretty obvious U.S. support of the mujahedin (1) the Soviets really had no response anyway and (2) supporting the Afghans actually created goodwill with some between the U.S. and Islamic states, and was also supported by people of practically every political stripe within the United States.

13. This is one interpretation of Poindexter's words and deeds, although probably not the truth. The more likely explanation is that the admiral was taking the heat for superiors, such as President Reagan, who had indeed authorized illegal and unconstitutional operations.

14. Indeed, an amount of similar explosive, Semtex, small enough to fit into a tape recorder, is what destroyed Pan Am 103 over Lockerbie, Scotland.

15. See Joseph Goulden, *The Death Merchant* (New York: Simon and Schuster, 1984), for the complete rundown on Wilson.

Chapter 10

If You're Not for Us, You're Against Us: Covert Actions at Home

BLACK OPS AND BLACK BAGS: COVERT ACTION COMES HOME

The man in the dark sedan parked across the street from the house was clean-cut and well dressed. His eyes focused on the rearview mirror, watching the Volkswagen microbus turn the corner and speed away. When he was sure it was gone, he picked up the walkie-talkie.

"One," he said into the microphone.

"Two," said the other voice.

"Clear," he responded.[1]

At the "clear" signal, two men in workman's coveralls got out of an unremarkable panel truck parked in the alleyway behind the north side Chicago house. After a brief look around, they walked up to the back door of the house; one of them knocked softly, just firmly enough to be heard in the house, but not loud enough to be heard next door. It was procedure to make sure the house was empty before setting about the next step: picking the lock. Within seconds, the door was open and the men slipped quietly inside, careful to close the door behind them. First, a quick check to be sure the place was empty—they had a ready-prepared cover story ("Gas company, there was a report of a leak. . . .") in case someone was home. Then they set to work; opening desk drawers and the filing cabinet, looking behind the books in the bookcase, checking anywhere a subversive might hide incriminating papers. If there was any evidence, these men would find it; this was hardly their first black-bag job. If there were any incriminating papers worth collecting, they would set up their specially designed photographic system—a camera, a frame to hold the camera steady at a fixed distance, and a bright lamp—to collect the evidence. They could do this in seconds, for they had a lot of practice. If there was anything merely embarrassing to the occupant, they'd grab that too.

These men were special agents of the Federal Bureau of Investigation (FBI). Along with the CIA, various police Red Squads, and even local sheriff's departments (sometimes directed by the local arm of the Ku Klux Klan), J. Edgar Hoover's FBI was conducting a covert war. Since it was *war*, dammit, there was no time or need to bother with minor technicalities of the law, such as search warrants or freedom of speech and assembly. This war against American dissent would be fought in the perilous ground beyond the U.S. Constitution.

It is essential to consider domestic black operations in any examination of American covert action. First, domestic operations (intelligence and covert political ops) are virtually always justified as quasi-foreign projects (e.g., "We're trying to find the KGB infiltrators in the movement"). Second, both foreign and domestic operations have arisen from the same roots:

- a cold war with a sinister, enigmatic, and implacable enemy;
- a black-and-white view of the world that allowed for no legitimate dissent (i.e., disagreement equals treason);
- the belief in a single, objective, and obvious "American" opinion, and the idea that anyone who did not share it was either duped by the Soviets or a traitor;
- the belief that only a scant few Americans understood the true subversive nature of the relentless foe; and
- the necessity for those who *did* understand to win at all costs.

It was this covert mentality that brought the CIA not only to Guatemala, Indonesia, and the rest of the world, but also brought black ops home. This mindset, too, brought covert operators, such as E. Howard Hunt and Frank Sturgis, into American domestic politics, where their names would become infamous. This chapter relates a brief history of these domestic operations, why they "came home," and how they were (and are) related to foreign black ops and U.S. intelligence agencies.

COINTELPRO

Perhaps no one epitomizes the covert mentality better than J. Edgar Hoover. The number one G-man saw conspiracies everywhere, and agents under his command conducted covert wars against the enemies he identified. Perhaps nothing epitomizes his attitude toward democracy better than the phrase he used to describe himself: "Seat of Government."

While this book focuses on foreign intelligence operations, it is important to keep in mind that these covert actions and the institutions and organizations that carry them out have serious domestic effects. They cannot help but become intertwined with the other domestic covert programs, even today. That is why we must, at least briefly, consider COINTELPRO.

COINTELPRO is the FBI acronym for COunter INTELligence PROgram. The name of the program suggests that the purpose is to thwart the intelligence gathering of America's enemies, i.e., to catch spies and expose traitors. COIN-TELPRO was, in theory, an FBI program designed to ferret out fiendish foreign agents nestled into American political organizations: KGB agents in the AFL-CIO, Red "outside agitators" in the civil rights movement, Soviet provocateurs manipulating the antiwar movement. This is how it was justified to presidents, attorneys general, the precious few members of Congress who were permitted to know, and the small number of FBI and CIA agents who objected. It may be that Hoover himself, and his supporters, actually believed this to be true. In practice, however, COINTELPRO was a political-action program aimed at destroying domestic political dissent, including:

- black-bag jobs undertaken without search warrants (these may number well into the thousands; some local FBI offices maintained a full-time black-bag staff);
- the use of black-bag material—i.e., the fruits of burglary—to blackmail or intimidate dissidents into silence (e.g., even if illegal material was found, such as marijuana, it would not be reported to police, but instead used as leverage to ensure the target's silence);
- extensive use of black propaganda: producing fake documents (letters, pamphlets) and using false "informers" (*agents provocateur*) to create tension and division within dissident groups, using forged letters to cause personal trouble for political foes (e.g., letters from a "friend" telling someone his spouse has been unfaithful);
- firebombing the cars of activists and making it appear the result of inter-factional conflict (purpose: to destroy dissident organizations from within);
- preparing and leaking phony snitch jackets for dissident leaders to make them appear to be government informants, thus destroying their credibility with their own organizations and followers;
- countless illegal wiretaps and electronic bugging; sometimes the fruits of these operations were also used to blackmail (or attempt to blackmail) targets, such as Martin Luther King Jr.;
- contacting the employer of a dissident "target" as part of an "investigation," an act calculated to either get them fired or at least cause trouble at work;
- conspicuously investigating individuals in an effort to have them socially ostracized and force their friends and communities to abandon them.[2]

When COINTELPRO was exposed in 1971, the FBI claimed to have ended the program. While this may technically be true, similar programs would emerge in the 1980s.

NO THIRD-RATE BURGLARY

The light switched on, and the men in the room froze. One of the men put up his hands, hollering, "Don't shoot!" There was nowhere to run, nowhere to hide, and they weren't going to shoot it out with the police. After all, they were there on a mission from the president of the United States. Surely the higher-ups would straighten this out. Ironically, these former CIA contract agents had been caught because they had used an amateur's trick: taping open the lock on the security door.[3] The crisis called Watergate was about to unfold; Richard Nixon's black operations were about to unravel; the wheels were about to come off his presidency.

It has become commonplace today, more than twenty-five years after the fact, to excuse the Watergate affair as a "third-rate burglary," as Richard Nixon dismissively passed it off. Indeed, while many right-wing writers and demagogues decry "revisionist" history, they themselves have been busy whitewashing and downplaying the facts and impact of the scandal. To the contrary, the Watergate burglary was itself merely the tip of the iceberg; there was an entire covert program and organization beneath it. When the light clicked on in the Democratic headquarters in the Watergate Hotel, far more than a few "burglars" were exposed.

Perhaps no American president understood the covert mentality like Richard Nixon. After all, Nixon had been the President Eisenhower's representative on the 54/12 Committee, which was responsible for authorizing covert operations in the Eisenhower administration. He had also been the White House operations officer for OPERATION ZAPATA. Moreover, Nixon often displayed a predilection for detecting conspiracies—or *konspiratsias*, as the Russians call them—whether or not they actually existed. It is not surprising that someone steeped in intrigue would turn to those methods when feeling threatened.

Aside from the Watergate burglary, which in itself *was* a relatively minor event, the president's men established and operated a covert organization, called ODESSA by G. Gordon Liddy, aimed at Nixon's political and personal enemies and rivals. The operations, eventually codenamed GEMSTONE, were often amateurish, but were sometimes effective.[4] These included:

- burglarizing the psychiatric records of Daniel Ellsberg in hopes of finding blackmail material;[5]
- planning the arson and burglary of the Brookings Institution (a think tank);
- an attempted break-in at McGovern headquarters, presumably to plant electronic bugs;
- a plan to wreck the air-conditioning system at the Democratic National Convention in Miami, to disrupt the convention;
- a plan to kidnap dissident leaders before the Republican National Convention, to disrupt protest activities;
- enlisting members of organized crime for these underhanded activities, thereby opening the door to possible blackmail;[6]

- soliciting money for and maintaining a large "slush fund" used for covert political operations, political payoffs, and hush money for the Watergate burglars;
- shaking down corporations for "contributions"—used for the covert operations—by promising favors (e.g., lucrative government contracts) or punishment (e.g., IRS audits);
- planning to use the IRS to "screw our political enemies" (in Nixon's own words);
- planning the assassination of political columnist Jack Anderson, going so far as to undertake a "practice run."

GEMSTONE included numerous black propaganda operations, notably:

- spreading false rumors of out-of-wedlock children about Democratic challengers Henry "Scoop" Jackson and George McGovern, and about Hubert Humphrey being stopped for drunk driving in the company of a call girl;
- using CIA personnel and facilities to produce a series of anti-Kennedy Chappaquidick cartoons in the event that Ted Kennedy entered the 1972 campaign;[7]
- fabricating a cable "proving" that John Kennedy had ordered the assassination of Ngo Dinh Diem,[8] and attempting to pass it off as authentic to *Life* magazine;
- forging letters from Democratic front-runner Edmund Muskie using derogatory ethnic slurs;
- a truly vicious rumor campaign, supported by the *Union Leader*, a New Hampshire newspaper, smearing Muskie's wife; this shameless assault led to the "tearful" Muskie interview that probably cost him the Democratic nomination in 1972;
- postcard mailings "from Muskie" in Florida, claiming Muskie was for busing and against J. Edgar Hoover and the space shuttle.[9]

Nixon's organization also orchestrated numerous black political actions, in which operatives posed as Democrats or antiwar activists while performing disreputable deeds, including:

- publicizing phantom "Democratic" political events that never happened (so people who tried to attend would become angry at the Democrats when there was no party or free beer);
- attempting to provoke violence at the Democratic National Convention in 1972;
- planting provocateurs with bizarre "quirks" among protesters at Republican events, to make it appear that Nixon's opponents were violent, Communist-inspired freaks;

- organizing a protest for "Billy Graham Day" in Charlotte, North Carolina, at which "protesters" would carry "extremely obscene" signs
  directed against Richard Nixon and Billy Graham; on the memo
  describing this operation, Nixon's Chief of Staff, Bob Haldeman, wrote
  "good" next to "obscene" and *"great"* next to "also toward Billy Graham."[10]

All of these actions were planned, organized, approved, and undertaken by a
small group of operators within the White House and the Committee to Re-
Elect the President (CREEP), including Jeb McGruder, Charles Colson,
Attorney General John Mitchell, G. Gordon Liddy, E. Howard Hunt, Donald
Segretti, and ultimately Nixon himself. While these were impeachably serious
conspiracies, there was an even larger covert game afoot.

THE HUSTON PLAN

By 1970, President Nixon was besieged by protests over the Vietnam War. Further, he was convinced that the scope and intensity of the dissent could not be
coming from *real* Americans; that something so damaging and "un-American"
as the antiwar movement could only have originated within the Kremlin. To
root out this fifth column, then, it was necessary to expose the Soviet origins of
the movement. To this end, he assigned a young staff attorney, Tom Huston, to
create a program to produce the critical evidence. The result became known as
the "Huston Plan."

In a nutshell, Huston recommended that President Nixon unilaterally relax
legal "restrictions" on: wiretapping and bugging American citizens and polit-
ical/social organizations, reading the mail of U.S. citizens, and surreptitious
entry (black-bag jobs) against U.S. citizens. Due to exigencies of national security, U.S. agents were to be free to operate without probable cause or search warrants; the ends justified the means. Huston himself clearly understood the issues
involved even as he was writing the plan; he wrote about black-bag jobs: "Use
of this technique is clearly illegal; it amounts to burglary."[11] The twenty-nine-
year-old lawyer understated the case, however; the inconvenient "restrictions" to
be set aside by presidential fiat were the Bill of Rights.

Every single recommendation of the Huston Plan was initially approved by
Richard Nixon on 14 July 1970, but revoked thirteen days later. The ultimate
irony of the Huston Plan was the reason it was never implemented. Illegality
wasn't enough to deter the president's men, nor was the fact that it violated the
majority of the Bill of Rights. What finally killed the plan was the opposition
of J. Edgar Hoover. Compounding the irony, however, was this: What Hoover
opposed was *not* the illegality; Hoover's FBI had already implemented most of
the actions recommended by Huston. No, the top G-Man nixed Huston's program because he didn't want the White House operation getting in the way of
his own unconstitutional programs. If White House operatives got caught, as

Hoover astutely anticipated they would, he didn't want to risk having *their* operations unravel and expose his own. In this, Hoover was supported by the CIA, which was concurrently running illegal domestic programs of its own.

CIA in the USA

When the CIA was created by the National Security Act of 1947, there was considerable concern and debate over the prospect that the Agency might turn into an American secret police. To guard against this, the CIA's charter specifically forbids it to undertake domestic operations.[12]

Despite this, throughout its history, the CIA has crossed the line, both literally, with regard to geography (it was restricted to *foreign* intelligence collection and operations), and figuratively, with regard to U.S. law. While these programs were always justified by the CIA on national security grounds, for all that they stomped on the liberties of law-abiding Americans, they produced virtually no relevant intelligence. These included operations codenamed RESISTANCE, MERRIMAC, LINGUAL, and CHAOS:

- RESISTANCE: a program to protect CIA college recruiters from pickets by infiltrating the antiwar movement, thereby spying on Americans undertaking constitutionally protected activities
- MERRIMAC: a program to alert the CIA to Washington-area protests at CIA facilities or against the CIA
- LINGUAL: a long-term CIA counterintelligence program for opening and reading the mail of literally thousands of Americans in a vain search for evidence of Soviet spies or agents of influence
- CHAOS: an approximately fifteen-year-long program to collect information on Americans and American political organizations

CHAOS, RESISTANCE, and MERRIMAC all depended on infiltrating domestic political and dissident groups. Under CHAOS, CIA agents black-bagged American homes and offices, without warrants, and shared the names of *suspected* "subversives" with local law enforcement offices. Ultimately, CHAOS produced files on over seven thousand American citizens and one thousand domestic political groups; it shared information with law-enforcement agencies on over three hundred thousand Americans.[13] One can only speculate about the effects on the lives of the people labeled by this activity.

While presumably acting as an impartial, nonpartisan government agency, the CIA has also undertaken programs to influence American public opinion. This has generally taken the form of gray propaganda, both gray gray and light gray—information discovered and disseminated from supposedly neutral sources. Generally this has been accomplished by selectively leaking information making the agency look good or its enemies look bad. These stories, while essentially CIA press releases, have been published in major American magazines and newspapers as if they were the result of independent and verified investigative reporting.[14] The problem with such actions by an intelligence agency in a democracy is that it amounts to lobbying the American people, as well as government, business, and the press, under a false cover; if one cannot tell where the story truly comes from, how can one judge its veracity? The CIA has also produced numerous "independent" books with the apparent intention of swaying American public opinion. The most famous of these is *The Penkovsky Papers*, a supposed memoir by a highly placed Soviet military officer, which today is generally regarded as a work of CIA disinformation.[15]

Finally, the CIA has attempted to prevent the publication of books about the agency and its operations. One of the first critical examinations of the CIA and its role in the United States and the world was *The Invisible Government* by David Wise of the *New York Herald Tribune* and Thomas Ross of the *Chicago Sun-Times*. When the CIA could not force the publisher, Random House, to withhold publication, it offered to *purchase* every copy. To his credit, Bennet Cerf, president of Random House, merely promised to print more copies.[16] While the CIA and the United States government have a necessary and legitimate interest in preventing the publication of facts that might (1) jeopardize national security, (2) jeopardize the lives of intelligence agents, and (3) reveal intelligence sources and methods, in most of these prior-restraint cases, these have not been key issues.

DEBATEGATE AND THE REAGAN ADMINISTRATION

William Casey would have been a good Russian. His fondness for the covert operation, or *konspiratsia*, was boundless. Even today, sorting out which programs and operations Casey authorized, both on and off the books, while he was DCI is as difficult as understanding some of his mumbled congressional "testimony."

In 1980, however, Casey was not yet DCI, but instead was serving as the campaign chairman for his friend, Ronald Reagan. Shortly before Reagan's debate with President Jimmy Carter, the Reagan campaign staff mysteriously came into possession of the Carter debate-briefing book. Reagan knew in advance every point Carter would make; thus rehearsed, the former actor had a ready stock of ripostes and one-liners. The debate was a critical event in the election of Ronald Reagan.[17]

There is no smoking gun that proves how the Reagan staff came up with the briefing book. It had to have been stolen by someone inside the Carter campaign—a spy, if you will—who passed it on to the Reagan staff. Perhaps Casey did not arrange this operation; perhaps he had nothing to do with it. Throughout his tenure as DCI, Casey claimed innocence, even suggesting that he would not have trusted such a find, in fear that it was disinformation planted by the Carter people. This very line of argument, however, fires both ways. Bill Casey would never have allowed Reagan to use the briefing book if Casey himself could not vouch for its authenticity. With his background in intelligence and his skeptical mind, Casey would never have vouched for its authenticity if he did not personally know where the book came from.

While Carter may have lost the election anyway, the more troubling issue is the use of a black operation in domestic politics. There are only four possibilities: (1) someone in the Carter campaign simply turned against Carter, most likely someone reasonably high up who had access to the briefing book; (2) Reagan operatives recruited someone in the Carter campaign to filch the book, and probably to provide other inside information as well; (3) a Reagan operative infiltrated the Carter campaign and passed the book on; or (4) a Reagan supporter black-bagged the Carter campaign to steal the book. Whatever the truth, the operation itself is disturbing and unprincipled; accepting the book was dishonorable.

Scarcely had the dust settled on the Gipper's 1980 victory when the drive began to increase covert operations inside America. One of these initiatives was a plan to revitalize the House Internal Security Committee and Un-American Activities Committee. While these never came to fruition, other domestic operations did.

Perhaps most disquieting was the CISPES investigation. CISPES was the Committee in Solidarity with the People of El Salvador, a group dedicated to changing U.S. policy toward El Salvador. In the 1970s and 1980s El Salvador was ruled by what might best be described as a "mortocracy": government by death. Ruled by a small group of wealthy elite, the country was controlled by death squads. Anyone who suggested even minor social, political, or economic reform was simply murdered. Moreover, while the death squads were not an official part of the government, it was plain that they worked for the ruling elite to insure that no reform occurred. This oligarchy was essentially supported by the United States government, and this is what the members of CISPES objected to.

It is an article of faith among the extreme Right, however, that CISPES was established and operated by Communist agents, although there is little or no evidence of this. Generally, CISPES members were liberal, progressive, and even socialist; many of them were clergy, nuns, businessmen, students, teachers, and homemakers. To some of the men in Washington, however, disagreement with U.S. policy—in this case, support for the government of El Salvador—meant that one was either a Soviet dupe or a traitor. It was essential, to the covert mentality, to root out the sources of Soviet influence and propaganda in the United States. Thus began the CISPES investigation.

Under the rubric of antiterrorism, the FBI began a program of infiltration, provocation, and harassment of CISPES members. Agents and informers joined CISPES. U.S. government provocateurs suggested that the organization carry out acts of violence and terrorism, and should supply weapons to the FMLN (the revolutionaries in El Salvador.[18] CISPES members were surveilled and photographed going about their daily business. FBI agents used the McCarthy-era tactic of interviewing the employers of CISPES members, relating that the employee was being investigated for possible involvement in a "terrorist" organization.

To this day, there is not a shred of evidence that either CISPES as an organization or individual CISPES members ever carried out or conspired to commit
even a single act of violence or provided material support for violence by the
FMLN or any other revolutionary or terrorist organization. The evidence *is*
overwhelming that CISPES was targeted with a COINTELPRO-type covert program merely for speaking out against government policy.

THE OPERATORS COME HOME

How can American law enforcement and intelligence officers justify to them-
selves activities like COINTELPRO, GEMSTONE, RESISTANCE, and the
CISPES investigation? How can a DCI read the CIA charter and still permit
CHAOS? Part of the answer lies in the nature of their business.

It is difficult to participate, let alone excel, in a profession without being
changed by the experience. This is even more true when the experience is as
intense as life-and-death struggle in black operations. While this does not
happen to all operators, most cannot help but become jaded and cynical. They
have worked, lived, and fought with revolutionaries, gunrunners, assassins, mercenaries, drug lords, fascists, Communists, religious zealots, and psychopaths.
They have seen their country and fellow countrymen obey the dicta of the
Hoover Commission Report: "We must learn to lie, cheat, subvert . . . and like
all American endeavors, do it the *best*." Having witnessed betrayal on all sides, it
is far too easy to fall into a Machiavellian view of the world.[19] Moreover, those
who become black operators are most often drawn from a pool of individuals who
already accept a common worldview: win at all costs, for us or against us, no-
holds-barred anti-Communism. This is further reinforced by the training reg-
imen of intelligence agencies and Special Forces, which includes a healthy dose
of political indoctrination.[20]

The problem occurs when they come home. Most black operators adjust to
American civil and political life without difficulty. Some, however, have been so
affected by their experiences that they cannot or will not distinguish between
foreign operations and domestic politics. Having lived in a LeCarré-esque world
of onion-layered conspiracy, where laws are inconvenient formalities to be circumvented and "truth" is that which will get you what you want, they simply
translate their skills into the American political dialect.

When Howard Hunt and Frank Sturgis and Bernard Barker were arrested in
the Watergate Hotel, they were merely implementing politics as they knew it.
When "someone" in the Reagan campaign orchestrated the theft of the Carter
briefing book, he was merely following the dictates of a conscience grown susceptible to "accommodation" in the clandestine world. When individuals who
have had access to intelligence sources and analysis take public positions on candidates, *as if this inside information conveys reasons to vote for or against someone, e.g.,*
". . . if you only knew what we know," they subvert the nonpartisan nature of the

intelligence agencies they represented, even though they are no longer employed by those agencies. Without the reality *and* appearance of nonpartisanship, intelligence agencies lose their ability to serve the Constitution and country by providing an unbiased (or less biased) source of information for decision makers.[21] They lose that which distinguishes them from the KGB.

One can draw two important conclusions from this. First, those who have been involved in black operations must be treated carefully in domestic politics, in particular if the suggestion is made to form a covert action organization or parallel private intelligence unit. Second, intelligence professionals ought to avoid partisan political activity that exploits their intelligence background in any way. An individual should always be able to base her decision to vote for or against a candidate or policy based on information that is publicly known, without relying on the interpretation and judgement of a special class of citizen (i.e., the spooks). This does not mean that former intelligence officers should not exercise their franchise, nor that they should avoid political activity. They should, however, avoid even the suggestion that they represent the views of their former agency—or even the views of "the intelligence community" or "former agents," for that matter.

COVERT OPERATORS, NATIONAL SECURITY, AND FREEDOM

Whenever those in government power seek to "relax" the strictures of law and the Constitution, the justification is *always* that the compromises are necessary to protect "national security." The problem with "national security" exceptions to constitutional provisions, however, is that the exceptions tend to broaden over time, often quite rapidly. While one might find good reason to surreptitiously bug the house of someone who may be an enemy spy or terrorist when faced with good evidence, i.e., probable cause, it is a considerable stretch to conclude that one is justified in investigating and black-bagging many thousands of individuals on the grounds that some of them *might* be aiding an enemy. Tom Huston eventually reached this conclusion:

> The risk was that you would get people who would be susceptible to political considerations as opposed to national security considerations, or would construe political considerations to be national security considerations, to move from the kid with the bomb to the kid with the picket sign, and from the kid with the picket sign to the kid with the bumper sticker of the opposing candidate. And you just keep going down the line.[22]

Further, domestic covert action like COINTELPRO (e.g., blackmailing dissenters, fingering them as Commies) plainly rips apart the fabric of the Constitution. These exceptions are always decided on in closed-door secrecy, not tested against logic and evidence by an impartial judge. The only arbiter of whether or not secret constitutional exceptions are *necessary* is almost always an individual who stands to personally benefit from them; it is precisely this circumstance the Constitution was written to block.

The Constitution *requires* a warrant for searches and violations of privacy to prevent the arbitrary exercise of police and government power over individuals. To obtain a warrant to search a home or wiretap a phone, the government must show a reasonable suspicion, *based on evidence*, that the individual has or is about to commit a crime. Moreover, this evidence must be presented to a judge, who is expected to exact a high standard of proof before allowing a serious covert use of police power. This is not to "protect the criminal"; it is to protect you and me (i.e., the innocent) from having our lives, families, and homes disrupted, and our reputations torn down.

Without these protections, *all* Americans are subject to arbitrary police and government power and harassment. In the past it was the Communists and socialists and antiwar activists and Black Panthers who were subject to these violations. The precedent set by domestic covert operations, however, means that anyone who opposes the current party in power may have *his* constitutional rights stripped, and in secret to boot.

Ultimately, what makes democracy work is not the elections or parties; it is what you do the morning after an election that your side has lost. You do *not* get your gun and head for the hills, as happens in so many countries. The reason you don't is because you expect that you and your family are reasonably safe from the capricious retaliation of political opponents backed by the power of the state. Political parties and policies may change, but the Constitution imposes boundaries, outside which are things *no government agent or official* can do to you. If these boundaries are broken down for "national security," it is an assault not only on "subversives," but on the very thing that guarantees the freedom of everyone.

The problem is that "national security" exceptions to the Constitution have become ubiquitous, not to mention iniquitous. Virtually *any* secret policy or domestic operation came to be justified under this umbrella during the cold war. No outside authority could check the power of the executive-branch institutions (e.g., the CIA and the FBI) because knowledge of even the *existence* of these programs was kept within the presidency, the CIA, or the FBI themselves. In essence, the executives in power were simply saying, "Trust me." When this unfortunate circumstance occurs, there is nothing left to distinguish a democracy from a monarchy or a dictatorship. Even a benign despot is still a despot.

WHERE THE LINE IS . . .

There is not a shred of evidence that any of the operations recounted in this chapter made the United States government or its citizens even a tiny bit more secure. They caught no spies, resulted in no valid prosecutions, produced no evidence of foreign control or influence of domestic political groups or activists, and yielded no proof that any of the targets had committed or planned violence. In a nutshell, this is the evidence that they were wrong.

There are, of course, politically motivated activities that do not warrant constitutional protection; there is a line that cannot be crossed under the protection of the Bill of Rights. It's not a hard one to see, and deserves to be defended with all the vigor and determination of the stalwarts who held the Alamo, Corregidor, or the Pusan Perimeter. When individuals or groups begin conducting acts of violence (e.g., physical injury to persons or property, or threats of thereof) or planning specific acts of violence, they have broken clear laws. Law enforcement agencies can easily obtain warrants to search, wiretap, and so forth, and constitutionally investigate and prosecute them. It's not that hard: no violence, no investigation.[23]

CONCLUSIONS

Americans are fond of saying that "You have a right to your own opinion," waving this proudly as proof of the freedom that exists in the United States. Indeed, we have in our Constitution a First Amendment, the "Crown Jewel" (as we teach in our American government classes)[24] that presumably guarantees not only the right to *have* an opinion, but the right to *say it out loud*. If you couldn't speak or write or sing your opinion, then there would be no difference between our freedom of speech and that of, say, Nazi Germany or the Soviet Union under the KGB. Anyone anywhere can have an opinion kept to himself, locked in his head; it is only the right to make it public that makes this a *freedom*.[25]

NOTES

1. Radio procedure for these operations was intentionally brief. This minimized the amount of time spent talking instead of watching, and also was cryptic enough that anyone picking up the signal would find the conversation impossible to follow.

2. See Morton Halperin et al., *The Lawless State: The Crimes of U.S. Intelligence Agencies* (New York: Penguin, 1976), chap. 4.

3. *Washington Post*, 18 June 1972, p. A1.

4. This accounting is drawn from *Washington Post*, 10 October 1972, p. A1; E. Howard Hunt, *Undercover: Memoirs of an American Secret Agent* (New York: Berkely Pub., 1974); G. Gordon Liddy, *Will: The Autobiography of G. Gordon Liddy* (New York: St. Martin's Press, 1980), pp. 196–204.

5. Ellsberg released the *Pentagon Papers* to the press.

6. Liddy, *Will*, p. 198.

7. Ibid., p. 218.

8. Hunt, *Undercover*.

9. *Seattle Times*, 9 November 1997.

10. See Sam Ervin, *The Whole Truth: The Watergate Conspiracy* (New York: Random House, 1980), p. 251.

11. Loch Johnson, *America's Secret Power: The CIA in a Democratic Society* (Oxford: Oxford University Press, 1989), p. 144.

12. Actually, the charter does not authorize "operations" of any kind; the CIA is *only* warranted for intelligence collecting, analysis, and coordination.

13. See Halperin et al., *The Lawless State*, chap. 5; Center for National Security Studies, *Operation Chaos* (Washington: Government Printing Office, 1976), p. 153.

14. See Victor Marchetti and John Marks, *CIA and the Cult of Intelligence* (New York: Dell Books, 1989), pp. 299–316.

15. Ibid., pp. 154–56.

16. Ibid., pp. 308–309.

17. See *Christian Science Monitor*, 24 May 1984, p. 3; and 7 November 1983, p. 23.

18. The issue is *not* whether or not the FMLN were Marxists. They were. The issue is that the United States was so concerned about maintaining the status quo that it supported a murderous regime similar in many critical respects to Stalinist Russia or Hitler's Germany. In this conflict, the United States was simply on the wrong side; had America forcibly supported change for social justice, the El Salvadoran revolutionaries would likely have turned to the United States, both as a model and for assistance, instead of Cuba and the Soviet Union.

19. It is not true, by the way, that Machiavelli's philosophy is amoral. Instead, it simply advocates a different morality in which the survival of the state is the highest moral value.

20. I'm not arguing that this indoctrination is bad. Indeed, it would be difficult to get individuals and teams to perform the tasks we ask of them, whether superhuman or merely inhuman, if they were not so *totally* committed to the cause. One must simply take care so as not to interpret the opinions of heavily indoctrinated individuals as though they were produced by objective analysis.

21. There is a flip side to this, however. If intelligence agencies prove *too* nonpartisan, some executives will (1) ignore the inteligence agencies altogether, relying on their own predispositions (their *cognitive map*) to interpret what they see on CNN, and (2) create their own private intelligence and covert operations organizations to circumvent the formal intelligence institutions (e.g., the North/Secord Enterprise).

22. Senate, Select Committee to Study Government Operations with Respect to Intelligence, *Final Report: Intelligence Activities*, "The Huston Plan," 94th Cong., 2d sess., 1976, S.Rept. 94-755, vol. 2, pp. 923–86.

23. Or conspiracy to commit violence; if they're planning it, we don't have to wait.

24. The author taught American government at a large university for three years.

25. Finally, let us suppose the extreme case: a domestic political organization supported or even created by a foreign power. Does this fact abrogate the rights of the Americans who belong to it? Does it make their expression of their beliefs less protected? Does it even necessarily mean that their opinions are *wrong*? What should a just government, relying on the consent of the governed and telling the truth, fear from opposing *ideas*?

Chapter 11

The Political Economy of Covert Action I: The National Interest and the Corporate Interest

Τhe room wasn't smoke-filled, but somehow it still retained the air of things best viewed in twilight and spoken of in whispers. As the men parted, there was no explicit agreement; there didn't have to be. Each understood the interests of the other, and each was prepared to act on their unspoken compact. The executive would provide resources, both in the target country and within the United States. The latter was especially important, so that the administration could mobilize friendly reporters and popular opinion to build political support, deny any government or corporate involvement, and bludgeon dissent where necessary. The other man was the secretary of state; he would use his powers, both statutory and persuasive, to ensure that the government of the United States would act against the target regime. There was no reason, he would later observe, to allow a country to go Communist just because of the irresponsibility of its own people.[1]

In studying covert action, we often focus on instances like Guatemala, Iran, and the Congo, and for good reason. All of these covert actions had numerous things in common. In every case, a national government was overthrown. In every case, the "Communist" or "pro-Soviet" nature of the deposed regime was dubious at best. In every case, important Western corporate assets were at risk. In every case, critical figures in CIA operations were handsomely rewarded.

- Walter Bedell Smith, who promoted the Guatemalan operation to President Eisenhower, was made a member of the board of the United Fruit Company (UFCO).
- Lawrence Devlin, the CIA station chief who filled Allen Dulles's mailbox with breathless cables about Patrice Lumumba, became an executive in charge of the fabulously lucrative Templesman Mining in the Congo.
- Gulf Oil, an American corporation, was awarded a handsome share of Iran's petroleum production after AJAX; Kermit Roosevelt, who masterminded the affair, was made a vice president of Gulf.

It is no accident that many of the highly reputed American covert operations have what might be called "corporate" happy endings. Whether it was The International Telephone and Telegraph (ITT) or Kennecott Copper in Chile, UFCO in Guatemala, or the Anglo-Iranian Oil Company (AIOC) in Iran, threats to American or Western corporate power have often motivated CIA black ops. This is not to say that every corporation has the CIA at its beck and call; that is plainly untrue. We cannot explain, for example, American actions in Laos, Vietnam, or Afghanistan by pointing to specific U.S. corporations. American foreign policy decisions, however, have *frequently* reflected the needs of global capitalism or the American corporate system, generally justified as the need to protect the principle of "private property rights." After all, who could be against that? (Hint: it's not nearly as simple as it sounds.)

This chapter examines the relationship between corporate power, the global system of capitalism, and CIA covert operations. It explores the nature of corporate influence on American national security and CIA decision making:

- how corporate America has influenced and even compelled U.S. covert operations;
- how U.S. transnational corporations have participated in these operations;
- why the corporate capitalist system has such a powerful claim on U.S. intelligence and government assets;
- what the resulting covert actions have been designed to protect or accomplish;
- how the U.S. national interest has adapted to reflect the corporate interest; and
- the effects of all this on the U.S. taxpayer.

ASK NOT WHAT YOU CAN DO FOR YOUR COUNTRY . . .

While corporate America is wealthy beyond imagining, it has seldom commanded the *kinds* of resources that characterize the power of the modern state: armies, navies, nuclear weapons, and intelligence agencies. Corporations have, on occasion, been able to purchase these items for the short term (well, not the nukes), but they generally rely on the United States government to protect their foreign assets and interests.

This is not to say that American transnationals, however, have remained aloof from black operations. Rather, they have often assisted, urged, and even coerced government covert actions, generally in three ways:

- providing operational support for covert operations;
- supporting and mobilizing economic warfare operations; and
- identifying or publicizing dangerous circumstances for the United States (structuring the "problem definition" of the government).

Operational support is the means by which black ops are carried out, including:

- intelligence information;
- money;
- personnel (especially indigenous employees who know their way around);
- facilities (houses, buildings, ports, training grounds);
- transportation (trucks, trains, cars, ships, aircraft);
- equipment (radio and television equipment, printing presses);
- civilian cover (helping infiltrate intelligence operatives into the country posing as corporate employees);
- smuggling (e.g., bringing in weapons in "machine parts" crates).

For example, during OPERATION FORTUNE (the aborted forerunner of SUCCESS in Guatemala), UFCO attempted to smuggle arms to Guatemalan insurgents in crates marked "agricultural machinery" aboard a United Fruit freighter.[2] When the 2506 Brigade was preparing for the invasion of Cuba at the Bay of Pigs, they trained in Guatemala on land owned by a certain North American transnational corporation (TNC). During the operation in Chile against Salvador Allende, ITT not only contributed large sums of money to Allende's opponents, but also directly offered a half-million dollars to DCI Richard Helms for covert action. Indeed, it would have been appropriate if Pinochet's soldiers had worn "ITT" patches on their uniforms, advertising their sponsor, as athletes do today. ITT also allowed American intelligence officers to use corporate "identities" to enter Chile, and the CIA returned the favor by introducing ITT people to the Chilean coup plotters; we still do not know all that went on between them.

Naturally, activities of this nature are dangerous, for if the target learns of the corporate hostility and the covert action fails, the firm has not only made a confirmed enemy, but also provided *legal* justification for punitive action against the company. How would Americans deal with a foreign company that had proven ties to an attempted overthrow of the U.S. government?

The second role corporations undertake in black ops is implementing "destabilization" programs by mobilizing the economic warfare resources of the advanced industrial nations and their corporations. In general, this kind of program is designed to cut off an offending country or regime from the rest of the world: no foreign money, no foreign markets to sell goods to, no imports from participating countries and companies, no spare parts for machinery and electronics, no foreign capital, and so forth. In many countries, these mechanisms of economic breakdown can be quite effective (see chapter 13).

The corporate role in this end of a covert action is quite natural. Many corporations will support other firms against the dangers of nationalization or expropriation; it is essential to make an example out of any regime that challenges the rights of corporate ownership, especially private property rights. In this, the bandwagon fills up fast. Moreover, if a company continues to do business with a targeted country, it might itself become the target of a lawsuit in international courts, designed to "recover" the value of "expropriated assets."[3] This kind of corporate action was effective against, among others, Iran (1952–1953), Chile (1970–1973), and Nicaragua (1980s).

The final role of the corporation in covert action is the most critical: mobilizing the forces of the U.S. government against an uncooperative regime. Since it is still considered bad form for a TNC to openly overthrow the government of a "host" country, it is still necessary to enlist a government agency to do the job when called for. To do this, corporations commonly employ what academics call "structuring the 'problem definition'" of the government. In an organization such as the U.S. government, the first step in making any policy is the "problem definition" stage: identifying some circumstance as a problem *for the government*. Throughout the cold war, this was a fairly simple proposition: Convince a powerful U.S. official that some foreign leader or regime was godless Communist, and the U.S. would launch a black op. This process was generally greased with a large dose of corporate propagandizing, both to the public and especially to key government and corporate officers, along with the able assistance of a highly-interconnected "Old Boy" network.

A classic example is the UFCO mobilization effort against the regimes of both Juan José Arévalo and Jacobo Arbenz in Guatemala. This was a masterpiece of political effectiveness. Even before Arbenz began his program of nationalization, UFCO had engaged Edward Bernays, one of the shrewdest masters of public relations ever born. Decades before Vance Packard, Bernays intuitively understood that people and governments respond to *perceptions* of reality. In 1928, he had written a book entitle *Propaganda*, in which he observed:

> The conscious and intelligent manipulation of the . . . opinions of the masses is an important element in democratic society. Those who manipulate this unseen mechanism of society constitute an invisible government which is the true ruling power of our country . . . it is the intelligent minority which need to make use of propaganda continuously and systematically.[4]

By 1950, Bernays had enlisted the help of the media in "uncovering" Communist subversion in Guatemala, persuading the *New York Times* and the *New York Herald Tribune* to send reporters to Guatemala, where they dined on the UFCO version of the nefarious Communist conspiracy at work. To ensure favorable coverage, the savvy PR man was careful to help the august newspapers select reporters who could view the matter objectively, i.e., hard-core anti-Communists. Their stories, placed as they were in distinguished and "objective" papers, piqued the interest of other major news organizations, and the "red advance" was soon being reported by *Time, Newsweek, U.S. News & World Report*, and the *Atlantic Monthly*. Despite President Arévalos's repeated proclamations that Guatemala was loyal to only the United States, and despite Guatemala's support for the United States in the Korean War, the other news organizations jumped on the red-scare bandwagon.

Another big gun UFCO brought to bear was Thomas G. Corcoran (aka

"Tommy the Cork"), a big-time political operator who knew practically everyone in D.C. Tommy the Cork had long-running intelligence contacts; among other roles, he had been counsel for the precursor to Air America, Civil Air Transport. Corcoran enlisted the help of his friend Walter Bedell Smith, who had only recently stepped down as DCI, was a current undersecretary of state, and was a close confidant of President Eisenhower dating back to World War II. Corcoran convinced Smith, who required little prodding, that the social reforms implemented by the Guatemalan government were the just the tip of a red iceberg. The Guatemalan land reforms, which were approximately as radical as those urged by the U.S. "Alliance for Progress" a mere seven years later, and less drastic than those *demanded* of the El Salvadoran government by the Reagan Administration, were promptly recognized as Communism on the march.[5] All told, UFCO accomplished this on roughly five hundred thousand dollars a year between 1950 and 1953.[6]

It probably didn't need to spend that much cash, for in essence, *La Frutera* was preaching to the choir. Dwight Eisenhower had been elected partly as a result of charges that the Democrats (and Harry Truman) had been soft on Communism, and his secretary of state, John Foster Dulles, was religiously committed to "rolling back" Stalin's evil minions. Moreover, Foster Dulles and his brother Allen, who happened to be the director of Central Intelligence, had both served as counsel to the law firm of Sullivan and Cromwell, who represented UFCO. The State Department official in charge of U.S. dealings in Latin America was John Moors Cabot, whose brother Thomas had once been president of UFCO.[7] This was serious political firepower, and UFCO quickly gained the support of the Central Intelligence Agency in protecting its investments, especially its hundreds of thousands of acres of uncultivated land. In reward, "Beetle" Smith would soon join UFCO's Board of Directors; this pattern would repeat itself over many other CIA covert actions.

The Guatemalan model of government mobilization essentially codified the means by which corporations could mobilize the clandestine forces of the United States for the cause of higher profits. In every case of U.S. covert intervention, the justification has been that either (1) the regime was (or was about to become) oppressive, or (2) planned nationalization of the economy was proof of Communist leaning, and the country was about to be swallowed up in the Soviet empire. As a general explanation for when and where the United States conducts black operations, however, neither holds water. First, the U.S. government has consistently supported some of the most oppressive and bloodthirsty regimes in the sad history of mankind, and sometimes installed those regimes in the first place, as seen in Chile (Pinochet), Indonesia (Suharto), El Salvador, Guatemala, Brazil, Zaire (Mobutu), and Saudi Arabia. Second, the United States gets on famously with *many* countries that have nationalized or socialized their economies (or large parts of it), including England, France, and Sweden. As mentioned above, the United States has promoted and even demanded land reform similar to Arbenz's in Japan, the Caribbean Basin, and El Salvador, recognizing that the concentration of land ownership in agricultural countries is *not* a free market, but rather

an unmerciful monopoly that perpetuates poverty and creates political instability. Even in avowedly Marxist countries that were Soviet clients, the United
States did not always follow a consistent pattern; as long as the government of
Angola allowed (and still allows) Chevron to pump its oil, the CIA never
received the kind of marching orders Richard Helms got from President Nixon.[8]

What has distinguished the motive for many covert actions has been a threat
to American corporate assets. Corporate America has often "helped" the government "find" the "Communists," essentially enlisting the covert and military power
of America; it has asked, "What can my country do for my profit margin?"

DEFENDING THE CORPORATE INTEREST

This does not mean that American foreign policy is controlled by individual corporations, whether it is UFCO, Gulf Oil, ITT, Chevron, or others. It is likely
that the power of the U.S. government has sometimes been co-opted to secure
specific foreign assets held by these and other U.S. TNCs, as in Guatemala and
Chile. The goal of the American policy in most cases, however, is not to protect
the individual corporation. If this were so, then there would be many more
instances of U.S./CIA intervention. Moreover, it would be simple indeed to
refute this as a major motivation of American foreign policy, for there are many
cases in which American corporations have been left to fend for themselves (e.g.,
Chevron in Angola), as well as cases of intervention where no obvious American
corporate investment was at stake (e.g., Laos and Afghanistan). Rather, the point
of U.S. intervention has been to safeguard the *system of transnational capitalism.*
This system is one in which large TNCs hold assets in many countries; in which
ownership of those assets conveys great economic and political power; and
through such power, the ownership of those assets are generally held to be invi-
olable (no matter how the assets were obtained in the first place).[9] This means
that, on occasion, individual companies are left to their fates if their loss does not
threaten the system of transnational ownership of foreign assets or set a precedent that might lead to an economic "domino effect." In other words, if a foreign country takes action that hurts a U.S.-based TNC but does not appear to
challenge the concept of "private property rights," e.g., corporate property
rights, then this is *not* a cause for U.S. covert action.

To understand why TNCs not only establish transnational economic relations but also conduct their own corporate foreign policies (complete with war-
making capability on occasion), it is necessary to understand the purpose of the
modern corporation. The goal of every corporation is *not* to produce goods and
services (e.g., cars or hamburgers). It is *not* to create employment, although many
Americans naively believe that this is so. One only has to look at the stock
market to see the fallacy in this belief: When American employment statistics
rise, the stock market falls. High employment rates in general are bad for corporations because employees represent a cost to the corporation. Moreover, high

employment (and a tightening of the labor market) generally requires corporate America to pay higher wages and salaries, thereby increasing costs. In other words, labor is a *liability*. What corporations are in business to produce, and any corporate executive will confirm this, is *profit*.

To raise the maximum possible profit, TNCs seek out a "favorable investment climate." While this may sound benign in the United States (although the people in, say, Flint, Michigan, or Youngstown, Ohio, might disagree), in the Third World, such a climate frequently means a political and economic system that Americans would almost universally call "oppression." Indeed, in the lives of the citizens of those countries, there is little difference between this "climate" and the harshest "Communist" regime. A favorable investment climate in the Third World often includes:

- extremely low wages, sometimes below subsistence level. Wages are often kept miserably low by death squads or murderous suppression of labor organizations, thereby assuring that wages and living standards (and democratic government) will never rise;
- exclusive ownership of the most productive land, for agricultural and extractive industries (e.g., mining, petroleum), at less than market value—often acquired through special "arrangements," i.e., bribes with local powers or by evicting small landholders and peasants at gunpoint;
- little or no corporate taxation, thereby assuring that little or no monetary benefits accrue to the citizens of the country;
- free, government-built infrastructure and public services (e.g., roads, electricity). In other words, people who struggle to earn $200 or $300 a year subsidize multibillion dollar TNCs;
- guarantees that no outside competition will be permitted. Domestic competition is sometimes allowed, in part to show that the TNC allows competition, but mostly because a Third World domestic competitor can be squashed by a TNC whenever the whim arises.

The ultimate result of this kind of "favorable investment climate" (aside from endless despotism) is to more or less permanently enshrine the TNC as the political and economic ruler of the country. As the "provider" of the country's foreign exchange income, the TNC holds a sword of Damocles over the government and domestic elite, not unlike the relationship between a crack dealer and an addict. Should the government attempt to take over the productive resources controlled by the TNC, disaster would almost certainly follow. Even if another TNC were recruited to take over and manage the resources and facilities, the inevitable interruption in cash flow would be disastrous for many countries. Most Third World countries perpetually live on the edge of financial catastrophe, and even a few weeks without hard currency could be calamitous, not to mention revolutionary. Moreover, it might be impossible to find a "replacement" TNC, as few would be willing to enter into an arrangement with a government that had set such a precedent. Finally, of course, a country embarking on such a course would likely find itself the target of a U.S./CIA-sponsored destabilization and also against the sharp end of a coup d'etat.

To establish and safeguard these investment climates, the United States government has spent billions of dollars and, more importantly, the lives of many good men and women. This "protective" role of the U.S. armed forces, proxies, and covert action has amounted to an enormous financial subsidy over the years (virtually impossible to estimate, but certainly in the tens, if not hundreds, of billions of dollars), allowing American TNCs[10] to operate and profit from potentially (and actually) risky overseas operations.

One commonly hears several justifications for the enormous profits reaped by corporations and corporate executives who pay their Third World laborers a dollar or two per day. One of the most persuasive, superficially, is that profit is the reward for risk, i.e., corporations "risk" their money by moving production facilities to "unstable" Third World countries, and therefore they *need* huge profits to offset the potential losses should one of the risky enterprises fail. At the same time they are clamoring for a "free market," however, one "unfettered by the government," they pursue a course that virtually removes the risk from these endeavors, both by benefiting from U.S. government largesse (i.e., the Overseas Private Investment Corporation, which "insures" American TNCs against foreign losses) and through direct U.S. action, e.g., covert operations, to reverse nationalization where it has occurred and deter other governments from following the same path.

A SYSTEM IS NOT A CONSPIRACY

It is common to denigrate individuals who question the role of corporate power in the making of foreign policy as "conspiracy nuts" or similarly belittling labels. That the U.S. government responds to corporate control, however, does not require smoke-filled rooms; the system of government produces "corporate-friendly" outcomes by design. One of the defining characteristics of the U.S. government as a set of organizations is the origin of the individuals who occupy both the top decision-making slots as well as those who comprise the foreign policy bureaucracy. These individuals come from a startlingly narrow segment of American society: Virtually all are, were, or will become business executives; many, too, are lawyers. A large proportion come from monied backgrounds, private prep schools, and Ivy League universities. This is obvious by simply examining the list of names of the individuals who have controlled American foreign policy and intelligence agencies: Bedell Smith, Allen and Foster Dulles, John McCone, George Bush, Bill Casey, and so on. In general, it is not necessary for American corporations to "enlist" their help against Third World social reformers, for these men and women already see the world the same way that corporate executives do. Even if a few decision makers come from different backgrounds with different perspectives, there are two great pressures to conform to the prevailing view of the world. First, to make a career within a large bureaucracy (such as the State Department), it is generally necessary to adopt the common ideology of the organization. Second, even if one does not come from a wealthy or corporate background, it generally possible to obtain such status and rewards *after* leaving the bureaucracy *so long as* one has been a suitably cooperative "team player." This does not apply only to the few government executives at the top (e.g., the secretary of state, DCI), for many of the individuals at lower levels can influence policy—and even whether or not covert operations are undertaken—by the kind of information they provide (or don't provide) and the interpretation they put on it.

Because of this common worldview, many social reforms in the Third World are perceived by American government leaders as Communist subversion rather than possibly justified social change. In essence, the U.S. position in many of the cases discussed throughout this book has been that *if a corporate asset is now owned by American interests, then: 1) the ownership is just, and 2) ownership cannot be challenged, even by the government of the country the asset resides in.*

When TNCs bleat about the sanctity of private property and the unfairness, not to mention the communistic motivation, behind the efforts of Third World countries to restructure and gain control of their own economies, it has to be taken with a grain of salt. First, when it comes to the issue of "private property," it is almost certainly true that the TNCs "own" the facilities, land, plantations, mines, and so on, that they use, and they have pieces of paper that say so. It is also true, at least in some cases, that these resources were obtained either by force, sometimes literally by chasing off peasants at gunpoint, or by chicanery, such as bribing local officials to "nationalize" land owned by small landholders, and so forth. Where were the private property rights of *those* people?

Second, one must examine the role TNCs play in "host" countries. How do Americans feel when Japanese conglomerates buy American property, banks, farms, telecommunications networks, and industries? Should Americans expect foreign-owned firms to operate in the best interests of the United States and the American people? If not, then why should Americans expect Third World citizens to placidly accept control of their economies and lives by foreign powers, either government or corporate?

CONCLUSIONS

The ultimate upshot of all this has been to the detriment of both the people of the Third World and the people of the United States. By supporting the power of TNCs against the governments of the Third World, the United States has:

- created or perpetuated a number of the most bloodthirsty and repressive regimes in human history;
- overthrown several democratic governments, *none of whom* gave any indication that they would turn their countries into Soviet clients or nationalist dictatorships;

- encouraged the export of American production and American jobs to low-wage Third World countries;
- guaranteed that those jobs stay in those countries by allowing and even encouraging regimes to repress any movement for higher wages;
- limited markets for American exports by allowing the repression of labor movements in the Third World, thereby preventing the growth of their middle classes and limiting their ability to buy American goods and services;
- *pressured American wages downward* by allowing TNCs to permanently shift production to very low-wage countries;
- destroyed American communities and families by shifting production to the "friendly climate" of Third World fascism.

These outcomes have been created in no small part because of American covert action. The secrecy of such operations, coupled with the "illegitimacy" of challenging the CIA and covert action, has made these actions possible. Covert action in the Third World has frequently subverted democracy and free markets.

NOTES

1. There were several meetings involving Harold Geneen and other ITT executives with Secretary of State William Rogers, Henry Kissinger, Richard Helms, and John McCone throughout 1970–71. See Anthony Sampson, *The Sovereign State of ITT* (New York: Stein and Day, 1973), chap. 11.

2. See Steven Schlesinger and Stephen Kinzer, *Bitter Fruit: The Untold Story of the American Coup in Guatemala* (New York: Doubleday, 1982), pp. 92, 102.

3. Cooperation is usually limited to actions against expropriation, which all corporations view as an assault on the capitalist system itself, and therefore on all of them. In cases where embargoes are attempted for other purposes, e.g., the U.S. wheat embargo against the Soviet Union, companies fall all over themselves to fill the void left by the boycotting firm.

4. Edward Bernays, *Propaganda* (New York: Horace Liveright, 1928), pp. 9, 31.

5. In breaking up the large land-holdings, Arbenz did *not* obtain ownership for the state. Instead, he distributed the land to 100,000 families, in essence *creating 100,000 new family businesses (farms)*. This was a far cry from Communism or even socialism; it was far more akin to Teddy Roosevelt's "trust-busting" than to Lenin's collectivization.

6. For a detailed recounting, see Schlesinger and Kinzer, *Bitter Fruit*, chap. 6.

7. Ibid., pp. 103, 106.

8. Essentially, get rid of Allende at all costs.

9. An excellent and more detailed description of the global capitalist system can be found in Michael Parenti, *The Sword and the Dollar: Imperialism, Evolution, and the Arms Race* (New York: St. Martin's Press, 1989), chap. 2, 6.

10. A transnational corporation is a corporation that operates across national boundaries, i.e., in many countries. This label more accurately reflects the nature and power of these entities than does "multinational."

Chapter 12

The Political Economy
of Covert Action II:
It's the Economy, Stupid!

BLACK OPS AND GREEN OPS

The farmers stood around the radio, listening to the faint signal, straining to catch a word or two. The army had risen up, and was taking over the government. Already, the radio reporter said, the president was dead. In a way, these campesinos were saddened, for this meant an end to a hundred years of democratic rule in their country. In a way, they were also glad, for it *seemed* like nearly a hundred years since any of them had had real meat to eat—other than rats, which didn't really count. Perhaps the army could bring order back to the economy; with the army came the Americans, and with the Americans came food and gasoline and new baseballs and Coca-Cola.

In many times and places, the people of foreign countries have enacted similar scenes, hoping and praying that their devastated economies could be rescued by someone who could bring back the dollars. Often, they do not know about the covert actions, conducted by another country, that have brought the events to pass; often, they are so desperate they do not care.

At the opposite end of the spectrum from the farmers are the string pullers. Covert action is attractive to decision makers for many reasons, as discussed in chapter 2. One of the most important of these is the apparent success that these black operations have had; critical foreign policy successes at relatively little cost. Frequently, enthusiasts for covert action point to victorious operations and assert that (1) they "worked," (2) the alternative was war, and (3) the other alternative was surrender to the Communists. While the overall "success" of American covert action will be assessed later, this chapter takes up one component of the historically "successful" covert actions: that the United States achieved its objective(s) in these cases *because* of the covert actions.

In fact, in many of the most successful cases of U.S. covert action, there were other U.S. forces at work besides the black operators. We might call these the "green ops," the use of American economic power to attain political objectives. Richard Nixon commanded all the legions of the U.S. government and private industry to make the economy of Chile "scream"; President Eisenhower and John Foster Dulles "encouraged" petroleum companies to undertake a devastating embargo of Iranian oil in 1953; thirty years later, when the United States stomped down on credits and spare parts for Nicaragua, the Nicaraguan economy crashed and burned. Because there were other "obvious" reasons for "victory" in these and other countries, the role of economic power has often been ignored as power politicians pronounce the lessons of history and covert operators scramble to claim a piece of the credit.

This chapter examines the ways in which American economic might has been used in support of, or parallel to, covert operations. The cases considered here are not the limited economic covert actions described in chapter 4 (e.g., influencing the 1948 Italian elections), but instead are big covert actions with big objectives: the overthrow of foreign governments. We will consider not only the nature(s) of economic power, but its opportunities and limitations, its historical uses, and the way it has interacted with and supported the CIA's black ops.

"MAKE THE ECONOMY SCREAM"

Richard M. Helms, director of Central Intelligence, walked out of the meeting with the president. Neither President Nixon nor Secretary of State Henry Kissinger were going to allow Latin America to become a "red sandwich," with Castro's Cuba on top and Salvador Allende's Marxist Chile on the bottom. The CIA was to spare no effort or expense in getting rid of Allende, and the primary treatment was to be economic. Helms's notes of the meeting record Richard Nixon's direct order: "Make the economy scream."

There was good reason to think that the United States could do it. While Chile had never been on the front burner as a major foreign policy or economic concern for the United States, the Andean country relied heavily on the American market and almost exclusively on American capital. The country's primary export was copper, and the copper industry, both mining and processing, was controlled by U.S. corporations: Anaconda Copper and Kennecott Copper *were* Chile's export earnings. Without exports to the U.S., Chile could earn no dollars; without dollars, Chile could buy nothing from other countries. From cars and trucks to gasoline to wheat and beef, copper exports paid the bill. Internally, Chilean electronics and telecommunications, including the country's telephone and television broadcasting facilities, were owned lock, stock, and barrel by a U.S. multinational, the International Telephone and Telegraph Company (ITT).

When Allende began his program of nationalization, which included expropriating facilities from Anaconda, Kennecott, and ITT, the corporations retaliated with a vengeance. Acting on their own, they sued Chile in both international courts and the U.S. court system, obtaining injunctions that tied up millions of dollars in Chilean exchange. More importantly, they mobilized the United States government: not only the CIA, but the State Department, Department of Defense (and the armed forces, especially their intelligence branches, special operations units, and foreign military training units), the Treasury, and the Department of Agriculture.

Together, the Treasury and the State Department proved decisive. The economic assault took several forms. First, working with Kennecott and Anaconda, the United States persuaded the world to stop buying Chilean copper; since 80 percent of Chile's export earnings came from copper, the country was essentially driven out of the foreign marketplace, since no exports means no imports.[1] Second, the U.S. government, through the Treasury and State Departments, virtually eliminated all foreign aid to Chile. In the seven years before Allende's election (1964–1970), Chile had received over $1.2 billion in aid from the U.S. Agency for International Development (AID), the U.S. Export-Import Bank, the World Bank, and other bilateral and multilateral agencies. Because Chile did not produce many things necessary to a modern society—including both manufactured goods like automobiles, machine tools, and television and radio equipment, as well as basic commodities like gasoline and even adequate foodstuffs—it depended on this foreign assistance to provide many of the things that kept the economy afloat and progressing, albeit at a slow pace. During the Allende years (1970–1973), Chile's foreign aid was reduced to about 1 percent of the pre-Allende total. Due to both the cutoff in export earnings as well as Allende's desire to carry through expensive social programs, Chile required about $1.25 million *per day* in foreign aid, i.e., more than the Soviets were shelling out to float Castro's Cuba, and which the Soviets did *not* provide to Allende.[2]

To exacerbate the increasing economic chaos and supply problems, the CIA undertook a subtle propaganda operation: CIA media assets and agents of influence began quietly reporting on shortages of critical goods *before they were scarce*. This whispering campaign produced the desired effect: People began hoarding these goods (e.g., sugar, gasoline, and toilet paper) so that actual shortages were created.

The final critical element in the destabilization was the trucker's strike. Modern economies, including Chile's, depend on transportation to move primary goods to processing plants, intermediate goods (i.e., parts) to assembly plants, and finished goods to market. In every country, a critical bottleneck is the trucking industry (this is why the Teamsters are such a pivotal organization in the United States). In early 1973, apparently to protest the decline in living conditions, virtually all truckers in Chile went on strike, rapidly creating severe shortages in almost every commodity. Moreover, despite the fact that the truckers' union had no strike fund, the truckers remained off the job for nearly a year. To this day, the CIA denies it funded the strike, but there has never been any other explanation for the ability of the strikers to go so long without any discernable source of income. It *has* been established that some "private" money went to fund the truckers, donated by U.S. business concerns and political "foundations," some of whom were connected to the CIA. This may be a case in which CIA representatives have technically told the truth, that the CIA did not directly pay out the cash, but instead funneled money to the strikers through proprietaries and cutouts, and arranged private sources of funding for the strikers (much as Bud MacFarlane and Oliver North solicited money for the contras from Saudi Arabia and Brunei in the 1980s). Anaconda, Kennecott, and ITT would have been good sources of cash for this purpose.

The economic quarantine devastated Chile. By 1972, production of most goods declined dramatically; e.g., wheat production was down 35 percent, the government was running a 40 percent deficit, inflation was running over 300 percent (but often goods were only available on the black market, at a rate even higher than this). The severe shortage of almost all goods was crippling, e.g., gasoline was rationed at about two and a half gallons per week, and even cabinet ministers were forced to stand in line for hours for bread.[3] By October 1973, the political preconditions for a military intervention had been created within the Chilean army and population; the actual military assault lasted a short time.

In the end, the U.S. economic action against Chile had two goals. The first was to create the conditions for either a revolution or military takeover. Since Allende had substantial popular support, and his policies in fact benefited the working classes, the American aim turned to reducing living conditions to the point where there would be a "popular" call for the military to "save" the country. This was essentially a no-lose proposition for the United States. If the Allende government was not overthrown, at least the second goal could be achieved no matter what: to drive living standards downward so far and fast that Chile could not possibly serve as an example of successful "socialist development." Even if Chile remained socialist, its economic disaster would deter other countries from considering the same path.

When the army coup d'etat ultimately took place, the economy recovered via an immediate and powerful assist by the United States, which permitted millions of dollars in aid, as well as American goods, parts, and expertise, to flow back into Chile. Even so, the impact of the American economic punishment was not quickly overcome. Inflation remained very high for several years; unemployment shot upward as the "free market" adjusted to the International Monetary Fund (IMF) austerity plan, except there was no social "safety net," so disease, mortality, and infant deaths rose rapidly, and access to medical care and education once again became the province of the wealthy. To rebuild the national infrastructure and physical capital (plants, machinery) after several years of embargo, the government and private firms had to borrow enormous sums of foreign money, and the external debt shot upward even faster than it had under Allende. Today, of course, if you can overlook twenty years of brutal repression, Chile is a success story.

The economic assault on Chile "worked" not because it created a popular uprising, and not because "the people" rejected Allende's Marxism, but because the population was beaten down enough that they were willing to trade their one hundred-year-old democracy for material survival. In the short term, the economic disaster, regardless of cause, excused the coup d'etat. Because of the entrenched democratic tradition in Chile and the strong military ethic supporting civilian control of the armed forces, it was the economic operation against Allende that made the coup permissible: The economic siege was the decisive action.

"Economic Sanctions Don't Work"

Chile is a prime example of what an economic behemoth like the United States can accomplish with economic muscle. It has become conventional wisdom among political leaders, academics, and pundits alike, however, that "economic sanctions don't work." If this is true, then the American people have done a poor job of selecting presidents; every American president since Franklin D. Roosevelt has imposed stiff economic sanctions against one country or another: The Soviet Union, other Eastern bloc nations, China, Japan, Germany, Korea, Cuba, Iran (twice), Brazil, South Africa, Chile, Nicaragua, and many others have felt the sting of Uncle Sam's wallet as it snapped shut.[4] Many more have caved in to the *threat* of economic sanctions initiated by America. As the case of Chile illustrates, however, sanctions *can* work; the right question is not *whether* sanctions can work, but instead, *under what conditions* do sanctions work?

Economic sanctions take many forms. The most direct is the cutoff of bilateral aid, e.g., when India exploded nuclear weapons in May 1998, the United States stopped $140 million in aid slated for the land of Gandhi.[5] The United States, home of many transnational banks that provide billions of dollars in loans to foreign governments (e.g., Citibank, Chase Manhattan), can "request" that the banks delay loans until some offending policy or regime is replaced. At a higher level, U.S. representatives can refuse or discourage multilateral aid—aid that comes from several countries, or from international organizations such as the World Bank or International Monetary Fund (IMF)—to an offending country. Because of the financial power of the United States and the predominating importance of U.S. contributions to those institutions, generally they do what the United States government asks. A more subtle approach is to simply downgrade the "credit worthiness" of a government, which generally results in reducing or eliminating credit, or making the target regime pay much higher rates of interest.

Another sanction is so common it scarcely creates notice: the embargo, cutting off trade between the United States and another country. Embargoes can be general, allowing no trade at all, as between the United States and Cuba since 1961, or limited to specific items, e.g., when the United States refused to sell oil, scrap iron, and steel to Japan in 1940.[6] "Limited" embargoes, however, can become quite extensive; sometimes the list of embargoed items for a single country can run into the thousands, such as the catalog of things that were not allowed to be shipped to the Soviet Union, including arms, electronics, many publications, machine tools, rare metals and minerals, and so on.

The potential power of an embargo increases exponentially when a country is *dependent* on the United States for critical economic or military ingredients.[7] These ingredients can be as simple as food (e.g., wheat), although food can often be obtained from other sources. Critical economic factors likely to influence a foreign regime are things like spare parts for American-made machines (e.g., factory machinery, cars, agricultural equipment, TV and radio components), or petroleum products (e.g., gasoline, diesel fuel, lubricants). Once equipment begins to break down, if replacement parts aren't available, one has to buy completely new items. This is often too costly, and moreover, it is not always as simple as buying a similar model from Europe or Japan; sometimes their machinery cannot be easily integrated—if it can be integrated at all—into a facility or factory based around U.S. hardware.

Military dependence also creates political leverage. Once a country adopts U.S. military hardware, especially the more sophisticated items like aircraft, electronics, and small arms, it is difficult to defy the wishes of the U.S. government without planning on restocking major (expensive) components of its armed forces. Once again, spare parts are the critical element; aircraft and modern electronics require constant maintenance, and F-16s without spare parts are just extravagant trucks.

One reason some political leaders conclude that sanctions don't work is because sanctions don't work *in all circumstances*. It is easy to point out cases in which sanctions didn't work, e.g., South Africa, Cuba (1960–present), Italy (1937), the Soviet Union(1919–1990), and Iraq (1990s). Yet this list merely helps to define the circumstances under which sanctions succeed or fail.

For U.S. economic sanctions to have an effect, they must meet several conditions. First, the restricted items (including money or credits) must be controlled by the U.S. government. If other entities (governments, businesses, or international organizations) can supply the goods or services despite U.S. policy, then there *is* no sanction; the target will simply get the goods somewhere else, and U.S. firms will lose the market. Second, the embargoed items must be impossible or prohibitively expensive to replace, e.g., an entire national radar warning system. Third, the cutoff must affect the *target group* within the target country. It does no good to merely starve the general public if the object is to change a government policy; the embargo must threaten something the target group cares about. Target groups can vary by time and place. Sometimes the aim of an embargo will be to influence the sitting government or dictator; often the military, or a coup-minded group within it, is the object; other times, the goal might be the middle class, in hopes of creating an uprising. If economic sanctions are not carefully thought out, they are a blunt instrument indeed.

The other reason the phrase "economic sanctions don't work" is so often pronounced is because of varying definitions of "work." It is probably true that economic sanctions by themselves rarely bring down a hostile foreign regime. Sanctions, however, have often created the conditions for rebellion, coup d'etat, and even electoral victory against U.S. foes.[8] Examples of such cases include Italy (1948), Iran (1953), Chile (1973), and Nicaragua (1980s).

In concert with covert action, economic sanctions have generally been used to *destabilize* a foreign government: to ruin the economy and make domestic living conditions so wretched that the military or the people will rise up against the government and install a new one that can get the economy moving again.[9] What makes this program so effective at times is that U.S.-backed insurgents usually *can* deliver on the promise to revitalize the economy; having wrecked the economy, the United States can pick it back up simply by ending sanctions. Generally, too, Uncle Sam quickly steps in with a generous aid package as soon as a cooperative regime takes charge. This is at least part of the story of how the recently deposed Suharto became president of Indonesia in 1965. Following a still-unexplained coup against Sukarno, American dollars flowed like water into the country to prop up the Suharto government. Let us turn next to some other examples of the use of economic power, which will illustrate the success and failure of green ops, as well as their interconnection with covert action.

IRAQ

Iraq is a good example of a condition under which sanctions probably cannot bring down a government, even in concert with covert action. Since the Iraqi invasion of Kuwait, virtually no military supplies have entered Iraq; foreign aid has been restricted to "humanitarian" aid; and Iraq has been able to earn very limited foreign trade by internationally imposed limits on the sale of Iraqi oil. Despite declining living conditions and several mutinous ethnic nations, Saddam Hussein's regime holds on.

One thing these sanctions show is that merely driving down the standard of living, even to brutal levels, is not guaranteed to create rebellions. One can learn this from modern conflict theory and research, which stresses two concepts: (1) *relative* deprivation of potentially insurgent groups, and (2) mobilization of insurgents. First, it doesn't matter how low living conditions sink for the ordinary people: As long as Saddam Hussein can provide an adequate lifestyle for key elements in his army, i.e., the Republican Guard, they will continue to stomp out the flickering flames of resistance. Moreover, the fact that the Republican Guard implements Saddam's brutal policies binds them to him, much as Anastasio Somoza's National Guard was forced to stand by him in Nicaragua. A democratic Iraq, controlled by the very people the Guards have made a living out of murdering and torturing, would seek justice. Within the core of Iraq, Saddam's omnipresent secret police and brutal methods of repression prevent the establishment of a revolutionary cadre around which the people might rally; around the edges (e.g., Kurdistan in northern Iraq), the still-intact Republican Guard can smash underarmed resistance movements. Finally, for immiseration to create rebellion, the population must believe that it is the government that is to blame. With years of indoctrination and limited foreign media penetration, Saddam has thus far managed to slap the blame for Iraq's economic woes on the United States and its allies.

COUNTERCOUP

The covert action that came to epitomize the clever, successful black operation, and which became the impetus for the many covert operations during the 1950s and 1960s was OPERATION AJAX against the Mosaddeq regime in Iran in 1953. The operator in charge, Kermit "Kim" Roosevelt, was swiftly awarded America's highest intelligence medal (which he could never wear, since he could not explain how it had been earned). Eventually, Roosevelt wrote a book about the operation, *Countercoup*, in which he justified and explained the exciting nuances of the operation.

In this case, however, as with many others, one of the biggest guns in the U.S. arsenal was economic. When Prime Minister Mohammad Mosaddeq threatened to nationalize the holdings of the Anglo-Iranian Oil Company (AIOC), not only did the black agents swing into action, but so did the green operators. With the backing of the American government, the government of the United Kingdom, and the "Seven Sisters" oil companies, an embargo was imposed on the purchase of Iranian oil. Iran had accumulated little in the way of foreign reserves (hard currency), in no small part because it had received so little for the oil pumped and exported by AIOC (about five cents on the dollar). Without hard currency, Iran's critical imports in industrial capital, manufactured goods, and food quickly dried up. This "inability to manage the economy" was seized upon by the Iranian military as a reason to support the shah, who quickly proved to be a much better economic overseer—a reputation backed, of course, by millions of dollars in U.S. aid and Western oil money.

CONTRAS, CORDOBAS, AND CREDITS

It is accepted without question by some that the "restoration" of democracy in Nicaragua is the result of the war fought by the contras and supported by the CIA, the U.S. government, individuals in the National Security Council, and private sources within the United States and around the world. The war in Nicaragua was viewed by some as the opportunity for the United States to show that subversion could work for *our* side as well as for the Commies; superficially, this appears to be true. Deeper inquiry, however, reveals that the change in government in Managua in 1990 was primarily, even if not entirely, the result of an overwhelming U.S. economic assault.

When the Sandinistas conquered the last of Anastasio Somoza's troops in 1979 and seized power, they inherited an economy already in ruins. The country owed a $1.6 billion foreign debt and held a mere $3 million in hard currency reserves. Moreover, there was about $300 million in war damage to repair, and this would only get the economy back to where it had been in the early 1970s. The World Bank estimated that Nicaragua would require about $300 million a year in aid merely to prop the economy back up to the 1977 level of GDP per capita, and even this minimal goal would take about a decade to accomplish.

It was not to be. In 1980, former CIA operative Cleto DiGiovanni proposed a plan to destabilize Nicaragua and bring about conditions that would require the country's leaders to cry uncle. The results of the destabilization program are summarized in table 13.1 (pp. 242–43). In 1981, the United States cut off all bilateral aid, but that was a drop in the bucket. When the real economic assault started two years later, the United States essentially vetoed multilateral aid to Nicaragua, including access to the International Monetary Fund and the World Bank. In 1985, the United States imposed a total embargo, essentially eliminating Nicaragua's ability to repair anything that broke down. Moreover, since the country had amassed such a huge and growing international debt, other countries would only sell goods to Nicaragua for hard currency (e.g., dollars). Yet the Sandinista government could not raise any hard currency, since its export markets (predominantly the United States) had been cut off. Since the Sandinistas couldn't *sell* goods for hard currency, they had no hard currency to buy foreign goods with—and no one would accept virtually worthless Nicaraguan money.

The impact of the credit cutoff and the U.S. embargo was breathtaking. From 1980 through 1984, Nicaraguan inflation was roughly 25–35 percent, and the wage index dropped from 100 to 68 (i.e., for every dollar a worker earned in 1980, he received only 68 cents in 1984). In 1986, the year after the embargo was imposed, inflation hit 682 percent and the wage index dropped to 19. Then things got *really* bad. By 1988, inflation hit an astonishing 14,316 percent, and the wage index dropped to 4; skilled office workers were making about $10 per month. Food consumption was scarcely above the starvation level, with the average calorie consumption dropping to about 1500 per day. In comparison, 1400 per day is about what you'd burn sitting in a La-Z-Boy watching *Jerry Springer* all day (basal metabolism); unfortunately, most Nicaraguans had to subsist on that while doing hard manul labor (e.g., farmwork, manufacturing). By the end of 1988, the Sandinistas had given in, implementing an IMF austerity plan that essentially dismantled their social and economic reforms in exchange for IMF credits to purchase foreign goods and capital equipment. Unfortunately for them, Hurricane Joan hit Nicaragua soon after, socking the country with additional millions of dollars in recovery costs.

By 1989, the austerity plan had reduced inflation to a "mere" 4,770 percent, and the Sandinistas agreed to supervised elections, including an opposition party, UNO, publicly backed by the United States. Through the National Endowment for Democracy, the United States funneled $30 million into the Nicaraguan election (about $30 for every voter; in comparison, in 1988, George Bush spent about $4 per voter to win the U.S. election). The candidate, Violetta Chamorro, had a simple platform: If she was elected, the United States would stop the contra war, send millions of dollars in aid, and resume trade. She was inaugurated in 1990. The "totalitarian" Sandinistas had held a fair election, lost it, *and turned over power*. Immediately, the United States forgave $250 million in bilateral debt; allowed renewed access to IMF, World Bank, and Import-Export Bank credits; and promised $700 million in direct aid, of which it delivered about half. Perhaps the biggest boon was the lifting of the embargo, which allowed American goods and spare parts back into Nicaragua. Sadly, the economy could not rebound like Wile E. Coyote; once it was stomped flat, it could not be easily pumped back up. Even today, after about a decade "back in the fold," it is scarcely attaining a Somoza-era standard of living.

There are two possible alternatives to the explanation that U.S. economic policies brought about the change in government in 1990: the contra war and Sandinista economic mismanagement. The contra war was certainly costly to an economy that was already in trouble due to decades of Somoza family looting. All told, however, the cost of the war has been estimated at about $1.15 billion: about $171 million in physical destruction by the contras, and about $978 million in lost production, including labor diversion (i.e., using people as soldiers instead of farmers). Moreover, while government military expenses amounted to a substantial portion of government revenue, many countries sustain such percentages during time of war and are not ruined (e.g., Israel).

Sandinista mismanagement of the economy has also been blamed for the economic disaster. Compared to other countries, however, the Sandinista regime fared *so far worse* than the worst "basket case" economies that it cannot possibly have been merely the result of mismanagement. By 1991, the accumulated external debt of Nicaragua (as a percentage of GDP) was about four times that of Mozambique (commonly considered *the* basket case); and five or more times worse than that of Zaire, Guinea-Bissau, or Somalia. To achieve such a disaster, the Sandinistas would have not only had to badly mismanage the economy, they would have had to mismanage several times worse than the worst Marxist regimes. Finally, the positive evidence of the impact of U.S. economic warfare has to be considered. Nicaragua is an obvious case of dependent economic development: Not only was over a third of Nicaragua's trade directed to and from the United States, but an even larger proportion of Nicaragua's working capital was of American origin. When U.S.-made machines began to break down, there was simply no way to get them back on line. Moreover, the Sandinista government managed to maintain inflation, wages, and the external debt within reasonable limits for the first six years of their rule, and for the first four years of the contra war (see table 13.1); yet within a year of the imposition of the full U.S. embargo, inflation had exploded from 22 percent to 682 percent, and the wage index plummeted from 52 to 19.

The impact of dependence reaches into virtually every aspect of life. For example, there were no bottle manufacturers in Nicaragua, and the United States had effectively squashed trade in such items, so Nicaraguans were forced to exchange bottles whenever they purchased a bottled product (e.g., Coca-Cola, beer). Because bottles are breakable, the national supply dwindled over time, thus making bottles an increasingly precious commodity and severely limiting access to bottled products.[10]

In the end, two things ended the Sandinista administration in Nicaragua. One was the devastation of the Nicaraguan economy, which produced such a precipitous and painful decline in the standard of living that the population became willing to accept virtually anything that would restore U.S. trade. While some of this was the result of warfare waged by the contras, by far the more substantial part was the result of inheriting an economy dependent on the United States, coupled with U.S. economic warfare. The other was an extraordinary political act: the willingness of the "totalitarian" Sandinista government to step down after losing the election. This in itself ought to call into question the "standard view" of both the Sandinistas and the role of the contras.

CONCLUSIONS

In cases in which economic pressure has been ineffective (e.g., Iraq, Libya, or Cuba, until recently), covert action has also proven ineffective. Historically, it is hard to separate out the effects of covert actions, on the one hand, and economic actions, on the other. Indeed, in most instances, these strategies have been viewed as complementary by the decision makers in Washington and Langley. It is possible to conclude, however, that in at least some cases, covert actions that "succeeded" could not have done so *without* the accompanying economic actions; the *necessary* component of the policy was economic. Conversely, the evidence for the success of the covert action is, in many cases, ambiguous at best. One must conclude that in some of these cases, the covert action merely produced gratuitous violence, when the end could have been achieved in other ways.[11]

Nicaragua-style campaigns of economic coercion are probably less likely to succeed in the future. First, the United States benefited from the cold war in isolating the Sandinista regime and Nicaraguan economy. Other countries who could have replaced America as the principal trading partner of Nicaragua hesitated to do so because the United States clearly saw this as a test of cold war loyalties. Today, however, if a country with a somewhat viable economy (as Nicaragua's was in 1980–85) seeks alternate suppliers in the face of a U.S. embargo, those suppliers, e.g., Japan, France, Italy, Canada, and even China, are likely to step forward. All that will have been accomplished is to lose the market for U.S. goods. Second, an effective U.S. embargo is less likely today in cases such as Nicaragua, or even Libya, for domestic reasons; it takes a deadly serious reason to stir up adequate public support for such actions. U.S. corporations make billions of dollars from overseas investments, and will not give that income up without a struggle. Short of outright expropriation of American assets, an Iraq-type provocation, or the special case of Cuba,[12] it is hard to see embargoes garnering adequate U.S. political support and cooperation.

The overall effect of these actions, however, has been to obscure or inflate the

Table 13.1
Comparative Chronology of Nicaragua, 1980s

Year	Internal Affairs	Contra War	U.S. Economic Acts
1980	Inflation: 35% Military exp: 20% Fiscal deficit: 29% Wage index: 100 External debt: $1.6B	Cleto DiGiovanni outlines plan to destablize Nicaragua. War cost: $1.6M	Still on good terms with Sandinista government
1981	Inflation: 24% Military exp: 22% Fiscal deficit: 22% Wage index: 91 External debt: $2.3B	First Reagan finding; Argentines begin training contras; AID funds anti-FSLN groups; War cost: $9.2M	Cutoff $9.8M in PL480 aid; all bilateral aid suspended
1982	Inflation: 25% Military exp: 19% Fiscal deficit: 35% Wage index: 81 External debt: $2.8B	Contra war begins (December), mainly cattle rustling. War cost: $32.1M	
1983	Inflation: 31% Military exp: 18% Fiscal deficit: 49% Wage index: 70 External debt: $3.4B	Contras target supplies, oil pipeline; attack on Corinto burns 3.4 M gallons of fuel. War cost:$164M	Nicaraguan sugar quota reduced 90%; U.S. kills multilateral aid; IMF and World Bank credit cut off
1984	Inflation: 35% Military exp: 24% Fiscal deficit: 41% Wage index: 68 External debt: $3.9B	Contras target exports: coffee, lumber, agricultural warehouses; CIA mines harbors War cost: $216M	
1985	Inflation: 22% Military exp: 34% Fiscal deficit: 42% Wage index: 52 External debt: $4.6B	War cost: $165M	Full U.S. embargo imposed; Inter-American Development Bank aid cut off
1986	Inflation: 682% Military exp: 39% Fiscal deficit: 42% Wage index: 19 External debt: $5.3B	U.S. Congress approves $100M for contras. War cost: $243M	

1987	Inflation: 912% Military exp: 41% Fiscal deficit: 37% Wage index: 7 External debt: $6.3B	Contra infrastructure offensive (power plants, transport) War cost: $408M	
1988	Inflation: 14,316% Military exp: 41% Fiscal deficit: 56% Wage index: 4 External debt: $6.8B	Contras sign cease- fire; U.S. Congress authorizes $18M in "nonlethal" aid. War cost: $178M	
	Sandinistas adopt austerity plan; it works, but gains wiped out by Hurricane Joan		
1989	Inflation: 4770% Military exp: 38% Fiscal deficit: 23% Wage index: ?? External debt: $8B	U.S. Congress authorizes $50M in contra aid	President Bush twice renews trade embargo; U.S. government, NED, and private donors give oppo- sition party (UNO) $30M
1990	Inflation: 12,338% Military exp: 40% Fiscal deficit: 52% Wage index: ?? External debt:$10.6B	Violetta Chamorro elected in February	U.S. forgives about $250M in bilateral debt; U.S. promises $700M aid, delivers about $350M

Military expenditures and fiscal deficit are expressed as percent of Central Government Expenditure.

Wage index is buying power of wages (1980=100).

External debt is in 1991 U.S. dollars.

Sources: Statistical Abstract of Latin America; U.S. Agency of International Development, *Latin America and the Caribbean: Selected Economic Data, 1992*; U.S. Arms Control and Disarmament Agency, *World Military Expenditures and Arms Transfers*, various years; CEPAL, *Notas para el estudio económico de América Latina: Nicaragua*, various years.

role played by covert action. In any future consideration of large-scale black operations intent on government overthrow, including Iraq and Libya, one must be very leery of analogies to past covert actions because it may not have been the black ops at all.

NOTES

1. See James Petras and Morris Morley, *The United States and Chile: Imperialism and the Overthrow of the Allende Government* (New York: Monthly Review Press, 1975), p. 92.

2. Yes, I agree; perhaps this *does* say something about just how much of a Soviet puppet Allende was. For the statistics, see ibid.

3. See Paul Sigmund, *The Overthrow of Allende and the Politics of Chile, 1964–1976* (Pittsburgh: University of Pittsburgh, 1977), pp. 228–35; and Edward Boorstein, *Allende's Chile: An Insider's View* (New York: International Publishers, 1977), p. 204.

4. Earlier presidents also used embargoes, dating as far back as Thomas Jefferson during the United States's conflict with England in 1807.

5. CNN (Cable News Network), 13 May 1998.

6. Technically, FDR did not embargo oil; he omitted oil from his final embargo order. Despite this, oil shipments stopped cold after the order. See Jerald Combs, *A History of American Foreign Policy* (New York: Alfred A. Knopf, 1986), p. 283.

7. For the academics, I am using dependence in the sense of a realist sanction/compliance relationship, not in the sense of structural conditions. An excellent summary of the distinction is Bruce Moon, "The Foreign Policy of the Department of State," *International Studies Quarterly* 27: 315–40.

8. There are two other reasons political leaders often say sanctions don't work. First, embargoes often hurt the constituencies of political leaders, e.g., U.S. wheat farmers in the embargo against the Soviet Union in 1980. It is far more politically acceptable to say that sanctions don't work than to admit one doesn't want to stand against evil. Second, political supporters of a foreign regime often say sanctions don't work in hopes of forestalling sanctions that might hurt the government they support. For example, this was a common theme among U.S. supporters of the government of South Africa during apartheid.

9. No, *all* the people will not rise up. Instead, what is required is that a cohort of insurgents is able to mobilize enough of the population to successfully rebel. This proportion can be remarkably small, so long as most of the population is apathetic or simply trying to stay out of the line of fire.

10. My thanks to Don Strickland for this story.

11. I am setting aside here two issues that are discussed elsewhere: (1) whether the ends were justifiable, and (2) the "structural violence" inflicted when one country wrecks the economy of another. Structural violence refers to the starvation, disease, and death that accompany poverty.

12. Cuba is a special case because of the dense concentration of Cuban-American voters in Florida, and because of the harsh anti-Castro position taken by their primary political organizations.

Part III

Off-the-Shelf

Chapter 13

Private Armies:
We Shoot for Loot

T he Curtiss P-40 screamed out of the sun, its six .50 caliber machine guns thumping out a drumbeat of death for the startled Japanese pilots below. The Japanese knew these snarling-faced aircraft all too well; the Flying Tigers, Chiang Kai-shek's small, brilliant air force, had sent dozens of the sons of Nippon to their ancestors. In a matter of seconds, the P-40s scattered the Japanese formation and sent several bullet-ripped enemy aircraft flaming into the jungle below. As they cartwheeled to their doom, the Japanese pilots knew something else; although the P-40s bore Nationalist Chinese markings, they were piloted by top-notch American aviators.

American history holds a proud place for men of high ideals and higher adventure, who didn't have to fight, but chose to anyway. These armed forces, ostensibly raised by private citizens, and ostensibly completely separate from the U.S. government, are remembered today with such heroic names as the New Orleans Grays, the Lafayette Escadrille, the Abraham Lincoln Brigade, and the Flying Tigers. More recently, the Cuban exile community has used the United States as a base and sanctuary for its ongoing war on Castro, and private organizations like the Alabama-based Civilian Military Assistance Group (CMAG) have openly provided military training to the contras from Nicaragua, as well as insurgents from other countries.

The use of American resources, territory, and government personnel, however, poses serious foreign policy problems for the United States, raising many questions: Is a private armed force really private, or merely a proxy for the CIA? Is an attack by a group trained in the United States an act of war *by the United States*? How should the United States respond if the target country retaliates? Doesn't the Nixonian Doctrine of hot pursuit apply when the sanctuary is the U.S. territory? Can the United States justifiably complain if a target government commits small acts of terrorism against insurgent training bases or individuals in the United States? If Americans fighting under a foreign flag are killed, how can the U.S. government stay out of the conflict? How can one be sure that "former" U.S. military personnel and intelligence operatives are truly "retired," and therefore not acting on the orders of the CIA or the U.S. government?

Furthermore, private armed forces operating on U.S. soil, even with the backing of the United States government, raise serious *domestic* political, legal, and law enforcement issues: Should these units be allowed to violate U.S. laws? Should private military units be allowed to attack other countries from American territory? Should they be allowed to purchase and possess military weapons, including machine guns, hand grenades, attack aircraft, explosives, and tanks? Should they be allowed to conduct military training in violation of state laws? To wage war effectively, or to train for war, private military units almost certainly must break numerous state, local, and federal laws; in effect, they are exempt from laws that ordinary American citizens must obey. These are critical issues in covert operations (where deniability is essential), and are often not considered in the least when covert operations are undertaken, or if they are considered, are explained away on an ad hoc basis.

This chapter analyzes two basic issues: first, the mobilizing of private American armed forces for foreign conflicts, and second, the problems raised when black paramilitary operations are based on and carried out from U.S. territory (whether they are government operations or not). It begins with the nature and background of America's private armed forces, the sometimes glorious history and sometimes the ignominious ends. It then explores the problems of "private" individuals, and how using sheep-dipped intelligence agents has seriously backfired on occasion. Most importantly, it explores the issues raised concerning covert operations with "private citizens."[1]

HAVE GUN, WILL TRAVEL[2]

While individual Americans can be found fighting or training fighters in almost any war, anytime, anywhere, they also inherit a tradition of fighting under foreign flags *as American units*. They fight for many reasons: it's what they've been trained for; some simply like the excitement of combat; others fight because they believe America will inevitably become involved in some future conflict. It is perhaps uniquely American, however, that Americans, from a country based on an *idea*, go out to *fight* in other countries for ideas. Whatever one calls it, be it liberty, freedom, antifascism, or anti-Communism, it is the *idea* that drives these men.[3]

Perhaps the most famous "private" American unit is The Flying Tigers (1937–1941), an American air force created by the legendary Claire Chennault to support the Nationalist Chinese of Chiang Kai-shek against Japan. By executive order, American military aviators were permitted to "resign" from American service to join the Tigers, with the understanding that they would retain rank and seniority if and when the United States entered the war. After the war, Chennault continued his personal excursion into international affairs, establishing

Civil Air Transport (CAT), a "private" airline that, among other things, covertly flew supplies to the beleaguered French garrison of Dien Bien Phu; CAT became better known after a name change to Air America.

Another prewar American venture was the Abraham Lincoln Brigade, comprised of American volunteers who fought the fascist forces during the Spanish Civil War (1937–1939). Roughly three thousand Americans served in the Brigade. Prior to both World War I and World War II, Americans served in the Canadian, British, and French air corps and armies, the most famous unit being the Lafayette Escadrille of World War I. Once the United States joined in, some of these units returned to American command, while others chose to remain with their "adopted" armed forces.

In the more distant past, privately raised American armed forces were quite common throughout the hemisphere. During the Texas Revolution (1836), American volunteers, such as the New Orleans Grays, flocked to Texas. You can see their flag displayed today at the Alamo, where they died to a man. It is even possible, although unproven, that Sam Houston was dispatched by President Andrew Jackson as an American agent to foment the rebellion against Mexican rule. Throughout the nineteenth century, private American citizens sought to extend the wealth, power, ideology, and territory of the United States by force of private arms. These filibusters, as they became known, were often either idealist liberators or arrogant conquerors, depending on one's point of view. Throughout Central America, men like William Walker raised small armies of Americans and led them against Mexico, Nicaragua, Honduras, and others—in Walker's case, against all three. Sometimes the goal would be to create a new state for the United States, sometimes to establish their own empires. Sometimes too, these were "liberal interventionists," intent on bringing the blessings of American-style democracy, capitalism, and Protestantism to the benighted brethren to the south, at the point of a gun if need be. Finally, although there is little historical documentation, many American corporations maintained private "security forces" in the countries of Latin America in which they had holdings. These "police" were generally better armed and more powerful than the army of the nominal "government," and helped protect the profit margins of powerful transnational corporations (TNCs).

Private military activities are not a thing of the past, however. When OPERATION MONGOOSE (the post–Bay of Pigs CIA program to overthrow Castro) was shut down, many Cubans and some Americans continued to train and carry out their own war against Castro. Throughout the 1960s, these men raided Cuba, sometimes driving powerboats into Havana Harbor to shoot up hotels, sometimes engaging in firefights with Cuban soldiers. One American organization that aided this effort was InterPen (the International Penetration Force), which served as a training unit for the exile forces and apparently conducted military operations against Cuban targets. More recently, the war in Nicaragua (1979–1989) spawned a plethora of private endeavors. Most of these were aimed at funding and supplying the contras, and few Americans directly engaged in combat with Sandinista forces (and none as "American" units per se); some contra training, however, took place within the United States.

WHERE YOU STAND DEPENDS ON WHERE YOU SIT:
SAFE HAVENS AND BLACK OPERATIONS

It is far easier to laud these groups than to criticize them. Sometimes they were "unofficial" units of the American military, and in most cases (but not all, e.g., some of the filibustering "armies") were comprised of valorous men of high ideals. There are good reasons, however, that private citizens are not *not* allowed to carry out their own personal wars against whomever they please.

Throughout its history, the United States has decreed, by legislative action as well as executive order, a variety of laws generically referred to as Neutrality Acts. The first of these was a proclamation by President Washington in 1793 regarding the war between France and England, among others, that forbade American citizens to commit, aid, or abet hostilities against any of the belligerent powers. Further, the proclamation committed the United States to prosecuting any citizens who violated international law to participate in the war.[4] The object was to prevent a war between a major European power and the fledgling United States. Throughout the nineteenth century, such concerns were less important, as most of the action concerning the United States occurred in the Western Hemisphere. To help evict European powers from the hemisphere and fill the power vacuum itself, the United States required small bands of fighting men for whom the U.S. government was not responsible, either politically or financially. These filibusters arose out of necessity, the inability of the federal government to control them, and the expansive use of private corporate money to build private armies intended to establish corporate empires in Latin America.

By World War I, however, America was once again concerned that a horrendous European war would entangle the country, and Congress passed a strengthened Neutrality Act forbidding the selling of arms to belligerents, travel by American citizens on flagged vessels of belligerents, or even travel into or through war zones by American citizens. Prior to World War II, in 1937 and 1939, several more Neutrality Acts were enacted.

The crux of the matter is simply this: The United States government reserves to itself the legal right to wage war, and individual citizens or groups of them may not war against other governments or political movements. *Any* citizen who does so is liable to prosecution resulting in fines and imprisonment.

Why have such laws? Is it not an element of freedom that any citizen should decide for himself if a foreign cause is honorable enough to fight for? There are two answers to this. First, from a philosophical perspective, would we want every citizen deciding every day which laws they believe are adequately just to obey, and which should be ignored? Of course not. With an adequate system of representative government in place, citizens are expected to obey every law, even those they disagree with, at least until they can convince the legislature to change them.

The more important answer is founded in political reality. When Americans commit acts of war against foreign countries, they invite retaliation. Such retribution is liable to spill over into the United States as American combatants return home, thereby spreading violence to our own shores. What, then, should the U.S. government do? Does it meekly accept foreign violence on American streets, or try to prevent it? In such circumstances, the chances for a government-to-government confrontation are high, thereby creating the possibility that a minor clash involving some Americans will drag all of America into the war.

Preventing privately funded or inspired violent attacks on another country from U.S. territory is even more important. In international law, governments have a legal responsibility to control their own domains, and especially to prevent violent acts from being undertaken against other countries. The United States has asserted, as in Vietnam, that if another country cannot control its own borders, then the aggrieved (attacked) country has a moral and legal right to send military forces across national boundaries to punish the assailants. While international law may have no serious enforcement power, if the United States permits foreign or domestic private armies to base themselves out of America and assault foreign countries, then the U.S. government surrenders the right to be outraged when foreign countries retaliate. Because the United States is so powerful, such retaliation cannot be overt; there will be no Cuban marines hitting the beach in Miami. Instead, it will virtually always take the form of terrorism against American targets, either within the United States or against American businesses or tourists overseas. Many CIA officers were chagrined when MONGOOSE and its Cuban offshoot, Alpha-66, began operating out of Miami against Cuba, for they understood the consequences of sacrificing moral authority.

MISS NELLI'S BOARDING HOUSE

The Dade County Sheriff's deputy wasn't quite sure what to do. Sure, he had stopped a carload of Cubans, and sure, they were armed with automatic weapons and hand grenades, and sure, this was *illegal*. Sure, too, he would be ordered to simply let them go. Some government big shot would step in, as usual, muttering something about "national security," and there the argument would end. Unlike the American citizens who lived in Dade County, *these* cowboys were above the law.

Many of them lived on Fourth Street near the Orange Bowl, where they trained for the liberation of Cuba, and were cared for by the proprietor of the boarding house, Miss Nelli Hamilton. She thought of them as "her boys." Periodically, some of them would disappear for a day or more, some arrested for driving around Miami brandishing their weapons, others off on some adventure against Castro's island. For a substantial period of time in the early 1960s, Miss Nelli's was the center of resistance against Castro.[5]

The domestic problems created by private armed forces are enormous. Simply training for military operations typically requires that a covert unit break numerous state and federal laws:

- possession of automatic weapons (federal);
- possession of explosives or explosive devices (federal);
- the Munitions Control Act, prohibiting the sale or export of most weapons without federal approval (federal);
- paramilitary training (many states);
- tax violations from raising money (federal, state);
- making and using false identification (federal, state).

When an operation reaches the point where actual raids or assaults are undertaken against a foreign target, a whole other set of laws is violated:

- the Neutrality Act, forbidding American citizens from participating in foreign conflicts (federal);
- customs and immigration laws when leaving and reentering American territory (federal);
- the Munitions Control Act (again), prohibiting leaving the United States with weapons and explosives;
- international antiterrorism agreements adopted by the United States.

When covert paramilitary units are based in the United States, and especially when they train there, a whole host of practical and related legal problems arise. Law enforcement officers will inevitably investigate what, to them, seems like a nefarious and illegal activity; then one has to come up with *some* reason why (1) they shouldn't cart him off to jail, (2) they shouldn't file a report, and (3) they shouldn't come back. In the United States, one must further deal with several levels of law enforcement:

- the FBI, which may think they're dealing with a foreign terrorist group or a bunch of "militia";
- the Drug Enforcement Administration (DEA), which may investigate to see if the unit is producing or running drugs;
- the Bureau of Alcohol, Tobacco, and Firearms (ATF), which will be watching for firearms and explosives violations;
- U.S. Customs, which will be on the lookout for import or export of weapons and munitions;
- state law enforcement, such as the state police and bureau of investigation;
- local law enforcement: city police, or the sheriff's department.

A covert paramilitary unit in training is going to run afoul of some or all of these agencies at one time or another. In practical terms, this means that dozens of people are going to have to be let in on the secret, thereby risking exposure of the existence of the unit and potentially creating a media investigation as well. If the participants are part of an actual government operation, they'll still have to have a verifiable government official vouch for them as "vital to national security." During MONGOOSE, it was a common occurrence for a CIA officer in Miami (often David Atlee Phillips) to bail out Cubans who had been arrested, for example, for driving around Miami brandishing submachine guns and hand grenades. In such cases, federal law enforcement will certainly back off (although perhaps maintaining some surveillance, as the FBI did of the Cubans involved in MONGOOSE). State and local law enforcement will probably not be too happy having machine-gun-toting *pistoleros* cruising around the neighborhoods.

For a paramilitary unit, effective training is realistic combat training. This requires the use of live ammunition, live fire exercises, field training in unit combat tactics (e.g., setting up an "L-shaped" ambush), serious PT (physical training), and so on. Without this kind of preparation, a combat unit cannot be combat effective; a paramilitary covert action is bound to fail. Moreover, to build true *unit* combat-effectiveness, the team has to train as a unit. Within the United States, however, such training is bound to attract the attention of neighbors, hikers, forest rangers, newspaper reporters, and law enforcement of all stripes (local, state, and federal). One cannot pop off clips of 5.56 ball ammo from fully automatic AR-15s anywhere in the United States without drawing serious and rapid attention from law enforcement. Even simple unarmed tactical training exercises are usually apparent for what they are to even a casual observer (i.e., a bunch of guys sneaking around the state park looks pretty darn suspicious for a variety of reasons). Such activities simply cannot remain hidden.

If the unit is *not* part of a government operation, things get much trickier. First, it might be "private but government sanctioned," meaning that the CIA or the president cannot sponsor the group, but approves of the group's existence and goals. In this case, law enforcement is liable to be asked *off the record* to turn a blind eye, and most will, if only to build up some credit with other government agencies. This raises a host of problems: Who will be responsible if something goes wrong, e.g., a citizen is accidentally shot by a member of the operation? The local citizenry will want to know why the group was allowed to violate the law before the incident, and what can the local law enforcement reply? There is no documentation of government involvement, so the locals can easily be hung out to dry.

There are two unavoidable legal issues entangled in U.S.-based private or covert armed forces. First, even if the enterprise is a U.S. government operation, there is no national security exception to most federal, state, and local laws. Second, if the laws being violated are not enforced on the covert unit, then someone else (another private army, for example, or perhaps a "militia" unit) is bound to argue that the law is being selectively enforced (which it generally is in these kinds of cases).

PRIVATE ARMY, PRIVATE WAR

The existence of private armed forces within the United States, answerable only to themselves, independent of duly constituted political authority, is a troubling thought. In the Western political tradition, one of the defining characteristics of a state (i.e., a national government) is that the state has a monopoly on the *legitimate* use of force. If an armed force is not controlled by the U.S. government, then disquieting questions arise: Who exactly *does* it fight for? *What* exactly does it fight for? The purpose of armed force is *force*, and both the people and government of the United States have a right to be concerned over whom the force will be used against.

If an armed force is not government sanctioned, then it is merely a private army. One concern about these is that such bodies of men have been and are still used to circumvent the American democratic process and to allow men of power to carry on their own private "foreign policy." In the past, this has been done out of personal hubris or greed, as when American corporate armed forces controlled the countryside in small Central American countries—but almost universally, these were not based in the United States, instead usually being comprised of indigenous "police." More recently, private paramilitary and cadre units have been created *precisely* to carry out foreign policies that have been rejected by Congress, the president, the voting public, and/or all of the above. Within the United States, there are some powerful individuals, corporations, and organizations that sometimes find their interests at odds with those of the American public or official government policy. Sometimes these powerful "elite" entities exist outside government, for example, the United Fruit Company, Standard Oil, and the World Anti-Communist League. Sometimes they rotate in and out of government, depending on which party wins the quadrennial election. Merely *allowing* any of these entities to create a paramilitary force or conduct military training sets a dangerous precedent, and is a step along the road toward private armies; from there, it is a shorter step toward *using* private armies.

It is also far too easy for such forces to create serious international incidents that could easily drag the United States into armed confrontation with another country. Cuban exiles operating out of Miami have, on at least one occasion, launched an assault on targets in Havana in the hopes of killing or capturing Soviet military and political personnel. While this probably would not have led to war with either Cuba or the Soviet Union, such an act would have, at best, created significant diplomatic problems for the United States; at worst, war would not be out of the question. Most likely, there would have been Soviet retaliation against American citizens (tourists, businessmen, or military personnel) in another country (e.g., an "accident" in East Germany). It is also possible, and even likely, that a private political armed force might *want* to create confrontation, thereby essentially enlisting the United States and the blood of its children in its own fight.[6] Finally, it is possible that such forces, trained and experienced in covert action, might try to incite the United States into confrontation by staging a provocation that appears to come from their enemy. While the author knows of no case where this has occurred, mysterious provocations of unknown origin exist throughout history, e.g., "Remember the Maine." In fact, the CIA itself has planned and executed at least one provocation in an attempt to induce overt

American intervention to bail out a faltering covert action. During OPERATION PB/SUCCESS against Guatemala (1954), Al Haney, a senior CIA officer in the field, ordered American black aircraft to bomb a Honduran airfield, blaming the attack on Jacobo Arbenz's Guatemalan air force.[7]

COLD WAR, HOT PURSUIT

On numerous occasions, the United States itself has claimed the right to send armed forces across international borders because the government in the target countries could not control insurgents there. On 16 March 1916, Mexican insurgents led by Pancho Villa crossed the American border into New Mexico, attacking the town of Columbus and killing seventeen American citizens. Within days, President Wilson dispatched General John "Black Jack" Pershing across the border into Mexico to punish Villa and his forces.[8] This was justified, according to the United States government, because the government of Mexico could not control the insurgents and the United States had a right to defend itself. During the Vietnam War, both the Johnson and Nixon administrations used massive bombing campaigns against the Ho Chi Minh Trail in Laos and Cambodia, asserting the right to do so since the governments of those countries were unable to fulfill their international obligation to assure that their territory was not used by one of the warring countries, in this case, the North Vietnamese. More recently, it was the Reagan administration that claimed the right to attack Nicaraguan (Sandinista) bases that were alleged to have been sending supplies to the Frente Farabundo Martí de Liberacion Nacional (FMLN) insurgents in El Salvador.[9]

These reasons are precisely why the Cuban 2506 Brigade and the Guatemalan insurgents of Castillo Armas were based *outside* the United States. If a force invading another country originates outside the United States, the American government can deny knowledge and responsibility with at least a hint of plausibility. Moreover, any retaliation cannot justifiably—by international law— occur against American targets. Conversely, if the attacking force is based in, and/or jumps off from, the United States, the U.S. government is legally responsible for preventing the attack under both international and U.S. law, can be held legally accountable for reparations, and, in the "Court of Public Opinion," as Adlai Stevenson put it, can be subject to reasonable and justified retaliation.

CONCLUSIONS

Private armies are a common aspect of covert operations since they can be (somewhat) plausibly denied. Wherever they are based, however, they create serious problems for the United States. Such activities violate the law (e.g., the Neutrality Act, customs and firearms laws, and so on.), encourage selective enforcement of the law, blur the line between the U.S. government and private organizations (decreasing deniability), and increase the chance of dragging the U.S. government into a foreign conflict.

In foreign affairs, the effect of these armies on world politics is to increase the number of belligerent nonstate actors, to diffuse the methods and technology of violence, and to create new sources of private power (especially in Less Developed Countries) or, more often, to reinforce existing, usually oppressive governments. Such armies also allow those in the U.S. government to avoid accountability by privately encouraging these forces while publicly denouncing them, and by permitting those currently "out of government" to implement their own personal foreign policies. As the 1990s draw to a close, we are witnessing an increasing number of private armed forces for hire. These are the legacy of the private armies of the cold war.

NOTES

1. This chapter deals only with private armed forces used *outside* the United States. Historically, there have been many private armies raised and used inside the United States—the various endeavors that "conquered the West"; corporate "security forces" used to murder and intimidate labor organizers and employees; vigilante groups; neo-Nazis and Klan groups; and the current militia movement—that have no legal sanction or basis.

2. With a fond nod of remembrance to Paladin.

3. There are, of course, some American mercenaries who, like mercenaries the world over, fight for the excitement, money, and so on. There are also those who have fought *against* freedom, such as those who worked with the Somoza regime or the government of Guatemala in the 1980s. Even in those cases, however, I believe *they* believed that their "anti-Communism" was synonymous with freedom.

4. George Washington, "Proclamation of Neutrality," 22 April 1793.

5. For an excellent account of the activities around Miss Nelli's, see Warren Hinckle and William Turner, *Deadly Secrets: The CIA-Mafia War Against Castro and the Assassination of J.F.K.* (New York: Thunder's Mouth Press, 1992), pp. 176–79.

6. This is the same motive that drives proxy forces to "accidentally" drag the United States into their conflicts.

7. The provocation failed because, there being a shortage of bombs for the *real* war, the American covert aircraft dropped water-filled practice bombs, instead. When it was pointed out by the press and international observers that there was scarcely any damage at all and that the bombs appeared to be practice ammunition, the provocation plan fell flat. In the warm afterglow of the successful operation to oust Arbenz, no one was ever disciplined for this action, and it remains largely unknown to this day. See Stephen Schlesinger and Stephen Kinzer, *Bitter Fruit: The Untold Story of the American Coup in Guatemala* (New York: Doubleday, 1982), p. 175.

8. For a summary, see Jerald Combs, *A History of American Foreign Policy* (New York: Alfred A. Knopf, 1986), p. 192.

9. See *Public Papers of the Presidents of the United States: Ronald Reagan*, vol. 1, (Washington: Government Printing Office, 1983), pp. 603–604.

Chapter 14

The Political Economy
of Covert Action III:
"Off-the-Books"

E very covert operator wants to be James Bond.[1] Of course, this virtually
never happens; real operators don't drive $120,000 cars (not on a govern-
ment paycheck, anyway)[2]; real operators can't go even-up with billionaires at bac-
carat; real operators can't pound down a bottomless supply of Dom Perignon.

And yet, here on the outskirts of San Salvador, the men in the mansion came
close. The opulent house was unusual for several reasons. The roof sprouted a
large array of antennae and satellite dishes, the traditional flashing neon sign of
a black operations base. The grounds were patrolled by tanned, alert men with
military-short hair, whipcord muscles, H&K MP-5 submachine guns, and avi-
ator sunglasses. In fact, *all* the men in the place looked like that. There were no
fat-cat types. Regular deliveries supplied American beer and cigarettes, steaks
(these men are always meat eaters), and the finest quality booze: Chivas, Jack
Daniels, Coors. Inside the house, there was a workout room to rival any American health spa, complete with Nautilus machines. The city's finest "working
women" knew their way around the place, too. For the American covert operators based in the big house, expense was no object.

This is because the entire operation—house, cars, booze, women, the whole
enchilada—was on the U.S. government tab. Had Congress known what it was
buying (running into the hundreds of millions of dollars), expense would indeed have
been a major object. Despite regular briefings by the heads of the various American
intelligence agencies and military branches (this was a U.S. Army operation), however,
the Solons on the Potomac never found out, for this operation was strictly "off-the-
books": a clandestine government operation run by government operators, paid for
with government money, but purposely concealed from anyone in government who
had the right to authorize it. This was an intelligence program *specifically designed* to
break the law, spawned by a clandestine intelligence organization within the U.S. government established to circumvent official U.S. intelligence agencies; in particular, the
CIA itself was bypassed *precisely because CIA officers might obey the law.*

Spy and action/adventure novelists sometimes put their operatives in secret organizations outside normal government channels: Adam Hall's supersecret Bureau, answerable only to the British prime minister, is one example.[3] The appeals of this kind of organization are, to novelists, enormous. Agents can blow away the bad guys with never a thought of being called to testify before Congress. Traitors? A bullet in the head is the answer; typical, trite, and movie-salable. Plausible deniability is nearly perfect, because there is no trail, not even inside the government itself.

In the last twenty years or so, such operations have also proven irresistible to responsible officers of the U.S. government, including at least one president, probably more than one DCI, members of the National Security Council, general officers in the U.S. Army (active and retired), and highly respected admirals. The organizations include such quasi-governmental organizations as the Iran/Contra Enterprise, a U.S. Army organization code-named YELLOW FRUIT, and the Intelligence Support Activity (ISA). It also includes various mechanisms set up to perpetually fund private covert operations, such as the Nugan Hand Bank and the possible looting of some of the failed savings and loans by intelligence operations (remember the hundreds of billions lost in failed S&Ls?).[4]

This chapter details the workings of the "off-the-books" operations: what they are, how they were established and what they did, why some of the highest government authorities turned to them, and the effects and implications of such activities.

WHAT "OFF-THE-BOOKS" MEANS

At first glance, an off-the-books operation or program might not look much different from an official covert action. Both are designed to be plausibly deniable, that is, the opposition knows something is occurring, but cannot prove who is responsible for it. Thus, whether the *sterile* assault rifles the contras off-loaded in Honduras came from covert CIA stockpiles or were provided by Richard Secord's Enterprise, from the outside, the operation looked the same.

There is, however, a world of difference. In the wake of the revelations of the Church Committee hearings, the United States established a set of laws to control covert actions. In the United States, according to this law (and the U.S. Constitution), covert actions are the province of official American intelligence organizations (primarily, but not exclusively, the CIA). Moreover, *every* covert action must be certified by the proper authority, in most cases the president.[5] In fact, covert actions against nations with which the United States is at peace can *only* be authorized by the president or DCI. Further, *every* covert action must be reported "in a timely manner" to the Senate Select Committee on Intelligence, thus providing (theoretical) control of these activities by the branch of government most reflecting popular sovereignty.[6]

Off-the-books organizations and operations, on the other hand, face none of these reporting and control mechanisms, for they are designed to circumvent them. First, off-the-books operations are intentionally not reported to some of the responsible authorities. Sometimes this means the president does not tell the DCI, or vice versa; sometimes it means that individuals lower down the chain of command create their own black organizations without authorization from either the president or the DCI. It virtually always means that Congress is cut out of the loop. One important implication is that funding comes from either a clandestine government source or private "donors." A *clandestine government source* is one in which federal money is budgeted for one thing, but through the magic of accounting—or lack thereof—is diverted to the covert operators. Without official government sanction, this is what lawyers call "fraud." By creating an off-the-books operation, a president can bypass anyone or anything that poses an obstacle, including the National Security Council, the Departments of State, Defense, and Treasury, Congress and its committees, and even the CIA itself; a DCI can bypass his own clandestine service (directorate of operations and deputy director for operations [DDO]). In other words, one *purpose* of an off-the-books operation, program, or organization is to hide the activities from government officers responsible for controlling such affairs. It is an operation secret from the people who have a *right* to know and a *responsibility* to protect the government, the Constitution, the people of the United States, and the president him or herself (from his or her own judgment in some cases).

The second purpose of these operations is to create an ongoing black organization that can carry out covert operations and intelligence functions (essentially a parallel CIA), whether or not the individuals who set it up have legitimate authority to do so. In 1986, a left-wing think tank called the Christic Institute sued a number of individuals, including Richard Secord, John Singlaub, Ted Shackley, and other "private" U.S. black operators, charging that they were part of a "Secret Team," a shadow government maintained by powerful members of the American far Right to conduct right-wing foreign policy and carry out covert operations in support of right-wing governments no matter the policy of the president or of Congress. This case (and the Institute) was largely smirked at in the mainstream media ("a conspiracy theorist's dream," "makes Oliver Stone look sane," and so on.), and viciously attacked in the conservative press. Long on passion but short on direct evidence of conspiracy, the suit was dismissed in 1988.

While the Christic thesis may have been overbroad, however, one thing is clear: During the Reagan administration, the director of Central Intelligence began operations to create a self-sustaining (i.e., self-funding) covert-action organization capable of sustaining and enforcing the administration's foreign policies and ideology regardless of the will of Congress, succeeding presidents, or the American people. Moreover, even before that effort, several organizations had been created to conduct private foreign policies and operations (at least as far back as the early 1970s). The most famous, and perhaps the only one many Americans know much about, is the Iran-Contra Enterprise.

THE ENTERPRISE[7]

The contra war in Nicaragua received mixed support, at best, from the American people. While the Pat Buchanan Right believed that the stakes were nothing less than capitalism, freedom, and a God-fearing society, to most Americans the threat did not seem so immediate, lethal, or eternal. The majority of Congress in particular was unconvinced, and in 1984 passed the first Boland Amendment, prohibiting the involvement of U.S. intelligence in any endeavors to overthrow the government of Nicaragua.

Anticipating this, President Reagan tasked Lieutenant Colonel Oliver North with keeping the contras together "body and soul." This fit in perfectly with the goals of DCI William Casey, who spoke often with North of creating a private black operations organization, self-funding and independent of congressional funding, which pretty much made it (1) independent of Congressional control, (2) beyond the legal responsibility of the president, (3) potentially beyond the control of the president, and (4) a private foreign-policy tool of whomever paid the bills.

What made the Enterprise go was the money. Some came from "donations" made by private donors (e.g., the Coors family) or foreign governments (e.g., Saudi Arabia, Brunei). Another way cash was raised was through the infamous weapons sales to Iran, a process that not only provided antitank missiles to a regime certified as "terrorist" by Ronald Reagan's own administration, but also, despite a professed goal of making friends with the Iranians, extracted an outlandish profit from the ayatollah's government. Some of the profit went to the Enterprise, and much of it also lined the pockets of the operators. Secord et. al. bought the weapons from the United States government for $12 million, and sold them to Iran for $30 million, scoring a nifty $18 million profit—a hefty 250 percent markup on a deal supposedly intended to "make friends." Of the $18 million profit, the contras received the princely sum of $3.5 million (about one-fifth of the proceeds); when the Enterprise was exposed, over $8 million remained in the bank accounts. Apparently the Enterprising "patriots" didn't think the contras were *that* bad off.

The immediate object of the Enterprise (aside from keeping Secord and friends off the breadlines) was to fund the contra war (that's the story, anyway). The Enterprise, however, was envisioned by some, including Bill Casey, as something of far greater scope and importance: It was intended to become a self-supporting, ongoing entity that could carry out covert operations both with and without the support of the lawful American government.[8] Through the exploitation of arms sales at enormous profits and "donations" from like-minded or fawning governments, individuals, and corporations, the men behind this plan could indeed have created a shadow military/intelligence organization, complete with CIA, army, navy, and air force. In the future they would have created, no matter who the American people chose to elect as president, foreign policy would have been made by the Enterprise.

From **HONEY BADGER** to **YELLOW FRUIT**: The ISA[9]

It was difficult to watch: the immolated bodies of American soldiers being defiled by Iranian "revolutionary guards," the burned-out hulks of American aircraft in the background, repeated on newscast after newscast. OPERATION EAGLE CLAW, the attempt to rescue the American hostages, was a disaster.

Even as they watched, horrified at the desecration and mortified at the failure, a few of the brightest covert operators in the U.S. Army vowed with grim determination to do it right next time. They would be disappointed with the second hostage rescue plan, HONEY BADGER, which literally never got off the ground. These were men of action, full of the spirit of "drive on" and "can-do" that makes American Special Forces special.

EAGLE CLAW had failed for many reasons: lack of adequate intelligence; lack of the right *kind* of intelligence, especially the tactical intelligence so necessary to "high-speed" counterterrorism and rescue operations; the use of a patchwork conglomeration of units not used to working as a team (army, navy, marines, air force—it's a minor miracle the Coast Guard didn't get some piece of the action[10]); inadequate training under realistic conditions; final control of the operation at long range (from D.C.) instead of with the commander in the field; and so on.

On 26 February 1981, the Army created the Special Operations Division (SOD). The objective was to create an *integrated* special operations unit: intelligence gathering, intelligence analysis, transport and aviation, special forces and covert action units, and funding sources all under a single command. Ultimately, the SOD would come to command both "white" (official army) and "black" (off-the-books) units.

The most important element was called the Intelligence Support Activity (ISA), so named because it sounded innocent, rather like the office that would supply the typewriters and carbon paper. Originally, the ISA was intended to provide the kind of intelligence to special operations (e.g., hostage rescues, counterterrorism strikes, anti-Communist insurgencies) that the army operators needed, and did not trust the CIA to provide. Eventually, the ISA would come to "own" safe houses, cars, and a fleet of aircraft, and provide a James Bond lifestyle for some of its employees.

To take the ISA completely off the books, intentionally hiding it from Congress and the even the army chief of staff, another operation, YELLOW FRUIT, was created. The purpose was to tap into U.S. Army dollars while bypassing the regular accounting system, evading even the procedures for funding secret operations. The heart of the scheme was a simple U.S. Army document called a 1080, "Voucher for Transfer Between Appropriations and/or Funds." Properly authorized, it allowed an individual to withdraw money from army accounts and deposit it elsewhere, even into private bank accounts. This made it possible for federal money to simply disappear from government accounts. Instead of buying, say, MREs[11] or uniform pants, thousands of dollars would simply disappear from the ledger, resurfacing to buy safe houses, high-tech electronics, cars, air travel, special weapons, and so on. This simple funding mechanism allowed ISA/YELLOW FRUIT to disappear from government records, thus making it a self-supporting private covert action force. Within about three years (1981–1983), over $324 million was *missing*—not including money legitimately accounted for. Expedience had lent itself to abuse: There was no accounting for expenditures, and the operation literally had officers walking around with suitcases full of cash.

The ISA/YELLOW FRUIT operation, aside from simply looting the U.S. Treasury, produced a large-scale off-the-books covert operations organization, complete with secret airfields; hidden caches of weapons and money; safe houses around the world; proprietary companies (including a butcher shop and meat warehouse in Panama); bases in Nicaragua, El Salvador, Honduras, Guatemala, and Panama; suitcases full of cash; and a stable of shooters ready to hit designated targets. Moreover, in contrast to the stereotypical infighting that characterizes Washington turf wars, the CIA did *not* want to control the ISA. DCI Casey knew about the organization but preferred that it stay within the army: *Army covert operations did not legally have to be reported to Congress.* By co-opting this group, the CIA could have had a black army hidden not only from the Soviets, but from the Congress and American people: Bill Casey could have had his cake and eaten it too.

Ultimately, the ISA/YELLOW FRUIT operation was exposed, with some of the principals undergoing *secret* courts-martial for fraud, malfeasance, theft of government property, and so on. Several spent time in Leavenworth, losing promising military careers and their pensions. Approximately one-third of a billion dollars was never accounted for or recovered.

Ultimately, the organization became an end unto itself, divorced from even the very army that spawned it. In fighting the war on terrorism, what had the $600 per night suites and $1,200 per month liquor bills purchased? The operation had assisted in the capture of the *Achille Lauro* hijackers; it had helicoptered the Lebanese prime minister secretly into Beirut.[12] That was about it.

MONEY, GUNS, AND DRUGS: THE NUGAN HAND BANK

It wasn't obvious how the man had shot himself in the head with the rifle, but there it was; body slumped over in the car, one hand seemingly holding the muzzle to his head, the other down by the trigger. Frank Nugan, cofounder of the Nugan Hand Bank, was dead. In his car, police found an appointment book with appointments and addresses of a constellation of former intelligence stars, including former DCI William Colby. Thus began the unraveling of one of the most puzzling confluences of intelligence and skullduggery in history; the real story remains hidden, on the run from truth, much like cofounder Michael Hand.[13]

The Nugan Hand Bank was established in 1973 by Francis John Nugan, an Australian lawyer, and Michael Jon Hand, former Green Beret and U.S. intelligence operator. Exactly where the two men raised enough cash to start their "bank" remains a mystery, although within a short time they were doing business with governments and (apparently) intelligence agencies. Once the bank was going, there were three basic sources of income. First, through Hand's connections in Indochina, the bank laundered considerable sums of drug money, so much, in fact, that it was more or less an open secret among some Australian and American intelligence officers. Second, because of its willingness to flout currency transaction laws and reporting requirements, Nugan Hand became a preferred institution for wealthy Third World dictators stashing away overseas nest eggs, including Ferdinand Marcos. Third, the bank raised deposits through what amounted to a huge pyramid scheme, i.e., paying early investors with more-recent deposits. Nugan and Hand were aided immensely in this aspect of the operation by the participation of a number of retired American military and intelligence figures, including former DCI William Colby; General LeRoy Manor (overall commander of the Iranian hostage rescue operation; involved in the air force end of covert operations for years), Dale Holmgren, former head of flight services for Air America; General Edwin Black, confidant of Allen Dulles and Richard Helms, who often flaunted his involvement with right-wing groups; Admiral Earl "Buddy" Yates, former chief of strategic planning for the Pacific region, and president of Nugan Hand Bank; and Guy Pauker, close advisor to Henry Kissinger and Zbigniew Brzezinski, and a probable CIA operative, who seemed *awfully* knowledgeable and connected to the Indonesian coup that overthrew Sukarno in 1965.

It is difficult to prove that Nugan Hand was an intelligence operation per se. It almost certainly was not a proprietary owned by an intelligence service, such as Air America. There are plenty of indications, however, that the bank was somehow connected to U.S. intelligence agencies. For one thing, the bank supported and arranged (via Michael Hand) covert arms shipments to U.S. proxy forces in Angola and Rhodesia at a time when such activities were coming under close scrutiny and limitation by the United States Congress (similar to the support the Enterprise supplied [or was supposed to supply] to the contras twenty years later).[14] There is some evidence that Nugan Hand also provided support for the Australian "coup" that ousted Prime Minister Gough Whitlam in 1975, an event also supported by the CIA (at the least; it is possible that the entire event was spawned by the CIA).

Another indication of the close ties between Nugan Hand and U.S. intelligence are the connections between the bank and U.S. intelligence operators, many of whom later became key figures in Iran-Contra. These include: Ted Shackley, former deputy director for operations (and "advisor" to Michael Hand); Thomas Clines, former CIA operator who assisted Nugan Hand on arms deals and helped slip Nugan out of Australia when the bank collapsed, and who would later be Richard Secord's right-hand man in the Enterprise; Richard Secord, friend of the bankers who helped connect Nugan Hand with Thomas Clines; and Edwin Wilson, who exploited his position with the CIA and naval intelligence, and his association with Secord, Clines, and Nugan Hand, to sell arms to Libya.[15]

Yet another reason to believe in the intelligence genesis of Nugan Hand is the lengths to which the CIA and the Australian Security Intelligence Organization have gone to frustrate attempts to investigate Nugan Hand and to look into the intelligence connections of the principals. Finally, there were so many ("ex") intelligence personnel involved in Nugan Hand that the place was, as they say, lousy with spooks. It is difficult to believe that so many bright, connected, and seemingly upright men would willingly participate in such a corrupt organization unless they believed (or *knew*, most likely) that it served another (secret) purpose.

In January 1980, under investigation by the Australian government, Nugan Hand collapsed. Frank Nugan put the rifle to his head; Michael Hand, after testifying that the bank was insolvent, disappeared, presumably with a considerable sum of cash. While there had been enough money to support covert actions, the bank ultimately bilked depositors—including many military and intelligence personnel who had entrusted their life savings to a bank represented by highly respected admirals and generals—out of (probably) hundreds of millions of dollars. Michael Jon Hand, former CIA operator, remains one of the world's most wanted men.

LOOTING THE U.S. TREASURY, PART II: THE SAVINGS AND LOAN SCANDAL AND BLACK OPS[16]

The United States taxpayers paid over $500 billion to cover the losses of failed savings and loans that were insured by the U.S. government. Spent in other ways, this would be approximately enough to cover the complete cost of a college education for one million Americans, or the entire defense budget for two years.[17] While there were several reasons for both the failure of the S&Ls as well as the financial disaster slamming into the U.S. Treasury, the dynamics aren't that complicated. In the early 1980s, many of the individuals operating in S&Ls began to make bad loans, investments they knew could not be repaid. From their perspective, this was okay, for the federal government insured their deposits, up to a point. If an S&L lost money on bad debts, it would get it back from Uncle Sam. From the perspective of the people receiving the credit, this was also a sweetheart deal: They'd never have to repay the loan, thereby essentially receiving gifts ranging into the millions of dollars. While this sordid tale is recounted elsewhere, there is another side of the story that has scarcely been reported: the possibility that some of these billions of dollars were intentionally looted from the S&Ls (i.e., the American taxpayers) to pay for off-the-books intelligence operations.

While the whole story is too complex to detail here, there are several facts that suggest at least some of the S&L money went to support black operations and, possibly, off-the-books organizations. The most important evidence is the intelligence connections of some of the individuals and organizations that received the "free" loans. While it is impossible to tell how much money went into the accounts of CIA assets or off-the-books organizations, it is likely in the tens of millions of dollars.[18]

"OFF-THE-BOOKS": SECRECY, DEMOCRACY, AND BLACK OPS

To be effective, it is often necessary for intelligence agents and operations to operate under some form of cover. In this context, there are two valid reasons to do so: first, to conceal the operation from the opponent (i.e., a clandestine operation); second, to avoid open intervention in the affairs of another state, thus averting confrontation and potential escalation of the conflict (i.e., creating plausible deniability). The founding fathers understood the need for secret operations, as well as the reasons for them. Many of the signatories of the Constitution served in the Congress that allowed President Washington his "contingency fund" with which to pay intelligence agents; they did not demand an itemized accounting, thereby demonstrating both a deep trust in the integrity of President Washington as well as an understanding of "need to know."

Nevertheless, the founding fathers also recognized the fatal allure of expedience: the siren song promising safety if one will only grant a few "temporary" constitutional exceptions in "exceptional" circumstances. Alas, all presidents have not the wisdom and integrity of the first one,[19] and the entire period of the cold war became one long exception, accompanied by an endless succession of claims of temporary authority that became precedent for each ensuing expansion of the power of the intelligence agencies and the executive branch. It was precisely to forestall the "rolling exception" that specific provisions were written into the Constitution; it was precisely the off-the-books operations that were viewed as the tools of tyranny. The damage these operations and organizations can do to both foreign affairs and domestically are presented below.

Off-the-Books Operations and Foreign Affairs

Off-the-books operations can seriously damage American foreign relations. First, while the organizations may indeed *not* represent American foreign policy, it is difficult to convince other countries of this. Weren't these men officers of the U.S. military and intelligence organizations? Hasn't the United States historically created proprietaries and cover organizations for covert actions using "retired" or sheep-dipped officers? Organizations like the Enterprise or the Nugan Hand Bank can simply drop broad hints about who they *really* represent, and any denial by the CIA or the U.S. government will be unbelievable.

Second, the mere existence of such organizations undercuts the power of the United States to carry out foreign policy. A "shadow CIA" can make its own foreign policy independent of the United States government. It can support or attack anyone it chooses, accountable to neither the president nor the Congress nor the American people. Such an organization can indeed conduct black operations *in opposition* to the U.S. government and the will of the people. Indeed, it is only answerable to those who pay the bills; it is an army for sale.

Third, the mere existence of such organizations can forestall the official institutions of U.S. foreign policy, preventing the president, State Department, and even the CIA from attaining foreign goals. This can occur because of what off-the-books organizations represent: *an alternative U.S. foreign policy*. If foreign regimes dispute current U.S. foreign policy, off-the-books operations allow them to evade U.S. policy (e.g., sanctions) until a more supportive U.S. administration is elected. Moreover, the ability of off-the-books intelligence organizations to raise money is important to foreign governments and elites, too: If official U.S. money is withdrawn to influence a regime, perhaps the black operators can shore up the foreign elite with some covert cash, thus providing the means to "wait out" formal U.S. sanctions.

One of the most important multipliers of American power has been the ability of the United States to speak to foreign affairs with a single voice: The old aphorism is that "politics stops at the water's edge." It is this that the off-the-books operations rip apart, for they actualize a second American foreign policy: Instead of multiplying American power and authority on the world scene, they divide it.

Fourth, these organizations create a dangerous potential for dragging the United States into an escalating conflict whether or not it is in the U.S. interest. This sword cuts two ways against the United States. Since the people involved in off-the-books operations are Americans, if they get into trouble, they are likely to appeal to the United States for help, and just as likely to become a cause célèbre in the United States. If some Americans, for example, were taken hostage, or tried as "pirates" and sentenced to be shot, the United States would certainly be forced to try to intervene on their behalf, even though the culprits might have taken part in acts of war (e.g., training insurgents, or even political assassination) against the foreign government. Moreover, when "private" U.S. citizens, especially "former" intelligence officers, undertake covert operations, it is always unclear that they are operating on their own: There is the very real possibility that they are indeed working on a government-sanctioned operation—as they will inevitably claim, in the hope of drawing U.S. intervention on their behalf.[20] Thus, anything that they do might be viewed by foreign governments as official acts of the United States.

Finally, the creation and support of private, off-the-books intelligence entities undercuts the authority of the United States's democratic example. If you are democratic, a foreign people might ask of the United States, and if democracy is so good, why do you need to bypass your Congress to accomplish things? If America must resort to such underhanded and authoritarian tactics in the name of national security, how much more necessary must these practices be to less developed and less secure countries? While there is a reasonable answer to this, it is a messy and complicated one; far simpler to squash off-the-books operations before they become a problem.

OFF-THE-BOOKS OPERATIONS AND AMERICAN DEMOCRACY

While the problems in foreign policy are a bad enough outcome (or potential outcome) of the existence of private, off-the-books intelligence organizations, the most dangerous issues arise domestically: What effect do these things have on the U.S. government, on American politics, and on Americans themselves?

One of the strongest arguments advanced by proponents of off-the-books operations is that the official intelligence organizations have become too hidebound, limited by rules written by bureaucrats, and prone to being "blown" or exposed by politically motivated leaks. From a purely practical point of view, however, there are excellent reasons to run covert operations through an institutionalized organization.[21] By using established institutions, one acquires the benefit of "institutional memory"—the accumulated wisdom of people who have conducted many such operations and devised a set of standard operating procedures (SOPs). While one size doesn't fit all, especially in black ops, SOPs provide a set of criteria, *based on past performance*, that allow intelligence executives and possibly inexperienced members of the executive branch to reasonably evaluate the potential benefits and costs of a covert action.[22]

Further, by examining a planned action through several different eyes, operational weaknesses unanticipated by the planners might be revealed; flaws can then be remedied, or the operation scrapped if they are too difficult. This latter possibility, of course, is precisely why, sometimes, covert and paramilitary operators do not want to pass a covert action through a careful screening process; they have become so committed to an operation that they will not permit it to be halted. During the planning for OPERATION ZAPATA (the Bay of Pigs), for example, Allen Dulles and Richard Bissell were pressing ahead so hard that they would not permit even a single day for the Joint Chiefs to war-game the assault, which almost certainly would have exposed some of the fatal flaws in the plan. Moreover, Dulles intentionally cut out the CIA's own intelligence division from the landing plans. This excluded, among others: Robert Amory, who had made twenty-six similar amphibious assaults during World War II, and would likely have informed President Kennedy that the United States Navy and Marine Corps had *never* carried out the kind of nighttime amphibious assault required by ZAPATA; and Sherman Kent, who might have reported that the CIA's intelligence analysis division believed that there was virtually no chance of a mass uprising against Castro. This is not to say that every covert action should suffer months of red tape and bureaucratic turf wars. It is essential for the success of covert operations, however, which by their very nature are iffy propositions, that they be examined for potential disaster by people who will ask the hard questions, and not merely approved by their own authors.

Another aspect of off-the-books funding that dangerously undermines *American* foreign policy is the solicitation of money from foreign sources. Did Saudi Arabia and Brunei simply *give* the money to the contras? Are we to believe that there was no quid pro quo? While some governments might fund American intelligence activities because the American black program actually serves their needs, accepting foreign lucre creates dangerous problems at best. First the foreign government that "buys" its share of the black op or program gains a measure of control: It can always cut off funding. Second, even if foreign control is not the intent of the American operators, they may find the organization cannot continue without the foreign money; they can become hooked. Third, foreign money provides a bit of blackmail leverage for the provider; the threat of exposure may be enough to compromise a black program, its officers, and even the presidency. Fourth, such funds may be provided with an *implicit* understanding of favors in kind; perhaps the United States will provide some airborne warning and control system (AWACS) aircraft, satellite intelligence, special equipment, Special Forces training, or even outright military protection. Even if there is no "deal," the foreign government might feel that it is "owed"; failure to pay back may produce hostility instead of the hoped-for goodwill from the initial payoff. Fifth and finally, government officers, even staffers from the National Security Council, can indeed offer quid pro quos in exchange for foreign support of off-the-books operations. These will not be tied overtly to the payoff, but rather take the form of "support for a request" or subtle nudges of policy in favor of the donor state. With an off-the-books operation, the quid pro quo can be hidden in the form of aid (economic or military), access to technology, intelligence, and so on. In this way, American foreign policy is manipulated in the interests of foreign powers.

Another critical and often overlooked issue is the effect that operations like YELLOW FRUIT have on the U.S. military. While there has always been political infighting and turf wars within the military, as within any large organization, the problems created by establishing a clandestine "army within the army" are horrendous. These "secret armies,"[23] reminiscent of the French Organisation Armée Secrète (who also "knew better" than their duly elected government), are a divisive force in the U.S. military, producing conflict where there is a need for unity. In any military action, especially in special operations, there must be *only one team*, and only one highest duty: to the Constitution of the United States. Individuals who create a private or off-the-books intelligence organization betray their oath and their duty, substituting their judgment and personal interests for that of those delegated the authority by the people of the United States. Perhaps most importantly, it is precisely the loyalty of the U.S. military to the Constitution that has preserved American liberty since 1776. Unlike the military in most countries, the United States Armed Forces are loyal to a Constitution, not a person or class or elite.

Finally, and most critically, off-the-books intelligence and covert operations groups are dangerously subversive of democracy, intending to evade the very controls established by the founders to prevent such activities. The founding fathers understood the power of the purse; they understood that activity in foreign affairs was largely a matter of money.[24] Without money, armies cannot be raised, spies cannot be paid, and so on. For Washington, Adams, Jefferson, and Madison, the power to tax was the power to make war, *and such power rightly belonged in the hands of the Congress.* Off-the-books operations prevent Congress from exercising any control whatsoever over potentially critical foreign-policy activities, including acts of war, entire wars, assassinations, coups d'etat, paying ransom for hostages, and selling high-tech weapons to terrorists. While one might accept that covert operations need to be secret, they cannot be left to the unchecked sole discretion of the president, the DCI, or the executive branch. There is a name for that kind of government: dictatorship.

Moreover, off-the-books operations get their funding and other support from untraceable sources: They are accountable to no one. It is even worse if they are created by and serve officials of the U.S. government, for these officials are thereby able to conduct their own foreign policies, disregarding those "inconvenient" checks and balances imposed by the Constitution. If the organizations are not answerable to the government (or someone in it), then they are merely private armies serving the demands of unelected entities, representing their own interests.

Even mere private funding of such organizations (e.g., U.S. government organizations) is dangerously authoritarian, allowing a few people, corporations, or governments to control the policies United States does and does not undertake. If a policy serves the American people, it should be justified to them and paid for by the U.S. Congress. By appealing to funding sources outside government, government officers (1) bypass (i.e., violate) constitutional limits on policymaking, (2) make themselves vulnerable to blackmail by the people, organizations, or governments that provide the funds, (3) violate operational security procedures ("need to know" seems to be ignored when one needs cash for personal, unauthorized foreign-policy ventures), and (4) risk creating the concept of "covert action for sale."

This does not mean that every government secret must be made public. There are indeed bad people and nefarious governments that might and do seek to harm or destroy the United States and/or its people. The need for operational security and policy secrecy, however, does not excuse covert operators from the authority of the president, Congress, and the U.S. Constitution. If an operation, program, or policy is deemed necessary by the proper authorities, it can be sanctioned with established procedures that maintain both accountability and operational security. Within the executive branch, this occurs through a national security advisory mechanism, such as the Forty Committee or 54/12 Committee. Committees such as these serve to protect both the president and the United States government by providing a final "reality check" on the kinds of operations carried out by the CIA (or other black ops organizations within the U.S. government), as well as probing the means used in these operations. Further, while the president is largely charged with conducting foreign policy, Congress cannot be left out of covert action; congressional involvement is required by both statute and the Constitution under the powers of making war, authorizing and expending U.S. funds, and perhaps even via archaic constitutional elements like issuing letters of marque (see chapter 19 for a thorough discussion of these issues).

CONCLUSIONS

Whether or not there is a "secret team" or a shadow government, as alleged by the Christic Institute, it is documented fact that there have been several efforts by U.S. officials, citizens, and organizations to create off-the-books black programs specifically intended to circumvent the U.S. Constitution and pursue private foreign policies in opposition to the will of the American people and the U.S. Congress. While some of these enterprises may have merely been private entities mainly out to make a buck, they have clearly allied themselves with specific ideological interests in American society and the U.S. government, and just as clearly served these ideological foreign-policy interests regardless of or in defiance of constitutionally arrived at American policy. They have not only undermined policies they disagreed with, but have also weakened the ability of every American president to carry out foreign policy—the *real* kind, backed up by the United States government.

NOTES

1. Slight exaggeration, probably.
2. Unless it's on *another government's* paycheck, like Rick Ames.
3. If you are reading this book and have not read any of the terrific novels by Adam Hall (pen name for the late Elleston Trevor), do yourself a favor and pick one up now. Hall takes a back seat to no one in this genre, including Le Carré, Fleming, Ludlum, Follett, McLean, and Ambler.
4. The funding of various political and guerrilla movements (contras, Kuomintang, mujahedin) at least partially through drug money is another set of examples; these are discussed in chapter 9.
5. Small or "minor" covert actions can be authorized by the DCI on his own authority; the DCI also determines what "minor" means, thereby creating quite a bit of latitutde in reporting black ops.
6. The issue of defining "timely" has proven quite a sticky wicket, as some DCIs (e.g., Casey) have been prone to report long-running covert actions only after they have been completed, thereby limiting congressional oversight to mere carping after the fact.
7. To my knowledge, it has always been unclear precisely why this organization was called "the Enterprise." I have wondered, however, if it is not related in some whimsical way to either the U.S.S. *Enterprise* or the starship in *Star Trek*.

8. See Bob Woodward, *Veil: The Secret Wars of the CIA 1981–1987* (New York: Pocket Books, 1987), pp. 539–40.

9. This section is drawn from the U.S. Army Intelligence and Security Command, article 15-6, *Investigation Into Special Mission Funds*, unpublished (the army investigation of YELLOW FRUIT); Tim Weiner, *Blank Check: The Pentagon's Black Budget* (New York: Warner Books, 1991), chap. 7; and Steven Emerson, *Secret Warriors: Inside the Covert Military Operations of the Reagan Era* (New York: G. P. Putnam and Sons, 1988).

10. At least I don't think it did; if any of you Coasties out there know differently, I'd love to hear the story.

11. "Meals, Ready to Eat," the current version of the C ration.

12. See Weiner, *Blank Check*, p. 195.

13. This account is drawn from Jonathan Kwitny, *The Crimes of Patriots: A True Tale of Dope, Dirty Money, and the CIA* (New York: W. W. Norton, 1987).

14. See ibid., chap. 8.

15. Ibid., chap. 7.

16. For a good account of the intelligence connections of the S&L raiders, see Pete Brewton, *The Mafia, CIA, and George Bush: The Untold Story of America's Greatest Financial Debacle* (New York: S. P. I. Books, 1992).

17. College education calculated at about $10,000 per year for five years; defense budget about $250 billion per year.

18. See Brewton, *The Mafia, CIA, and George Bush.*

19. Granted, the world is a far more complex and immediately dangerous place than in 1792. Still, a free people led by men and women of integrity is perhaps the most powerful weapon, as it was then.

20. One good indication of whether or not captured operators are really working for the government is this: If they truly serve the government, they will deny it to the death (usually; this is what they're supposed to do); if they're on someone else's payroll, they'll practically always claim they work for the CIA. This is not an infallible indicator, but a pretty good rule of thumb.

21. If you're going to run them at all; but that is an argument for a different chapter.

22. It may come as a surprise, but very few people come to the National Security Council (or the 54/12 Committee or whatever arrangement exists within the current administration) with much or any experience in either black ops or the process of evaluating (or "selling") them. One reason so many black ops blow apart so spectacularly is that individuals in authority often do not even know the right questions to ask. Also, standard operating procedures in black ops should not be regarded as a hard-and-fast set of *rules*; they can be superceded by good ideas, but the burden of proof should always be on the individual who wants to deviate from standard procedure to explain why.

23. I am referring here to off-the-books corporations that are clearly unconstitutional and intended to bypass properly authorized controls. There is a very real need for special operations forces such as SEAL Team Six and Delta, and sometimes a very real need for them to operate in secret even from the rest of the military. This does not relieve them, however, of the responsibility of operating within an established military command structure and within the bounds of constitutional civilian control of the military.

24. The other sources of power being lawmaking capacity (largely inapplicable to foreign affairs) and moral suasion.

Part IV

Democracy, Foreign Policy, and Covert Action

Chapter 15

"Hell, Mr. President, We *Are* Involved!": Covert Action, Operational Limits, and Prestige Investment

They quietly get the president off the dance floor, away from the formal ball. The small group of advisors gather around as he joins them in the conference room. Under other circumstances, he cuts a striking figure in his tuxedo, the embodiment of vigor, but this night his face drains as they give him the news.

The covert operation is failing. On a distant beach, tough, American-trained men are fighting and dying heroically, struggling to overcome lost surprise, failed air strikes, flawed intelligence, poorly planned logistics, a surprisingly tough enemy, and just plain bad luck. Around the president, the advisors press for "support." The CIA had promised there would be no need for U.S. military intervention, but the operation is going to hell in a hurry; there is a U.S. carrier battle group nearby, and a brigade of U.S. Marines, first to fight. "Launch the aircraft, Mr. President," they advise.

The president has been in office a mere three months; he is nervous. He has made it plain to the CIA that there would be *no* open American intervention. The operators at the CIA had promised there would be no need; either the operation would succeed, or the 2506 Brigade would "melt into the mountains" and take up guerrilla warfare. A minute before, indeed, the chairman of the Joint Chiefs had said, "It's time for this outfit to go guerrilla." There is no plan, replies the deputy director for plans, to go guerrilla.[1] The Brigade is not been trained or briefed for it, despite the promise; it is hemmed in by a swamp and by twenty thousand of Castro's men, and the mountains are eighty miles away.

Under enormous time pressure, the president ponders his options, trying to restrain his anger. He does not want to be viewed as yet another *Norte Americano* cowboy riding roughshod over Latin America. He knows about what happened in Guatemala 1954, and does *not* want the U.S. Marines to be viewed as an extension of the fruit and tobacco companies. Moreover, he has the solemn word of legendary CIA operator Allen Dulles and DDP Richard Bissell ("One of the

smartest men in government," JFK calls him) that there will be no need for
American assistance. Finally, scarcely believing that the 2506 Brigade *cannot* "go
guerrilla," Jack Kennedy stands his ground: "I don't want to get involved."

His military advisor, Admiral Arleigh Burke responds with exasperation:
"Hell, Mr. President, we *are* involved."[2]

And that, as it turns out, is the critical issue with covert action. Once a
black operation begins, what happens if it blows apart? What happens if the
hand of the United States is exposed? How do you know when to bite the bullet
and escalate to open intervention, and when to cut your losses and actually exercise plausible deniability? To maintain deniability, American intelligence agencies set operational limits on covert undertakings, ensuring that there can be no
proof of U.S. involvement. Frequently, however, once the operation is underway,
covert operators have sought to change these ground rules, as happened in
Guatemala (1954), Indonesia (1958), Cuba (1961), and ultimately Laos and
Vietnam. In this chapter, we examine the key issues of failing covert operations,
the pressure to rescue a failing operation with overt intervention, and the potential for loss of "credibility" should one of our actions fail. Further, a set of key
questions is developed; questions that a president should receive adequate
answers to before approving any black operation. Operations *do* fail; the hand of
United States intelligence *is* sometimes revealed. What happens then? The
answer to that question is not only about contingency plans; it also bears heavily
on another more critical issue: Should the United States even be involved in
covert action?

COVERT ACTION, DENIABILITY, AND OPERATIONAL LIMITS

It is the concept of plausible deniability that defines covert action; if the government doesn't want to conceal its involvement, it can simply send in U.S.
armed forces, weapons, equipment, and money under the United States flag. For
a number of reasons, however, the United States sometimes desires or needs to
mask its activities:

- to avoid open intervention that invites or justifies counterintervention by
  another country;
- as a corollary to the above, to avoid confrontation with a nuclear-armed
  opponent;
- to prevent open engagement that could escalate the intensity or violence
  of a conflict;
- to disguise open intervention in another state's affairs if the revelation of
  the intervention could itself cause the operation to fail or backfire (e.g.,
  manipulating an election);
- to carry out a policy that violates American or international law (and thus
  escape potential consequences);

- to carry out an action that violates one's own established policy (e.g., we don't negotiate with terrorists).

Some of these reasons are politically and ethically defensible, and some are not. All of them, however, are used to prop up the notion that some acts of government need to be, if not entirely secret (i.e., clandestine), at least unattributable. The idea is not to keep the opponent from knowing what the CIA or some U.S.-backed secret army is doing; of course they know. Rather, the idea is to not slap them in the face with it, to avoid forcing them to respond or to escalate to a higher, more dangerous, and more confrontational level.[3] Thus, when one undertakes a covert action, there are usually, initially at least, good reasons to keep the operation deniable.

To achieve deniability, intelligence organizations establish *operational limits*: restrictions on the kinds of operations and tactics that can be employed, the origin of operational personnel (e.g., can U.S. military personnel be used or not?), the source of equipment and money, and so on. By adhering to these restraints, it becomes difficult for someone—whether the opponent, another government, or the press—to identify or prove the operation or program is an action of the U.S. government. Covert operations thus provide two benefits: First, they lessen the likelihood that an opponent will intervene against U.S. interests; second, if the opponent *does* overtly intervene, it becomes by definition an act of aggression, and the United States has stolen a march in world—and American—public opinion; *we* are merely *defensive*.

To achieve deniability, operational limits typically focus on minimizing connections between the United States government and the individuals and organizations involved in a black op. This generally means limits on:

(1) Personnel
- Few or no Americans can be involved.
- No Americans can be exposed to capture (and subsequent appearance on CNN).
- Exposed or involved Americans must be either truly acting on their own or they must be sheep-dipped to separate them from the government.

(2) Equipment
- must be (generally) of non-American origin; and
- must be (generally) available on world market.

(3) Money
- must come from non-U.S. sources; or
- must be laundered to wipe out any backtrail to U.S. intelligence or known intelligence front groups.

If these limits are followed, plausible deniability is usually achieved; observers may *suspect* U.S. involvement, but certainly cannot prove it.

Based on what we know about black ops, almost all covert actions begin with such limits—probably with the best of intentions. Historically, however, when a covert operation falters or appears in danger of failing, intelligence officers in the field often request that the limits be expanded or lifted altogether, calling for air strikes, U.S. troops, and so on. This is the kind of activity that can lead to protracted, costly, fruitless, and sometimes self-defeating interventions. While field officers can be excused for becoming caught up in the moment (and movement), occasionally headquarters personnel (e.g., the DCI or DDO) and higher-ups (i.e., National Security Council officials) also change their tune in the heat of battle. Allen Dulles said about the Bay of Pigs:

> We felt that when the chips were down—when the crisis arose in reality, any action required for success would be authorized rather than permit the enterprise to fail.[4]

> I have seen a good many operations which started out like the Bay of Pigs— insistence on complete secrecy—non-involvement of the U.S.—initial reluctance to authorize supporting actions. This limitation tends to disappear as the needs of the operation become clarified.[5]

Dulles's DDP, Richard Bissell, also said about the Guatemalan operation (1954):

> You can't take an operation of this scope, draw narrow boundaries of policy around them, and be absolutely sure that those boundaries will never be overstepped.[6]

Unfortunately, each step past the boundary increases the risk that the United States's role in a covert operation will be exposed; this is presumably why operational limits are agreed upon in the first place.

BREAKING THE GLASS

There are numerous examples of covert operations, both successful and failed, in which a president has been pushed by CIA executives, military advisors, the National Security Council, and even operators in the field to ignore previously agreed upon operational limits. Virtually all of these were intended to rescue failing operations, including:

- Guatemala, 1954: OPERATION SUCCESS depended on a rebel air force to maintain the appearance of a real rebel army. When two of the CIA planes were shot down, Allen Dulles went to President Eisenhower and told him bluntly that unless the United States replaced the aircraft, the operation would have "zero" percent chance of success. Despite his resolve to avoid even the appearance of intervention, Ike relented, and allowed Dulles to arrange for replacement aircraft provided by Anastasio Somoza of Nicaragua.

- Guatemala, 1954: In the same affair, CIA operator Al Haney attempted to incite overt America intervention in Guatemala by activating a CIA provocation plan: A CIA plane disguised as a Guatemalan Air Force plane flew over Honduras, dropping bombs on a Honduran airfield. Close examination revealed that the bombs were practice bombs filled with water rather than explosives; the provocation fizzled, although the United States had prepared for military intervention by stationing a Marine Corps expeditionary force off the Guatemalan coast.

- Indonesia, 1957: American aircraft, pilots, naval vessels (at least submarines), and probably paramilitary "advisors" were eyeball deep in the uprising against Sukarno. As it was failing, Secretary of State John Foster Dulles said to Undersecretary Christian Herter that he'd like to give formal recognition to the rebels and land U.S. forces "to protect the life and property of Americans; use this as an excuse to bring about a major shift there."[7]

- Cuba, 1961: As the 2506 Brigade was surrounded at the Bay of Pigs, U.S. officials repeatedly pressed President Kennedy for overt American intervention, despite the fact that the CIA had constantly reassured the president that no U.S. forces would be needed or involved. Kennedy was pressed for air strikes, U.S. fighter cover for "exile" aircraft (which he authorized), and naval gunfire support from U.S. Navy ships "observing" the operation. A U.S. Marine Brigade was also standing by offshore—we can only speculate as to the reason, since there are no available documents that suggest there was any *plan* to employ them.[8] Earlier, both Eisenhower and Kennedy had publically declared they would defend the U.S. base at Guantanamo Bay, and both had privately wished that Castro would attack it to justify U.S. intervention.

- Laos, ca. 1960–1971: In a program that lasted more than a decade, a small, efficient CIA operation designed to contest and deny the Laotian highlands to the Communists by creating, training, and modestly equipping Hmong village militias evolved into a full-scale secret war. The militias were turned into strike forces, attacking the Ho Chi Minh trail in support of America's goals in Vietnam rather than the objectives of the Hmong themselves. This scaling-up of the war provoked large scale North Vietnamese retaliation, which ultimately destroyed the Hmong homeland and led to the Communist victory in Laos.

- Vietnam, 1954–1965: U.S. involvement in Vietnam began with small covert operations, including the use of Civil Air Transport for supply, interdiction, and tactical air strikes for the French at Dien Bien Phu; efforts to manipulate the election of 1956 in hopes of defeating Ho Chi Minh; sabotage of North Vietnamese infrastructure and economic targets throughout the late 1950s and early 1960s; and running covert seaborne raiding teams into North Vietnam in the early 1960s, which ultimately helped produce the Gulf of Tonkin incident.

- Kurdistan, 1997: This is an unclear example, for which there is some—but not conclusive—evidence. While we can be certain that the Kurds believed U.S. air strikes would help them defend Kurdistan and Irbil, we do not know if U.S. field operators actually requested this aid, nor whether such an option was contemplated at higher levels of government. It is also possible, although not confirmed, that in fact Kurdistan *was* promised air support, either explicitly or implicitly, by someone in the Bush or Clinton administrations.

These represent only some of the more prominent examples. It is possible, and perhaps likely, that there are many other cases of pressure to escalate failing black ops. In fact, such tension probably arises within virtually every faltering operation; there are powerful reasons for it.

PRESSURE FROM WITHIN: FAILURE AND EXPOSURE IN COVERT OPERATIONS

Government is a complex organism that responds to pressure. Unfortunately for political theorists, pressures come not from one direction, but from many different directions, and from opposing and competing directions simultaneously—e.g., keep the Commies out, but don't get us in a war, or roll back the reds but don't risk nuclear confrontation. Oh, and do it *cheap*.

It is these pressures, among others, that produce covert operations, especially the competing desires to (1) stand up to the opponent, (2) *do something*, (3) *be seen* doing something to satisfy domestic constituencies, (4) don't use American blood (at least not too much), (5) be frugal with American money, (6) don't do anything so openly that we get dragged into a war, and (7) win, dammit. All these intentions stretch the foreign policy Gumby in different directions, and sometimes his arm tears off; something gives, forcing decision makers to decide *which* goals shall be pursued and which shall be sacrificed.

It is not supposed to be like that with covert action. The whole concept relies on plausible deniability to assure that the scenario is "no lose"; in a failing operation, the United States can neither be forced into a war, nor lose credibility in the eyes of the world, precisely because the United States *was never involved anyway*. The very core of the concept is that one can say, "Oh, well, tomorrow is another day," and take the loss. The ultimate contingency plan in the event of failure is to deny involvement.[9]

Two problems arise by the very nature of this concept. First, there is a natural tendency to try to retrieve failure by adding just that *little bit* more that will put the operation over the top. It is always a few more aircraft, a couple of air strikes, five hundred more men that will retrieve the operation. This is exacerbated by the nature of the people who occupy high government positions (accustomed to success) and by the career-decapitating effects of failed operations on political and intelligence careers. For intelligence operators, asking for expanded or abolished operational limits is the "no lose" option: A major black op disaster spikes your professional future in any event, so *why not* go for the whole enchilada? Ask for some gunships or cruise missiles, or perhaps a battalion of marines to "safeguard American property." All the president can do is say no, and if the answer is yes, the operation and career are still breathing. Moreover, it is the nature of Americans to single-mindedly pursue success in the belief that, given enough willpower, Americans can do anything. By actually adhering to operational limits and falling back on plausible deniability, a president would be admitting failure, an outcome to be avoided if at all possible.

The second problem is that an American role in a black operation tends to become exposed. This is especially true of larger operations, which typically are designed to achieve far-reaching and conspicuous political objectives, such as overthrowing a government or reversing a major policy of a foreign regime. When such events occur, they usually spur suspicion that the United States was involved, especially when large-scale and expensive resources appear with no readily explainable origin.

The timing of such exposure, however, is sometimes critical to the outcome. Ordinarily, if the political objective can be attained in a way that is not easily reversed, e.g., the new government is in power and the opponents are in prison or dispersed, then deniability may only be necessary until the operation is over and a more or less stable situation created. If the U.S. hand is exposed at this point, the United States may lose some regional goodwill, but that is about all. Moreover, even if the exposure comes years later, there may be substantial political cost; had the shah of Iran achieved power in 1953 on his own, the United States might not have reaped the whirlwind of Khomeini and his legacy.

On the other hand, if a CIA hand in an operation-in-progress is exposed, this may clear the way for overt and powerful counterintervention by another power, or for even appeals to the United Nations (UN), the Organization of American States (OAS), and so on. Political pressure from such bodies may force the United States to suspend an important operation.

Most importantly, however, is the difficult dilemma forced upon a president when a faltering covert action is unmasked: Should he push ahead with the operation, knowing that the whole world is watching the intervention, or should he let the operation go under, and thus allow the whole world watch it *fail*? President Eisenhower put it this way: "Where the flag goes, it must succeed."

Once the role of the United States has been revealed, the stakes immediately get much higher. First, the potential for a wider event increases: A U.S. opponent, either invited or uninvited, may involve itself, or "counterintervene," as may regional or global organizations (e.g., Organization of African Unity [OAU], OAS, UN). Second, once an operation has been revealed as American, the prestige and credibility of the United States is sunk into the affair. If the allies, proxies, and covert operators cannot drive the operation to victory, *it becomes a defeat for the United States*. No longer is the covert action a "no lose" proposition. Allowing the mission to fail may carry substantial global strategic penalties for the country. America may lose the ability to deter aggression by showing itself to be weak and vacillating, not tough enough to carry through the objectives of a major power. Opponents and potential aggressors may decide that the United States will not stand up to a hard challenge. An act of abandonment, then, may be viewed as an invitation to a world of aggressors. The United States may lose the ability to attract allies in the Third World as they see that the United States does not stand fast by its friends and its commitments.

The other option, once one's hand is exposed, is to jump in headfirst, committing whatever equipment, money, and manpower is necessary to carry the program through to victory, in the belief that if the flag is revealed, it must be sustained by honor, comittment, and success. There is, of course, the risk that one might not succeed even by openly intervening, and merely become bogged down waging a costly war in a place without much strategic value. Moreover, covert actions lend themselves to easy support of unsavory or unpopular characters (e.g., Mobutu, Suharto, Pinochet). If U.S. sponsorship of such regimes is revealed, the exposure deeply undermines the moral position of the United States, making it harder for the people of the United States and the world to distinguish between the good guys and the bad guys. If the United States is to have any credibility in the world, seizing the moral high ground is a key political objective, but it is one easily sacrificed by the hypocrisy of poorly covered or thought out covert actions.

To conclude, covert actions are only "no lose" as long as plausible deniability holds. Once exposed, the choices are bleak indeed: overt intervention or meek withdrawal. Such operations do indeed suffer from a high exposure rate, and this ought to be enough to give pause to executives considering black operations.

CREATING PROVOCATIONS

Perhaps the most dangerous circumstance within a black op occurs when the operators create or invent a provocation; usually an act of aggression by the target that can be seized upon to justify retaliation and sometimes overt intervention, such as the faked bombing of the Honduran airfield during OPERATION SUCCESS. *Creating* a provocation is subtly goading an opponent into an attack or act that, say, insults your national honor. This is accomplished by running a deniable black operation that forces or tricks an opponent into an overt response. In this case, the provocation (attack) is real, although the public telling of the story must be controlled by the intelligence agency (or government) and confused, or else people might think the opponent's action is justified. In this case, propaganda assets such as news-media outlets are important to provide the proper spin on precisely who is at fault. *Inventing* a provocation, on the other hand, is actually attacking your own territory, allies, or installations in such a way that it appears to have been carried out by the enemy. This was the nature of the Honduran airfield bombing in 1954. It has also been suggested that part of OPERATION ZAPATA was a plan for Cuban exiles to attack the U.S. base at Guantanamo Bay dressed as if they were Castro's troops.

For a provocation to succeed, one must understand that the audience is not the opponent, who generally knows whether or not it has assaulted American or allied targets.[10] Instead, the targets of the provocation are (1) world public opinion, to justify retaliation and counterintervention, and (2) the American public, to justify retaliation as well as to whip up an outcry to "satisfy our lost honor," thereby pressuring hesitating American leaders into jumping on the bandwagon. In cases like this, the provocation is employed with the full knowledge of the president and American leadership, or at least those executives responsible for national security decision making.

There are a few examples of the use of such provocations in American history. Aside from the "bombing" of Honduras in 1954, the CIA also arranged for an airdrop of "Communist" weapons inside Guatemala to help build the case against Jacobo Arbenz. The infamous El Salvador White Paper was a clear attempt to create a Soviet-manufactured insurgency and sell it to the American people. During the contra war, there were numerous attempts by the contras to entice Sandinista forces to follow them across the border into Honduras, thereby creating an incident that would have buttressed the claim that the Sandinistas were a Soviet-inspired aggressor bent on regional domination, and perhaps creating enough of a war fever within the United States to lead to open U.S. intervention.

We also have evidence, in the form of National Security Council minutes, of presidents and advisors wishing for provocations. On 3 January 1960, President Eisenhower said he would move against Castro "if he were provided with a really good excuse." Failing that, he said, perhaps we could think of manufacturing something that would be generally acceptable.[11] Perhaps, Ike thought, if we cut off relations with Cuba abruptly, Castro would be goaded into attacking Guantanamo Bay (or Gitmo, as it is known in naval parlance). During this meeting, Secretary of State Christian Herter suggested that the United States fake an attack on Gitmo to justify a full-scale U.S. invasion.[12]

The most dangerous kind of provocation, however, is the one carried out by the operators themselves, without presidential approval; in effect, a plan to force a president to intervene. This had to be the motivation with the fake bombing of the Honduran airfield in 1954, as there is no evidence that the operation was approved by President Eisenhower. It was possibly true during for the Bay of Pigs operation, in which the skids were greased for U.S. intervention in case the fifteen hundred men of the 2506 Brigade could not defeat Castro's two hundred thousand-man army.[13]

The use of provocations in black ops is a dangerous proposition. At the very least, "set up" provocations are a misrepresentation to the American public, involving the risk of a serious (and possibly politically fatal) public-opinion backlash if the truth ever comes out. One of the critical factors in the turn of American public opinion against the Vietnam War was the revelation that the

Gulf of Tonkin incident had been set up by the United States. More importantly, the creation or invention of a provocation to build support for a foreign-policy objective abrogates the very notion of government accountability. Responding to legitimate threats is one thing; acting against fictional challenges is quite another. Finally, if an opponent truly is aggressive, expansionist, and so forth, it will almost certainly provide a *real* justification for American action sooner or later, and then the United States can mobilize all the forces at its command— not only covert assets, but economic and diplomatic ones as well, and most powerfully, the willingness of the American people.

COMING HOME TO ROOST

Black operations can create more problems than they solve, especially if they either fail or lose plausible deniability. These problems arise from several sources.

First, an operation may not be provided with adequate planning or resources to succeed. During the CIA support of Kurdistan in the early 1990s, it was always unclear what would happen should Saddam Hussein's army move in force against the Kurds; as was found with the Poles in 1939, great fighting spirit is ultimately no match for tanks and aircraft. During the Bay of Pigs, it was always unclear to the president and his advisors precisely how the plan would "work." Would the Cuban exiles actually *defeat* Castro's army? Would Castro's forces simply defect? Would the Cuban people rise up around the exile Brigade? No one could explain this, and this lack of understanding was a critical factor in the fiasco.

The second, complementary problem is the lack of a good cover story. The only way the United States can maintain deniability is through a plausible alternative explanation for an event created by a CIA operation, and deniability is the characteristic that allows a "no lose" operation. When the cover is blown off a CIA black operation, the credibility and prestige of the United States is placed on the line. Without serious attention to the cover story, *every* covert action carries substantial risk of high political cost.

Third, it is always necessary to give adequate thought to contingency plans: What happens if the operation fails? What most decision makers do not want to face up to is that in many cases, the contingency plan must be to simply leave the field, with the operation (and sometimes personnel) unacknowledged. This is, of course, a ruthless and cold-hearted option. The point is *not* that such an option should be exercised frequently, but instead that this very idea should give one pause *before* a black op is approved.

Finally, many of the fiascos that have arisen from black ops gone bad are the result of disagreements between decision makers, intelligence executives, and field operators over (1) what the operational limits for a covert action *are*, and (2) what they *should* be. In many cases, operational limits have been left ambiguous or unstated at all, perhaps not even discussed with the president. Sometimes too, CIA executives have believed that operational limits expressed by a president are not "real" limits, but, like some European speed limits, are merely "advisory guide-lines." This was almost certainly the case in the Bay of Pigs:

> We believed that in a time of crisis we would gain what we might lose if we provoked an arugment [about commitment of U.S. forces] .
>
> Allen Dulles[14]

With such beliefs extant in the intelligence bureaucracies, it is essential that a president and his representatives establish (ahead of time) not only clear oper-ational limits but also the *nature* of those limits:

- *Covert only*: If the operation fails, there will be no attempt to retrieve it that risks revealing the role of the United States. This is way virtually all covert actions are initially portrayed by intelligence agency proponents.
- *Covert preferable, limited overt*: The operation should be kept covert as much as possible, but some acknowledged U.S. support may be available if nec-essary.
- *Covert first, overt follow-up*: The policy begins with covert action, but the objective is so important that the United States will openly act if the black op fails.

It is far better to examine the potential costs of moving to overt intervention in the calm calculation before the covert action than to cobble together a disaster-retrieval operation after it has blown apart.

THE KEY QUESTIONS

To avoid the some of these problems, every covert action plan should contain answers to key questions that ensure that the operation *serves* national policy objectives rather than *creating* them. Among these are:

- Can the operation/program stay covert?
- Can it succeed on its own?
- Once insurgent training is underway, can it be called off? What are the political costs of cancellation?
- Does U.S. involvement impose any moral obligations on the United States (e.g., Kurds, Hmong)?
- What is our response if the we lose deniability?
- If our hand is exposed, can we simply throw it in, or must we escalate?
- Can the president refuse to bail out failing operation?

CONCLUSIONS

The questions presented above, considered in total, give rise to a larger question of national ends and means: Is a black operation the best way to achieve a specific policy objective? Once a United States hand in a black operation has been exposed, the prestige and credibility of the country is automatically and involuntarily sunk into the operation; *every* black op carries this risk.

NOTES

1. General Lyman Lemnitzer, testimony before the Taylor Commission, meeting 17, *Paramilitary Study Group Report*, John F. Kennedy Library, Boston, Mass.

2. See Peter Wyden, *Bay of Pigs: The Untold Story* (New York: Simon and Schuster, 1979), p. 270.

3. For the purposes of this chapter, we are discussing the nonconfrontational reasons for covert action, rather than the "hide the policy" reasons.

4. "My Response to the Bay of Pigs," Allen Dulles Papers, Seely G. Mudd Library, Princeton, N.J., box 244.

5. Ibid.

6. See Richard M. Bissell, "Reflections on the Bay of Pigs: Book Review of Operation Zapata," *Strategic Review* 12, no. 1 (winter 1984): 380.

7. Dulles-Herter Telephone Notes, 8 December 1957, 10:16 AM, John Foster Dulles Papers, Telephone Series, Dwight D. Eisenhower Library, Abilene, Kans., box 7.

8. For the entire documented story of the pressure to intervene, see John Nutter, "To Trap A President: JFK, CIA, and the Bay of Pigs" (The Conflict Analysis Group, 1996, photocopy), available from the author.

9. There is another possibility, of course: that a covert action be taken with the understanding *by the president* that should it fail, the United States will overtly intervene. In this case, overt intervention is the contingency plan, and the covert action is merely employed at the beginning in hopes of attaining the objective cheaply and quietly. The author knows of no historical case where this was true, but would be happy to hear from operators who know of such plans (and would be especially happy to see corroboration or documentary evidence).

10. This is not always true, however; there can be unintended attacks resulting from ambiguous events. For example, both sides might respond to gunfire of undetermined origin, and both truly believe they are firing back in self-defense.

11. Gordon Gray, "Memorandum of Meeting with the President," 3 January 1960, p. 6. Dwight D. Eisenhower Library, Abilene, Kans.

12. Ibid.

13. For a thorough examination of this thesis, see Nutter, "To Trap a President."

14. "My Response to the Bay of Pigs."

Chapter 16

Innocents Abroad:
Covert Action and the
Advising Process

"**M**istakes were made." It was a hard admission for the president to make, and in many ways he still felt he had been right; at least his *intention* had certainly been good. Still, he was responsible for a covert action program that was full of blunders. He had allowed and aided a National Security Council assistant in organizing and soliciting funds for a dangerous and perilously unconstitutional off-the-books black organization. He had okayed a support program for the Afghan mujahedin that was so "leaky" it has been estimated that perhaps one weapon in ten actually reached the Afghans; many of those went to Afghan insurgents that quickly demonstrated hostility toward the United States in the form of terrorism. A substantial portion of the highly advanced weapons sent to Afghanistan simply disappeared into the international terrorist underground, at least some destined to be aimed at Americans. After declaring Iran a "terrorist state" and pressing America's allies to embargo arms sales to it, he okayed the shipment of antitank TOW missiles, HAWK antiaircraft missiles, and combat aircraft spare parts to the ayatollah. After vowing a "hard line" against terrorism—"We shall never deal with terrorists"—he approved an operation to ransom hostages in exchange for military hardware, eventually getting suckered in the bargain. The hostage he *really* wanted back was already dead when the first exchange was made, and then the terrorists simply snatched more hostages after they released some. Yes, indeed, mistakes were made.

Presidents and their advisors rarely have experience managing covert action, much less in managing the institutions of government that plan and carry out covert operations. To the unwary, covert action appears to be a cost-free way of attaining big results. This perception is fostered by the CIA, which largely has a monopoly on covert planning,[1] and more importantly, a monopoly on the information necessary to evaluate whether or not a covert action is advisable, or likely to succeed or fail. Moreover, the operators who conceive of covert actions typically become advocates of them, often exaggerating the chances of success and minimizing the likelihood and costs of failure. There are few institutional safeguards against this, often because presidents discard established evaluation procedures and attempt manage covert action with an informal, streamlined process—"streamlined" in this case being a synonym for "loose and haphazard"—and also because DCIs tend to be drawn either from the covert action branch of the CIA (and therefore gung ho on covert action) or from big business (and therefore susceptible to "capture" by the organization). This chapter examines the nature of the advising process that produces covert actions, focusing on the potential sources of bias in favor of approving black operations inherent in the manner in which presidents are advised.

COVERT ACTION: PLAYING WITH HOUSE MONEY?

To an executive used to getting quick action, getting a government agency to move must seem like bailing water with a fork; implementing policy must seem to move at the speed of tectonic plates. Moreover, due to the size, complexity, and ill-understood dynamics of the world political, economic, and strategic systems, the outcomes of any policy are uncertain at best, and often perverse; because the various international actors (i.e., governments, agencies, and substate organizations such as insurgent and terrorist groups) can adjust to any given U.S. policy, the result is often the opposite of what was intended. Further, there are virtually *no* meaningful policies a U.S. president can enact that will not stimulate substantial domestic opposition.

This is why black operations must seem so powerfully appealing. The action is simple and direct: Fix an election here, eliminate an opponent there, and engage actions in which effect rapidly follows cause—or so it seems. Further, there is no Congress to debate with and schmooze, no hard questions from Sam Donaldson to evade, no public-opinion polls to worry about. Perhaps most importantly, there is little or no chance of losing political capital; covert action is *perceived* as a "no lose" proposition. All these together create a disposition that makes it easy to approve black operations. One of the most important elements in this process is persuasive power of the CIA.

WHEN THE UMPIRE GETS TO BAT:
THE CIA AND THE COVERT ACTION ADVISING PROCESS

The CIA was originally conceived as an impartial intelligence coordinator, or clearing house, that the president and Congress could rely on to sort out conflicting intelligence analyses and prognostications produced by the "political" intelligence organs government: the army, navy, air force, State Department, and so forth. As each of these has particular axes to grind—e.g., the air force sees the most critical threat from enemy bombers and missiles, the navy recognizes

Soviet nuclear submarines and missile frigates as most threatening, and the army discerns the fearful might of the Red hordes—with substantial payoffs at the end of the budget process, the CIA embodied the hope for a detached arbiter. What the country and the president needed was an analytical organization that could sort through the overwhelming, biased, and contradictory "intelligence" that flowed into the White House from all these sources and produce a single, useful set of "facts."[2]

As soon as it was chartered, however, this role went by the boards. The CIA began conducting black operations in 1947 (e.g., the Ukranian operations and the liberation of Albania), and thus lost its impartial arbiter role; in the fight against Communism, the CIA stepped up to bat, and as a "player," could no longer also serve as umpire. Instead, much as the army views land warfare as the crux of national power and the navy believes in the pivotal role of seapower, so too the CIA came to be an advocate of what it does: covert action. Almost from its inception, the CIA promoted covert action as the means to American security. Somewhere between nuclear annihilation and surrender to the godless Communists lay the third option: covert action, run by the CIA. While it does not happen in every instance, the fact that both black ops and the information necessary to evaluate them flow from the same source creates serious (and sometimes realized) potential to bias the national security advising process in favor of approving covert operations.

One of the critical elements in producing an almost unexamined fire for covert action in the fledgling CIA was the Office of Strategic Services (OSS) background of the early CIA operators and executives. Even though Wild Bill Donovan had been cut out of the deal, his men had not (see chapter 3 for a full discussion). A complementary dynamic that has produced a less than detached attitude toward evaluating prospective black operations lies in the origins of the directors. When Robert Gates was confirmed as Director of Central Intelligence (DCI) in 1991, he was the first professional intelligence officer to advance within the CIA to the directorship from the analytical branch. Every other director with intelligence or CIA experience had come from operations/clandestine services. It is only natural that individuals who have spent their careers planning, carrying out, and in some cases actually leading covert endeavors will look favorably upon black ops in general. Further, if an operation is important, a DCI or deputy director of operations (DDO) often takes a personal role in it, from handpicking the personnel to actually planning the details to serving as an actual operations officer. In such cases, the executive can easily develop a personal stake in not only the success of the operation, but also pushing the operation forward. There is a natural tendency for intelligence executives to become advocates rather than evaluators.

> [A]n eager operational group, presenting a plan of action, can and must be expected to put on its best face. If there are operational plans in government, or elsewhere, there have to be enthusiastic people to conceive them, develop them for approval, and become advocates in the process.
>
> DDP Richard M. Bissell[3]

There is, moreover, an inherent loyalty that bonds compatriots within such close-knit enterprises, and a DCI who is a former operator may either find it difficult to say no to a cherished plan brought forward by a former comrade, or perhaps more easily surrender to the enthusiasm of a "true believer" committed to a particular cause, country, or action plan.

One of the few exceptions to this dynamic was Richard Helms, an intelligence professional who rose to become deputy director for plans, and eventually DCI. Although he had been chief of the Clandestine Services, Helms was never enamored of black ops, believing that the most powerful influence the CIA could have on the world was to provide timely and insightful intelligence and analysis to the United States government.

In addition to the dynamics of the office of DCI, the CIA itself exhibits some characteristics of typical organizational behavior. Although in many ways, the CIA is a special organization, it is still an institution made up of people, and therefore subject to the dynamics of organizational sociology and psychology. One of these dynamics working within the CIA is the bifurcation between analysts and operators (or, as it is sometimes crudely put, between the "professors" or "thinkers" and the "knuckledraggers"). In this culture, the analysts believe that the operators fail to understand the complexities and uncertainties of global and local politics, societies, and economies, while the operators believe that the analysts will talk any issue to death before taking action. Because they see the complexities of a circumstance, analysts are often in the position of counseling restraint and of pointing out the uncertainties in and potential problems created by a covert operation. Operators, on the other hand, view this as counseling *inaction*. After all, they signed on to *fight* the enemy, not to talk about them. Because of this institutional tension, sometimes the analysis and information provided by the analytical branch of the CIA is denigrated by operations planners as too timid, sometimes it is ignored, and sometimes the intelligence branch is cut completely out of the loop.

During the planning of ZAPATA, for example, the CIA's analysts predicted repeatedly that there would be no uprising in Cuba in response to the landings at the Bay of Pigs: If they weren't already imprisoned or in Miami, any opposition to Castro would be rounded up at the first sign of trouble; besides, to most Cubans, Castro was still the popular leader who had ousted Batista. This information, the product of manifold intelligence sources appraised by expert analysts, and known by DCI Allen Dulles and DDP Bissell, never reached Jack Kennedy. It was never passed on to him by the intelligence executives, who instead presented a rosy picture indeed of the masses of Cubans just waiting to join up with the liberators of the 2506 Brigade. Moreover, the planning and preparation of ZAPATA was deemed by the DCI to be so secret that, although word of it was all over the street in Miami and was being reported in newspapers in Latin America, his own intelligence analysts could not be consulted.

Cutting out analysis is a particularly dangerous proposition for a black operation. Ideally, a covert action is the judicious use of just the right amount of force at a key time and place. These operations depend critically on plentiful, accurate intelligence; they require good analysts to determine whether or not they can be effective, or "work." By cutting out the analytical branch, whether for "security" reasons or because its conclusions put the kibosh on a favorite covert endeavor, the operation is forced to rely on ad hoc intelligence, untested by national or regional experts, and devoid of analysis.[4] Moreover, virtually by definition, one eliminates any possibility of pessimistic information flowing through to the decision makers who may need it to gauge whether or not to give the go-ahead. This plainly biases the decision making process by, in essence, only presenting the up side.

Finally, there is a common sociological dynamic at work that helps perpetuate a culture of covert action within the CIA (or indeed within any institution that combines intelligence and black ops functions): It is easier to promote someone with a notable career path highlighted by bold deeds. While an analyst or spymaster[5] may have produced startlingly accurate analyses or delivered insightful intelligence from the heart of the enemy government at a critical moment, there are two aspects of this activity that, perhaps, diminish its effect on personal career advancement. First, a lot of intelligence work, the actual work of collecting information, whether from satellites or spies, is deeply classified even within the CIA. These are not successes that can be bandied about over a scotch and soda, for the mere existence of most intelligence sources is extremely secret. On the other hand, while covert actions are theoretically secret, the real secret is supposed to be CIA involvement; the activities themselves are often visible to all the world. This means that they *can* be a subject for discussion and reputation building within the agency. Further, larger covert programs, e.g., MONGOOSE, are essentially open secrets within the CIA.

Second, black operations are perceived by many as "where the action is." While the analysts in Langley write papers, the operators are out in the field *doing something!* As one climbs the professional ladder in the CIA, it's a major bonus if someone can point to him and say, "*He's* the guy that saved Jamaica." Directors tend to be chosen from men with a reputation for "getting things done," and covert action is where the doing is.

PRESIDENTS, POLITICIANS, AND PLANS

"How could I have been so stupid?"

In the aftermath of the ZAPATA disaster, President Kennedy expressed his anguish at having personally approved such a fiasco. To Jack Kennedy, it was virtually inconceivable that he, along with his Special Group comprised of the handpicked cream of the "best and brightest," could produce such a debacle. What JFK did not understand, however, was that no matter how bright the president and his advisors, only by asking the right questions can one get the right information to make the right decision. Sadly for JFK, neither he nor his advisors had the experience or knowledge to ask these questions and to demand answers.

In recent years, it has been a rare president who has assumed office having much foreign affairs preparation at all. Only three of the ten postwar presidents (Eisenhower, Nixon, and Bush) have possessed such seasoning; the others having come from the Senate or from governors' mansions. Typically, such a lack of experience is imagined to be remedied by the president's advisors, who are supposed to have enjoyed considerable foreign-policy experience and education.

Often, however, presidents pack their advising staff and National Security Council (NSC) with friends, political operators, business executives, and lawyers. Jack Kennedy relied most heavily on his brother Bobby in making national security decisions; Ronald Reagan appointed as his National Security Advisor William Clark, a judge whose primary qualification seemed to be that he had helped Reagan get elected. While such advisors typically provide the president with a few individuals he or she can trust, these individuals rarely bring along knowledge of the history of covert action, especially the pitfalls that line the path of black ops. Without such background, it becomes nearly impossible to contest a proposed covert operation; after all, "we can always deny it." Further, even more rarely is there an advisor who understands the way the advising process favors the approval of whatever covert actions bubble up from the DCI.

The presidential appointee process also reduces the ability of the executive branch to evaluate covert actions, in two ways. First, the revolving door of the NSC produces an organization with very little "institutional memory." What worked in the past? What led to disaster? What aspects of prior covert actions led to loss of deniability? There are no training manuals for this kind of thing, and presidential appointees (almost all of whom are new to their offices and the national security process) are at the mercy of those career officers who have been in Washington or Langley for perhaps decades. Even if the "new guys" want to question a black operation, without bureaucratic experience or historical knowledge, they have no ammunition. In addition, presidential nominees who have experience and have proven themselves healthy skeptics are often "unconfirmable;" individuals with a record of concern about intelligence activities or covert action find their nominations dead on arrival at the U.S. Senate (e.g., Morton Halperin, Ted Sorenson).

Another problem arises when a president and a DCI misunderstand their relationship. Typically, a president might expect a DCI to be the impartial arbiter on intelligence affairs, the president's personal intelligence spymaster. In this role, the president expects that the DCI is only going to bring forward those operations that the DCI thinks should go forward. Given an experienced DCI, a president may reasonably expect these to be necessary operations with a high probability of success, involving little risk of the United States, the CIA, or the president getting caught holding the bag. On the other hand, an experienced DCI is likely to perceive his role as (1) the representative of the CIA, (2) the advocate or defender of the CIA, and (3) a long-term civil servant more attuned to a "national interest" than, say, a former governor subject to the gale winds of partisan politics.

The difference in how each perceives the role of DCI is critical to understanding the decision-making process for covert action. Perceiving that the DCI is the president's personal intelligence advisor, a president is more likely to defer to the "experience" and "impartiality" of the director in deciding whether or not a black operation should proceed. After all, in this scenario, the DCI's *job* is to prescreen these activities, ever watchful for the effect they may have on the president.

The decision-making logic of the president would be substantially different, however, under a different set of understandings. Suppose the president perceives the DCI as the executive of an organization with its own rules, goals, and culture. Further suppose that the CIA is perceived as an organization not *above* politics, but *part* of a political system, competing for status and resources against other government bureaucracies. Under this scenario, rival policies that percolate up to the national security decision makers might be viewed as what they are: bids for power, prestige, money, and a privileged seat at the policy-making table.

Yet another kind of misunderstanding can lead to foreign policy embarrassment or disaster. Sometimes the impetus for covert action flows not *up* from the CIA to the president, but *down* from the president to the CIA. Here, there is a complex, difficult, or urgent foreign-policy problem (e.g., Saddam Hussein, Afghan-based terrorist armies), and the DCI receives an order to *do something*: Give the president a plan to eliminate the irritant. In these cases, presidents propose objectives and the DCI does the best he can. This may result in very difficult, impossible, or mutually exclusive objectives, e.g., get rid of Saddam Hussein but *don't* assassinate him. Under such pressure, the CIA may indeed come up with a plan, albeit sometimes not a very good one, and one the agency would not put forth on its own. The political problem arises when a DCI brings such an endeavor to the president. As the initiator, the president is predisposed to view the proposed operation favorably. If the DCI, on the other hand, hints that the plan is not too promising, he is in effect admitting that the CIA has failed at the mission; something any high-ranking executive is loathe to do. In such cases, the DCI or operations officer presenting the plan may try to reveal the underlying concern by a lack of enthusiasm. This signal, however, may escape a gung ho president and NSC, especially if they are relatively inexperienced in handling operational briefings. Further, such hinting may only serve to irritate the president or members of the council. This carries the risk that the DCI might lose credibility with or access to the president, and also that the president might even attempt to bypass the CIA for black operations, as happened in the Iran-Contra and YELLOW FRUIT affairs. DCIs are loathe to run this risk, since it might not only lead to dangerous waters for the country (e.g., a possible constitutional crisis if the president goes off the books), but also because of potential damage to the CIA as an organization.

Having said all this, one must also recognize the difficult position of the DCI, being asked to serve conflicting roles. As the nation's principal intelligence officer, the DCI must attempt to act as the presidential intelligence advisor; no one has access to more information or (potentially) better analysis. As the head of the Central Intelligence Agency, the DCI is responsible for maintaining the quality and morale of the organization; this can only be accomplished if the director champions his own agency. As the coordinator of America's intelligence community, the DCI is asked to resolve conflicts between essentially competing intelligence organizations, in which his own agency is often one of the contending parties. Such conflicts are not only over budget allocations, but more importantly over the collection and interpretation of intelligence information itself. Is the threat from Saddam Hussein more critical than the potential for an India-Pakistan nuclear war? Is the best response to terrorism cruise missiles or a black operation to wipe out terrorist training bases? The answers to questions like these are pivotal in establishing U.S. foreign policy and in coining status for the various intelligence organs of the government.

Several other organizational and small-group dynamics also probably enter play from time to time to encourage a favorable disposition toward black operations. One of these might be termed "role overload," in which a president and his advisors are forced to wear so many hats at once that they cannot give adequate attention to any single policy action. In any single day, dozens of decisions must be made, and the time to consider any one of them is limited. This kind of time pressure effectively prevents the president and NSC from deeply probing any single operation unless it is perceived as truly critical.[6]

Second, careful evaluation is sometimes hindered when advisors hesitate to effectively criticize a proposed operation, even when they perceive obvious major flaws. This may be occasioned by "groupthink," an unwillingness to openly challenge "what everybody thinks."[7] During the consideration of ZAPATA, for example, several advisors later reported that they remained silent about what they perceived as flaws in the operation because they believed that if these things were indeed flaws, surely some of the other brilliant people in the room would say something. No one did. Another interpersonal dynamic that can silence advisors is an unwillingess to kill an operation for fear of being labeled a "can't-do" kind of guy. Presidents and government executives value hard chargers who get things done; there is less value perceived in preventing a fiasco by incisive criticism.

Finally, presidents often feel pressure to approve covert actions for fear they will be branded as "soft" or "indecisive." Theoretically, the cancellation of an operation or program is not public knowledge, but such things almost inevitably leak, and presidents understand this. The threat of such leakage was a critical factor in President Kennedy's decision to launch the Bay of Pigs operation; if he canceled the operation, he would have turned loose fifteen hundred Cubans, who would have reported how he had "chickened out" or "not stood up to Castro," on the streets of Miami. This motivation, in effect, the pressure to *do something*, is probably also behind the mediocre efforts to oust Saddam Hussein in the mid-1990s.

REINVENTING THE WHEEL, REINVENTING THE WHEEL . . .

Many presidents have entered office with the intent to restore power and vitality to American foreign policy. President Kennedy called it "vigor" (he pronounced it "vigah"); Ronald Reagan talked about "unleashing" the CIA. Typically, such sentiments are a response to perceived bureaucratic inaction or ineffective foreign-policy ventures. This is often ascribed to "red tape" or overly complicated decision-making processes, and new presidents often try to dispense with the formalities for two reasons. First, they seek better control over the reins of government, trying to wrest power away from bureaucracies and career civil servants. Second, they usually look for ways to streamline decision making, and often end up eliminating various advisory committees, such as the 54/12 Committee, which monitored covert actions under President Eisenhower. Sometimes, too, new presidents enter office so enamored of covert operations and James Bond affairs that they may attempt to bypass the DCI and DDO and control CIA black operations directly out of the White House, without the supervision or judgment of experienced CIA executives. Finally, active presidents also often assert "presidential preeminence" in foreign affairs, making both a political and constitutional claim that in foreign relations, efficiency, decisive action, and unity of purpose are called for, and these can only be found in the office of the presidency. Therefore, according to this view, it is essential that the president be able to act without formal constraints, especially in critical situations.

Breaking down these institutionalized processes, however, often creates more inefficiency than it avoids. First, small advisory bodies are scarcely large bureaucracies. Often, presidents who drop these committees end up establishing ad hoc covert action advisory groups, usually without adequate concern for representing the spectrum of organizations, experience, and knowledge required to evaluate black ops. It essentially becomes a diminished, haphazard form of the eliminated committee.

Second, there are very good reasons these committees exist. They permit evaluation of potentially risky foreign-policy activities by individuals with a range of experience and expertise. They also tend to have broad enough representation that various black ops from different parts of government do not step on each other or work to cross-purposes. Moreover, these committees tend to be rather small anyway; they hardly comprise a thick layer of bureaucracy that could hold up a conspicuously necessary covert action.

CONCLUSIONS

The covert action evaluation and approval process that has evolved within the American political system predisposes the president to green-light black operations, largely based on two premises: first, that black ops are low-risk because

they are deniable, and second, that the president and close advisors know little
enough about the history of these activities to believe the preceding premise.
Moreover, the various conflicting roles played by the DCI figure largely into this
one-sided process; at least for a CIA sponsored black operation, it is difficult if not
impossible for a president and NSC to acquire necessary *and independently verified*
information to evaluate the possible costs of an operation. All the data for making
the "go/no-go" decision are provided by an agency with a vested stake in "go."

How can this bias be overcome? The first and most important single thing
is to ensure that the president and his advisors acquire broad background education in covert action, learning both some history as well as analysis of issues raised
by black ops. Second, one or more close advisors should have or acquire a deep
knowledge of historical covert actions, to fill in the gaps in the broad background
knowledge of the president. Third, a president must make explicit the nature of
the presidential-DCI relationship. This may reduce blunders created by misun-
derstandings, and at the very least make it clear to the DCI where his responsi-
bilities lie. Fourth, every covert action should be evaluated for approval by a
standing group within the NSC; members of this group must include individuals
with experience and background knowledge of covert operations. Fifth, the covert
advisory group should have direct access to the CIA's directorate of intelligence
(DI) in order to verify critical information that bears on the potential success or
failure of covert operations. Failing this, the president should insist on receiving
data and analysis from the DI that supports the premises of the covert action as
well as data that challenges the premises. Sixth, wherever possible, the NSC
should explore alternate channels of information to validate the assumptions of
the operational plans. Seventh, every covert operations plan should contain sec-
tions detailing (1) how the plan will "work," e.g., the logic by which the desired
outcome is produced by the action, and (2) the potential costs of exposure. Finally,
members of the advisory committee should have direct, private access to the president, either face-to-face or by written communication, in order to express mis-
givings that they might hesitate to bring up before the group.

It is essential that those who make critical decisions about American national
security do so by considering the most complete information and range of outcomes possible. Not only do these processes and operations influence events around
the world, but they also have profound effects on democracy, freedom, and a government of the people. It is to these concerns that we turn next.

NOTES

1. It is true that the U.S. Armed Forces, as well as some law-enforcement agencies,
may carry out clandestine activities during peacetime, e.g., secret operations by SEAL
Teams to plant electronic monitoring devices inside the USSR or China. These are mainly
clandestine missions, however, and not the kind of covert operations that are apparent to
the world but unattributable to the United States.

2. Eventually, this became the National Intelligence Estimate (NIE), which has proven to be nearly as prone to political influence as the separate reports from the various agencies and military intelligence offices. Like any negotiated document, an NIE is full of compromises that often reflect the bargaining power of the various intelligence organizations rather than their reasoning ability.

3. Richard M. Bissell, "Reflections on the Bay of Pigs: Book Review of Operation Zapata," *Strategic Review* 12, no. 1 (winter 1984): 380.

4. Analysis is a critical part of the intelligence process; it is the process of making sense of what the raw intelligence information means. Analysis, for example, explores or reveals contradictory intelligence, and helps us sort out the real from the illusory, the probable from the unlikely. It is a grave mistake to think one can simply read raw intelligence and understand what is happening (or going to happen).

5. No, this is not a term used within the CIA, except in derision.

6. It must also be said, however, that even a lot of National Security Council attention does not guarantee good results. Both ZAPATA and EAGLE CLAW (Iranian hostage rescue) received huge amounts of presidential attention.

7. The primary work on groupthink is Irving Janis, *Groupthink: Psychological Studies of Policy Decisions and Fiascoes*, 2d ed. (Boston: Houghton Mifflin, 1982).

Chapter 17

Covert Action and Democracy

"When the president does it, that means it is not illegal."

Richard M. Nixon[1]

". . . we operated from the premise that everything we did do was legal."

Oliver North[2]

He had often described himself as "nondescript"; the man in the gray flannel suit. He believed that this was one of the things that made him a good secret agent. Slowly, deliberately, he raised the umbrella, opened it. Behind the platform, the seated men flinched. Fortunately, the umbrella wasn't loaded.

The nondescript man was William Colby, director of Central Intelligence, and he had just shown the Church Committee and the world one of the CIA's clandestine weapons, the "nondiscernable bioinoculator"—in other words, a concealed dart gun. Perhaps, as a "bioinoculator," it had been intended to inject a target (an opposing politician, or maybe a security guard) with a knockout shot, or perhaps something to make him ill. At least, that is what Colby said it was for, and these would indeed be useful and valid intelligence purposes. Given the CIA's history with botulism, tularemia, anthrax, brucellosis, and sleeping sickness, however, there was good reason to believe the umbrella's designers had more permanent and lethal ideas in mind.

It was 1975, the "Year of Intelligence," and the DCI was struggling mightily to save what he could of the CIA. Congressional committees were probing the history of CIA operations, especially covert actions, and for the first time, powerful voices in the United States government were challenging specific operations and programs of American intelligence agencies: the assassination plots; secret wars; "black" companies such as Air America; assassinations carried out under the guise of PHOENIX in Vietnam; intervention in the political affairs of neutral and friendly countries; domestic intelligence operations,

298

including spying on loyal Americans and American political organizations; disruption and harassment of domestic political activists and organizations; and potentially devastating biochemical, neurochemical, and psychological experiments conducted on American citizens without their consent or knowledge.

As these revelations slugged America in the gut, one rapid body blow after another, many Americans began to voice the unthinkable: If *this* is what happens, should there even *be* a CIA? Hadn't the CIA become a sort of American gestapo, as some members of Congress had feared during the debate of the National Security Act in 1947? Was the CIA a "rogue elephant" or an invisible government, making its own foreign policy, heedless of the will of the people, holding itself above the authority of the presidency? Don't these secret organizations *inherently* subvert democracy?

These are indeed the critical questions. For nearly twenty-five years, they remained unasked, bottled up by the stopper of cold war bipartisanship as well as the stifling fear that merely to pose such questions was un-American or would be shamelessly exploited to slap a "red" label on the questioner. With the revelations of the Church Committee and the exposure of the *Family Jewels* (a CIA-produced digest of illegal and unconstitutional CIA programs and operations, compiled under DCI James Schlesinger) the stopper was pulled, unleashing a whirlwind of harsh criticism at the CIA, culminating in calls to completely shut down the agency. The CIA had enough powerful supporters, however, and there is enough reasonably indisputable need for intelligence collection and analysis that there was never any serious consideration of closing the doors at Langley. Nevertheless, it is also apparent that covert action and the institutions it has created have shaped American democracy, and perhaps distorted or even subverted it. How has covert action and its institutions affected American democracy?

It is to these issues that this chapter is devoted. We first examine the effects of the "covert mentality" on American democracy. This is followed by the constitutional and legal basis of covert action, an analysis of the inherent conflict between covert action and democratic government, and a description of how the United States has attempted to resolve these issues. Finally, the practical problems and outcomes of these efforts are explored, concluding with a discussion about whether covert action can, in the long run, be controlled.

THE COVERT MENTALITY AND AMERICAN DEMOCRACY

One critical effect of covert action, as a standard mode of operation, on the United States has been that created by the entrenchment of the "covert mentality" within elements of the executive branch, intelligence agencies, Department of Defense, and even Congress itself. This worldview, produced by the nature of the cold war and the conspiratorial perceptions it engendered, has led powerful individuals in these institutions to endeavor to "win at all costs," sacrificing even the Constitution if necessary. It is a dangerous world, says this view, and Americans must do whatever is necessary to preserve the country. "Whatever is necessary" is a particularly subjective notion, however, and has been interpreted to allow:

- spying on Americans for their political beliefs;
- opening the mail of Americans not suspected of any crime;
- harassing and disrupting legal American political groups simply for their dissenting views;
- testing neurochemical and biological agents (such as LSD) and toxins on American citizens without their consent or knowledge, covering up these activities, and destroying evidence of them;
- engaging in secret wars with neither the consent or knowledge of Congress;
- engaging in acts of war or acts that created a high probability of war without the consent or knowledge of Congress;
- purposely concealing these acts or intentionally misleading members of the government who have a right to know about such activities;
- employing the policies and resources of intelligence agencies to further the goals of private corporations and political groups;
- subverting democratic processes and sponsoring the functional equivalents of coups d'etat in friendly and allied countries;
- creating private, off-the-books intelligence and operations organizations in deliberate attempts to evade U.S. law;
- negotiating with terrorists and paying ransom for hostages;[3] and
- arming insurgent and terrorist organizations with modern weapons in spite of their anti-American positions.

These operations are practically all illegal and unconstitutional; these operations have produced virtually no significant intelligence or advantage against America's foes in the cold war. By themselves, they have indirectly yet substantially damaged American democracy. It is likely that such abuses would not have occurred without the entrenchment of covert action as a (or *the*) standard mode of operation during the cold war, for the perpetrators of these actions understood that they were violating the Constitution. That is why they developed such elaborate defenses of their deeds. As a group, these actions caused greater damage than the individual operations did, however; they undermined democracy and constitutional government itself. It is to that we turn next.

COVERT ACTION AND THE CONSTITUTION

At the genesis of the cold war, there was really no question about the Constitution. To the individuals charged with safeguarding America, it was a black and white issue: win or die. The Constitution, it would often be remarked, is not a suicide pact. In essence, the Constitution could be suspended on the flimsiest claim of "national security." While there *was* some concern over the possibility of CIA domestic operations, there was scarcely a question about the power of the president to conduct foreign covert actions against the Commies.

There is no mention of covert action or similar operations in the Constitution. There is discussion of war, treaties, armies, and militias, and even legitimizing private armed forces; secrecy and deniability, however, are nowhere to be found. Moreover, while it is often asserted that the Constitution confers primary authority for foreign affairs on the president, there is little in the document itself to support this. According the Constitution, the president is authorized to:

- serve as commander in chief of the armed forces;
- receive foreign ambassadors;
- appoint ambassadors to foreign countries (with the advice and consent of the Senate); and
- negotiate treaties with foreign governments.

Congress, by comparison, receives substantial foreign-policy authority:

- most importantly, the power to declare war;
- the power to raise and maintain armed forces;
- the power to raise money for government purposes;
- the sole power to authorize expenditures for government activities;
- the power to ratify treaties with foreign governments; and
- the power to grant letters of marque.[4]

A simple reading of the document indicates that congressional authority is, generally, more appropriate for undertaking covert action than are the powers allotted the president. Covert action, especially major operations, often involves raising armies (or what amounts to armies, even if they are foreign armies), carrying out acts of war or engaging in full-scale wars (even if fought by foreigners under foreign flags), and sponsoring attacks by private citizens on the people, land, commerce, and armed forces of hostile countries. While the founders did not explicitly consider deniable operations in the Constitution, the authority granted to Congress certainly seems to indicate a congressional role in such actions. Given the propensity for covert action to approximate acts of war, it is likely that the founders would have considered congressional approval a *necessity* for proxy wars or operations with a substantial risk of escalation into war.

Historically, these powers largely refer to formal, declared wars with foreign countries, and thus it can be argued that these provisions provide no constitutional basis for covert action. We should recall, however, that many of the founders had long experience with nondeclared wars, militia operations, and unconventional border wars. Many had served through the sporadic violence leading up to the French and Indian War, had participated in the "deniable" operations in which both the French and English attempted to recruit the various Indian nations as proxy armies, and had fought in nearly continuous Indian wars for decades. Given this experience, it seems probable that the founders at least thought about such activities; most likely, they considered them to be within the purview of Congress via the power to fund or not fund such "nonwar" enterprises.

In terms of practical politics, too, the founding fathers understood a necessity for secret operations, creating the president's "contingency fund," a fund that simply received an annual sum of money for intelligence operations. No accounting was required for this money; Congress took it on faith that the president would use it wisely, not abuse the funds, and be honest. Of course, the president was named Washington. Further, both Presidents Jefferson and Madison engaged in what was essentially covert action in Tripoli and East Florida, respectively.

It is unclear how prevalent covert action was during the early years of the republic, although the cases recounted in chapter 3 suggest that it was not uncommon during the drive toward Manifest Destiny, the "acquisition" of the Panama Canal, and the creation of the prototype Office of Strategic Services (OSS) before World War II. It was after 1945, however, that covert action became a centerpiece of American foreign policy. At the very least, the individuals involved in the debate at the time of the National Security Act of 1947 did not believe there was liberal constitutional authority for covert action. Over time, however, the perceived requirements of survival during the cold war led to reliance on black operations, and the widespread employment of these methods became, essentially, constitutional precedent. The CIA, as an executive-branch agency, was viewed as an arm of presidential power, carrying out the sometimes unsavory and brutal necessities of fighting off the Commies. Today, ironically, it is the very laws passed by Congress to control and limit covert action that are used as the legal justification for black operations.

COVERT ACTION AND THE LAW

Harry Truman, the man who signed the CIA into existence in 1947, would later say that he had never envisioned the agency becoming involved in peacetime cloak-and-dagger operations. Yet, as discussed in chapter 2, the ink was barely dry before secret arms shipments were being dropped to Ukranian rebels, deals were cut with the Corsican syndicate to control the Marseilles waterfront, Italian elections were being massively and covertly funded, the abortive Albanian uprising was launched, and black organizations were being created in Eastern Europe under OPERATION RED SOX/RED CAP to stir up armed rebellion against Soviet occupation.[5]

When the CIA was chartered by the National Security Act of 1947, it was assigned a variety of critical intelligence roles. Almost as an afterthought, the act ascribed to the CIA the authority to undertake "other such functions and duties related to intelligence affecting the national security as the National Security Council may from time to time direct." From 1947 until 1974, this astonishingly innocuous phrase was wellspring of American covert action, the statutory authorization for the expenditure of billions of dollars, the loss of thousands of lives, and the creation of several political circumstances that might have triggered nuclear war.

Congress, for the most part, accepted the authority of the executive branch to conduct black ops. First, Congress did receive occasional reports from the CIA regarding covert action, even though these communications were restricted to special committees whose members often remained uninformed by choice. Due to a variety of political dynamics—the perceived need for absolute secrecy, the fear that any dissent would be construed as treason, the need to appear tougher on Communism than one's political opponents, a small number of "in the know" Congressmen, and the aura of invincibility and omniscience around the CIA in its first twenty years or so—Congress acquiesced to virtually every covert action about which it was informed. It asked no hard questions and made no effort to learn of activities the CIA did not tell it about. This acquiescence by Congress essentially created a new presidential and executive authority by virtue of the precedent it created.

Moreover, it can be argued that Congress implicitly legitimized covert action over time, even without actually creating explicit statutory authority, by continually authorizing billions of dollars for black operations. While this has some merit, there are two powerful rejoinders. First, while Congress certainly allocated money for covert action, the legislative bodies were never certain how much was being authorized, how much was being spent, and what the money was actually paying for. Intelligence funding of all kinds—including not only covert action, but also intelligence gathering and analysis, counterintelligence, and so on—has always been hidden or buried in numerous funding bills unrelated to intelligence; the intelligence budget itself has been "black." Congress never knew (nor generally desired to know) the extent of funding, *and therefore could not begin to determine the extent of covert action*. Second, because Congress as a whole had little or no knowledge of the extent of U.S. covert operations, and because what knowledge it possessed was sometimes disinformation disseminated by U.S. intelligence agencies themselves (i.e., Congress sometimes received and believed the same cover stories as the rest of the world), the claim that Congress assented to covert action in general by not asserting limits is probably specious. Few members of Congress, if any, knew of the secret war in Laos, or of ZAPATA or AJAX or SUCCESS or MONGOOSE, or of the assassination plots, or the training of Tibetan insurgents, or the conspiracies against Salvador Allende or Gough Whitlam, or the deals with the Corsican Mafia. Given congressional assent to the National Security Act, it might be reasonably believed that Congress accepted a small amount of "other activities"; it is something else to claim that this implies agreement to, essentially, a foreign policy largely comprised of black ops. One cannot claim that because Congress did not object to things it was unaware of, it therefore approved of them.

In 1974, with the exposure of the CIA's ten-year operation against Allende, coupled with congressional outrage that the CIA and the president had explicitly lied to Congress about CIA actions in Chile, both the House and Senate acted to regain a say in foreign policy, which had largely been abrogated to the presidency during the cold war. Committees and commissions were established to study covert action and the intelligence community in general. In the House, the Pike Committee self-destructed, but the Senate's committee, chaired by Frank Church, produced an investigation that, while incomplete and for good or ill, exposed the CIA's dirty laundry.

Aghast at the kinds of activities the CIA had been carrying out (generally responding to presidential command, however), Congress intervened in the covert action process for the first time in 1974. The Hughes-Ryan Act of 1974 *prohibited* any expenditure of U.S. money for CIA overseas operations "unless and until the President finds that each such operation is important to the national security of the United States and reports, in a timely fashion, a description and scope of such operation to the appropriate committees of Congress." Thus, for *every* covert action, the president is *required* to sign a finding, a formal summary and approval of the operation, and to tell Congress about it. There were, of course, some loopholes in Hughes-Ryan. It related only to *CIA* covert actions, and thus presumably exempted black ops by other intelligence organizations, military units, the Department of Agriculture, and so forth.[6] Second, the notion of a "timely fashion" became a matter of some dispute. Congress intended that the president report covert operations *before* they took place, unless the action required such great urgency that prevented prior notification.[7] This broad language was incorporated to allow a president, in theory, the flexibility to respond to the rapidly shifting sands of world events; in practice, these phrases were treated as loopholes through which one might evade the intent of the law. In an attempt to remedy this, Congress passed the Intelligence Accountability Act, commonly referred to as the Intelligence Oversight Act, in 1980. This act requires the president to report *all* important covert actions to Congress, not only those undertaken by the CIA. Thus, a president could no longer evade Hughes-Ryan reporting requirements by working black ops through government agencies other than CIA; through the Treasury or Drug Enforcement Administration, for example, or the Department of Defense. Further, the Intelligence Oversight Act required the president to inform Congress of covert actions *before* they are carried out, but permitted an exception in cases of extreme emergency. Even in such cases, however, the leadership of the House and Senate must be informed within forty-eight hours of the onset of the operation.

The obvious and critical loophole in the Oversight Act is that, if presidents are required to report "important" covert operations, it is thereby established that they need not report "unimportant" operations. The Oversight Act itself does not define important and unimportant, and thus a whole new set of exceptions has been created. Who's to say whether an operation is important or unimportant? What if an "unimportant" operation suddenly escalates to an international crisis?

Such possible exceptions notwithstanding, the Oversight Act seems to have had a substantial impact on the CIA. One of the reasons that the North/Secord Enterprise was created was precisely because individuals in the National Security Council, DCI William Casey, and probably President Reagan himself *believed that CIA officers would follow the law.* Thus, neither the president nor the DCI could risk using the CIA to violate either the Boland Amendments or the president's executive orders barring the shipment of arms to terrorist nations (in this case, Iran). While this indicates progress in bringing black operations back within the purview of the Constitution, there still remain such problems with covert action in general as to render it a persistent and potentially fatal problem for democratic government.

COVERT ACTION AND DEMOCRACY: CAREFUL BALANCE OR MORTAL COMBAT?

The most serious effect of both covert action and the rise of its institutions is the impact of secret policies and decisions on the ability of the people to hold the government accountable for its actions. Covert actions can impair or destroy accountability, since the very nature of a covert action is to lay the responsibility off on someone else, to prevent government action from being seen as government action. Covert action and the secrecy surrounding it can also permit government policy and power to be appropriated for private ends, as in the cases of Guatemala and Chile. Further, the evolution of "secret knowledge" within the government inherently produces secret power: individuals and organizations that hold sway over others without answering to anyone or being subject to checks and balances. For example, the desire to permit a president to secretly (and deniably) order an assassination by explicitly *not* ordering it places tremendous, yet invisible and unaccountable, power in the hands of the DCI (or even in the hands of those lower down the CIA chain of command). Moreover, responsibility for—or even mere knowledge of—some covert operations or programs, especially those that are illegal, places one in a precarious position; those who can hold it over your head have a subtle yet real influence over you. Consider the difficulties George Bush had in trying to deny that he had known about the arms for hostages deal. If a president or a DCI for example, could be proven to have known about something more important to the American electorate or Congress, e.g., some of the domestic operations, the threat of exposure and fear of impeachment or removal from office would provide decisive leverage for those who held the information.

THE EVOLUTION OF PLAUSIBLE DENIABILITY

Another basic problem created by the mere employment of covert action as a policy option is the way in which, in recent years, the basis of covert action, plausible deniability, has become a travesty. Originally, plausible deniability meant that U.S. involvement in an election, sabotage, or war could not be proven; that even if such activities were in the interest of the United States, it was at least possible that some other government or group was behind the action. The idea was to enable the United States to undertake necessary political and military actions without the risk of exposure that could cause the operation to boomerang against the United States or openly throw down the gauntlet to the Soviets.

Plausible deniability, however, has come to be intentionally misconstrued by high government officials in what may have been deliberate attempts to subvert American democracy.[8] This modified version of plausible deniability asserts that, while members of the executive branch may have approved a covert operation, *the president did not know or officially approve.* Typically, this kind of deniability is used to protect a president when undertaking an operation that is illegal, unconstitutional, or would never obtain congressional approval or funding. This occurred not only in Iranscam, but earlier in events like the assassination operations, in which Allen Dulles and Richard Bissell "understood" President Eisenhower to mean that he wanted Patrice Lumumba killed.

It is understandable that subordinates strain to protect the president from having to give direct, nasty, and potentially illegal orders. The typical solution has been for presidents to make intentionally vague statements which are interpreted by subordinates as explicit marching orders: "Get rid of Castro." "Do something about Lumumba." "Keep the contras together body and soul." Beating around the bush in this manner is presumed to spare the office of the president from being sullied by the sordid truth of a bullet in the head or a painful death from botulism. This method has also been used by CIA executives and National Security Council officials to cover themselves by claiming that they knew what the president wanted, even if an explicit order was never given. In this way, *any* individuals involved are shielded from prosecution *and* accountability.

THE OVERSIGHT MYTH

Even though Hughes-Ryan and the Oversight Act represent steps toward accountability, there remain two inherent problems with congressional oversight. First, oversight committees themselves are by nature fraught with contradictions. Some representatives and senators simply don't want to know what the intelligence agencies are doing. This results from (1) squeamishness about the kinds of things that might be going on—they don't want to know about the bullet in the head either, (2) a fear that they might accidentally divulge classified information and perhaps ruin an operation or get somebody killed, (3) fear that they might be blamed for a leak, and (4) the fact that sharing information also imposes a share of the *responsibility* for each black operation on the legislator. In general, in the intelligence committees, silence is presumed to mean assent: If you do not object to a covert action, you therefore give it your stamp of approval. Many, if not most, legislators prefer to avoid anything to do with potentially risky operations.

Moreover, especially since the crumbling of the bipartisan consensus in foreign policy, covert actions have been the subject of substantial partisan politicking. Since politics does *not* stop at the water's edge anymore, every covert action is seen as an opportunity to score political points. If a black operation is successful, there is a tremendous incentive to "leak" it, thereby making one's political side look powerful, clever, and decisive. If an operation fails, the opposition party benefits by exposing it. Thus, covert actions are more difficult than ever to keep covert. This changed, politically-charged environment also encourages presidents to undertake plainly illegal off-the-books operations in an effort to avoid both the legal process of reporting to Congress and the extralegal "check" represented by leaks.

The most important limit on congressional oversight, however, is this: It is up to the CIA, other intelligence organizations, or the administration to inform Congress of covert operations. Congress, however, has no way to independently verify that what it is being told is, in fact, correct and the whole story. If a DCI or undersecretary of state for Latin America tells the congressional oversight committees something, the committees have little choice but to accept it; where would they get the information to dispute it? In other words, true oversight of covert operations comes from CNN.[9] Without a separate agency to gather, analyze, and report information regarding covert activity, Congress is blind. Only a CIA confession can expose CIA wrongdoing; only the news media can expose non-CIA covert actions.

Over the years, one of the significant arguments against congressional oversight is the problem that members of Congress, or their staffs, might leak classified information, whether inadvertently or on purpose (perhaps to embarrass the president or the CIA, or to expose an ongoing operation that the member disagrees with). Sometimes intelligence operators claim they must, as Oliver North put it, make a choice between "lives and lies"; either protect an operation by lying to Congress, or see one's own people killed should an operation be unmasked.

The hole in this argument is gaping. One merely has to look at the kind of people habitually entrusted with secrets during a covert operation: shady arms dealers, mercenaries, foreign insurgents (many of whom may want to expose the U.S. operation in hopes of triggering direct intervention), smugglers, drug runners, Mafia dons and hitmen, and so on. While not all covert operations employ these kind of individuals, many do. Are these individuals and groups really more trustworthy than U.S. Senators? Moreover, when the United States undertakes a covert operation, it is rare indeed that the activity is *not* known to the opposition. Were the Soviets unaware of U.S. sponsorship of the secret army in Laos, of U.S. support for the 2506 Brigade, or of the buy-off of the Corsicans in Marseille? Of course they knew. Did the Iranian government know about the deal to trade arms for hostages? Did the Soviets and Sandinistas know about the arms and supplies being provided by the Enterprise? Of course they did. Then, we might ask, *precisely who is being kept in the dark on these operations?* Precisely, it is the American people and their representatives, the Congress of the United States. The choice between lives and lies is most often a false dichotomy.

Accountability is further prevented by the inability to actually punish covert operators or intelligence executives who knowingly and shamelessly violate the law or the Constitution. These operators, whether directed by superiors or operating as rogue agents, possess three powerful lines of defense that can be used in even the most flagrant cases: (1) I was just following orders, (2) I'm more patriotic than you are, and (3) you can't prosecute me anyway.

First, in covert action, "I was just following orders" is sometimes a viable defense. This is due to the fact that intelligence officers have to rely on their immediate superiors in the chain of command; if the DCI gives an operator an assignment, he might reasonably believe it has been approved by the president. It would be rare and almost certainly unique if a mid-level CIA executive or field officer actually received written authorization from the president. It simply doesn't happen. The executive or field agent has no way to tell if a presidential finding has been signed or if the operation has been reported to the intelligence committees, as required by law.

Second, it may occasionally be a useful defense to claim that while an operator knew a black op was illegal, it was necessary and served the national interest, so he did it anyway. A defiant stand, well made, can often draw powerful political allies to one's side. This is especially true if there was substantial prior support for one's political position, and if the law itself was controversial and narrowly passed. Further, powerful political allies can raise the specter that any prosecution would be politically motivated for partisan political gain, that the Congress had criminalized differences of opinion on policy matters. This is exactly what happened during the Iran-Contra hearings, as Oliver North essentially defied Congress in its own house by declaring that Enterprise would not have been necessary if Congress had had the guts to do the right thing.

Finally, covert operators under indictment may find themselves in the enviable position of having the knowledge to *graymail* the government. Graymail, as the name implies, is a nebulous form of coercion similar to blackmail, in which the defendant claims that he or she must reveal classified information in order to receive a fair trial. Sometimes this may be true, if, for example, there are classified documents showing that an officer did indeed receive orders from above for a controversial operation. Sometimes, however, this claim is merely a thinly veiled threat to blow ongoing operations and expose intelligence methods and personnel. The concept is that the judge will rule that since the classified information cannot be exposed, a fair trial is therefore impossible, and the charges must be dismissed. Graymail schemes have several variations. First, it can be part of an "I was following orders" defense, in which the classified documents are supposedly the presidential findings or authorization to undertake the operation for which the intelligence agent is being prosecuted. Second, if the indicted officer operated for the administration still in power, the administration itself might classify critical documents *after the fact* when some of its covert operatives are already indicted. Such documents might be, for example, intelligence reports that show that the executive knew that an operation violated federal law, that it was being exploited by drug cartels to smuggle cocaine into the United States, or that it violated an executive order prohibiting the sale or transport of weapons to a "terrorist" government or organization. In this way, it is possible for a president or administration to order or allow its black operators to intentionally flout a law with impunity; no trial can ever occur.

One might suggest that individuals who undertake such operations face other penalties: the loss of career, retirement benefits, and reputation. Based on the outcomes of the Iran-Contra figures, however, such results seem unlikely. It is quite simple for people with vast experience and contacts in the black world to move into private black operations and "security consulting" ventures. Indeed, most can earn far more than their government salary or retirement income through book deals, movie rights, speaking engagements, think tank positions, serving on assorted boards of directors, writing newspaper and magazine columns, delivering radio or television talk shows, and various "consulting" gigs, and even direct fund raisers from supportive organizations.

There is a statute and a legal procedure intended to enable the use of classified information in criminal trials. In cases in which classified material is necessary for prosecution, the government is supposed to provide it to the judge, who screens it for relevance and determines if it is necessary to the defense. This procedure, however, was intended for trials in which the defendant was being vigorously prosecuted by the government as a spy or a traitor, rather than circumstances in which those in power supported the indicted individual. In the latter case, the administration may simply withhold the information, classify it, or, in some cases, even destroy it in order to hinder the prosecution of someone it favors. You may recall a certain marine lieutenant colonel who openly admitted to shredding government documents precisely to keep them from federal investigators.

DEMOCRACY, ACCOUNTABILITY, AND BLACK OPERATIONS

The glue that holds a representative democracy together is the notion of *accountability*: Those who hold power in government are answerable to the people for their actions. If the government performs badly, it is the right and responsibility of the public to vote new officeholders into power. Without reasonably accurate information about both what the government is doing and how it is performing, the ability to assess these things is destroyed, and so too is self-government.

Within the covert institutions of the United States government, there are two dynamics that sometimes or often limit or distort the ability of the American public to accurately assess and hold their political authorities to account. First, black operations are inherently meant to be secret. Even if the United States is carrying them out, they are not supposed to be widely known or acknowledged.

Thus, by its very nature, covert action *must* diminish accountability, and therefore diminish democracy. Sadly, this notion of deniability has been mangled in recent decades. Throughout the cold war, there were secret wars and covert "political actions" being waged on every inhabited continent; actions in the Ukraine, Albania, Italy, Cuba, Guatemala, Chile, Indonesia, Australia, Laos, and Burma represent a tiny fraction of these activities. Generally, the United States knew what the Soviet Union was doing, and generally the Soviet Union knew what the United States was doing. From whom was the secret war in Laos secret from? Who did not know that it was United States and CIA money that rebuilt the Corsican Mafia and permitted it to become the major heroin conduit into the neighborhoods of the United States? Who was kept in the dark about U.S. training and support for Tibetans, Kurds, Ukranian partisans? While it may not have been the primary goal, a central inherent *effect* of covert action was to keep such knowledge from the citizens of the United States.[10] In fact, for most of the cold war, the American people were incapable of evaluating the foreign affairs of their own government because those foreign affairs were largely black operations.

Second, the widespread acceptance of covert action in the political life of America produced a tremendously dangerous dynamic in political discourse: the acceptability of "secret information" as justification for policy. Whenever a foreign policy activity was criticized by dissenters, it became allowable to reply (with a long-suffering smile, for effect), "If you only knew what I knew, then you would understand why we're doing this. So don't ask questions or you'll get Americans killed." Secret information is necessary to the security of some operations, but is anathema to democracy. Too much of this medicine, and the cure could kill the patient.

CONCLUSIONS

In the end, one is led to conclude that as long as the United States engages in covert action, the kinds of abuses characterized in the Church Committee Report and the many histories of black operations are inevitable. Perhaps they are not the rule; perhaps there are many "good" black ops that are necessary to the safety of the American people and that do not substantively harm democratic government. Nevertheless, as long as covert action is a common U.S. government practice, and as long as covert action spawns institutionalized organizations, the risk to democratic control of government is very great.

Covert action and the institutions it has grown have seriously damaged democracy and popular sovereignty in the United States. It has enabled presidents and intelligence executives to carry out foreign policies that are antithetical to liberty and for which the executives cannot be held accountable. It has enabled presidents to proclaim a public policy to the American people and do precisely the opposite under cover. This activity has been so corrupting that the concept of plausible denial has evolved from meaning "The United States wasn't responsible for this act" to "We did it, but we didn't tell the president, so he can't be prosecuted."

The culture of covert action has produced a series of private, self-perpetuating organizations beyond the control of the government and elected representatives. Congressional oversight is chimerical, as Congress has no means to independently verify what they are being told by intelligence agencies. Knowledge of covert action subjects government officials to possible blackmail, especially if they were "in the loop" on illegal or unconstitutional covert actions. Moreover, operators who conduct illegal covert actions are rarely if ever prosecuted, either for fear of graymail, or because a sitting government can choose to withhold necessary evidence to get indictments dismissed. Even if convicted, penalties imposed are *never* more than wrist slaps, and frequently viewed as badges of honor within the intelligence community, as, for example, in the cases of Richard Helms and Claire George.

Finally, the role of secret information biases the democratic decision-making process. Control over information provides covert action organizations with the practical power of "self-oversight," and with the power to define their own agenda. Moreover, since covert action *requires* lying to one's own people, it cripples the ability of the people to make a judgement on the efficacy of their own government, and creates a cynical view of democracy and government. As long as America maintains a large and powerful organization to conduct covert action, American foreign policy will remain at the mercy of secret institutions.

NOTES

1. See Bill Moyers, *The Secret Government: The Constitution in Crisis* (Washington: Seven Locks Press, 1988), p. 94.

2. Ibid., p. 60.

3. It is inherently bad to do this, although often no one explains why. The reason is that Americans are so easy to take hostage that if one pays ransom for them, the terrorists will simply take more hostages, thus repeating the process and trapping the United States into a role as terrorist cash cow and arms supplier. This is basically what happened during Iran-Contra: As soon as a couple of hostages were released, several more were taken.

4. Oddly, granting letters of marque may be the closest that the Constitution comes to control of covert action. A letter of marque is a commission for private citizens ("privateers") to raid foreign commerce and attack the enemy in time of war. Given the perceived importance of privateering during the Revolution and the War of 1812, as well as the need to get the maritime states on board during the Constitutional Convention, it is not surprising that the practice is mentioned superficially. Legal acceptance of privateering, however, ended with the Declaration respecting Maritime Law, signed in Paris in 1856 (although not signed by the United States until later).

5. All of these activities began or occurred between 1947 and 1949. The CIA still refuses to acknowledge RED SOX/RED CAP.

6. There may not have seemed any reason to expressly forbid covert operations by nongovernmental organizations (e.g., the Enterprise or beer companies) since they were presumably already forbidden by the Neutrality Act.

7. Any student of covert action can tell you, however, that covert actions undertaken in haste are highly risky in terms of potential for success, possibility of exposure, unforseen consequences, and, not least, human lives. If an intelligence agency asks for many "urgent" black ops, it is doing something badly.

8. You can believe that those involved in Iran-Contra weren't deliberately trying to thwart the will of Congress and the American people if you want to.

9. Not just CNN, of course, but any news organization that might get wind of unreported covert operations.

10. It is almost certainly true, however, that a CIA or U.S. intelligence goal in some (many?) covert operations was to keep knowledge from Congress and the American public.

Part V

Conclusions: Déjà Vu All Over Again

Chapter 18

A Circle in a Spiral:
What Covert Action Accomplished

T hey're called "jockstrap medals," because, the joke goes, you're only allowed to wear them on that particular piece of apparel under your clothes. Like everything else, including the brand and amount of toilet paper consumed at Langley, decorations within the CIA are highly secret; after the medal is pinned on, the recipient gives it back, where it is secured in a safe for a later time. It may be returned to the honored officer upon retirement, or perhaps never; the reasons for the award may remain secret for decades. The idea, with considerable merit, is that if such awards were exposed to the public (and therefore the opposition) then bad people might start asking questions: What is this medal for? Where was this agent operating? Thus, enemies of America might be able to ferret out information about CIA operations, personnel, and methods.

There can be no disputing the courage, intelligence, and patriotism of virtually all the individuals who carried out covert action, both during the cold war and afterward.[1] Bravery and brains in the field, however, do not necessarily prove the effectiveness of the policies they served. If we reflect on the cold war (a big "if"; while there is a lot of credit-claiming, there is little reflection), the role of covert action stands out. There was a lot of it, and it seemed to occur wherever there were important issues at stake. It is difficult, however, to assess the role covert action played in the outcome of the cold war. Was it critical to holding the cold war line against the Soviets? Was it marginal? Were the costs of covert action worth it? What did covert action *accomplish*?

How Can We Judge?

When we think about how to answer these questions, several important problems immediately crop up. The greatest obstacle to accurately judging the contribution of covert action toward the "winning" of the cold war appears to be the

315

secrecy surrounding many of the black operations. How can we take into account that which we do not know? How can the CIA, and black ops in general, be accurately "credited" in the ledger of cold war victory?

These are important questions, and ones that must be considered fully and thoughtfully. Some individuals, both within and without the CIA, argue that a public accounting is inherently incomplete and therefore futile; *of course* covert operations were critical in winning the cold war. This, they claim, is apparent to anyone who knows the *whole* story, and not just the public disasters. Unfortunately, their corollary is that it is still a dangerous world, and thus the whole story can never be made public; when the operators claim that they won the cold war, the American people just have to take their word for it.[2]

If this country is to be a free and democratic society, however, there are three reasons this argument must be rejected. First, in even a "representative" democracy, the intelligence agencies must be accountable to someone: In a republic, that means the representatives or delegates of the people. This does not require that every black operation be exposed on CNN or on the CIA's Web site; it *does* demand that every black operation be disclosed and justified to those who are responsible for the activities of the government. Second, it is quite unlikely that there are many significant covert operations that do not appear somewhere in the public record. Covert action, after all, almost always has visible effects (e.g., a dramatic change in a government's policies or leadership); it is only the *cause* of such changes that is denied by the United States government, and many of these are confirmed cases, or at least those that present highly credible evidence, of U.S. black ops. Moreover, it is likely that we know about practically all of the significant *successful* covert actions through the first fifteen or twenty years of the CIA's existence. Allen Dulles was not shy about seeking "covert publicity" for his agency; through 1975, the Church Committee exposed the bulk of significant CIA covert operations.[3] Third, even an examination of black operations that considers only the acknowledged covert actions is useful, and contains at least the possibility of a decisive evaluation. If the record shows that covert action had a highly positive effect on American foreign affairs, then it would take a series of "hidden" or unknown covert disasters to outweigh the positive. Conversely, if the impact of the known covert actions is strongly negative, then we might ask (1) how many and what kind of "unknown" successes it would have taken to transcend these, (2) how likely it is that these occurred, and (3) how likely it is that such successes would not have reached the public record by now? In this case, if we cannot assume a large number of significant successful black ops, then the scales must weigh against covert action.

JUDGING SUCCESS AND FAILURE

To evaluate the "success" of covert action, several things must be considered. First, one must weigh both success and failure so that the balance of costs and benefits can be assessed. Second, the overall purpose served by covert action needs to be taken into account; on the whole, what did covert action contribute toward a successful end to the cold war? Third, long-term and external costs and benefits must be considered. Are there effects produced by specific operations that remain with us today? Are these to American benefit or detriment? Have there been long-term effects, too, of the mere act of widely using covert action, and in creating the organizations that carry it out?

One final difficulty in appraising the role of covert action is that of the *counterfactual* (i.e., something that did not happen). Any assessment is colored by three facts: (1) There was a lot of covert action at critical times and places during the cold war, (2) many of these programs were successful, at least in the tactical sense, and most importantly, and (3) the United States won the cold war. Is it not obvious then, that covert action played a critical, and perhaps decisive, role in that victory?

This is fundamentally the argument for covert action, and appears to place the burden of proof on those who might argue that covert action was not important in the overall scheme of things. After all, the argument goes, if Guatemala and Chile and Nicaragua had become Soviet beachheads, the United States might well have faced a real-life *Red Dawn*,[4] with Soviet and Cuban paratroopers landing in Yourtown, U.S.A. At the least, Soviet control over critical resources (e.g., Angolan oil) or geographic choke points (e.g., the Straits of Hormuz or Straits of Molucca) could have coerced the United States into allowing the Soviets to communize most of the world. The basic premise of this line of reasoning is that since covert action squashed these outposts of aggression, the Soviet invasion was forestalled, and this enabled the United States to win the cold war: QED.

It is a great leap, however, to conclude that it was the covert actions that led to or even contributed to victory. The kind of argument that claims because one thing followed another, the first event *must* have caused the second is a logical fallacy historians label *post hoc ergo propter hoc*, meaing "after this, therefore because of this."

It is a great leap because there is no simple battle to examine or decisive engagement to study; no Midway or D day or Inchon. Instead, proponents of black ops point to the countries that *would have been* lost without covert action to "save" them. The critical aspect of this claim is that it too is based on a counterfactual: What *would have* happened had not U.S. intelligence intervened in the target countries (i.e., the countries would have become Soviet clients and bases for further subversion and aggression), and what *would have* resulted in that case (each falling nation would have pushed over its neighboring domino, resulting ultimately in either World War III or a United States so hopelessly surrounded, vulnerable, and compromised it would have surrendered to Soviet occupation).

This line of reasoning overlooks a number of things. First, it assumes that the targets of the covert operations would indeed have allowed their countries to become, essentially, "owned" by the Soviet Union. This is likely a faulty assumption. There is little or no evidence that Mohammad Mosaddeq or Jacobo Arbenz or Salvador Allende or Sukarno or Gamal Abdel Nasser were Soviet puppets. The errors were in mistaking nationalism for Communism, and in driving nationalists into the arms of the Soviet Union. Second, it assumes an extraordinary level of aggression on the part of the Soviet Union that may or may not have been accurate; many prominent scholars of Soviet foreign policy have concluded that there was no innate drive for world conquest on the part of the Soviet Union. Third, it assumes that the Soviets would have gone about this "chessboard" game around the world more or less unconcerned about the U.S. nuclear arsenal; that the threat of American nuclear weapons would have eventually become too feeble to deter the Soviets from adventures that threatened critical U.S. interests.[5] Fourth, often overlooked are the costs of covert action: how these might have made the cold war more bloody; how they might have made the ensuing "peace" more difficult to manage.

To conclude, one cannot say that merely because covert action seemed to keep some countries out of the Soviet camp, that it played a necessary role in the outcome of the struggle. Rather, one must look at the operations, and evaluate *what* was contributed and *how* it was supposed to influence affairs. The burden of proof rests on neither side, but in the middle.

SUCCESS AND FAILURE: A BRIEF LEDGER

Let us examine the balance sheet for American covert action during the cold war. How successful were the major operations? What were their outcomes? How did they effect the "correlation of forces"[6] or "balance of power"? Are there effects of these operations that are with us today?

- Ukraine, 1947–??: It is unclear just how large an operation the CIA mounted to support rebellion within the boundaries of Soviet occupation. One can only imagine, however, the U.S. response to a foreign power supplying weapons to the Michigan Militia, Aryan Nations, and Posse Comitatus. Given Stalin's innate fear of America, these operations probably had little effect on Soviet attitudes toward America. The biggest cost, probably, was simply getting fifty to a hundred thousand courageous anti-Soviet Ukrainians killed (along with those of many other nationalities); this probably deprived the United States of some substantial intelligence resources during the height of the cold war.
- Iran, 1953: Overthrow of the cantankerous but nationalist (*not* Communist) Mosaddeq enabled the shah of Iran to sit on a moderately authoritarian throne for about twenty-five years. The shah served to stabilize the Persian Gulf, assisting American interests, for example, during the Dhofar rebellion in Oman. It was the 1954 coup, however, that set the stage for the eventual emergence of the revolutionary Islamic state in 1979. The ascendance of the ayatollah damaged the United States in untold ways: the loss of prestige engendered by the hostage crisis; the support for terrorism that killed more than two hundred marines in the Beirut barracks; the impetus for the Reagan administration trading arms

for hostages; serving as a catalyst or demonstration for regressive and repressive theocracies that seem to be inherently anti-American.

- Guatemala, 1954: This action replaced an emerging democracy with a revolving-door authoritarian system that evolved into one of the most murderous regimes in history, comparable to any of the Soviet-style regimes in repressing and murdering its own citizens. "Success" here turned an Argentinian physician, Ernesto Guevara, into Ché, and convinced many South and Central Americans that the United States would never permit self-determination, helping produce a generation of Latin American revolutionaries hostile to the United States.

- Tibet, 1950–1981: The CIA helped the Dalai Lama escape Chinese Communist captivity and trained hundreds of Tibetans to fight the invading Chinese. While it achieved worthy goals, the covert program was never more than a minor irritant to the Chinese. "Keeping the spirit of resistance alive" is a spiritually useful goal, but there was never any chance of liberation, and the program merely encouraged some Tibetans to take unnecessary risks with their lives. Tibet remains under the Red Chinese boot.

- Indonesia, 1957–1964: America's client, Suharto, ascended to power in a coup in 1964, almost certainly with the assistance of the CIA. Suharto emerged as yet another despot, looting his own economy, repressing his own people, perpetuating an economic system of bribery and kickback, and suppressing any possibility of economic competition or free markets.

- Congo, 1959-1960: American sponsorship of the coup that beat Patrice Lumumba to death destroyed an imperfect democracy and replaced it with the government of Joseph Mobutu, who was as repressive as any Soviet client state, looted his own country as badly as the Belgian colonialists, and stamped out any semblance of a "free market." Billions of dollars in diamond revenue have been soaked from the Congo/Zaire, with virtually none benefitting the people who live there. The CIA officer in charge of the coup became an executive of the diamond company that profited enormously by the former postman's death. Statues of Patrice Lumumba stand all over Africa as a comment on the behavior of the United States toward democracy and self-determination.

- Cuba (ZAPATA), 1961: Spectacular failure at the Bay of Pigs helped entrench Castro in Cuba; obvious and arrogant lying about U.S. involvement sacrificed American credibility—America's word was no longer good.

- Cuba (MONGOOSE), 1961–1965: Continuing efforts to sabotage the Cuban economy, assassinate Castro, and plan for another invasion convinced the Soviet Union that Cuba could only be defended with nuclear weapons, leading directly to the Cuban Missile Crisis. Even though we didn't vaporize ourselves, the chances of it happening were tremendously heightened by the activities of MONGOOSE.

- Brazil, 1961–1964: The overthrow of the Goulart regime by a CIA-backed army faction stamped out another Latin American democracy, ushering in an era of death squads that once more undermined the ability of the United States to claim that there was a real difference between the United States and Soviet Union.

- Chile, 1964–1973: Actions here replaced a democracy with a harsh authoritarian regime. There was no evidence that Allende was a Soviet puppet or likely to turn the country into an outpost for Soviet expansionism. U.S. action was largely spurred by and served corporate, rather than American, interests.

- Laos, 1957–1973: While this was a small-scale operation supporting the Hmong and Laotians, CIA involvement was reasonably successful in both holding off the Communists, both Pathet Lao and Vietnamese, and keeping the war a local, rather than regional, affair. The political decision to use the Hmong to help fight the war in Vietnam destroyed the prospects for keeping Laos out of the superpower war; slapped in the face, the Soviets and Vietnamese were forced to respond, destroying the Hmong villages and exposing the United States as a fair-weather ally.

- Vietnam, 1950–1973: United States involvement in Vietnam began with covert action dating back to the French colonial period immediately after World War II, in which heroic Air America aircrews flew in supplies to Dien Bien Phu and Ed Lansdale sought to rig elections for U.S.-backed candidates. While U.S. arrogance certainly played a role in both entering the war openly and in rosy expectations of victory, covert action in the 1950s was the first foot into the quagmire. Indeed, the "DeSoto Patrols" that resulted in the Gulf of Tonkin Incident were in part carried out as support for covert operations inserting South Vietnamese commandos (and possibly U.S. Navy SEALs) into North Vietnam as part of "Project Alpha." By establishing an American presence and interest in Vietnam, the black operators committed the prestige of the American presidency and the credibility of the U.S. government, and staked out Vietnam as a place where America would fight. Unfortunately, covert action is intended precisely to avoid this outcome. Further, the dispatch of "advisors" to the Montagnards encouraged them down a path of destruction, where they were abandoned by the United States.

- Australia, 1973–1975: The participation of CIA assets (at the least) in the ouster of Prime Minister Whitlam doesn't seem to have had any lasting effects on U.S./Australian relations, although there is a residual undercurrent of resentment on the Australian left.

- Angola, 1975–1980s: American-backed guerrillas were paid by the CIA to destroy American oil facilities, while Castro's Cuban "volunteers" defended the interests of U.S. oil companies. In the end, this "Marxist" government is happy shipping as much oil as possible to America. Commercial transactions continue unabated, while tens of thousands of Angolans (and a few CIA-hired American mercenaries) paid with their lives in essentially gratuitous violence.

- Afghanistan, 1979–1988: This is the poster child for successful covert action. While this was more proxy war than true covert action, the provision of American weapons (especially Stinger missiles) and the role of the United States in organizing international support for the mujahedin was decisive in stalemating and then defeating the Soviet army, an event that played a catalytic role in the collapse of the Soviet Union. Against this remains the costs still to be paid, including the creation of an militant and insurgent theocracy (which is no friend of the United States and allows dangerous anti-American terrorist groups to operate openly), the training of perhaps thousands of potential terrorists in modern insurgency and military techniques (some of whom are already attacking Americans), and the provision of a large arsenal of modern weaponry to these groups (including probably hundreds of Stinger missiles, some of which will almost certainly one day be turned on American airliners). On the whole, giving a good shove to the Soviet system was worth it, but we should be aware that all the bills are not yet paid.[7]

- Nicaragua, 1981–1987: Covert action against Nicaragua, and the desire to keep the contras together "body and soul," resulted in a series of illegal activities and produced a constitutional crisis of near-Watergate proportions. Ultimately, American covert action required the Sandinista government to spend more than it wanted on military affairs. The decisive activity, however, was probably the American economic war that broke the back of the Nicaraguan economy, driving Nicaraguans to vote for the American-backed candidate. The Nicaraguan economy remains a near basket case even under a "free market."

- Iran, 1980s: Approaches to Iran in the 1980s by a somewhat bizarre assortment of National Security Council personnel and hirelings (e.g., Bud MacFarlane and his Bible, Albert Hakim, Manocher Ghorbanifar) merely highlighted the divisions in the United States for the Iranian government. Even worse, the Iranians (and Islamic Jihad) successfully played the NSC amateurs for suckers, extracting thousands of weapons for a few hostages, only to turn around and snatch more (readily available) hostages off the streets. Worst of all, efforts to bypass American law, the Constitution, and presidential executive orders produced a series of programs in which numerous crimes were committed, including impeachable offenses by the president,[8] offenses that should have resulted in the removal of the DCI, efforts by the DCI to bypass his own organization precisely *because* it had become law-abiding, the payment of ransom for hostages, renting out American foreign policy to foreign governments, and establishing off-the-shelf covert organizations to perpetuate a capability to evade American law and thwart democratic processes. The domestic impact was an acute schism in popular support for American foreign policy, the final killing of bipartisan cold war policy, and the resurrection of a mini-McCarthyism that divided people into two categories: (1) Americans, and (2) those who opposed contra aid. All these dynamics combined to further erode the confidence of Americans in their government, and in the very process of governing in general.

- El Salvador/Guatemala, 1960s–1980s: Covert training of armed forces (not the School of the Americas, but the dispatch of American "advisors" to the host countries) over decades helped produce the two most murderous armies this side of Hitler's *Einsatzgruppen*. This created a lot of people in small Central American countries who hate the United States, but this didn't really seem to damage American foreign relations, since the campesinos are powerless anyway.

- Libya, 1981–1989: A CIA-backed premature uprising in 1984 helped Gadhafi identify underground political foes so he could execute them. Hard to see the gain here.

- Iraq, 1980s–1990s: Covertly arming Iraq through the 1980s in its war with Iran, the United States helped Saddam Hussein build up the armed forces that would eventually be turned against Kuwait and American troops. Once Saddam turned against U.S. interests, covert efforts to build up the Kurds were aborted by Kurdish disunity, U.S. timidity, and the hostility of other U.S. allies (especially Turkey) toward an independent Kurdistan on their borders. The Kurds were led down the garden path, only to be stomped out by Saddam's army while the United States stood by impotently. Additional efforts to foment a coup against Saddam merely funneled money to a group of Iraqi officers whose plans were mainly in their heads; those serious coup assets remaining in Iraq were exposed as a result of their cooperation with "the Accord," thereby helping Saddam purge his own government and army.

IT'S THE ECONOMY, STUPID: ONE LAST TIME

The overall outcome of covert action can be instructively assessed against three dimensions: economic effects, political effects, and contribution toward the outcome of the cold war. Let us first examine the economic consequences.

These are not too difficult to fathom. The first and simplest observation is that there were many U.S. covert operations that were undertaken at the specific request of, or in support of, specific corporations: the United Fruit Company, the Anglo-Iranian Oil Company, The International Telephone and Telegraph Company, Anaconda Copper, Templesman Mining interests, and so on. Even so, it is far too simplistic to suggest that the CIA was simply the iron fist behind these companies, for there were times (not many, admittedly) when CIA operations perversely assailed American firms (e.g., Chevron Oil in Angola), or when there seemed to be no economic interest at stake (e.g., Laos).[9] It is also too easy to point to the American covert operators or those with intelligence connections who benefited financially from their own operations, e.g., Kermit Roosevelt, Lawrence Devlin, the Dulles brothers, Bedell Smith, Richard Secord, and so on.

The larger economic conclusion is that American covert action supported American economic interests by repressing the development of free markets and economic competition in the Third World. Far too often, covert action was used to establish or prop up any Tom, Dick, or Mobutu who claimed to be anti-Communist. Inevitably, these despots enacted a basic three-pronged anti-Communist "plan":

(1) I am against the Soviets.
(2) I own everything in my country.
(3) If you disagree with #2, you are a dead man.

By supporting these tyrants, American covert action sometimes installed state-controlled economies every bit as government dominated as the Soviet Union's. Moreover, many of the black operations destroyed regimes that were economic nationalist rather than Communist. As the colonial powers withdrew or were forced out of the Third World, many of the fledgling governments attempted to regain control of their own national economic resources, e.g., diamond and copper mines, coffee and banana plantations, and so on. These resources represented the only chance for national economic development or progress, and despite decolonization, often remained in the hands of First World corporations, who extracted the mineral and agricultural wealth of the Third World with very little benefit accruing to the host country or its people. If you don't like the idea of non-Americans buying up big American companies and owning *your* job, imagine an America in which *all* the auto makers and software companies and banks and mines and utilities are owned by foreign companies, with all the profit being sucked out of the United States. That is what many of these economic nationalists were trying to overcome; that is what too many covert actions perpetuated.

For the purposes of this examination, the key consideration is this: These "kleptocracies" were made possible in large part by U.S. covert action. The deniability of covert programs allowed the United States government (and sometimes private organizations and firms) to support truly vicious regimes while publicly professing a commitment to democracy and free markets; without the deniable nature of such support ("Gee, we don't *know* how Lumumba got killed . . ."), there would have been many more political battles in the Congress and in the streets of the Shining City on a Hill.

One direct economic effect of the creation and support of these Third World dictatorships is the ongoing hemorrhage of American jobs overseas. One of the prime tenets of modern economic development theory is that investment and production in Less Developed Countries will benefit the whole world, including those in the economically advanced countries, *because the Third World workers will*

use their increasing income to purchase First World (e.g., American) goods. Thus, when
American factories move to Indonesia or Brazil, for example, American workers
should ultimately benefit. This *only* happens, however, if those Third World
workers are paid high enough wages to afford American goods, and these wages
only rise when there is a strong labor organization to force them upward. When
the government is a brutal dictatorship, though, the first ones up against the
wall are the labor organizers. No labor organization, no rising wages, no money
to buy American goods. By paying for dozens of covert actions which have
installed oppressive and economically *anticompetitive* regimes, American taxpayers have paid to send their own jobs overseas.

POLITICAL OUTCOMES OF COVERT ACTION

Since about 1942, the United States has been the most politically important
country in the world. It has been powerful enough to essentially structure, or set
up the rules for, the postwar global economy; it has been the militarily preemi-
nent superpower; it has led the world in technological innovation; it has served
as the educator for most Third World elites; and it has seen its culture diffuse
across all national boundaries.

Despite these potentially decisive attributes, the United States chose to
fight many cold war battles under cover, mostly for the reasons discussed in
chapter 2, such as the desire to not openly confront the Soviet Union and thereby
risk nuclear war. It was probably also due to the desire to not *openly* intervene in
the affairs of other nations, to avoid potential local backlash. In so doing, however, the United States, to some degree, squandered and diminished the
immense power of its political, economic, diplomatic, and cultural assets.

By carrying out covert operations at all, the United States appeared to the
world to be playing the same power politics game as the Soviets. To the Third
World, U.S. covert intervention was perceived as merely an updated manifesta-
tion of colonialism: Instead of openly "owning" Third World countries, America
simply used its transnational corporations to suck the natural and productive
resources out of the Third World. The United States had emerged from World
War II as the emancipator of the colonies, looked to by Africa, Asia, and Oceania
as the hope for political liberation and economic self-determination. Unfortunately, in its zeal to repress anything that anyone called Communist, the United
States came to symbolize the status quo. America put tyrants into power,
absolved them as "authoritarian" rather than "totalitarian"—the point being
that *our* dictators aren't as bad as *their* dictators—and told the huddled masses
yearning to be free that liberation would have to wait: The cold war was more
important. In particular, the moral authority of the United States was badly
undercut by American willingness to overthrow *democratically elected regimes*, even
when they showed no real indication of joining the Soviet orbit or of permanently seizing power. By undertaking the covert line of action, the United States

validated Soviet propaganda that claimed the United States would never allow nations to choose their own course, that America was to be feared. Even assuming the best of intentions, covert action blurred the line between the Soviets and the Americans.[10] In the words of the Hoover Commission, by learning to lie, cheat, subvert, and set aside American standards of fair play, *we made ourselves look like our enemies.*[11]

This was a pivotal sacrifice, as the United States came out of World War II with an enormous reservoir of goodwill. It is possible, even probable, that the cold war could have been even more successfully managed by using that goodwill to establish a set of international norms advantageous to the United States, in effect determining what the rules of competition would be. Instead, by playing the game with secret armies, rigged elections, trumped-up coups d'etat, paid-off antiunion head busters, student front groups, and exploding cigars, the United States stooped to a competition anyone could play. Moreover, by undertaking such widespread and numerous covert operations, the United States opened a Pandora's box of accusations; virtually any coup, assassination, guerrilla war, riot, or outbreak of the flu could be blamed on the United States. No matter how outlandish the allegation, when compared to admitted and provable U.S. black operations, it would appear reasonable. After all, the United States *did do* these things frequently, and establishing a pattern of conduct is a valid point of evidence even in American trials.

Another important outcome of the way covert operations were sometimes handled was the increased development and power of both organized crime and the drug cartels. While the Sicilian Mafia and *Unione Corse* may have eventually reemerged and prospered in any event, the decision to employ them in government operations certainly hastened their rebirth after World War II, and made them more powerful than they might otherwise have been. Moreover, U.S. intelligence connections seemed to have played a significant role in establishing and protecting the "French Connection" heroin smuggling operation that made these syndicates far richer and more powerful than they would have been had the government been their antagonist.

U.S. covert action programs also essentially established the Kuomintang (KMT) Army in the Golden Triangle, which developed into the world's largest heroin exporter; assisted the Afghan heroin trade by both ignoring it as the price of mujahedin cooperation and by establishing smuggling routes that ran in both directions; and, if not actually *encouraging* Latin American cocaine trafficking by U.S. clients and mercenaries, then at the very least set up a transport/smuggling system that ran out of and into the United States with no controls or supervision at all: "Nice group the boys chose," said Robert Owen.[12]

Another tragic consequence of covert action was the sacrifice of American responsibility to people who believed America was as good as its word. One of the reasons to stay in Vietnam, we were often told, was that by pulling out, the United States would prove itself an unreliable ally; such loss of credibility would damage our alliances and even, we were told, lead the Soviets into more reckless aggression. Given the history of U.S. covert operations, however, it would be hard to conclude that the United States was anything *but* an unreliable ally. By leading on such peoples as the Kurds, Montagnards, Hmong, Cuban exiles, Tibetans, Angolans, and many others, the U.S. government showed how ruthlessly it could play power politics, casting them overboard into the jaws of bloodthirsty regimes. Like a cagey player in a game of Diplomacy, America's word was its bond, right up until the moment it stomped on your fingers to cast you off the cliff.

Finally, covert action frequently did not remain hidden; even when successfully denied, the United States often found itself drawn into open conflicts, trying to balance credibility and nuclear destruction on the razor's edge. The entire involvement in Southeast Asia began as a series of black programs; the Cuban Missile Crisis arose in large part due to the Soviet response to ZAPATA, MONGOOSE, and a continuing U.S. plan to invade Cuba. While covert action was supposed to avoid precisely these risks, in practice it led America into confrontations that might otherwise have been avoided, had the government either not become involved at all or entered selected conflicts with a stronger hand at the beginning, perhaps deterring Soviet or Chinese "adventurism."

WINNING AND LOSING THE COLD WAR

The $64,000 question, of course, is whether the United States and the Western allies could have triumphed in the cold war without the prolific use of black programs. As a couterfactual, this is a difficult question that admits of no real proof. It is, however, a critical question, and one which we *must* attempt to answer if we are to learn anything from the cold war that we may carry into the new millennium—which will almost certainly include new cold wars.

The answer is that the United States would have been victorious in the cold war, and probably at far less cost to both America and its proxies, without most of the covert programs it engaged in. First, nuclear deterrence protected not only the continental United States, but also America's closest allies (NATO and Japan). Further, the U.S. nuclear umbrella was also effectively extended over critical countries that were hostile to the United States, such as revolutionary Iran. Second, the structural economic power of the United States and the Western capitalist system tied most of the Third World to the West in a way the Soviet system could never hope to replicate. Third, the Soviets were so heavy-handed in their domination of their own clients that (1) few countries and peoples saw them as a true "liberating" alternative to the West, and (2) contrary to the "Once a Soviet satellite, always a Soviet satellite" school of thought, some countries did indeed kick out the Soviets, e.g., Egypt, China, and Ethiopia.[13] Fourth, historical experience very early in the cold war showed that there was *not* a single monolithic Communist bloc, and that when new Communist countries emerged (e.g., North Korea, North Vietnam, Laos, Kampuchea, and Mozambique), they typically chose to serve their own interests rather than some master plan for world domination passed down from Moscow. Geographically contiguous Communist countries tended to act gratifyingly like contiguous capitalist countries, e.g., they attacked each other to redress historical insults and injuries as in China-Vietnam, and Vietnam-Kampuchea. Cuba is the only example of a Soviet client serving as a base for regional or global subversion, and it was Cuban troops who ended up defending Chevron Oil in Angola. Indeed, Angola and Yugoslavia provided examples of "Communist" states that desired both independence from the Soviets and trade and investment from the capitalist West. Fifth, the Soviet system, due to its inherent inefficiency and inflexibility, could not adapt to a changing global economy driven by technological innovation. The Soviet economy was a Potemkin village for at least a decade—and probably two— before the collapse, unable to compete in the global marketplace. Only its enormous natural endowment of oil kept it from failing years before it did; it had nothing adequate to trade for petroleum, and could only have invaded the Middle East Persian Gulf. Without computerization, the USSR could never have kept up even in defense systems; as computer technology diffused throughout the Soviet Union, the oppressive mechanism of the KGB was bound to break down. Finally, there is indeed the human spirit to consider. Could the Soviet government have gone on oppressing its own people forever, contrary to the visible examples of Europe and the Americas?

There are many reasons that the cold war ended in an American victory. Perhaps covert operations made a contribution; the most obviously important one is probably Afghanistan. Even in that case, however, it was simply the last straw that broke the back of a tottering system. Without posing highly imaginative counterfactuals (e.g., "Without the Corsican mob, France goes over to the Soviets, and, unlike Egypt, can't kick them out"), it is difficult to find a claim for covert action that outweighs the apparent damage it did to American foreign policy, the people of the Third World, and American democracy.

POSTSCRIPT: FIGHTING FIRE WITH WATER

While it is easy in hindsight to be critical of actions undertaken by those "in the trenches" in different historical times, it is important to recognize that there *was* a real enemy who would have done in the United States if possible, who *did* lie, cheat, steal, and carry out all manner of nefarious and malicious activity. What alternative was there, then, to fighting fire with fire?

One possibility might be called "fighting fire with water." Rather than fighting the Soviets at their own level (subversion, assassination, and so on), the United States might have attempted to use Soviet intervention against the USSR by (1) exposing Soviet covert actions and subversion, (2) supporting national independence movements, and (3) attempting through diplomatic, cultural, economic, and educational programs to raise the U.S./Soviet rivalry into those planes of competition where the United States had a marked advantage. This would have drawn clear moral boundaries between the United States and the Soviets, rather than blurring them, as widespread covert programs did. It would also have enabled the United States to enlist Third World populations in far greater scale, as they might have viewed the United States as less interventionist and more willing to support national self-determination. The United States *could have* placed itself on the side of anticolonialism and revolution; this was the way the tide was flowing, and was the natural philosophical road for the United States to take. Alas, it was the road not taken, and instead it was the Soviet Union that was allowed to swim downstream.

One of the keys to this strategy would have been the enhancement and exploitation of American credibility *in the sense of honesty*. Much as the integrity of the Allied governments and media were a potent weapon in the war against Hitler's Germany, so too could it have bestowed tremendous power in the war against Communism and tyranny. A credible U.S. Information Agency (USIA) and State Department could have been a powerful combination in mobilizing the people of the Third World against Soviet intervention and subversion, except for one thing: The United States was *also* intervening and subverting their governments. When the United States said that it was not involved in a fixed election or an assassination or a guerrilla war or a harbor mining, it was not remotely believable. Jack Kennedy was right when he said that one of America's great treasures was the well-known integrity of Adlai Stevenson; but enthralled by secret operations, James Bond, and a small group of courageous fighters, JFK blew it, too. The masters of covert action, through their own black programs, undercut any other alternatives; once credibility and honor are lost, they are difficult or impossible to redeem.

In the end, it was probably impossible for the United States to have adopted a policy toward covert action other than one it did. Domestic pressures from the McCarthy far Right sharply limited political and foreign policy options; the system of transnational corporations was the lens through which Third World economic and political independence was viewed; and the early, seemingly easy, success of the CIA at shaping political events made it the obvious choice. In the end, however, there were more than *three* options.

NOTES

1. Almost all of them, anyway. There have been a few motivated by more crass considerations.

2. It is important to note, however, that this is not the viewpoint of everyone, or even the majority, within the intelligence community and the CIA. There are many individuals who understand the necessity of accounting to the public and its representatives, as well as the dangers of a government that is *too* secret.

3. In fact, we probably know enough about the most successful intelligence

(spying) operations as well, although they are beyond the scope of this examination. After all, both the United States and the Soviet Union have prosecuted and punished many critical spies, such as John Walker, Chris Boyce, and Oleg Penkovsky.

4. This is the John Milius movie about a Soviet-Cuban invasion of the United States, starring Patrick Swayze and Charlie Sheen.

5. If this were the case, for example, what exactly was it that kept the Soviets out of Iran? Surely they knew that the United States military could not kick them out had they invaded.

6. This is a Soviet phrase that roughly approximates "Who is ahead?" which is different from the concept of balance of power as it is used by international relations scholars.

7. The costs are worth it in terms of reducing the risk of nuclear war. On the other side of the ledger, we must weigh the increased danger that terrorists or rogue nations will obtain (more available) former Soviet nuclear weapons and use them. Moreover, it is likely that the Soviet Union would have collapsed, anyway. Facing pressures from the West—economic competition, an arms race, increasing Western technological superiority, Western computer and communications technology that made censorship more difficult, increasingly rebellious satellite states, and even blue jeans, rock and roll, and disco—as well as internal pressures—an increasingly inefficient, repressive bureaucracy, the rise of technocrats over ideologues, population pressure from ethnic minorities and increasing ethnic nationalism, an increasingly inefficient and unadaptive economic system, and the effect of militant Islam on the Southern Crescent republics—the political economic system was a pool of gasoline waiting for a match. One of the sparks just so happened, in this instance, to be Afghanistan.

8. In the opinion of this author (and many others), these were (1) clearly impeachable offenses, (2) offenses that were clearly subversive of American democracy, and (3) far more serious than Watergate.

9. Although even in cases such as Laos, one might argue that U.S. intervention was demanded not for Laos itself, but the fear of falling dominoes that might eventually topple an American economic interest.

10. There was a real line between the Soviets and the Americans, in my opinion. The brutalities of the Soviet Union and China are far beyond anything ever conducted by the United States; the Japanese internment camps and Indian reservations, while harsh and unjust, were not Gulags (the Trail of Tears comes very close, however, although on a smaller scale). This does not, however, absolve the United States of the murderous actions of American-supported foreign regimes such as Indonesia, Guatemala, and El Salvador.

11. This was unintentional, of course, for we assumed that covert actions would indeed remain covert. This naive assumption has continually plagued American administrations since Harry Truman.

12. Owen was the courier for Oliver North's contra supply operation. He made this comment about the known drug traffickers hired by the CIA ("the boys"), North, and the contras. See Bill Moyers, *The Secret Government: The Constitution in Crisis* (Washington: Seven Locks Press, 1988), pp. 25, 87.

13. In the wake of the fall of the Soviet government, it would be interesting to study whether or not the Soviets had a "who lost China" dispute.

Chapter 19

Meet the New Boss: Covert Action and Foreign Policy in the Twenty-First Century

T he cold war always provided the rationalization for covert action: It is a dangerous world; the Constitution is not a suicide pact; the Soviets don't play by any rules, so why should we? Since the bear is no longer in the woods, what should we expect from covert action? What will happen to the long-established covert operation organizations? If you've been paying attention, the answer should be evident: more of the same.

With the collapse of the Soviet Union, the most important reason for covert action disappeared: There is no longer a need to engage in deniable political and military actions for fear of provoking the Soviets into a military confrontation and potential nuclear war. Moreover, the demise of the global Communist movement[1] means that it is no longer necessary to respond to every shift in political winds in every country: The dominoes have fallen, alright, but they turned out to be *red* ones. Every coup and insurgency need not call forth a response from Langley lest the power vacuum be filled with Red hordes. There may be "hot spots," but they won't be ignited by Moscow.

While the world looks dramatically different than it did in the pre-Gorbachev days, with precious few powerful foes of the United States, covert action will continue to serve, for good or ill, as a staple of American foreign policy. There are four reasons for this:

(1) All the old foes aren't dead and all the old issues aren't resolved.
(2) Established covert bureaucracies will survive by *finding* new roles for themselves.
(3) Covert action will continue to appeal to presidents for the same reasons it did in the past.
(4) The post–cold war "New World Order" opens up all kinds of new possibilities and targets for covert action.

ALL THE DRAGONS AREN'T SLAIN

With the collapse of the Soviet empire and the disintegration of the Soviet Union itself, the world hoped that it had seen the last of the deadly, bipolar, zero-sum ideological politics that had driven the cold war. While this has largely occurred, not every cold war foe has melted away like the Wicked Witch of the West. China is a growing power, and, while not yet a superpower, possesses the raw capacity to challenge its foes for regional domination and even Asian hegemony. Cuba remains a problem for American foreign policy, and may remain the target of covert action, depending on the ideological predilections of the occupant of the Oval Office. Iraq will require some form of American intervention in the near future, and an American president will be loathe to take the necessary steps to completely restructure the Iraqi political system (i.e., military occupation of the country); thus, covert action (coup d'etat) will be the policy of choice.

Aside from serving the ideological goals of the American state, covert operations have also been frequently employed to safeguard the interests of American corporations and the transnational capitalist system in general. While those interests might no longer be threatened by agents of the Soviet state, the continuing failure of Western-prescribed economic development policies, along with a growing gap between rich and poor nations and an increasing number of middle-income countries sliding into poverty, will give rise another generation of Third World economic nationalists who will question the wisdom of allowing their economic resources to be funneled out of their countries for pennies on the dollar. When such nationalist parties and leaders arise, they will be dealt with in the manner of Patrice Lumumba, Salvador Allende, Jacobo Arbenz, and Michael Manley: The sanctity of corporate property, no matter how it was acquired, will be ferociously defended. Because these new leaders cannot be attributed to an overt threat like Soviet subversion, they will likely be disposed of by covert operations supporting or manufacturing proxy "opposition parties" whose connection to American corporations and intelligence will be denied by the United States. The new cover story will incorporate democracy and human rights.

AGENCIES IN SEARCH OF A MISSION

There is a saying among those who study the behavior of large bureaucracies and organizations that "there is a problem for every solution." So too with covert action; having established large, expensive, and powerful covert action organizations with influential constituencies, it is virtually impossible to dismantle them; they will *find* tasks for themselves.

The dust hadn't settled from the crumbling of the Berlin Wall before national intelligence agencies were looking for new tasks and threats. Much as the intelligence (spy) branches found some (e.g., industrial espionage, terrorism), so, too, the covert action organizations will find new and "vital" assignments to keep themselves alive. While there may be some "downsizing," this will be a temporary blip. As noted above, some threats remain, and many new threats have evolved out of the power vacuum left by the end of the U.S./Soviet rivalry. As the black operators "found" their own missions and targets during the cold war, so too will they continue to "identify" circumstances that can "only" be remedied by covert operations.

In addition to new threats, there are two other reasons that will be put forth to maintain a capable (and large and generously supported) covert action agency. First, proponents will say, it might not be a bad idea to keep the skills and expertise of black operations alive. While *this* cold war is over, there is no guarantee that there will not be future cold wars, or hot wars, where the skills of the black operators will again be vital. The United States does not want to get caught in the same situation it was before World War II, having to learn covert operations skills from someone else because America's skills had been allowed to atrophy.

Second, a very good reason to maintain a modest covert operations capability is simply to keep the most dangerous black operators "in the fold." This is not to suggest that every paramilitary spook is a loose cannon or mercenary; to the contrary, most are patriotic, order-obeying officers. There are some operators, however, who *will* continue to practice their craft, whether within the American intelligence system or outside it. Having witnessed the results of Soviet nuclear weapons engineers renting themselves out to the highest bidder, it is better to keep American-trained black operators working *for* us.

THE CONTINUING APPEAL OF BLACK OPERATIONS

As discussed in chapter 3, covert operations are enormously appealing to decision makers, and that will not change in the future. Presidents will continue to hear the lyrics of the black ops siren song: cheap, deniable, easy to get out of if things go wrong. With little foreign policy experience or historical knowledge, chief executives and cabinet members will dip a toe into the covert action pool, easing into secret wars and rigged elections and the odd coup here and there, little understanding the dangerous undertow lying a step beyond. The powerful attraction of these operations will be exacerbated by the end of the cold war. While there was a Russian bear to focus on, the world seemed reasonably simple: oppose the Soviets. In the new world, things are not so clear, and covert action seems to promise simple, direct solutions to complex problems.

Domestic political considerations, too, will continue to encourage covert action. Should American politics remain as polarized as it is at the end of the twentieth century, there will remain powerful incentives for presidents to conduct their own "black" foreign policies to avoid the incessant back biting and second-guessing by Congress. Moreover, Americans will be increasingly unwilling to commit their armed forces to "another Somalia" or "another Bosnia." In this case, the only option may seem to be covert action.

COVERT ACTION AND NEW WORLD ORDERS

The most powerful arguments for continuing and widespread covert operations will be the plethora of "new" international threats and issues that emerge from the ferment of post–cold war uncertainty. Highest on this list will be nuclear, biological, and chemical threats—from either "rogue" states or terrorist organizations—and terrorism in general.

Iraq remains a concern because of its potential for military aggression against important oil-producing countries, and because of it ongoing chemical and biological weapons programs.[2] Saddam Hussein will remain a serious threat to the United States as long as he remains in power. Any number of inspections and cruise missile strikes will only delay the day of reckoning, and the United States, having withdrawn its offensive ground capability and allowed its Gulf War coalition to dissolve, will be unwilling to build up the armed forces and unable to establish the political support necessary to go back in and finish the job. Inspections and embargoes are only short term methods to "manage" the increasing peril; if the threat of Iraqi terrorism and biological holocaust against America is to be stamped out, covert action seems to be the apt tool. This is unlikely to result in outright assassination, as it is not only against the law, but Saddam is a very difficult target; American black ops will focus on the difficult task of assembling a junta to overthrow the dictator—or, to turn around a popular aphorism, just because they're out to get you doesn't mean you're not paranoid. Two other "rogue states" will also likely be targets for ongoing covert action, due to their continuing nuclear, chemical, or biological programs: Libya and North Korea. In each case, the grip of the leadership is strong enough as to make outright overthrow difficult if not impossible, and black operations will be directed at eliminating specific targets related to the nuclear/biological/chemical threat: destroying production facilities, disrupting smuggling operations, and perhaps even assassinating the technicians, engineers, and scientists involved in the "research."

Nonstate actors, such as irredentist groups, separatists, and terrorist organizations, like the one commanded by Osama bin Laden, may also try to create or purchase chemical, biological, or nuclear weapons. Many of these organizations are based in countries hostile to the United States (e.g., the Sudan, Afghanistan), and cannot be apprehended or prosecuted by standard means (e.g., arrest and extradition). Moreover, "safe" military actions, e.g., fifty cruise missiles blasting apart mud huts, has so far proven unable to deter or disrupt major terrorist organizations. Eventually, the United States may settle on establishing its own insurgents within some of these relatively lawless areas; this is the only way to "take the war to the terrorists" short of direct U.S. special operations.[3] Further, some countries, like a few of the former Soviet Republics with available nuclear weapons, prefer not to cooperate with or allow American law enforcement personnel to operate within their borders. It is likely that there are already teams of

American covert operators working inside these states without the knowledge or sanction of the host governments, and in general, these teams must work covertly and deniably.

Another prominent target for covert action will be terrorist organizations, even those who are not nuclear/biological/chemical threats. Covert action in this area will probably not be so deniable, because American presidents will want to be seen *doing something* about terrorism. Terrorist groups are nebulous targets by nature, having no specific location, capital, or easily identifiable members; they are extremely difficult to identify and apprehend. When an outrage occurs, American leaders will need to take public retribution, and "overt" covert action fits the bill.

Moreover, even if terrorist leaders can be identified and located, apprehending them can be another thing entirely. Many governments hesitate to arrest and extradite even notorious and obvious terrorists, for fear that (1) their own people will be kidnapped and held hostage for the terrorist's release, or (2) their own people and country will be targeted by terrorists in revenge. This was the unspoken rationale when France released terrorist Abu Nidal. It is very unlikely that the United States will ever create a "Wrath of God" unit like Israel used to kill the Munich Massacre terrorists, but it is possible that there may be a covert, *very* deniable American unit used to kidnap terrorists and "mysteriously" deliver them across a border and into the hands of American law enforcement in a *moonlight extradition*. These activities will have to be extremely well covered, as they may be conducted in countries with which the United States wants to maintain good relations.[4]

The desire to deal decisively with drug production and drug cartels will also lead to continuing support for covert action. Generally, the United States cannot use overt military intervention to wipe out drug producers, as this would cause wars with the "host" countries. Moreover, even small-scale military operations are liable to be viewed with hostility by the governments of the countries from which drugs are exported as a violation of national sovereignty ("What?! You don't think we can handle our own problems?"), and might even cause some governments to fall. Such actions could even result in the host government army defending their national honor by fighting against the U.S. forces; in essence, the United States could force them into an alliance with the drug dealers. Finally, an overt operation into a drug enclave is bound to take some casualties, whether from small arms, mines, antiaircraft missiles, mines, or boobytraps. Thus, any kind of close interdiction or "search and destroy" operations will have to be done covertly. Another option that the United States may eventually settle on is simply hiring foreign armies or mercenaries to fight the drug cartels on their own turf, although there will be not only the danger of exposure, but also that the U.S. hirelings will simply take over the drug production and become a bigger, better cartel, as happened with the KMT Army in the Golden Triangle.

Related to the problems of retribution and deterrence of terrorists, rogue states, and drug cartels is the ever more apparent problem that cruise missile attacks and bombing raids are not especially effective against "soft targets" like terrorist leaders and drug lords. Many of these organizations can only be destroyed by cutting off the head, and the only certain way to do that is through a covert special operation, with deniable Special Forces personnel on the ground, shooting the bad guys. Once the United States has bombed the hell out of enough mud huts, this will become apparent.

The relative international disorder that has emerged from the end of the cold war and the dismantling of the Soviet empire also provides many opportunities for covert operations: Aside from nuclear weapons to retrieve, there will be elections to influence, pro-American political parties and leaders to sustain or buy, resurgent Communists to subvert, economic nationalists to stamp out, and so forth. Further, as peacekeeping and peacemaking operations become more common for American forces, covert actions will be the cutting edge, employed to protect the peacekeeping forces. For example, a deniable covert operation might be used to destroy an insurgent arms depot, or to preemptively assault and break up an insurgent unit preparing to attack American peacekeepers. By allowing the overt American units to skirt open combat or avoid the appearance of "taking sides," covert operations can contribute to the peacekeeping mission.

CONCLUSIONS

Covert action is here to stay. Most of the important justifications for it during the cold war are gone, but it is so ingrained in American intelligence, the military, and the political elite that, despite a track record of limited success and catastrophic failure, it will remain a weapon of choice.

NOTES

1. Unless, like the John Birch Society, you believe this is all a ploy to get America to let its guard down; or unless, like those in the self-styled "patriot" movement, you believe that America is *already* controlled by totalitarian forces.

2. See "CIA: Iraq Could Quickly Revive Arsenals," *USA Today*, 10 November 1998, p. 1.

3. I am not saying this is a good or bad idea. Rather, it is an idea that will be considered (if it hasn't already), and one that will more likely than not be adopted.

4. There may also be some cases, however, where the foreign government is quite happy to be rid of the terrorist without having to take responsibility for the arrest.

Chapter 20

Same as the Old Boss:
The Power of Covert Institutions
and the End of the Cold War

In light of historical experience, what can we say about covert action? Sadly, for all the courage, imagination, blood, sweat, and tears poured into black operations, the record is not very good. It is difficult to argue that they had much of an impact on the outcome of the cold war, or even that they substantially assisted the countries they were directed toward. Instead, they produced numerous fiascoes; alliances full of blackmail potential with the Mafia and drug cartels; sordid uncontrolled assassination plots; encouragement and abandonment of indigenous peoples who trusted the United States; the overthrow of several democratic governments (some of whom have not yet recovered, e.g., Guatemala); outrageous intervention in the political affairs of close allies (e.g., Australia); the spread of modern military technology into insurgent and terrorist hands; the facilitation of the American drug epidemic, and therefore the crime epidemic; the renting out of American foreign policy to corporations and foreign governments; the sacrifice of American credibility and honor; attempts to create private off-the-books covert action organizations to circumvent constitutional and governmental control; despotic intrusions into the lives of law-abiding American citizens; outrageous violations of Americans in mind-control experiments; and powerful support for tyrants around the world.

This is not a call for the abolition of the CIA. In its intelligence capacity, the CIA plays a critical role in American security. Rather, it is simply the recognition that recurring abuses of power are the cost of doing covert business. Due to the inherent nature of covert organizations, the concept of accountability will remain chimerical, based on the nature of the men and women who make up the agency. Law-abiding CIA operators will obey the law; lawless operators, in the belief that the ends justify the means, will evade or scornfully break any laws or rules they choose to, and there isn't very much we can do about it.

The existence of these organizations inherently diminishes democracy, thereby producing a government of men and not of laws. Because of its overpowering appeal, however, covert action will indeed continue, serving the same masters it always has: expedience and power.

Spookspeak:
A Glossary of Fun and Useful Terms

Agent: A person who acts in the interest of an intelligence organization. Professionals never refer to themselves or the agents they control as "spies." See also *opposition, spooks*.

Agent of influence: A politically powerful person who serves the interest of a foreign country, often publicly, as many U.S. lobbyists; sometimes secretly, e.g., Manuel Noriega and shah of Iran when they were on the CIA payroll. These differ from a standard *agent* in that agents of influence can actually affect or alter the policies of the government, corporation, or organization they hold office in.

Agent provocateur: An agent who infiltrates an opposition organization and attempts to induce members to do illegal or stupid things, with the intent to embarrass the organization, make it look criminal, or get the members in trouble. Agents provocateur may also try to sow dissension within an organization, attempting to pit members against each other to destroy the group. See *COINTELPRO*.

Agitprop: *Agitation propaganda*; propaganda intended to create unrest in another country. Soviet origin.

Asset: An agent or organization who works for or is controlled by an intelligence agency.

Backstopped (identity): When a cover identity or story can be verified by apparently independent people, organizations, and documents. If an agent says he was employed by "Smith and Jones Co." and someone can call the phone number and talk to "Mr. Smith" who confirms the employment, the identity is backstopped. Backstopping is critical to successful *cover*, especially *deep cover*. See *cover*.

A better world: Where you go when an intelligence organization kills you. Usage: "We sent him to a better world." Mossad origin.

Black-bag job: To illegally break into a home or office. Sometimes used as a verb, as in "We black-bagged the office," or even shorter, "We bagged the bedroom." Performed to find information, install listening devices, or sometimes to plant incriminating evidence to frame someone, either for prosecution or for-blackmail. See *COINTELPRO*.

Black operations, black ops: Covert or clandestine operations. Also referred to as *going black* or *operating in the black*.

Black propaganda: See *propaganda*.

Blowback: Negative consequences of an operation, especially when it has failed. Examples include the pubic trial of Francis Gary Powers, the Iran-Contra hearing, and the sinking of the British ship *Alfhelm* by American agents during PB/SUCCESS. Within intelligence organizations, often refers to the organizational and personal consequences to those who fail spectacularly, as in the firings of Allen Dulles and Richard Bissell after the Bay of Pigs.

Blown: When a cover story has been exposed or proven false.

Bona fides: Proof that someone is who he says he is; credentials. Alternately, proof that someone can do what he claims he can do. For example, if a foreign agent claims to represent a group of "moderates" in revolutionary Iran, we might ask him to establish his bona fides.

CIA: Insiders never say *"the* CIA," but simply "CIA," as in "This is Mr. Smith from CIA."

Clandestine op: An action or program in which the action itself is hidden and ideally unknown. For example, an agent breaking into an embassy safe to photograph the codebooks is performing a clandestine act (i.e., there is no conceivable cover that could innocently explain this activity). In contrast, an assassination might be a covert action (everyone knows it happened, they just don't know for sure who did it). See *covert action*.

Closure (mission closure): Leaving no loose ends that can be traced back to the country that initiated a covert action. When *operators* undertake a mission with complete closure, they can carry nothing that can be traced back to their own country or true employer. They will carry foreign weapons, wear foreign clothes, eat native food, and at the extremes may even have dental work replaced (in particular, American dental work is very distinctive). Complete closure also requires that no wounded be left behind; if you can't keep up, you're dead, and your body will be destroyed. See *sterile*.

COINTELPRO: *COunter INTELligence PROgram*; long-running FBI program to spy on, intimidate, and blackmail U.S. citizens and organizations (virtually all of them engaged in constitutionally protected activities), including Martin Luther King Jr., the Southern Christian Leadership Conference, Vietnam Veterans Against the War, the Black Panthers, and so on. Activities under COIN-TELPRO included *thousands* of black-bag jobs on Americans (hey, judges are busy guys—why bother them for a little ol' search warrant?), blackmail, planting and forging "evidence," and trying to coerce Martin Luther King into suicide.

Company, the: Euphemism for CIA.

Compartmentalization: Making sure that the various groups and individuals in an operation or intelligence organization have no contact with or knowledge of each other; thus, if one agent or team is *blown* or captured, they can only reveal to the opposition information about their part of the operation or organization. See *need to know*.

Contract agent: An agent who is not a formal member of an intelligence organization, but is simply a paid employee on a temporary contract. Within *the Company*, formal CIA agents are "officers." However, to provide deniability, sometimes CIA officers are "discharged" or "retired," then hired back on as contract agents.

Cover: A fictional identity or story ascribed to an agent or organization to hide their true identity, purpose, and supporters, and initiators. A good cover story is what makes covert actions deniable. Corollaries to the concept include:

Organizational cover: A cover story based on an agent being a member or employee of an organization, e.g., "I'm a reporter for the Toledo Clarion," or "We're a branch office of Zenith Technical Services." Generally, CIA uses real organizations and corporations for such cover, sometimes letting a corporate officer in on the secret so that there's no internal ruckus when the "employee" doesn't show up for work. This is by far the most common kind of cover in current intelligence operations.

Light cover: A quick-and-dirty cover story that won't hold up if carefully challenged. This ranges from making up a false name on the spot to using a business card you just printed up to providing a false driver's license and a phony employee ID card. Used when dealing with individuals and organizations that won't ask too many questions and that you'll only have to deal with once, or when you have to make up a cover on the spot. Remember when "Rockford" used to print up business cards in his car? That's light cover.

Deep cover: Extensive cover story, carefully prepared and *backstopped*. Used when the cover has to hold up to the media, foreign governments, drug lords, and perhaps even hostile intelligence agencies. Very expensive and time consuming, since it generally involves obtaining real identification documents (or *very* good forgeries), opening real offices and real corporations, establishing real acquaintances and friends, and so forth. For an agent, deep cover could involve living in a foreign country for years "undercover"; for an operation, probably involves creating numerous front corporations or organizations to muddy the waters (as happened in Iran-Contra).

Cover organization: An organization (business, media, political, social) created by an intelligence agency to provide cover; an organization that looks *legitimate* but the people in it really do covert operations. Examples include Permindex, Zenith Technical Services, Hortalez and Co., the Dodge Corporation, and Southern Air Transport. See *front organization*.

Covert Action: An action or program to alter the policies or personnel of government, undertaken in such a way that the true initiators and perpetrators of the action are disguised, or at the very worst, cannot be proven.

Cowboy: (1) An *operator* or *agent* who exceeds his authority, disobeys direct orders, gets out of control, or initiates serious covert actions on his own; (2) A private operator who undertakes covert action on his own, without the sanction of an intelligence agency. See *going private*.

Cutout: An intermediary agent, usually *witting*, used to ensure that agents in an operation do not come into direct contact with each other. Suppose, for example, that Allen gives the secret missile plans to Bob, who passes them on to Chuck. Bob is simply the courier, and Allen (the source) never knows the true end recipient of his intelligence. In covert action, cutouts are intermediary organizations and corporations commonly used to hide sources of money, supplies, and equipment. These are typically temporary organizations with names like "World League of Anti-Bolsheviks" or a corporation that is the subsidiary of a subsidiary, and so on down the line. Threatened with exposure, a covert action network simply closes down the intermediate corporations, and investigators hit a dead end. For the Iran-Contra conspirators, the appropriately named "Dodge Corporation" served as a cutout to launder money.

Delaware Corporations: See *proprietary company*.

Demoralization (operation): A program or operation that attempts to undermine the will or morale of an opposing country or force. This is usually accomplished by providing or broadcasting information that portrays the opponent's leaders as corrupt or inept and their cause as hopeless. Often tied to *black propaganda*. In OPERATION PB/SUCCESS against Guatemala, rebel aircraft didn't have real bombs, so they dropped Coke bottles, which *sounded* like bombs, thus demoralizing the people and the army. Ed Lansdale's "Filipino Vampire" operation is another example.

Destabilization: A program to create circumstances under which a coup d'etat, revolt, or uprising will occur. Generally involves programs to destroy a country's economy ("Make the economy scream," said Nixon to Helms) and clandestine/covert support for local opposition forces. Sometimes includes public promises to make the economy better if a regime change occurs. First used referring to Chile (1970s); other examples include Cuba (1961–present) and Nicaragua (1980s).

Disinformation: False information used to make the enemy look bad. Examples include: "AIDS is a CIA experiment" (Soviet origin, 1980s); wartime movies; "They're dragging babies out of incubators!" Another purpose is to fool the enemy into believing something that isn't true. This kind of disinformation is often "leaked" to the opponent by devious means, such as double agents (false traitors) or "captured" documents. See *propaganda, black*.

Disposal: Not as cold-blooded as it sounds, since it doesn't refer to killing people (usually). The disposal problem is what to do with an agent or group that you no longer need. With ordinary agents, it's a problem because they may not want to be "fired," and they might know a lot of secrets (national security or simply embarrassing). In a *covert action*, it's hard to simply "lay off" a guerrilla movement without making it look like you're simply abandoning them (which you are): examples include the Hmong (Laos), the Kurds (Iran, Iraq, Turkey). Even if the covert action has not begun, if you've merely trained but not deployed a covert fighting force, disposal becomes a problem. One of the reasons President Kennedy went ahead with the Bay of Pigs was that there seemed to be no practical way to simply disband the Cuban exile brigade without having them spread the word that they were ready but Kennedy wouldn't stand up to the Commies.

Enemy: See *opposition*.

Executive action: CIA euphemism for assassination. Also refers to the capability to perform assassinations (i.e., off-the-shelf).

Family Jewels: a compendium of unconstitutional, illegal, and immoral activities performed by the CIA during the '50s, '60s and '70s. Compiled under DCI James Schlesinger (he sent out a memo ordering all CIA employees to report any CIA operation they knew of that might have been illegal); revealed to Congress and the public by DCI William Colby (many in the CIA have never forgiven him for this). The *Family Jewels* reports on CIA activities regarding assassination of foreign leaders, domestic spying and political action, and mind-control experiments.

Farm, the: Camp Peary, Virginia. CIA summer camp where campers learn swift and silent killing, breaking and entering, lock picking, safe cracking, surveillance techniques, forgery, and so on. Go to Williamsburg, drive around until you see forested areas along the road, fenced with chain-link and barbed-wire, with white and blue "U.S. Government—No Trespassing" signs. That's it. See *tradecraft*.

Front organization: An organization created by an intelligence agency in which few if any members know of the intelligence sponsorship, such as the World Assembly for Youth, the Congress for Cultural Freedom, and the National Students Association. In contrast, in a *cover organization*, members know that they're involved in an intelligence operation, who really pays the bills, and so on. (The line between cover and front organizations is often blurry in real life).

"Going private": Taking the skills, contacts, and equipment you have acquired in government service and (1) selling them on the open market, or (2) using them to pursue your own private foreign policy.

Graymail: To protect oneself from prosecution by threatening to reveal classified (or simply embarrassing) information against the government. Often, *operators* or *cowboys* who have performed illegal or unconstitutional acts, or acts against U.S. interest, will claim that their defense rests on classified information; that they cannot get a fair trial without revealing secrets; and that therefore the charges should be dismissed. Often they are. Examples include Oliver North, Claire George, Johnny Roselli, numerous drug dealers, and a slew of S&L crooks.

Gray propaganda: See *propaganda*.

Haunted: Anyplace crawling with spooks. See *spook*.

Indian Country: Where the bad guys live or an area they control; dangerous territory.

Jedburghs: During World War II, special three-person teams were parachuted into France to coordinate activities of the French resistance. This was a joint SOE-OSS-Free French program, and teams generally consisted of an Englishman, an American, and a Frenchman. These teams were known as Jedburghs after area they trained in.

King George's cavalry: Money. When all else fails, buy 'em. . . . Obviously, British origin.

Knuckledragger: Generally derogatory name for people who do the violent work in a covert operation. Sometimes refers to simple thugs, or more often to *Special Forces* types who are highly skilled in violence. Named after the characteristic of gorillas; thus, often considered by State Department types as brawn without brain.

Heavy squad: A bunch of *knuckledraggers*. Soviet usage.

Intelligence: In American terminology, evaluated information; i.e., information that has been judged as to credibility, the reliability of the source, and verified and cross-checked as much as possible.

Legitimate: True information or a true background (as opposed to a cover); also, an individual or organization not involved in intelligence ("Delta Airlines is legitimate"). Compare to *notional*.

Measles, to get the: To put a member of the opposition out of commission temporarily. Used when an assassination is too risky or not appropriate. For example, to arrange an auto accident (typically Soviet); have one beaten in a "robbery"; perhaps actually inoculate him with an illness. For example, if you need to get a shipment of "farm implements" through customs, and the number-two man is on your payroll, you might arrange for his supervisor to "get the measles" that week.

Mighty Wurlitzer: The CIA propaganda machinery and the world press which pick up and either unwittingly or wittingly rebroadcast propaganda. See *playback*.

Moonlight extradition: Kidnapping. Generally performed on individuals located in countries with which the United States has no extradition treaty.

Morale ops: See *demoralization*.

Need to know: A philosophy of intelligence organizations that prevents leaking or spying by giving to individuals members only the information they need to carry out their duties and activities. If you don't need to know it, you won't be told. See *compartmentalization*.

Neutralize: To kill someone; occasionally, to make him less effective or remove him from a position of power without killing. Generally, professionals understand that neutralize means "kill," although they'll seldom admit this, relying instead on the second definition whenever they are exposed advocating neutralization in, say, a manual they've written for some insurgent group. One example of neutralization short of lethal was the CIA plan to make Castro's beard fall out. See *a better world*, *on vacation*, and *measles*.

Notional (identity): False identities employed in a covert action, e.g., individuals, organizations, and identities that are made up. If CIA operator Bob creates a false company called, say, Universal Export, fills its bank account with U.S. government money, and then sends the money on to the guerrillas in Kurdistan, Universal Export is a notional corporation. Compare with *legitimate*.

Office of Strategic Services (OSS): Freewheeling and highly successful forerunner of the CIA, and training ground for many of the covert "buccaneers." Created by the legendary Wild Bill Donovan.

On vacation, send someone: To put someone temporarily out of commission, e.g., "The Minister of Defense needs a vacation. . . ." This can be performed by temporary kidnapping, a reasonably severe beating, drugging the target to make him ill for a few days, and so on. See *measles*.

Operator: A complimentary term for a slick or highly effective intelligence officer or agent (i.e., one who gets the job done). Also often used to describe outstanding snake eaters. Sometimes similar to *cowboy*.

Opposition: What intelligence professional call those on the other side—the opposition is never called "the enemy."

Plausible denial: What you have when no one can prove that you initiated or supported a covert action. Essentially two levels; the best when your *cover* is so good that few or none suspect your responsibility; less good is when your involvement is suspected or known, but simply can't be proven. Plausible denial is the key concept in covert action.

Playback: When *gray* or *black propaganda* disseminated by an *asset* is picked up and portrayed as fact by the *legitimate* press. The epitome of skill in propaganda ops, and a potentially serious problem for democratic societies.

Propaganda: Information (false or true) intended to influence someone. Comes in three basic flavors: *white*, in which the true source is known (example: Voice of America, or a public statement by the president); *gray*, in which the true source is concealed, usually by passing it out through an "independent" or foreign source; and *black*, in which the source is supposed to be the opposition (to make them look bad and sow dissension), e.g., to "discover" a list of people to be shot if the revolution succeeds in order to undermine the revolutionary leadership.

Proprietary company: A corporation that looks like a *legitimate* business enterprise but is in fact owned and operated by an intelligence agency, e.g., Air America. CIA proprietaries are theoretically not supposed to turn a profit or compete with legitimate business. Also formerly called *Delaware Corporations*, because so many were chartered there due to the state's lenient regulations.

Provocation: An act that is commonly understood as justification for retaliation against an enemy. Sometimes an event designed to look like enemy action which you actually perform yourself, to justify your own actions.

Provocateur: See *agent provocateur*.

Psyops: *PSYchological OPerationS*; operations aimed at influencing what a leader, organization, or people are thinking. See *demoralization*.

Ring the gong: Raise a ruckus by claiming that some earthshaking event is about to happen. Doing this in error is the CIA equivalent of crying "wolf!"

Sheep-dipping: Establishing a *cover* for an *agent* or organization by creating events and having them behave in ways that fit the cover: visiting the right places, reading the right books, going to meetings, and so on. Often used to provide cover for U.S. military or CIA personnel who "retire" or are "discharged," then begin working for a *cover organization* (all the while retaining government seniority and rank). The idea is to use them on *operations*, but the government can claim they're acting on their own. Often, it's difficult to distinguish between a sheep-dipped operator and a *cowboy*.

Snake eaters: From a particularly enjoyable survival technique taught to these units. See *Special Forces*.

Special Forces: Highly skilled soldiers trained in special techniques like infiltration and stealth, hand-to-hand combat, survival, diving, demolitions and explosives, special weapons, parachuting, and intelligence; includes SEALs,

Green Berets (formally called Special Forces), U.S. Marine Force Recon, British Special Air Service (SAS) and Special Boat Section (SBS), Soviet *Spetznaz*.

Special Operations Executive (SOE): World War II British equivalent of *OSS*. Highly successful espionage and sabotage organization, which led to widespread belief in the effectiveness of *special ops* and *covert action*.

Special ops: Small-scale commando-type activities, usually sending a small group of highly skilled *snake eaters* against a target of high strategic value, often behind enemy lines. Examples include the raid on the Son Tay POW camp in North Vietnam (1970), the attempted hostage rescue from Iran (1980), and the fictional *Guns of Navarone*.

Spook: An intelligence *agent*. The term applies to both those engaged in government work as well as private operators.

Stay behind (nets): *Agents* and small organizations intended to stay in place after an enemy has captured their area, to provide a ready-made spy/sabotage network. Throughout the cold war, such networks were prepared in NATO countries for the event of a Soviet invasion, as part of OPERATION RED SOX/RED CAP.

Sterile: Equipment and people that are not traceable if they are captured. In a *covert operation*, one ideally uses foreign-made equipment captured from the enemy or purchased on the open market by a *cover organization* which conveniently goes out of business without a forwarding address right after the transaction. For example, when the U.S. began supporting the Afghan mujahedin in 1979, American agents purchased Egyptian-made AK-47s to send to them; thus, the United States maintained *plausible deniability*. See also *closure*.

Termination: Euphemism for killing someone. Real life intelligence professionals have used this one. No one *ever* says "Terminate with extreme prejudice"—it's from spy novels.

Tradecraft: The skills necessary to be a *covert operator* or an *agent*, including surveillance/countersurveillance, secret meetings, using codes and ciphers, breaking and entering, money laundering, bribery, working undercover, and so on.

Unwitting/witting: When a individual knows they're part of an intelligence operation, they are said to be witting participants. Unwitting participants are people used in an operation without their knowledge, e.g., a courier paid to deliver an envelope, or an office secretary who thinks the shipment really is "machine parts."

Wet squad: An assassination team. Named due to the spilling of blood. Soviet usage (they also call assassination "wet work").

White Propaganda: See *propaganda*.

Who, me?: A chemical used in *psyops*; secretly apply a little to someone's clothing and it smells like they've had an "accident."

Wrath of God: Israeli hit squad that seeks out and kills terrorists. Very successful killing the men responsible for the Munich Massacre, until they killed the wrong guy (a Swede—oops). According to the Israeli government, no longer active.

Bibliography

"Afghanistan's Gold." *The Middle East* (September 1997).

Agee, Philip. *Inside the Company: CIA Diary*. New York: Bantam Books, 1975.

Asprey, Robert. *War in the Shadows: The Guerrilla in History*. Garden City, N.Y.: Doubleday, 1975.

Bakeless, John. *Turncoats, Traitors, and Heroes*. New York: J. B. Lippincott, 1959.

Bernays, Edward. *Propaganda*. New York: Horace Liveright, 1928.

Bissell, Richard M. "Reflections on the Bay of Pigs: Book Review of Operation Zapata." *Strategic Review* 12, no. 1 (1984).

Blum, William. *The Forgotten CIA*. London: Zed, 1986.

———. *Killing Hope: U.S. Military and CIA Interventions Since World War II*. Monroe, Maine: Common Courage Press, 1995.

Boorstein, Edward. *Allende's Chile: An Insider's View*. New York: International Publishers, 1977.

Braden, Tom. "I'm Glad the CIA is 'Immoral'." *Saturday Evening Post*, 20 May 1967.

Brewton, Pete. *The Mafia, CIA, and George Bush: The Untold Story of America's Greatest Financial Debacle*. New York: S. P. I. Books, 1992.

Campbell, Rodney. *The Luciano Project: The Secret Wartime Collaboration of the Mafia and the U.S. Navy*. New York: McGraw-Hill, 1977.

Casey, William. *The Secret War Against Hitler*. Washington: Regnery Gateway, 1980.

Center for National Security Studies. *Operation Chaos*. Washington: Government Printing Office, 1976.

"CIA: Iraq Could Quickly Revive Arsenals. *USA Today*, 10 November 1998.

CIA—The Pike Report. Nottingham, U.K.: Spokesman Books, 1977.

Cline, Ray. *Secrets, Spies, and Scholars*. Washington: Acropolis Books, 1976.

Colby, William, and Peter Forbath. *Honorable Men: My Life in the CIA*. New York: Simon and Schuster, 1978.

Combs, Jerald. *A History of American Foreign Policy*. New York: Alfred A. Knopf, 1986.

Constantine, Thomas. "The Threat of Heroin to the United States." Testimony before the House Committee on Government Reform and Oversight, Subcommittee on National Security, International Affairs, and Criminal Justice, 19 September 1996.

Coors, Joseph. Testimony at Joint Hearings before the House Select Committee to Inves-

tigate Covert Arms Transactions with Iran and the Senate Select Committee on
Secret Military Assistance to Iran and the Nicaragua Opposition. Vol. 100-3. Washington: Government Printing Office, 1987.

Copeland, Miles. *The Game of Nations.* New York: Simon and Schuster, 1969.

Cusack, John T. "Turkey Lifts the Poppy Ban." *Drug Enforcement* (fall 1974): 3.

Draper, Theodore. *A Very Thin Line: The Iran-Contra Affairs.* New York: Simon and
Schuster, 1991.

Dulles, Allen. "Response to the Bay of Pigs." Allen Dulles Papers. Seely G. Mudd
Library, Princeton, N.J.

Dulles, John Foster. "The Evolution of Foreign Policy." *Department of State Bulletin,* 25
January 1954.

Emery, Fred. *Watergate: The Corruption of American Politics and the Fall of Richard Nixon.*
New York: Random House, 1994.

Ervin, Sam. *The Whole Truth: The Watergate Conspiracy.* New York: Random House, 1980.

Ferguson, Gregor. *Coup d'Etat: A Practical Manual.* Dorset, U.K.: Arms and Armour
Press, 1987.

Ford, Franklin. *Political Murder: From Tyrannicide to Terrorism.* Cambridge: Harvard University, 1995

Foreign Relations of the United States, Vietnam, V.III. Washington: U.S. Government
Printing Office.

Friedman, Alan. *Spider's Web: The Secret History of How the White House Secretly Armed Iraq.*
New York: Bantam Books, 1993.

Gosch, Marvin, and Richard Hammer. *The Last Testament of Lucky Luciano.* New York:
Dell, 1981.

Goulden, Joseph. *The Death Merchant.* New York: Simon and Schuster, 1984.

Gurr, Ted Robert, ed. *Handbook of Conflict.* New York: Free Press, 1980.

Halperin, Morton, Jerry Berman, Robert Borosage, and Christine Marwick. *The Lawless
State: The Crimes of U.S. Intelligence Agencies.* New York: Penguin, 1976.

Hamilton-Merritt, Jane. *Tragic Mountains: The Hmong, the Americans, and the Secret Wars
for Laos, 1942–1992.* Bloomington: Indiana University, 1993.

Hersh, Burton. *The Old Boys: The American Elite and the Origins of the CIA.* New York:
Charles Scribner's Sons, 1992.

Hersh, Seymour. *The Dark Side of Camelot.* Boston: Little, Brown & Co., 1997.

Hickey, Gerald Cannon. *Free in the Forest: Ethnohistory of the Vietnamese Central Highlands,
1954–1976.* New Haven: Yale University, 1982.

Hinckle, Warren, and William Turner. *Deadly Secrets: The CIA-Mafia War Against Castro
and the Assassination of J.F.K.* New York: Thunder's Mouth Press, 1992.

Hoover, J. Edgar. *Masters of Deceit: The Story of Communism in American and How to Fight
It.* New York: Henry Holt and Co., 1958.

Hunt, E. Howard. *Give Us This Day.* New York: Arlington House, 1973.

———. *Undercover: Memoirs of an American Secret Agent.* New York: Berkley Pub., 1974.

Hunt, Linda. *Secret Agenda: The United States Government, Nazi Scientists, and Project
PAPERCLIP, 1945–1990.* New York: St. Martin's, 1991.

Janis, Irving. *Groupthink: Psychological Studies of Policy Decisions and Fiascoes.* 2d ed.
Boston: Houghton Mifflin, 1982.

Johnson, Loch. *America's Secret Power: The CIA in a Democratic Society.* Oxford: Oxford University Press, 1989.

Kaplan, Fred. *The Wizards of Armageddon.* New York: Simon and Schuster, 1983.

Kornbluh, Peter, ed. *Bay of Pigs Declassified*. New York: New Press, 1998.

Kwitny, Jonathan. *Endless Enemies: The Making of an Unfriendly World*. New York: Viking Penguin, 1984.

———. *The Crimes of Patriots: A True Tale of Dope, Dirty Money, and the CIA*. New York: W. W. Norton and Co., 1987.

Lefeber, Walter. *The American Age: United States Foreign Policy at Home and Abroad Since 1750*. New York: W. W. Norton and Co., 1989.

Liddy, G. Gordon. *Will: The Autobiography of G. Gordon Liddy*. New York: St. Martin's Press, 1980.

Lorenz, Marita. Interview on *CIA: Executive Action*. Arts and Entertainment Network, 1992.

"Lucky Luciano." *Biography*. Arts and Entertainment Network, 1998.

Luttwak, Edward. *The Coup d'Etat: A Practical Handbook*. New York: Fawcett, 1969.

MacArthur, John R. *Second Front: Censorship and Propaganda in the Gulf War*. New York: Hill and Wang, 1992.

McCoy, Alfred. *The Politics of Heroin: CIA Complicity in the Global Drug Trade*. Brooklyn, N.Y.: Lawrence Hill Books, 1991.

McDowall, David. *The Kurds: A Nation Denied*. London: Minority Rights Press, 1992.

Maheu, Robert, and Richard Hack. *Next to Hughes*. New York: HarperCollins, 1992.

Mangold, Tom. *Cold Warrior: James Jesus Angleton: The CIA's Master Spy Hunter*. New York: Simon and Schuster, 1991.

Marchetti, Victor, and John Marks. *CIA and the Cult of Intelligence*. New York: Dell Books, 1989.

Marshall, Jonathan, Peter Dale Scott, and Jane Hunter. *The Iran-Contra Connection: Secret Teams and Covert Operations in the Reagan Era*. Boston: South End Press, 1987.

May, Ernest. *American Cold War Strategy: Interpreting NSC-68*. Boston: Bedford Books, 1993.

Michigan State University Vietnam Advisory Group. "All Reports of the Michigan State University Team in Public Administration." In *Reports and Documents*. Saigon: Michigan State University Vietnam Advisory Group, 1955–1960.

Moon, Bruce. "The Foreign Policy of the Dependent State." *International Studies Quarterly* 27.

Moyers, Bill. *The Secret Government: The Constitution in Crisis*. Washington: Seven Locks Press, 1988.

Nolen, Barbara. *Spies, Spies, Spies*. New York: Watts, 1965.

Nutter, John J. "Terrorism: A Problem of Definition or Epistemology." Paper presented at the annual meeting of the American Political Science Association, Washington, D.C., September 1983.

———. "To Trap a President: JFK, CIA, and the Bay of Pigs." The Conflict Analysis Group, 1994. Photocopy.

———. "Unpacking Threat: A Formal and Conceptual Analysis." In *Seeking Security and Development,* edited by Norman Graham. Boulder: Lynne Reinner Publishers, 1994.

———. "The Blue Helmets are Coming! Local Insurrection in America." The Conflict Analysis Group, 1997. Photocopy.

O'Neill, William. *American High: The Years of Confidence 1945–1960*. New York: Free Press, 1986.

O'Toole, G. J. A. *Honorable Treachery: A History of U.S. Intelligence, Espionage, and Covert Action from the American Revolution to the Present*. New York: Atlantic Monthly, 1991.

Parenti, Michael. *The Sword and the Dollar: Imperialism, Revolution, and the Arms Race.* New York: St. Martin's Press, 1989.

Parker, Phyllis. *Brazil and Quiet Intervention, 1964.* Austin: University of Texas, 1979.

Patterson, Thomas. *Major Problems in American Foreign Policy: Documents and Essays.* 2d ed. Vol. 2. Lexington, Mass.: D. C. Heath and Co., 1984.

Payne, James. *The American Threat: National Security and Foreign Policy.* College Station, Tex.: Lytton Publishing, 1981.

Pearson, John. *The Life of Ian Fleming.* New York: McGraw Hill, 1966.

The Pentagon Papers. New York: Bantam, 1971.

Petras, James, and Morris Morley. *The United States and Chile: Imperialism and the Over-throw of the Allende Government.* New York: Monthly Review Press, 1975.

Phillips, David Atlee. *The Night Watch: Twenty-Five Years of Peculiar Service.* New York: Atheneum, 1977.

Powers, Thomas. *The Man Who Kept the Secrets: Richard Helms and the CIA.* New York: Pocket Books, 1979.

Prados, John. *President's Secret Wars: CIA and Pentagon Covert Operations Since World War II.* New York: William Morrow and Co., 1986.

Public Papers of the Presidents of the United States: Ronald Reagan. Vol. 1. Washington: Government Printing Office, 1983.

Robbins, Christopher. *Air America.* New York: G. P. Putnam and Sons, 1979.

———. *The Ravens: The Men Who Flew in America's Secret War in Laos.* New York: Pocket Books, 1989.

Sampson, Anthony. *The Sovereign State of ITT.* New York: Stein and Day, 1973.

Sasson, Jean P. *The Rape of Kuwait: The True Story of Iraqi Atrocities Against a Civilian Population.* New York: Knightsbridge Publishing, 1991.

Schlesinger, Stephen, and Stephen Kinzer. *Bitter Fruit: The Untold Story of the American Coup in Guatemala.* New York: Doubleday, 1982.

Siekman, Philip. "When Executives Turned Revolutionaries." *Fortune,* September 1964.

Sigmund, Paul E. *The Overthrow of Allende and the Politics of Chile, 1964–1976.* Pittsburgh: University of Pittsburgh Press, 1977.

Smith, Joseph Burkholder. *Portrait of a Cold Warrior.* New York: Ballantine Books, 1976.

———. *The Plot to Steal Florida.* New York: Arbor House, 1983.

Smith, Robert Barr. *Men At War: True Stories of Heroism and Honor.* New York: Avon Books, 1997.

Smith, William French. "Drug Traffic Today: Challenge and Response." *Drug Enforcement* (summer 1982): 2–5.

Snyder, Glenn H. "The 'New Look' of 1953." In *Strategy, Politics, and Defense Budgets,* edited by Warner Schilling, Paul Hammond, and Glenn Snyder. New York: Columbia University, 1962.

Sorenson, Theodore. *Kennedy.* New York: Harper and Row, 1965.

Stevenson, William. *A Man Called Intrepid.* New York: Ballantine Books, 1976.

Taylor Report. Paramilitary Study. John F. Kennedy Library, Boston, Mass.

Tower Commission Report. New York: Random House, 1987.

Treverton, Gregory. *Covert Action.* New York: Basic Books, 1987.

U.S. Army Intelligence and Security Command. Article 15-6: *Investigation Into Special Mission Funds.* Unpublished.

U.S. Comptroller General. *Controlling Drug Abuse* (March 1, 1988): 7–9.

U.S. Drug Enforcement Administration. "The Heroin Labs of Marseille." *Drug Enforcement* (fall 1973): 11–13.

U.S. Senate. Committee on Foreign Relations, Subcommittee on Terrorism, Narcotics, and International Operations. *Drugs, Law Enforcement, and Foreign Policy.* 100th Cong., 2d sess., 1988. S. Rept. S100-165.

———. *Final Report of the Select Committee to Study Governmental Operations with Respect to Intelligence Activities.* Book 1: "Foreign and Military Intelligence." 94th Cong., 2d. sess., 1976. S. Rept. 94-755.

———. *Final Report of the Select Committee to Study Governmental Operations with Respect to Intelligence Activities.* Book 4: "Supplementary Detailed Staff Reports on Foreign and Military Intelligence." 94th Cong., 2d. sess., 1976. S. Rept. 94-755.

———. *Final Report of the Select Committee to Study Governmental Operations with Respect to Intelligence Activities.* Book 6: "Supplementary Reports on Intelligence Activities." 94th Cong., 2d. sess., 1976. S. Rept. 94-755.

———. *Final Report of the Select Committee to Study Governmental Operations with Respect to Intelligence Activities.* "The Huston Plan." 94th Cong., 2d. sess, 1976. S. Rept. 94-755.

———. *Interim Report of the Select Committee to Study Governmental Operations with Respect to Intelligence Activities.* "Alleged Assassination Plots Involving Foreign Leaders." 94th Cong., 1st sess., 1975. S. Rept. 94-465.

———. *Staff Report of the Select Committee to Study Governmental Operations with Respect to Intelligence Activities.* Book 7: "Covert Action." 94th Cong., 2d. sess., 1976.

United States War Department, Strategic Services Unit. *The Overseas Targets: War Report of the OSS.* Vol. 2. Edited by Kermit Roosevelt. New York: Walker and Co., 1976.

Warner, Roger. *Backfire: The CIA's Secret War in Laos and Its Link to the War in Vietnam.* New York: Simon and Schuster, 1995.

Walzer, Michael. *Just and Unjust Wars.* New York: Basic Books, 1977.

Washington, George. "Proclamation of Neutrality." 22 April 1793.

Woodward, Bob. *Veil: The Secret Wars of the CIA 1981–1987.* New York: Pocket Books, 1987.

Wyden, Peter, *Bay of Pigs: The Untold Story.* New York: Simon and Schuster, 1979.

"X" [George Kennan]. "The Sources of Soviet Conduct." *Foreign Affairs* 25 (July 1947).

Index